THE FOURTH CRUSADE

The Medieval World

Series editor: Julia Smith, University of St Andrews

Alfred the Great
Richard Abels

The Western Mediterranean Kingdom
David Abulafia

The Cathars
Malcolm Barber

The Godwins
Frank Barlow

Philip Augustus
Jim Bradbury

Medieval Canon Law
J. A. Brundage

Crime in Medieval Europe
Trevor Dean

Charles I of Anjou
Jean Dunbabin

The Age of Charles Martel
Paul Fouracre

Margery Kempe
A. E. Goodman

Bastard Feudalism
M. Hicks

The Formation of English Common Law
John Hudson

Cnut
K. Lawson

The Age of Robert Guiscard
Graham Loud

The English Church, 940–1154
H. R. Loyn

Justinian
J. Moorhead

Ambrose
John Moorhead

The Reign of Richard Lionheart
Ralph Turner / Richard Heiser

The Welsh Princes
Roger Turvey

English Noblewomen in the Later
Middle Ages
J. Ward

THE FOURTH CRUSADE

EVENT AND CONTEXT

MICHAEL ANGOLD

PEARSON

Longman

Harlow, England • London • New York • Boston • San Francisco • Toronto
Sydney • Tokyo • Singapore • Hong Kong • Seoul • Taipei • New Delhi
Cape Town • Madrid • Mexico City • Amsterdam • Munich • Paris • Milan

PEARSON EDUCATION LIMITED

Edinburgh Gate
Harlow CM20 2JE
Tel: +44 (0)1279 623623
Fax: +44 (0)1279 431059
Website: www.pearsoned.co.uk

First edition published in Great Britain in 2003

© Pearson Education Limited 2003

The right of Michael Angold to be identified as
author of this work has been asserted by him in accordance
with the Copyright, Designs and Patents Act 1988.

ISBN 0 582 35610 5

British Library Cataloguing in Publication Data
A CIP catalogue record for this book can be obtained from the British Library

Library of Congress Cataloging in Publication Data
A CIP catalog record for this book can be obtained from the Library of Congress

10 9 8 7 6 5 4 3 2 1

Set in 10.5/13pt Galliard by Graphicraft Limited, Hong Kong
Printed in Malaysia

The Publishers' policy is to use paper manufactured from sustainable forests.

CONTENTS

CONTENTS

LIST OF MAPS AND PLATES

Maps

Plates

ACKNOWLEDGEMENTS

We are grateful to the following for permission to reproduce copyright material:

Maps 1 and 2 adapted from Map 1 in *The Franks in the Aegean*, published by Longman, reprinted by permission of Pearson Education Ltd (Lock, P., 1995); Maps 3, 4, 5 and 6 adapted from a map in *Cambridge Medieval History IV*, Part 2, published and reprinted by permission of Cambridge University Press (CUP, 1967).

Plate 1 from *Dumbarton Oaks Papers*, 22 (1968) reproduced with permission of Dumbarton Oaks Research Library and Collections, Washington, D.C., copyright 1968; Plates 2 and 3 reproduced with permission of The Bridgeman Art Library.

In some instances we have been unable to trace the owners of copyright material, and we would appreciate any information that would enable us to do so.

SERIES EDITOR'S PREFACE

O n 12 April 1204 the soldiers of the Fourth Crusade and their Venetian allies sacked the city of Constantinople. Heart and symbol of the Byzantine empire, Constantinople – the Queen of Cities – was the largest, richest Christian city of that era. Its sack attracted the attention of people of that day as much as of this. Was this event, which shattered a civilisation but did not end an empire, one of the 'events which make history'?

In this incisively written book, Michael Angold offers us a fresh and cogent approach. His theme is the complexity of an 'event' such as this. It was, he suggests, an accident with a certain logic behind it. He explains how we can view it as a combination of long-term structural trends and very short-term political decisions. But, he argues, we must pay equal attention to the attitudes, knowledge and cultural assumptions of all participants. An event such as this is not merely what happened but what people believed to have happened. Michael Angold also demonstrates how the meaning and significance attributed to this event is by no means the same thing as its consequences.

The first part of this book thus explores what happened from a range of viewpoints, Byzantine, Venetian, French, papal. It pays as much attention to the opinions which westerners and Byzantines held about each other as to the sequence of political decisions and miscalculations which led the crusaders to such an uplanned outcome. The medieval politics of competing interest groups, financial exigency and prejudice are shown for what they were. Its second part turns to the aftermath of the city's sack. Differing perspectives on what had happened make clear how deep western ambivalence was. While some participants faced strategic decisions, others found the occasion for opportunistic profiteering. In drawing up the cultural balance sheet, Michael Angold brings his great expertise in Byzantine history to bear. He assesses the both the psychological and the political impact on Byzantium, and explores the economic and religious consequences for all parties. He explains why, although western rule of Constantinople itself lasted no later than 1261, the restored Byzantine empire was never able to recover fully. With the city stripped by the French of many of its most precious religious relics and its population plummeting, the very heart had been ripped out of the empire.

As his analysis unfolds, Michael Anglod reflects on the historian's purpose. The historians he scrutinises are the chroniclers and commentators of the twelfth and thirteenth centuries as well as the distant but not dipassionate scholars of the twentieth and twenty-first centuries. What's in an event? Who, or what, makes an event? These are his guiding questions throughout. I welcome this sparkling contribution to the Longmans Medieval World as much for its valuable reflections on the historian's craft as for its wealth of new insight into the gripping story of the Fourth Crusade.

Julia M. H. Smith

PREFACE

This book is not intended as a conventional narrative of the events surrounding the conquest of Constantinople in April 1204 by the Venetians and the soldiers of the Fourth Crusade. I do not believe that there is a need for another narrative of the history of the Fourth Crusade. In his *The Fourth Crusade. The conquest of Constantinople*, Donald Queller has provided a definitive catalogue of events. What happened after the crusader conquest is covered in admirable fashion by Peter Lock in his *Franks in the Aegean 1204–1500*. What I aim to do is to provide the anatomy of an event. This centres on how the course of events took shape, which is essentially a dialogue between the forces, long term and short term, which played on the leading figures of the crusade, and the decisions that they made. It is also an examination of the consequences – again long term and short term – produced by the fall of Constantinople to the Fourth Crusade.

1204 is an event that has been hanging over me ever since many years ago I embarked on a study of the Nicaean Empire, the creation of which was one of the immediate consequences of the fall of Constantinople to the crusaders. I was interested in how the Byzantines reacted to a 'cosmic cataclysm' and wondered how it had changed the course of Byzantine history. I concentrated on administrative history. It struck me that despite many continuities the institutional changes effected during the period of exile marked a decisive change in the structure of the Byzantine Empire. After the return of the seat of empire to Constantinople the new administrative system was not capable of sustaining old imperial ambitions with the result that 'imperial authority became increasingly illusory'. That still seems to me a fair judgement.

On this reading, the fall of Constantinople in 1204 was a decisive turning point. But this flies in the face of a powerful current of modern historical thinking that does not rate events and personalities as significant factors in the process of historical change: they are merely involved in surface change. To quote Fernand Braudel, they 'fade from the picture when we contemplate these vast phenomena, permanent or semi-permanent, conscious and subconscious at the same time'. He is referring to those underlying structures shaped 'by geography, by social hierarchy, by collective psychology and by economic need'.[1] Braudel's assumptions seem to suit the fall of Constantinople. On the surface, it seemed to make little difference. Byzantine civilisation survived – not much changed. The Latin regime established in the aftermath of the crusade at Constantinople lasted a bare fifty years and left scarcely a trace behind. If the Byzantine Empire as an institution emerged, as I believe, greatly weakened, this, it could well be argued, was the result of long-term developments, not the impact of a single event. Were important changes not taking place before 1204 in the structure of the Byzantine Empire? Had not the emergence of localised power structures and the infiltration of western commercial and political interests already gone a long way towards undermining the institutional strength of the Byzantine Empire? It is these quite plausible assumptions that I wish to test. But it soon becomes clear that this is just one approach – and a rather traditional one at that – to an event of considerable complexity.

It is based on the assumption that the event can be established as objective fact. This is easier said than done. The event is in the end a construct based on the information available. But this, whether it comes in documentary or narrative form, has been shaped with particular ends in view. But it is exactly this process which creates the event which only exists because it was recorded in the way that it was. This might be used as an argument to invalidate the study of events on the grounds that they can never be established in a truly objective fashion. I have preferred a different approach: to accept this process as central to the event for the good reason that much of the impact of an event depended on how it was remembered; on how it was shaped by historians. It means paying particular attention to the sources, not so much as a quarry for facts, but as part of the process of the creation and assessment of the meaning of the event. It was largely through recollection of the past that the particip-ants and the opponents of the Fourth Crusade reacted to those forces, long term and short term, with which they had to contend. Equally, their successes and failures would be remembered in ways designed to influence succeeding generations.

Note

1. F. Braudel, *A History of Civilizations* (Harmondsworth, 1995), 28.

ABBREVIATIONS OF SOURCES
MOST FREQUENTLY CITED

Acropolites	*Georgii Acropolitae Opera*, ed. A. Heisenberg (Leipzig, 1903), rev. edn. ed. P. Wirth (Stuttgart, 1978). I: *Historia, Breviarium historiae, Theodori Sentariotae additamenta*; II: *Scripta minora*
Andrea, *Contemporary Sources*	A. J. Andrea, *Contemporary Sources for the Fourth Crusade* (The Medieval Mediterranean 29) (Leiden, 2000)
Chronicle of the Morea	*The Chronicle of Morea*. Tò Χρονικὸν τοῦ Μορέως, ed. J. Schmidt (London, 1904)
Chronicle of Novgorod	J. Gordon, 'The Novgorod Account of the Fourth Crusade', *Byzantion*, 58(1973), 297–311
Clari	Robert de Clari, *La conquête de Constantinople*, ed. Ph. Lauer (Les classiques français du moyen âge) (Paris, 1924)
Devastatio	A. J. Andrea, 'The *Devastatio Constantinopolitana*, a special perspective on the Fourth Crusade: an analysis, new edition, and translation', *Historical Reflections*, 19(1993), 131–49
Gesta Innocentii III	*Gesta Innocentii Papae III*, ed. J. P. Migne, *Patrologia cursus completus, series Latina*, 214, xviii–ccxxviii
Gunther of Pairis	*The Capture of Constantinople: The* 'Hystoria Constantinopolitana' *of Gunther of Pairis*, ed. & transl. A. J. Andrea (Philadephia, 1997)
Henri de Valenciennes	Henri de Valenciennes, *Histoire de l'Empereur Henri de Constantinople*, ed. J. Longnon (Paris, 1948)
Martin da Canal	Martin da Canal, *Les estoires de Venise: cronaca veneziana in lingua francese dalle origini al 1275*, ed. A. Limentani (Florence, 1972)
Migne *PG*	J.-P. Migne, *Patrologia cursus completus, series Graeca-Latina* (Paris, 1857–66)

Migne *PL*

J.-P. Migne, *Patrologia cursus completus, series Latina* (Paris, 1844–80)

Mesarites I–III

A. Heisenberg, *Neue Quellen zur Geschichte des lateinischen Kaisertums und der Kirchenunion*:
I. *Der Epitaphios des Nikolaos Mesarites auf seinen Bruder Johannes*,
II. *Die Unionsverhandlungen vom 30 August 1206. Patriarchenwahl und Kaiserkrönung in Nikaia 1208*
III. *Der Bericht des Nikolaos Mesarites über die politischen und kirchlichen Ereignisse des Jahres 1214*
in *Sitzungsberichte des Bayerischen Akademie der Wissenschaften, Philosophisch-philologische und historische Klasse. Jahrgang 1922–1923* (reprinted in A. Heisenberg, *Quellen und Studien zur spätbyzantinischen Geschicte* (London, 1973))

Nicetas Choniates

Nicetae Choniatae Historia, ed. J.-L. van Dieten (Berlin/New York, 1975), 2 vols (Vol. I cited in notes)

Pokorny

R. Pokorny, 'Zwei unedierte Briefe aus der Frühzeit des lateinischen Kaiserreichs von Konstantinopel', *Byzantion*, 55(1985), 203–9

Reg.

The letters of Pope Innocent III in the editions cited:
Migne PL: (see above), 215 and 216 ed. Haluscynski: *Acta Innocentii PP. III (1198–1216)*, ed. P. Th. Haluščynskyj (Pontificia Commissio ad redigendum codicem iuris canonici orientalis, Fontes, ser. III, 2) (Vatican, 1944)

Tafel and Thomas

G. L. F. Tafel and G. M. Thomas, *Urkunden zur älteren Handels- und Staatsgeschichte der Republik Venedig* (Fontes rerum austriacarum, 3 vols) (Vienna, 1856–7)

Villehardouin

Villehardouin, *La conquête de Constantinople*, ed. E. Faral (2nd edn, Paris, 1961), 2 vols.

A NOTE ON TRANSLITERATION
OF PROPER NAMES

It is difficult to be entirely consistent. Where Greek names are reasonably familiar I have preferred to use the Latin or Latinised form, e.g. Nicaea and not Nikaia, Adrianople and not Hadrianoupolis, Cantacuzene and not Kantakouzenos. But where Greek names are relatively unfamiliar I have preferred a Greek form, so Kamateros and not Camaterus. With French surnames I have usually translated 'de' by 'of'. I have anglicised French first names, so Gautier becomes Walter; Thibaut Theobald. I have usually been guided by the system of transliteration adopted by the *Oxford Dictionary of Byzantium*.

MAPS

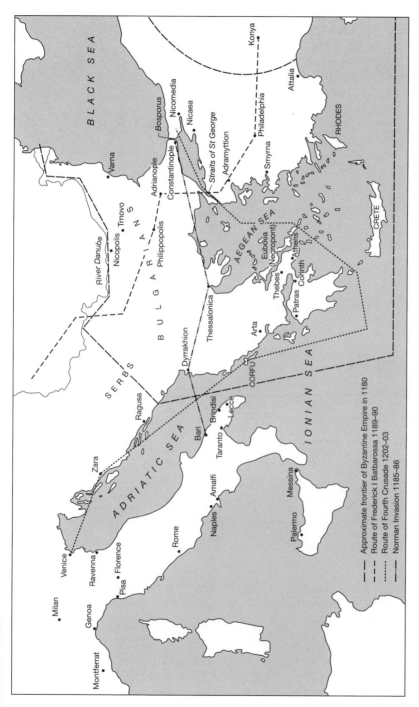

Map 1. The Byzantine Empire on the eve of the Fourth Crusade.

Source: adapted from Lock, P. (1995) *The Franks in the Aegean* (pub. Longman), Map 1. Reprinted by permission of Pearson Education Ltd.

Map 2. The Latin Empire of Constantinople under Henry of Hainault, 1206–16.

Source: adapted from Lock, P. (1995) *The Franks in the Aegean* (pub. Longman), Map 1. Reprinted by permission of Pearson Education Ltd.

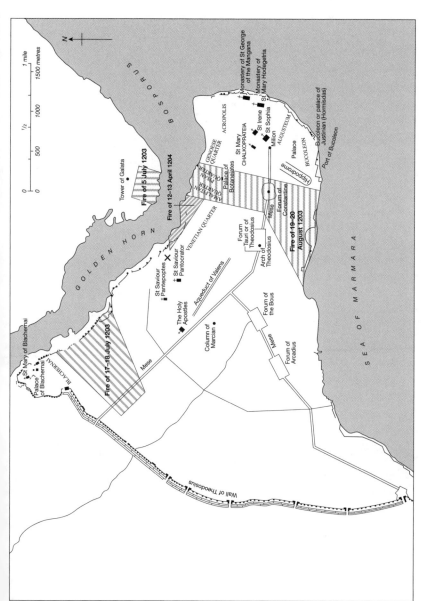

Map 3. Fire damage at Constantinople, 1203–4.

Source: adapted from *Cambridge Medieval History IV*, Part 2 (pub. Cambridge University Press, 1967), using information from Madden, T. F. (1992) 'The Fires of the 4th Crusade in Constantinople' in *Byzantinische Zeitschrift*, 84/85, pp. 72–93 (pub. B. G. Teubner).

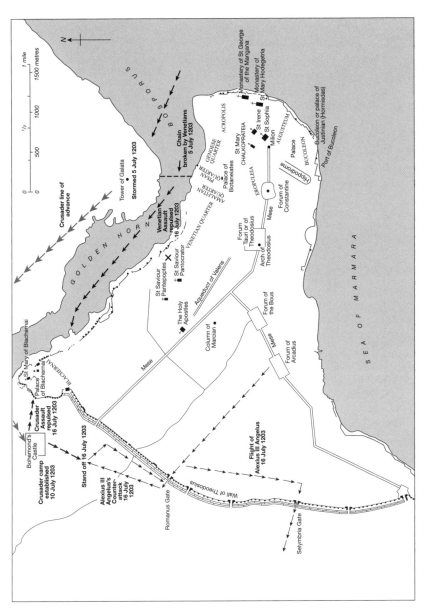

Map 4. The first crusader siege of Constantinople.

Source: adapted from *Cambridge Medieval History IV*, Part 2 (pub. 1967), published and reprinted by permission of Cambridge University Press.

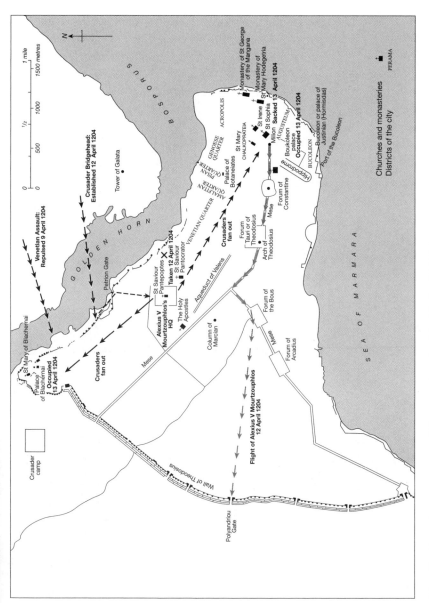

Map 5. Crusader conquest of Constantinople, 12–13 April 1204.

Source: adapted from *Cambridge Medieval History IV*, Part 2 (pub. 1967), published and reprinted by permission of Cambridge University Press.

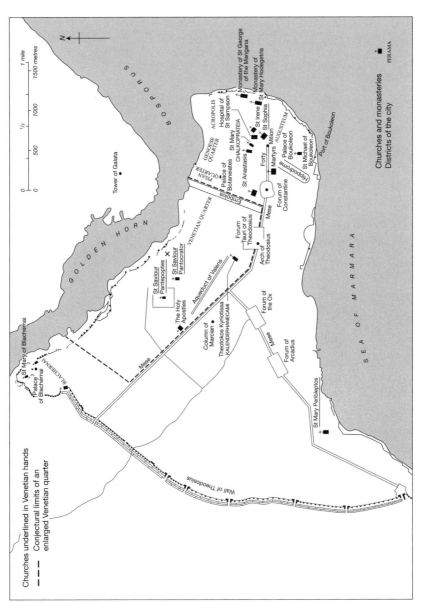

Map 6. Constantinople under the Latins.

Source: adapted from *Cambridge Medieval History IV*, Part 2 (pub. 1967), published and reprinted by permission of Cambridge University Press.

Part 1

THE FOURTH CRUSADE

chapter 1

SOURCES AND PERSPECTIVES

I

The conquest of Constantinople in April 1204 by the Venetians and the soldiers of the Fourth Crusade still has the capacity to amaze and sometimes to enrage. The sequence of events has often been recounted and, thanks most recently to the work of D. E. Queller, is scarcely in doubt. It begins with Pope Innocent III issuing a crusading bull on 15 August 1198. This was the first important act of his pontificate. The recovery of Jerusalem was always among the pope's chief concerns, but at first there was only a muted response to his appeal. He had to wait more than a year before the crusade began to take shape, when the count of Champagne together with many other prominent figures of northern France and the Low Countries took the cross. These crusaders then concluded a treaty with Venice in April 1201, which secured shipping to transport them to their destination: Egypt no less, but this was kept a secret. By the summer of the next year it had become apparent that the crusade might have to be aborted because troops were not reaching Venice in the numbers anticipated. It meant that the crusade leaders could not pay the Venetians in full. It was therefore agreed to help the Venetians conquer the Dalmatian port of Zara. At the same time, the crusade leaders made a deal with a Byzantine prince: they would put him on the throne of Constantinople and he would support the crusade with men and money. The crusaders were as good as their word. The young Alexius Angelus was duly crowned emperor in St Sophia on 1 August 1203. The new emperor agreed to pay the costs of the Venetian fleet for a year from the end of September and retain the crusaders in his service until the beginning of March, when it was assumed that they would set sail for the Holy Land along with Byzantine reinforcements. It never happened. Relations between the crusaders and Byzantines quickly deteriorated, leaving the crusaders marooned outside the walls of Constantinople. In February

1204 the crusade leaders finally decided on the conquest of Constantinople. Their first assault on 9 April was driven off by the defenders, but
a new attack three days later was successful. The crusaders had conquered Constantinople and overthrown the Byzantine Empire. Robert of
Clari, who was there when the city was stormed, catches the scale of the
crusaders' victory when he proclaims that 'never was there seen nor won
in all recorded time so great, so noble or so rich a prize, not in the time
of Alexander nor in the time of Charlemagne nor before nor after'.[1]

Establishing the sequence of events is only a beginning. The meaning
or significance of the conquest of Constantinople elicits contradictory
judgements. For Sir Steven Runciman 'there was never a greater crime
against humanity than the Fourth Crusade'. Its 'effects were wholly
disastrous'.[2] It made the schism between the Latin and Orthodox churches
irreparable. D. E. Queller is not much interested in the consequences of
the conquest of Constantinople. He is content to observe that it 'was
the most improbable of outcomes'.[3] John Godfrey described it felicitously
as 'a tale of men enmeshed in the toils of their own miscalculations'.[4]
Others have seen the fall of Constantinople as the all too likely consequence of the failure of the Byzantine system of government, while
Michael Hendy has dismissed it as 'one of the most boring and stultified
topoi of all medieval history'.[5] Such a range of views points to underlying
disagreements over the interpretation of the conquest of Constantinople.
Was it just an accident or was it a natural consequence of deteriorating
relations between Byzantium and the West? Does the moral dimension
have any place in the assessment of an event that occurred so long ago?
Are events even worth bothering about? Are they not just the froth of
history? 'Ce n'est que l'écume' was a mantra of those loosely dubbed the
Annales school, who dismissed narrative history or *l'histoire événementielle*
as irrelevant to the proper study of history, which required the investigation of deep structures and long-term trends. Paradoxically, it was
work by two of the most distinguished Annalistes – Georges Duby and
Emmanuel Le Roy Ladurie – which demonstrated the limitations of
such a blanket dismissal of the study of events. While Duby demonstrated
the value of placing an event in its historical and historiographical context,[6]
Ladurie elaborated the notion of the 'key event'. This he understands as
a liminal zone where existing circumstances are changed out of all recognition. As he puts it: 'Once one has reached this zone, factors which are
often mysterious delineate poles of necessity within fields of possibilities:
once they have surfaced their existence is obvious – but a moment before
their appearance, they were as unpredictable as they were unprecedented.'[7]
In other words, there are some events which are capable of effecting
transformations unlikely or even impossible otherwise.

It would be unrealistic to suppose that a new set of circumstances emerged out of nothing. It is true that at the outset none of the participants in the Fourth Crusade envisaged or sought the eventual outcome. But there was a long history of tension between Byzantium and the West made still more intractable by the mutual obligations imposed by the crusade. Equally, a recurring pattern of Byzantine history was one of periods of stable and effective government interspersed with dynastic crises which left Byzantium vulnerable to foreign intervention. In other words, the potential for significant change was already there. 1204 acted as a catalyst. In other circumstances it would not have been unreasonable to expect the Byzantine Empire to recover from its difficulties at the end of the twelfth century and to reclaim its domination of the Levant. It did not happen and the reason it did not happen was because the fall of Constantinople to the crusaders crystallised trends that had been working against Byzantium for a century or more. It meant that a new logic would begin to apply.

The assumption being made here conforms to Ladurie's idea of the transforming power of the event: that there are moments when, for whatever reason, long-term trends impinge directly on the surface of events, creating a new set of circumstances which make possible the replacement of the old order and certainties by others. But this is to objectify. It is trying to understand the processes of historical change from a modern standpoint. It can be done with very little attention being paid to how contemporaries regarded the events in which they were enmeshed. So we have to probe a little deeper and consider a possibility ignored by Ladurie. Is an event not somehow an artificial creation: a conspiracy between modern historians and their sources? Historians are almost bound to be the prisoners of the distorted image of the truth contained in their sources. However discerning they may be, they never quite escape the inadequacy of their material. This is perhaps the most serious objection to narrative history that has to be addressed. It goes without saying that the investigation of past events begins as an exercise in historiography. It soon becomes clear that contemporaries were interested in establishing what happened, insofar that it enabled them to ascribe meaning to events, in a way that inevitably distorts and eventually mythologises the past. This process is important in itself because an understanding of the past, however distorted, was integral to the priorities and ideals of a society and not just to some vague sense of identity. Happily, contemporaries were often bitterly opposed about the interpretation that should be put on events. These conflicts allow modern historians the latitude they need to exercise their historical judgement as to the significance of an event. Even where there is no

Fresco with the figure of a Franciscan friar. Part of a cycle of St. Francis, fragments of which are preserved in the Kalenderhane Cami, Istanbul. This was originally the church of the Theotokas Kyriotissa, taken over during the Latin Empire by the Franciscans. It is one of the few traces of Latin occupation of Constantinople that has survived.

Source: *Dumbarton Oaks Papers*, 22 (1968), Plate 24, Detail of Friar from Upper Left Scene. Reproduced with permission of Dumbarton Oaks Research Library and Collections, Washington, D.C., copyright 1968.

conflict or where an agreed interpretation eventually obtained, modern historians can penetrate behind the mask of self-deception thus created by earlier chroniclers and historians, because at some stage the interpretation will lose its value and either be quietly dropped or given a new twist.

But can we ever do more than play back what our sources tell us? With the proviso that we cannot escape seeing and understanding the past through the spectrum of our sources, we can adopt a variety of strategies in our approach to the sources. The most common is simply to identify the inaccuracies and distortions they contain and seek to rectify these. Less common is the exploitation of these inaccuracies and distortions. Their value lies in the way that they represent at one or two removes the understanding of the past entertained by the leading players in any event. That understanding would have little objective value, but objectivity has done much to sanitise and neutralise the past. Greater subjectivity gave the past more immediacy and cogency. The past was understood as a guide to present actions. Decisions were shaped by a view of the past. The assumption is too often that events unfolded in some mechanical way; or that the participants were at the mercy of events. In fact, events are made up of thousands of deliberate decisions: some successful, others not. In the case of the Fourth Crusade it is possible to work out the process of decision-making, at least for the most important decisions. We are best informed about the crusader leadership and theirs was the active role, but its members had to take into account other decisions: those made by the Byzantine government and, above all, those taken by the papacy. Nothing will have worked out exactly as planned, but our sources are rich enough to allow us an insight into the way in which events are shaped. The understanding of the past they reveal – however distorted it might seem to us – was essential to the way problems were confronted and decisions made. In that sense, our sources are not just a guide to the unfolding of events, but part of the historical process.

II

The conquest of Constantinople in 1204 by the Venetians and the soldiers of the Fourth Crusade produced a veritable torrent of contemporary narratives and comment. It reflects the intense interest that the fall of Constantinople aroused among contemporaries. Perhaps the only comparable event of the Middle Ages hitherto had been the crusader conquest of Jerusalem in 1099. It raises the question of whether the importance of an event is to be judged by the degree of contemporary interest.

There are three major narrative sources for the events of 1204. On the Byzantine side there is the *History* of Nicetas Choniates. His account of the fall of Constantinople and its aftermath constitutes Books VII–IX of his history of Byzantium in the twelfth century. Nicetas Choniates was born around the middle of the twelfth century.[8] He made his career in the Byzantine administration, eventually reaching the position of grand logothete under Alexius III Angelus (1195–1203). The grand logothete was the administrative head of the Byzantine civil service. It does not mean that Nicetas Choniates therefore belonged to the inner circle around the emperor, which was responsible for the formulation of policy. It does mean, however, that he was extremely well informed about the reaction of the Byzantine regime to the new crusade which was assembling at Venice. He had connections throughout the Byzantine administration and the Patriarchal Church – his brother Michael was archbishop of Athens. Nicetas Choniates lived through the events of 1203–4. He has left an eyewitness account of events. Nothing he says can easily be dismissed. He presents the Fourth Crusade as a Venetian-inspired act of revenge against Constantinople. It was certainly much more complicated than this. What he is expressing are the fears of the Byzantine government as they confronted the news that Venice was cooperating with a new crusade. Nicetas Choniates is a great historian in the sense that he knows how to shape events. We may now disagree with the meaning that he ascribes to events, but it will have been shared with most of the Byzantine elite. To that extent, Choniates allows us access to the reactions to and assessments of the Fourth Crusade which prevailed in Byzantine ruling circles.

On the surface, Choniates saw the fall of the city of Constantinople to the crusaders as divine judgement for the sins of the Byzantines. More subtly, he presented 1204 as the culmination of the deterioration of Byzantium's body politic. His explanation, as Jonathan Harris has recently reminded us, centres on 'the character and actions of the imperial incumbent'.[9] Emperors failed to measure up to the demands of the time and failed to provide the drive and direction needed. To blame the emperor when things went wrong was a normal Byzantine procedure. But Nicetas Choniates was an acute enough historian to use it to explore Byzantium's internal weaknesses as the Fourth Crusade approached. It enabled him to reveal its vulnerability to an attack from the West. Equally, it set in relief the dynamism of the West, which only exposed Byzantine weaknesses. A reading of Nicetas Choniates suggests that in one way or another the West would dominate Byzantium. It is an impressive analysis, which fits with a modern prejudice that empires fall because of internal weakness rather than because of external pressures.

Recently, Paul Magdalino has urged caution about accepting Nicetas Choniates's interpretation of events.[10] He takes issue not so much with Nicetas Choniates's largely flattering portrait of Manuel I Comnenus, but with modern historians' willingness to overinterpret Choniates, so that they trace Byzantine decline back to the reign of Manuel I Comnenus. Nobody would wish to deny that it was only after Manuel's death that the first ominous cracks in the Byzantine body politic opened up, but this does not mean that there were not already weaknesses. It was these that, good historian that he was, Nicetas Choniates sought to probe. Magdalino prefers Cinnamus's more optimistic interpretation of Manuel Comnenus's achievements, which was a reflection of the official line. However, any criticism that Nicetas Choniates made of Manuel Comnenus was measured and careful. He recognised the emperor's abilities, even if he was not above criticism. Nicetas Choniates's sober assessment of Manuel's reign therefore enhances the reliability of his treatment of events leading up to the fall of Constantinople. This needs to be emphasised because after 1175 when Cinnamus's narrative abruptly ends there is no Byzantine historian against which to test Choniates's version of events.

It is worth speculating about how the course of Byzantine history in the last two decades of the twelfth century would appear to us if by some unhappy chance only the first books of Nicetas Choniates's history survived. It would certainly have come across as a time of extreme difficulty, but also as a time when the Byzantine government dealt quite effectively with its foreign enemies. The Normans of Sicily may have taken Thessalonica in 1185, but they were then unceremoniously expelled from the Byzantine Empire. The passage of the Third Crusade in 1189–90 was a menacing episode, but ended with the German Emperor Frederick Barbarossa following the route across Anatolia that the Byzantines indicated. The demands made by Frederick Barbarossa's son the Emperor Henry VI in 1197 were circumvented; it is true, more by luck than good management. A Venetian fleet sent to the Straits in 1196 with a view to intimidating Constantinople seems to have returned home, having achieved very little. The frontiers in Anatolia were under severe pressure from Turcoman nomads but had not given way. The only serious loss was in the Balkans, where the emergence of the Second Bulgarian Empire pointed to a significant weakening of the Byzantine Empire. A superficial reading would be that Byzantium still had reserves of strength and diplomatic skill which should have enabled it to face down the challenge of yet another crusade. A more considered appraisal might find very worrying the increased tempo and intensity of foreign pressure over the last two decades of the twelfth century. When, it has to be asked, would the breaking point come? What Nicetas Choniates reveals in his *History* are the weaknesses below the surface of events. Byzantine political society was deeply divided. Different factions and family groupings pursued their interests at the expense of anything else – certainly the common interest. But division went deeper than this. In the provinces there was a sense of alienation from the capital, while in Constantinople the people had reclaimed the streets. There was a lack of respect for authority of any kind. It was a reaction to a failing system of government, which lacked a consistency of purpose with the consequent impact on decision-making.

These are the essentials of Nicetas Choniates's interpretation of events. Persuasive as it is it still needs the closest of scrutiny, simply because it has defined the fall of Constantinople from a Byzantine angle. There are other contemporary Byzantine sources but they do not have Choniates's authority or his imaginative grasp of historical situations. They may be more limited but there is always the possibility that they may also be more objective for being less directly involved. They come in the shape of letters, homilies and other rhetorical pieces. The most important are from the pens of Eustathios of Thessalonica,[11] Nicholas Mesarites[12] and Nicetas's brother Michael, the archbishop of Athens.[13] It has to be said that they bear out Nicetas Choniates's understanding of events.

Something of the fatalistic atmosphere that prevailed in Constantinople is caught in the account of events embedded in the Novgorod chronicle.[14] There is a distinct possibility that it was the work of Antony of Novgorod, who is known to have been staying in Constantinople immediately before the arrival of the Fourth Crusade. Antony is best remembered for his *Pilgrim Book*, which describes Constantinople, its churches and shrines on the eve of the crusader conquest. The Novgorod account is the work of somebody present in Constantinople. It concentrates on the flux of palace politics as a background to the crusader assault. It then recounts the looting of St Sophia and the hewing down of the silver sanctuary screen (*templon*). The author of the account may bewail the plundering of innumerable churches and monasteries, but he plays down the horror of the sack of Constantinople. The Franks may have robbed monks and nuns and priests, but they killed only a few, while 'they expelled from the city the Greeks and Varangians who remained'. The Novgorod chronicle preserves one telling detail: the icon of the Hodegetria was saved thanks to 'good people'. Since we know it passed more or less immediately into Latin hands this suggests some respect by the conquerors for Byzantium's religious treasures.[15] The author concludes: 'And thus, in the dissension of the emperors, perished the empire of the God-preserved city of Constantine and the Greek land. The Franks now have it.' The Greeks had only themselves to blame. The lack of animus against the Franks is striking. It seemed almost a matter of indifference whether Constantinople was in the hands of the Greeks or the Franks. The Russians still remained aloof from the religious rivalry of Constantinople and Rome. The value of the Novgorod chronicle is its neutrality. It confirms the line taken by Nicetas Choniates: that Byzantium's internal weaknesses moulded the events leading to the conquest of Constantinople by the crusaders.

Of the two main western narrative sources Geoffrey of Villehardouin's account of the conquest of Constantinople has attracted far more attention than Robert of Clari's.[16] Much of the modern historiography of the Fourth Crusade revolves around the reliability of Geoffrey of Villehardouin's narrative.[17] Whether intended or not, a major theme of Queller's book is the vindication of Villehardouin. Thanks to Queller's efforts there seems very little point in impugning Villehardouin's good faith. He did his utmost to present an accurate and honest account of the events that led from the calling of the Fourth Crusade to the conquest of Constantinople in April 1204. Villehardouin was well placed to act as the 'official' historian of the Fourth Crusade.[18] He was born around the middle of the twelfth century into the baronage of Champagne. He became marshal of Champagne and accompanied Henry, count of Champagne, on the Third Crusade. Henry stayed on and became king of Jerusalem, while Villehardouin returned to Champagne and served Henry's son, Theobald, the new count. Theobald was at the centre of the planning of the Fourth Crusade, one of the first of the leaders to take the cross at the tournament of Ecry in November 1199. Villehardouin's role is highlighted by the way he was chosen as a member of the embassy despatched to Venice to organise the details of transport and commissariat. He retained the trust of the crusade leaders after Theobald's sudden death in May 1201. The death of Theobald is likely to have increased Villehardouin's standing in the counsels of the crusade leadership. He it was who proposed Boniface of Montferrat as the new commander of the crusade army. This does not mean that Villehardouin was one of the leaders of the crusade, only that his advice was sought and respected by the leaders. He was present when virtually all the major decisions were taken. This gives his testimony great weight. It meant, of course, that he became an apologist for the crusade leadership.

At one or two points in his narrative he is not as candid as he might have been. It is, however, difficult to pin the charge of deliberate distortion upon Villehardouin, because any 'spin' is subordinated to his relentless narrative. His history is a most original production. It is the first prose history written in the French vernacular (as opposed to being translated from a Latin original). It has been usual to assume that in writing his history Villehardouin took as his model the *chanson de geste*. However, as R. Hartman has urged, this was done in anything but a straightforward manner.[19] Villehardouin chose to write in prose in order to distinguish his history from works in verse, be they *chansons de geste* or romance. Verse was for entertainment. Prose was for truth. That said, there were bound to be reminiscences of *chansons de geste*. It was impossible to escape their influence, when they enshrined so much of the warrior ethos that underlay the crusades. But why should Villehardouin have taken it upon himself to write a history of the conquest of Constantinople? The fact that he wrote it in prose rather than in verse indicates, as we have urged, the seriousness of his purpose. Villehardouin leaves precious few clues. He ends his history with the death of Boniface of Montferrat in September 1207. He celebrates the marquis as 'one of the best of barons and the most generous and one of the best knights who was in all the world.'[20] This is as close to emotion as Villehardouin allows himself to come in his history. He treats Boniface's death as the end of the adventure, which had begun at the tournament of Ecry. Villehardouin was a survivor who felt the need to celebrate his companions-in-arms, now dead or departed. One of his few indulgences is to list participants in particular actions. It serves as some sort of roll-call of honour. Villehardouin is last heard of alive in 1212. There is therefore a good chance that he began writing his history soon after Boniface's death in 1207.

There is no indication in the text as to the intended audience. There is, however, a fairly rich manuscript tradition. Five manuscripts from the thirteenth and fourteenth centuries survive. Still more indicative of its popularity are the continuations it inspired, of which that of Henry of Valenciennes is the most important.[21] The earliest manuscripts of Villehardouin's *Conquest of Constantinople* point towards a northern French provenance, but E. Faral – the most recent and authoritative editor of the text – preferred a different group even though the manuscripts are only from the fourteenth century. These seem to have a north Italian connection.[22] It does not seem very likely that Villehardouin would have set out to address a northern Italian audience. It is far more probable that northern Italian interest derived from the Latin Orient. This suggests the plausible hypothesis that Villehardouin's *History* attracted two distinct audiences: the first in the Latin Orient and the second in northern France. Villehardouin will have maintained his links with Champagne, where his son had succeeded him as marshal. He will also have been aware that criticism of the Fourth Crusade was already building up in northern France. This would surface in Robert of Clari's account of the crusade.

Villehardouin's narrative is likely to have been written before Clari's, for the good reason that, while Robert of Clari records the death of Henry of Hainault in 1216, Villehardouin fails to. There is, on the other hand, no way of telling whether either author was aware of the other's work. Where they touch is in their allotment of responsibility for the failures that occurred after the conquest of Constantinople. Robert of Clari blames the leaders, who took more than their fair share of the booty, leaving very little for 'poor knights' such as himself. This was symptomatic of the arrogance of the leadership and pointed the way to the defeat of the Frankish crusaders at the hands of the Bulgarians in March 1205. Villehardouin is careful to answer the charge about unfair division of the spoils and suggests that it was the greed of the rank and file that was the crusade's real moral failure. What is clear is that both narratives were written against a background of the debate that quickly developed about the validity of the Fourth Crusade. The series of disasters that the Franks suffered at the hands of the Bulgarians called into question the legitimacy of an enterprise that instead of rescuing the Holy Sepulchre destroyed Christian Byzantium.

Robert of Clari was a Picard knight, who along with his brother Aleaulmes, a priest, joined the contingent of Peter of Amiens. He was just a 'poor knight' as he describes himself: part of the rank and file. It was even more extraordinary that he should have thought to compose an account of his adventures. He was back in his native Picardy by 1206 when he gave relics obtained from the Great Palace at Constantinople to the local monastery of Corbie. A second batch of relics followed in 1213. Clari's account of the conquest of Constantinople, in marked contrast to Villehardouin's, pays particular attention to the relics housed in the imperial palace. It is therefore more than possible that his narrative was designed at one level to explain the circumstances that allowed him to obtain such precious relics. The monks of Corbie needed some sort of authentification. For his part, Clari had to justify his acquisition of these relics, now that military failures were beginning to cast doubt on the legitimacy of the crusade.

Clari's account survives in a single manuscript dating to around 1300 which suggests that it never circulated very widely. The use of the Picard dialect indicates that it was intended for local consumption. The original manuscript may possibly have been lodged with the abbey of Corbie.[23] Clari's account has never commanded the same respect among modern historians as Villehardouin's narrative. Clari was not close enough to the leadership to know in detail what was happening. He had to rely on camp gossip. At best, he is thought to provide the perspective of the rank and file. His account is far more discursive than Villehardouin's focused

The Deesis mosaic in the South Gallery, St. Sophia, Istanbul. Detail of the central figure of Christ. Thought to have been set up as an offering of thanks for the recovery of Constantinople by the Byzantines in 1261.

Source: South Gallery, Byzantine, 14th Century, Hagia Sophia, Istanbul, Turkey, Bridgeman Art Library.

narrative. Clari includes a long section on Isaac Angelus's seizure of the throne of Constantinople in 1185 and works in the Byzantine adventures of Conrad of Montferrat, brother of the crusade leader. Best known is his excursus on the 'Marvels of Constantinople'. These digressions make Clari a more interesting read than Villehardouin but seem only to confirm that he was not a serious historian. However, the work of P. F. Dembowski, C. P. Bagley and J. Dufournet now requires that we pay more attention to Clari's history.[24] We can no longer dismiss it as the artless storytelling of a veteran. It is carefully constructed. The digressions are an essential part of the narrative: Clari's account of recent Byzantine history not only explains why the crusaders were sailing to Byzantium, but also provides its justification, in that it reveals that Byzantium was essentially corrupt. The inclusion of Conrad of Montferrat's experiences in Byzantium explains his brother Boniface's interest in supporting the claims of the young Alexius, but also suggests a precedent for the crusade's support for a claimant to the throne of Constantinople. The 'Marvels of Constantinople' provide an opportunity for Clari to explain about the relics, but also to buttress his condemnation of the arrogance of the leadership of the crusade. Far more obviously than Villehardouin, Clari provides an interpretation of the events in which he participated. It is intended to justify the morality of the conquest of Constantinople. The Greeks were a worthless people. Clari wished to make clear that the disasters that occurred after the capture of the city did not invalidate the action of the crusaders. These calamities were to be explained by the arrogance of the leadership who had failed to accept their gift from God with proper humility.

This brief assessment of the three major narrative sources for the fall of Constantinople begins to reveal how complicated an event it was. The course of events may be relatively straightforward, but the meaning ascribed to the event itself is complex. Nicetas Choniates explains it as the culmination of Byzantine political and social instability; Robert of Clari also suggests that Byzantium's political weakness was an underlying factor, but introduces its deteriorating relations with the West as another. Frankish contempt for the Greeks colours Villehardouin's account. If the sources are agreed on the importance of underlying factors, they stress the significance of the consequences even more. Villehardouin hailed the conquest of Constantinople as a nigh miraculous vindication of the crusade. He gave praise to the Lord: 'And well ought they praise our Lord; since they never had more than twenty thousand men under arms between them, and with God's help they had conquered four hundred thousand or more, and that in the strongest city which was in all the world; a great city and the best fortified.'[25] The disasters that followed this glorious achievement required explanation. The conquest of Constantinople was not the uncomplicated victory that it had first seemed to be. Clari and Villehardouin made their assessment in moral terms.

Whereas most episodes of medieval history depend upon one or two contemporary narratives, the fall of Constantinople in 1204 is remarkable for the number of contemporary accounts. They are mostly short, but this does not matter. Their existence is proof of the impact that the event made on contemporaries. They add very little in terms of new information, but they do provide a different slant on events. The fall of Constantinople provides one of the central episodes of the *Gesta Innocentii Papae III*, which was written in 1208.[26] It is a defence of Innocent III's record. It is notable for the way it relies on papal correspondence with the crusaders – sometimes in a doctored form – in order to strengthen the papal case that Innocent III had neither approved of the diversion of the crusade to Constantinople nor condoned the atrocities committed during the sack of the city. The *Gesta Innocentii Papae III* adds another twist: in order to exonerate the crusaders its author singles out the Venetians as the villains of the piece. The diversion of the crusade and the conquest of Constantinople are blamed on the Venetians, who were in any case under papal ban for their assault on the city of Zara.[27] The events leading up to the conquest of Constantinople were a test of papal authority. It was clear that Innocent III had lost control of the Fourth Crusade. He sought to recover some prestige by apportioning blame and by accepting the outcome as another example of God moving in mysterious ways. It also forced Innocent III to confront the exact purpose of the crusade. He decided that the conquest of Constantinople 'gave hope that the province of Jerusalem would the more easily be liberated from the hands of the pagans'.[28] It fitted well with the way in which Innocent III was extending the scope of the crusade to include other targets than Jerusalem. One of the justifications that he used – as for example in the case of the crusade against the remnants of the Hohenstaufen regime in Sicily – was that it would facilitate the recovery of Jerusalem. This was largely casuistry.

The historiographical interest of the *Gesta Innocentii Papae III* is heightened by juxtaposing the text with the letters of Innocent III to the crusaders which provided the foundations of the account contained in the *Gesta*. It allows us an insight into the way that the raw material of a text was shaped by the author and increases our awareness of the gap between the event as it unfolded and the event as it was presented by one party.[29]

A different perspective emerges from three personal accounts of participation on the Fourth Crusade. The most substantial is Gunther of

Pairis's *Hystoria Constantinopolitana*.[30] It provides an account of his abbot Martin's involvement in the Fourth Crusade. The purpose is both to exonerate him and to authenticate the relics which he brought back from the crusade to the Alsatian abbey of Pairis. Abbot Martin was one of those prelates who was unhappy with the diversion of the crusade to Zara in pursuit of Venetian interests. He left the crusade and stopped off at the Roman curia, where he sought papal approval for his actions, before making his way to Syria. He arrived at Constantinople only on 1 January 1204, to find the crusade army in a tight spot. Once the city had fallen, Martin devoted himself to the acquisition of relics. While others plundered the imperial palace, he made his way to the monastery of the Pantokrator which had been the burial place of the emperors John II and Manuel I Comnenus. Having seized a string of relics, which Gunther carefully itemises,[31] Martin secreted them aboard a vessel and then sailed to Acre in order to complete his pilgrimage. There was something underhand about his acquisition of relics, but his actions were justified on the grounds that 'the Western church would rejoice forever, illuminated by the inviolable relics of which these people [the Greeks] had shown themselves unworthy'.[32]

Like many other German prelates of the time, Abbot Martin found himself in a difficult position because of the struggle between Philip of Swabia and Otto of Brunswick for the German crown. Participation on the crusade was a way of avoiding involvement. This was what prompted Bishop Conrad of Halberstadt to go on the crusade. He was excommunicated for supporting Philip. He therefore took the cross, 'judging it wiser to fall into the hands of God than into human hands'. An account of his adventures is included in the anonymous *Gesta episcoporum Halberstadensium*.[33] The intention is once again to exonerate the actions of the bishop and to authenticate relics which he brought back from the crusade. Conrad was another of those prelates deeply disturbed by the diversion of the crusade first to Zara and then to Constantinople. The account devotes no more than a paragraph to the conquest of the city. As soon as he could, Conrad made his way to Acre in order to obtain absolution from his original excommunication. The anonymous account concentrates on the bishop's spiritual state, lest his gift of precious relics to the cathedral of Halberstadt and other local foundations be called into question.

The third account centres on Bishop Nivelon of Soissons,[34] one of the leading prelates on the Fourth Crusade. Its author is anonymous, but is likely to have belonged to the cathedral clergy of Soissons and the bishop was almost certainly his source of information about the Fourth Crusade. The bishop was among the first to take the cross. He does not seem to have had the same reservations about the diversion of the crusade as the two German prelates. After the conquest of Zara he was among the emissaries sent by the crusaders to the papacy in order to obtain absolution. He failed to convey the pope's deep-seated objections to a further diversion to Constantinople. He was one of those who preached to the assembled crusaders as they prepared for their assault on the city walls, assuring them that their cause was a just one, because the Greeks had seceded from the Church of Rome. As a final mark of the trust placed in him by the crusade leadership, he was entrusted with the coronation of the new Latin Emperor Baldwin. The anonymous author of the account presents the Fourth Crusade as a continuation of the third. He has no qualms about the legitimacy of the crusade. He celebrates the deeds that men of the bishop of Soissons's contingent accomplished during the storming of Constantinople. But most of all he itemises the relics that the bishop sent back to Soissons after the conquest of Constantinople and then again when he returned to France after the defeat at the battle of Adrianople in March 1205 in order to seek support for the Empire of Constantinople.[35] The account closes with a notice of two miracles effected through these relics. The three accounts are united by personal concerns which in the end focus on the acquisition of relics, which provide both a justification for the crusade and for involvement on the crusade. They were some token of divine approval.

More difficult to place is another short anonymous account – the *Devastatio constantinopolitana*.[36] It is a bald factual account, brimming with accurate dates and figures. There is no personal slant, though it is quite clear that it was the work of an eyewitness who provides details lacking elsewhere. It ends oddly and abruptly with the membership of the Fourth Lateran Council which assembled in 1215. The connection is hard to fathom. It may possibly relate to one of the topics discussed at the council: the status of the Orthodox under Latin rule. This required exact and concise knowledge of the circumstances leading to the conquest of Constantinople. This the author provided. The spareness and objectivity of the account are immediately apparent. The hints of criticism directed towards the Venetians would be in line with papal thinking about the Fourth Crusade.

These narrative accounts provide a variety of perspectives on the events surrounding the Fourth Crusade and reflect contemporary understanding of the meaning of the fall of Constantinople. There is, however, one major lacuna. There is no contemporary Venetian account of events.[37] The first official Venetian account in any detail was the work of the Doge Andrea Dandolo writing in the mid-fourteenth century.[38] Almost a century earlier Martin da Canal had included a section on the Fourth Crusade in his history of Venice,[39] which had semi-official encouragement, but it was written in French and seems to have been intended for the Franks of Outremer. Martin da Canal has the Venetians acting in the interests and with the approval of the papacy. This is a travesty, but it is how the Venetians would like their part in the events of 1204 to be remembered. The Venetians were happy to mythologise their history as a means of proclaiming their imperial destiny. Da Canal catches this process at an early stage. The legends associated with the acquisition of the relics of St Mark provided the bedrock of the 'Myth of Venice', which was then elaborated with the help of more recent history: two events, in particular – the Peace of Venice of 1177 and the conquest of Constantinople in 1204 – were brought into play.[40] The Peace of Venice was remembered less for the way Venice acted as arbiter between papacy and empire and more for the privileges bestowed upon it by Pope Alexander III. This required that the events of 1204 were presented in such a way that Venice's role had papal approval. There would have to be the lapse of some considerable time before it would be possible to rewrite history to this degree. The lack of any contemporary Venetian account is all the more serious because the Venetians held the initiative and because their Doge Enrico Dandolo was the most respected of the crusade leaders and made a decisive contribution to all major decisions. It means that it is easy to blame the Venetians, on the grounds that they pleaded, so to speak, the fifth amendment.

Events have to be reconstructed. In the case of the conquest of Constantinople in 1204 this has to be done largely on the basis of the contemporary narrative sources. It is not so much just piecing together the course of events, as approaching their historical significance on the basis of contemporary judgements. At a later date it is normally possible to test narrative sources against documentary sources, remembering always that they will only represent a particular kind of truth, often no more than intentions. Most of the documentary sources for the Fourth Crusade have been preserved in two archives: the Archivio di Stato at Venice and the Vatican archives. The Venetians took great care to keep texts of the treaties that they made with the crusaders.[41] These served as title deeds to their claims to their territories and rights in the former Byzantine Empire. They were of more immediate value than some narrative of events. To an extent the existence of these documents compensates for the lack of a Venetian chronicle of the Fourth Crusade. The papal letters to the Fourth Crusade provided the material for the *Gesta Innocentii Papae III*. They are the record of papal intentions rather than what happened. However, the Vatican archives have also preserved some replies by crusade leaders, such as Boniface of Montferrat and Baldwin of Flanders. These allow us an insight into how the crusaders reacted to papal pressure and admonition. Their reactions provide a commentary on how events took shape.

There have also survived three letters sent back home by the crusade leadership. Two were written after the first conquest of Constantinople in August 1203 and the third was a general report sent in the summer of 1204 by the new emperor of Constantinople Baldwin of Flanders. Of the two letters written after the first siege of Constantinople one was a semi-official circular letter back home issued in the names of Baldwin of Flanders, Count Hugh of St-Pol and Count Louis of Blois. The recipients included Innocent III and Otto of Brunswick.[42] The other was a letter of Hugh of St-Pol, which survives in two versions. The first was addressed to his 'Dear Friend' Henry, duke of Brabant, and was preserved in the *Cologne Annals.*[43] The second was sent to the otherwise unknown R. de Balues, one of the count's vassals.[44] It contains precise details of the agreement made in August 1203 between the crusade leaders and the young Alexius. These are missing in the other version, which may therefore have been despatched a few days earlier. The letters are not dated, but must have been written in late August or early September 1203. They provide a more detailed account of events than the circular letter, which is mostly useful for the views of the crusade leadership in the aftermath of their establishment of the young Alexius on the throne of Constantinople. Hugh of St-Pol gives details that are not available elsewhere. He is very good on the arrival of the young Alexius at the crusader camp on the island of Corfu in May 1203 and the furore this caused. He then goes on to provide a blow-by-blow account of the crusaders' first siege of Constantinople, which is the fullest and most vivid that has survived.

One of the purposes of Hugh of St-Pol's letter was to defend the involvement of the crusaders in the affairs of the Byzantine Empire. He denounces those defectors who abandoned the crusade at Zara and sought refuge with the Hungarian king. He claimed that they had put the crusade 'army in mortal danger'. He swept aside the gathering criticism of the doge, describing him as 'a discreet and prudent man, capable of making difficult decisions'. He insisted that the decision to support the Byzantine pretender was justified by the return of the Church of Constantinople to the Roman obedience. He claimed that the patriarch of Constantinople had given his oath to visit Rome in order to receive the pallium.[45] Finally, Hugh's letter reveals that in September 1203 the crusade leadership was still determined, but now with Byzantine aid, to accomplish their 'avowed intent' and invade Egypt.[46]

The Pala d'Oro, St. Mark's, Venice. Altarpiece in gold and enamel inlaid with precious stones, originally commissioned from Constantinople by the Doge Ordelafo Falier (1101–18). Detail of Christ in Majesty with the Mother of God below, flanked by the Doge Ordelafo Falier and Empress Eirene. The figure of the Doge replaced that of a Byzantine Emperor, when the Pala d'Oro was remounted in 1209 following the conquest of Constantinople.

Source: courtesy of Byzantine Basilica di San Marco, Venice, Italy/ Cameraphoto Arte Venezia/Bridgeman Art Library.

This is equally apparent from the circular letter, which aimed to explain and justify the events that brought the crusaders to Constantinople. The letter begins with an apology for the attack on Zara – 'the city of transgression', as it is termed. It was a matter of necessity. The agreement with the young Alexius is justified on the grounds that the crusaders lacked the necessary supplies for a campaign against the Saracens, as previous crusaders had found to their cost. The crusade leaders had also been led to believe that the young Alexius would be welcomed at Constantinople. To their astonishment this was not the case. The crusaders were treated as though they were some infidel army come to 'pollute holy places and to overturn the Christian religion'. They realised that they 'had necessarily either to perish or to conquer' – an ominous choice of words. Their resolution had paid off. Alexius III Angelus fled and Constantinople opened its gates to his nephew, the young Alexius. The crusade leaders were confident enough to send ambassadors to the sultan of Egypt to announce their imminent arrival.

After his coronation as emperor of Constantinople on 16 May 1204 Baldwin of Flanders despatched another circular letter to the West.[47] It provides a more detailed account of events than the previous one, but its main purpose was to celebrate and justify the conquest of Byzantium. The main justification was that Constantinople had long been opposed to both the Roman Church and the kingdom of Jerusalem. It was now thanks to the crusaders restored to the Christian religion. The Latin emperor insisted that the crusaders intended to complete their vow and make their way to the Holy Land. He begged the pope to come to Constantinople, so that he could hold a General Council of the church which would solemnise the unification of the two churches.

A letter written by the new Latin emperor of Constantinople provides an appropriate ending to a survey of the sources for the conquest of Constantinople. It contains a celebration of the apparently fortunate outcome of an extraordinary enterprise. It has been necessary to devote so much space to the sources because it is impossible to divorce the study of the event from the study of the sources, for the event and its significance are a function of the sources.

III

When the Emperor Baldwin despatched his circular letter to Pope Innocent III in May 1204, he had every reason for optimism. The subjugation of the Byzantine provinces was going ahead without meeting real resistance. It did seem possible that he would be able to fulfil his crusader vow. Instead, his defeat at the battle of Adrianople in April 1205 at the hands of the Bulgarians and his subsequent disappearance meant that the Latin Empire of Constantinople would never fully replace the Byzantine Empire. The shape that it took was radically different from what had seemed possible just a week or two before the battle. If the Latin Empire itself has always seemed a broken-backed creature, this does not mean that the crusader conquest of Constantinople was *sans lendemain*. It confirmed the Latins for the next two centuries or more as the dominant force in Romania – the name given to the old Byzantine Empire by the Latins. This was possible because of the bases they established in the aftermath of 1204 in the Greek lands and the islands. These allowed the Latins – mainly in the shape of the Venetians and subsequently of the Genoese – to dominate the sea routes of the region. Control of the land mass was not a matter of concern, except perhaps in the Peloponnese, where Geoffrey of Villehardouin – a nephew of the chronicler – had created the principality of Achaea in the aftermath of the conquest of Constantinople.

An event has to be judged by its consequences, both short term and long term. The Latin Empire is in a sense a judgement on the events of 1204. Looked at in this way, history as the study of events is not a simple matter of establishing what happened. Why things turned out in the ways they did is not always a matter of blind chance. Every turn required a conscious decision. The history of the Fourth Crusade is a story of a thousand or more decisions often at cross purposes. These decisions were hardly ever made upon a whim. They were often made on the basis of past experience or of a sense of interest shaped by past experience. If events themselves were conditioned by an awareness of the past, they in their turn would make their own contribution. But this required that their meaning be crystallised. This was a process that had to take into account the consequences that the events were to have. It involved the distortion and mythologising of the events to conform with particular interests, or with a particular standpoint. Events can only be understood as part of a living process.

But how the past is understood varies from society to society, from age to age. But more than this the attention given to the past will also vary. The modern 'scientific' approach to the past is not very helpful in understanding how past generations viewed the past. In the first place, the past no longer has the same practical importance that it used to have for the conduct of affairs of state. History sadly is not 'scientific' enough. In the Middle Ages there was due respect for accuracy and the truth on the part of historians, but there was equally a demand that the past should be presented in such a way as to be useful – politically, ideologically and morally. This involved a process of assessment and refinement which normally distorted the past in the interests of the present. It was the way an event was created. The past was understood as a series of events; events made the past utilisable and accessible. The modern zeal for revealing the structures underlying events produces an understanding of the past that is quite divorced from the thought processes of the past.

This is not in any way to deny the importance of underlying structures. It is only to observe that isolating them does violence to the full historical context. The proper meaning of these structures is best apprehended through events. What gives an edge to the study of the crusades in general, and the Fourth Crusade in particular, is the clash between the Latin West and Byzantium; it was a struggle between two civilisations in the course of which each acquired a clearer sense of identity. The First Crusade presupposed that Byzantium and the West were linked by an essential unity of faith. It soon became clear how far from the truth this was. Out of this confrontation which culminated in the events of the Fourth Crusade it emerges how differently the Latin West and Byzantium had evolved. Nicetas Choniates famously observed that Byzantine and Frank 'had not a single thought in common'.[48] There is a degree of exaggeration but it reflected the truth that each was the product of a very different system. The main features of the Byzantine system can be traced back to the time of Justinian. This does not mean that it was entirely sclerotic. The Byzantines always displayed an ability to adapt to new circumstances. Byzantium survived and functioned so effectively and for so long because of the city of Constantinople. It was a metropolitan civilisation. This was normally a strength, because the Byzantines had hitherto been able to throw back the enemies that assailed its walls. The Fourth Crusade demonstrated that having a metropolis as capital could also be a fatal weakness. Its fall threatened Byzantium's very existence.

In its way, Latin Christendom was just as much an offshoot of the Roman Empire as Byzantium. It too looked backwards to some Golden Age in late antiquity. But it had been forced to reinvent itself more radically than Byzantium ever had. There were perhaps three things that distinguished Latin Christendom from Byzantium in the era of the crusades. The first was the power of the papacy. It exercised prerogatives that in Byzantium would have belonged to the emperor – something which the Byzantines found increasingly scandalous. The second was the ideology of chivalry, which imparted to Christianity a warrior ethos. The Byzantines by way of contrast sought to keep religion and war separate. Finally – most obviously among the Italian city states – there was a commercial drive in the West never matched by Byzantium. The Byzantine establishment appreciated the vigour and the virtues of the Latins and made a concerted effort to harness the talents of Latin merchants and soldiers to the needs of Byzantium. The Fourth Crusade was proof of how dangerous a strategy this was. But more importantly, the character of the structural differences separating Byzantium and the West will emerge more clearly through the events themselves rather than if they are taken out of context.

But the first task is to discover the extent of the historical information and understanding that the Byzantines, on the one hand, and the crusaders and the Venetians, on the other, possessed about each other as they embarked upon the Fourth Crusade. It must be remembered that crusaders and Venetians may have disposed of similar information about Byzantium, but their understanding was likely to be very different. The crusaders and the Venetians constituted the positive element in the unfolding of events, but this does not mean that the Byzantines can be dismissed as if their actions made no significant difference to the shape of events. Why, given their history and their political and diplomatic skills, were they unable to avert catastrophe? Constantinople had faced and overcome in the past more apparently serious threats than the Fourth Crusade. We must begin with the Byzantine assessment of the danger presented by the new crusade.

Notes

1. Clari, §LXXXI.10–13.
2. S. Runciman, *A History of the Crusades*, II (Cambridge, 1954), 130.
3. D. E. Queller and T. F. Madden, *The Fourth Crusade: the Conquest of Constantinople*, 2nd edn (Philadephia, 1997), 203.
4. J. Godfrey, *1204. The Unholy Crusade* (Oxford, 1980), vii.
5. M. F. Hendy, *The Economy, Fiscal Administration and Coinage of Byzantium* (Northampton, 1989), no. III, 26, n. 92.
6. G. Duby, *Le dimanche de Bouvines, 27 juillet 1214* (Paris, 1973).
7. E. Le Roy Ladurie, *The Territory of the Historian* (Hassocks, 1979), 111–31.
8. The fundamental study on Nicetas Choniates remains A. P. Kazhdan, *Kniga i pisatel' v Vizantii* (Moscow, 1973), 82–119. See also his introduction to *Niceta Coniata Grandezza e catastrofe di Bisanzio*, ed. R. Maisano (Verona, 1994), ix–lv; A. P. Kazhdan (with S. Franklin), *Studies on Byzantine Literature of the eleventh and twelfth centuries* (Cambridge, 1984), 256–86, which concentrates on the literary side of his work.
9. J. Harris, 'Distortion, divine providence and genre in Nicetas Choniates's account of the collapse of Byzantium 1180–1204', *Journal of Medieval History*, 26(2000), 19–31, at 31.
10. P. Magdalino, *The Empire of Manuel I Komnenos 1143–1180* (Cambridge, 1993), 18–26, 477–82. Cf. M. J. Angold, 'The Road to 1204: the Byzantine background to the Fourth Crusade', *Journal of Medieval History*, 25(1999), 257–78.

11. St Kyriakidis, *Eustazio di Tessalonica, La espugnazione di Tessalonica* (Palermo, 1961); Eustathios of Thessaloniki, *The Capture of Thessaloniki*, transl. J. R. Melville Jones (Canberra, 1988). See P. Magdalino, 'Eustathios and Thessalonica', in *ΦΙΛΕΛΛΗΝ. Studies in Honour of Robert Browning* (Venice, 1996), 225–38.

12. Mesarites I, no. II; Nicholas Mesarites, *Die Palastrevolution des Johannes Komnenos*, ed. A. Heisenberg (Würzburg, 1907). See Kazhdan (with Franklin), *Studies*, 236–42.

13. Michael Choniates, *Τὰ Σωζόμενα*, ed. S. P. Lampros (Athens, 1879–80; repr. Gröningen, 1968), 2 vols.

14. Chronicle of Novgorod.

15. R. L. Wolff, 'Footnote to an incident of the Latin occupation of Constantinople: the Church and the Icon of the Hodegetria', *Traditio*, 6(1948), 319–28.

16. J. Dufournet, *Les écrivains de la quatrième croisade: Villehardouin et Clari* (Paris, 1973), 2 vols; J. M. A. Beer, *Villehardouin. Epic Historian* (Geneva, 1968); R. Hartman, *La Quête et la croisade: Villehardouin, Clari et le Lancelot en prose* (New York, 1977); G. Jacquin, *Le style historique dans les récits français et latins de la quatrième croisade* (Paris/Geneva, 1986); C. P. Bagley, 'Robert de Clari's *La conquête de Constantinople*', *Medium Aevum*, 40(1971), 109–15.

17. E. Faral, 'Geoffroy de Villehardouin: la question de sa sincérité', *Revue historique*, 176(1936), 530–82; C. Morris, 'Geoffrey of Villehardouin and the Conquest of Constantinople', *History*, 53(1968), 24–34.

18. J. Longnon, *Recherches sur la vie de Geoffroy de Villehardouin* (Paris, 1939).

19. Hartman, *La Quête et la croisade*, 21–60.

20. Villehardouin II, §500, 314.

21. Henri de Valenciennes.

22. Villehardouin I, xliv–li.

23. Clari, iii; W. Maleczek, *Petrus Capuanus. Kardinal, Legat am vierten Kreuzzug, Theologe (+1214)* (Vienna, 1988), 208.

24. P. F. Dembowski, *Chronique de Robert de Clari: étude de la langue et du style* (Toronto, 1963); Dufournet, *Les écrivains de la quatrième croisade*; Bagley, 'Robert de Clari's *La conquête de Constantinople*'.

25. Villehardouin II, §251, 54.

26. *Gesta Innocentii III*, 214, cc.18–228.

27. Ibid., §lxxxvii.

28. Ibid., §xciv.

29. See Andrea, *Contemporary Sources*, 7–176.

30. Gunther of Pairis.

31. Ibid., 125–7.

32. Ibid., 91.

33. A. J. Andrea, 'The Anonymous Chronicler of Halberstadt's Account of the Fourth Crusade: Popular Religiosity in the early thirteenth century', *Historical Reflections*, 27(1996), 457–77; A. J. Andrea, *Contemporary Sources*, 246–63, at 246.

34. A. J. Andrea and P. I. Rachlin, 'Holy War, Holy Relics, Holy Theft: the Anonymous of Soisson's *De terra Iherosolimitana*, an analysis, edition, and translation', *Historical Reflections*, 18(1992), 157–75; Andrea, *Contemporary Sources*, 230–8.

35. Pokorny, 188–92.
36. *Devastatio*; Andrea, *Contemporary Sources*, 212–21.
37. The fundamental work remains A. Carile, *La chronachistica veneziana (secoli XIII–XVII) di fronte alla spartizione della Romania nel 1204* (Civiltà Veneziana, 25) (Florence, 1969).
38. Andrea Dandolo, *Chronica per extensum descripta*, ed. E. Pastorello (Rerum Italicorum Scriptores, 12, 1) (Bologna, 1938).
39. Martin da Canal. See G. Fasoli, 'La *Cronique des Veniciens* di Martino da Canale', *Studi medievali*, ser.ii. 2(1961), 42–74; A. Pertusi, 'Maistre Martino da Canal, interprete cortese delle crociate e dell'ambiente veneziano del secolo XIII', in *Venezia dalla prima crociata alla conquista di Costantinopoli del 1204* (Florence, 1965), 103–35; Carile, *Chronachistica veneziana*, esp. 172–93.
40. On the Myth of Venice, see E. Muir, *Civic Ritual in Renaissance Venice* (Princeton, 1981), 13–61.
41. Tafel and Thomas I–III.
42. Tafel and Thomas I, no. cxi, 428–31. See Andrea, *Contemporary Sources*, 79–85.
43. *Chronica Regia Colonienses*, ed. G. Waitz (MGH, SS, 18), 203–8; Tafel and Thomas I, 304–11.
44. Pokorny, 203–9. See Andrea, *Contemporary Sources*, 177–201. There are traces of two other versions of this letter.
45. Pokorny, 209.173–89; Andrea, *Contemporary Sources*, 199–200.
46. Pokorny, 209.190–204; Andrea, *Contemporary Sources*, 200–1.
47. Tafel and Thomas I, 502–11. See Andrea, *Contemporary Sources*, 98–112.
48. Nicetas Choniates, 301.

chapter 2

THE VIEW FROM BYZANTIUM

I

The fall of Constantinople to the Venetians and the soldiers of the Fourth Crusade was not simply a matter of western aggression. Byzantine weakness and miscalculations were just as important. It would be a harsh judgement, but not without some foundation, that the Byzantines had only themselves to blame for the way events turned out. After all, the fatal slip was for a faction at the Byzantine court to send the young Alexius Angelus to the West in order to seek help in an internal political dispute. This was a less surprising decision than it might at first seem. Byzantium had been relying heavily on western help since at least the middle of the eleventh century when Frankish mercenaries and other westerners began to be recruited on a large scale into the Byzantine armies. At the same time, Byzantium came to depend on the Venetians for naval support. Alexius I Comnenus's decision to appeal to Pope Urban II for military aid in 1095 was an extension of this reliance on the West. There can be little dispute that the First Crusade altered the nature of Byzantine relations with the West, but it would take some time before it became apparent exactly how. In his testament for his son John, Alexius I Comnenus singled out the challenge from the West as among the greatest dangers confronting Byzantium.[1] John II Comnenus followed his father's advice to the extent of seeking to cut his ties to the West and to operate within Byzantium's traditional boundaries. His goal was to recover the lands lost to the Turks in Asia Minor, but years of campaigning brought few tangible rewards. Towards the end of his reign John II Comnenus changed tack. He sought closer relations with the papacy and the German emperor, as well as with the crusader states.

It was left to his son Manuel I Comnenus (1143–80) to work out the full implications of this change of policy. He was faced almost immediately with the passage of the Second Crusade. This aroused all the old fears about western ambitions against Constantinople, but Manuel Comnenus's handling of the crusade leaders – none other than the German emperor and the king of France – tended to confirm the wisdom of his father's change of policy. Thereafter Manuel Comnenus worked for acceptance by the West, but on terms appropriate to a Byzantine sense of self-importance. Traditionally, Byzantine emperors understood that they were the head of a 'Family of Kings' by virtue of their claim to be Roman emperors. In practice, this was little more than a matter of protocol. But it could be adapted to make sense of Byzantium's relations with the West, which had come to impinge more directly than before on Byzantine interests in the Levant. For all their horror of abroad, Byzantine diplomats remained shrewd observers of the societies and political systems where they needed to exercise influence. They were able to appreciate the political strengths conferred on Latin rulers by the feudal pyramid. It was exactly as such that a member of Manuel Comnenus's inner circle, the historian John Cinnamus, described the political system of the West.[2] This may now appear to be a travesty, but it was how the West appeared to an observer at the Comnenian court. As understood at Byzantium, it was a system that was quite compatible with the Byzantine 'Family of Kings'. What was not was the power of the papacy, which was coming under increasingly close scrutiny. It was apparent that the character of papal authority was very different from that of the patriarch of Constantinople. The pope exercised political privileges in the West not dissimilar to those enjoyed by the Byzantine emperor in his dominions. To a Byzantine observer the western political system appeared to revolve around the papacy rather than any imperial or royal figure.

It therefore looked as though the papacy was the key to Byzantium's inclusion within a Latin political framework. Manuel Comnenus understood that he had first to end the religious divisions which separated the churches of Rome and Constantinople. He was aware of the theological complexities, but believed that he could find a political solution satisfactory to both Rome and Byzantium. There he was wrong. Papal circles remained suspicious of his intentions. Nor did posing as a protector of the crusader states win him papal approval. By and large, Byzantine interest in the Holy Land was regarded in the West as an unwarranted intrusion.[3] By the end of Manuel Comnenus's reign it was clear that his policy of rapprochement with the western powers was not working.[4] Byzantium had no place in a Latin political system, as its exclusion from the Peace of Venice in 1177 demonstrated.

Manuel's interest in the West had never been just a matter of *Realpolitik*. He was genuinely attracted by the chivalric ideal of prowess and generosity. It was a warrior ethos that appealed to a soldier-emperor. Manuel appreciated the military and commercial skills of westerners and hoped to tap them for the benefit of his empire. After his death he was remembered both at Byzantium and in the West as a ruler who had deliberately welcomed westerners into his service and entrusted them with positions of power and responsibility.[5] Nicetas Choniates accused Manuel of placing noble-born Byzantines under *homunculi* who were little better than barbarians.[6] Whether this was indeed the case is another matter. Apart from his brother-in-law, Baldwin of Antioch, none of Manuel's top commanders was of western origin. Nevertheless, in the course of Manuel's reign it became something of a stock charge against the emperor. In the mid-1150s a Byzantine bishop could exclaim:

> I can't believe that a Philhellene and lover of freedom would docket a Hellene with barbarians nor a free man with people who are slaves by nature. I can't abide the sort of people who use the barbarian tongue, nor those apparent servants of Mars, if I can describe them thus. They are the kind of people who are on such good terms with the barbarians that they prefer the barbarian to the Hellene, alleging against the Hellene, though a hero, a lover of the Muses and Hermes, that of the two he is the inferior.[7]

The bishop was trying to obtain a sinecure for an uncle, but these are strong words critical of a perceived bias at the Comnenian court in favour of the Latins. This was fostered by the young Manuel who was an enthusiast for tournaments and wished to measure his prowess against Frankish paladins, such as Raymond of Antioch who visited his court early in his reign. Manuel accorded a warm welcome to Latins passing through the Byzantine Empire. He himself was the son of a Hungarian princess. His first wife was a German and his second wife a crusader princess. Nieces were married off to German, Hungarian and crusader rulers.[8] These dynastic marriages produced many western connections, so much so that Manuel took an especial interest in marriage law particularly as it affected 'those figures who have come to settle in the Queen of Cities from foreign lands ruled over by kings and princes'.[9]

The Latins were a presence at the Comnenian court and presented the Byzantine elite with a problem which continued to divide Byzantine society. Paul Magdalino has argued that there was never any clear split under Manuel Comnenus into pro- and anti-Latin factions and that Manuel made no attempt to strengthen his own position by building up a Latinophile party at court.[10] This is true insofar as faction at the Byzantine court was always a matter of family interest and that family-based alliances were always shifting. However, there were also issues that divided the Byzantine establishment and in the twelfth century the Latin question was perhaps the most important. Though easy enough to simplify, it was enormously complicated. A combination of the crusades and the union of churches ensured that it always remained at the forefront of public interest.

II

In the course of Manuel Comnenus's reign Byzantium found itself in an increasingly false position: the emperor's efforts at a rapprochement with the West sharpened mutual suspicions, while his reliance on – and admiration for – westerners opened up internal divisions, which he was not always able to control. The crusade only accentuated the mixed feelings that the Latin question aroused. The Byzantines understood, even if they did not entirely approve, the crusade to be an armed pilgrimage undertaken with papal blessing. It was not until after the fall of Constantinople in 1204 that Byzantines began to comprehend the system of indulgences which underpinned the crusade. From the start the Byzantines suspected with justification that, even if the crusade itself was not directed against Byzantium, it was used as a cover by western rulers, such as Bohemond or Roger II of Sicily, who did have designs on Byzantine territory. In many ways, the Second Crusade was more worrying than the first, because it brought home to the Byzantines that the crusade was here to stay, that the western presence was a permanent problem. Because it was initiated by the pope the crusade underlined the question of the union of churches. The twelfth century was punctuated with negotiations and conferences designed to end the state of schism which existed between the churches of Rome and Constantinople. It became increasingly apparent to Byzantine churchmen that the 'stumbling block' that prevented the restoration of normal relations between the two churches was the papal claim to a *plenitudo potestatis*. This was interpreted as a demand for the submission of the Church of Constantinople to the papacy.[11]

Manuel Comnenus dismissed these fears as unrealistic. In pursuit of papal approval he was willing to make various concessions to the Latin Church. In the 1160s he took on as a religious adviser an Italian theologian Hugh Eteriano. This coincided with a doctrinal controversy over the meaning of Christ's words: 'My Father is greater than I.' It had originated in the Latin Church and had been raised at the Byzantine court by a Byzantine diplomat just back from a mission to the West. Manuel may have engineered the whole affair as a way of proving his loyalty to the papacy. With Eteriano's support he adopted what he took to be the official papal line on this question: that according to His divinity Christ was the equal of the Father; as a man Christ was, however,

His inferior. This produced a nigh unanimous condemnation on the part of the Byzantine bishops, because it threatened to divide the incarnate from the divine Christ in the manner of the Nestorians. Manuel eventually faced down opposition to his theology, but it was perhaps the most serious challenge to his authority in the closing years of his reign. It sparked off a wave of anti-Latin sentiment on the streets of Constantinople. Eteriano related that 'Latins were pointed out as objects of hatred and detestation'. There were those among the younger generation of court aristocracy who supported the bishops' stand against the emperor. Underlying Byzantine distrust of the West was always this religious dimension. Latins represented a threat to Orthodoxy.[12]

They also challenged the Byzantine view that their empire represented the perfect Christian order. Eustathius, archbishop of Thessalonica, was an apologist for traditional views on the hierarchical ordering of society. These he enunciated in response to the lack of respect for authority that he found in Thessalonica.[13] This breakdown of a sense of order was a theme of Byzantine writers in the last decades of the twelfth century. It contrasted with the discipline which characterised westerners. Another archbishop, Michael Choniates of Athens, had occasion to intervene in a dispute in the neighbouring town of Euripos or Chalkis on the island of Euboea. He was exasperated that the people of the town were incapable of ordering their affairs. This was shameful, when contrasted with the self-discipline shown by the Latins. The archbishop concluded: 'One sees Celts, Germans and Italians assembling in an orderly fashion and debating with a sense of decorum, but, as for the Byzantines [*Rhomaioi*], they get infuriated at the slightest pretext and reduce any meeting called for the common good to a shambles.'[14] Eustathius of Thessalonica was all too aware of the unruly character of his city, but was impressed by what he had learnt about the government of Venice. It struck him as an almost perfect example of Aristotle's mixed constitution.[15]

It is Nicetas Choniates in his *History* who has paid the greatest attention to the challenge to Byzantine self-satisfaction that came from the West. Nicetas Choniates used selected westerners to bring out what he saw as Byzantine weaknesses. His treatment of the West was to an extent a device of self-criticism, but this was not just a literary procedure. It mirrors one of the most obvious methods of evaluating a society – comparison with others. In the past this only had the effect of confirming the Byzantine view of their empire as verging on the perfect Christian society. To judge from Nicetas Choniates's *History*, a comparison with the West now revealed Byzantine deficiencies. Comparisons of this kind in a medieval context usually lead on to the conclusion that these inadequacies are the result of a failure to implement the traditional order.

They are often a prelude to a call for a return to the past, the first step being a reformation of the moral order. Nicetas Choniates is strong on the sins of the Byzantines, which have brought down upon them a series of disasters, culminating in the conquest of the city by western crusaders. However, he does not use the apparent strengths of western society to manufacture a defence of the traditional Byzantine order. A reading of his *History* leaves the distinct impression that he was aware that the West had practical skills of government and military organisation which Byzantium could not match. This sneaking admiration for the West did not turn Nicetas Choniates into a lover of Latins. Some of the bitterest criticism of Latins is to be found in the pages of his *History*. It was more that as a good civil servant Nicetas Choniates was able to provide a reasonably objective assessment of the strengths and weaknesses of the empire's enemies. In doing so he laid bare some of the weaknesses of Byzantium.

One of the heroes of Choniates's *History* was Conrad of Montferrat. He was 'brave and prudent beyond measure' in the historian's estimation.[16] His family had long-standing connections with the Byzantine court. His brother Renier had married Manuel Comnenus's daughter Maria and had been given the title of Caesar, but had then fallen victim to Andronicus Comnenus. After the latter's overthrow Isaac Angelus immediately set about reviving the links between the imperial dynasty and the house of Montferrat. Conrad of Montferrat duly married the emperor's sister. His arrival in Constantinople coincided with a serious rebellion against Isaac Angelus. Nicetas Choniates contrasts the emperor's passivity in the face of this threat to his throne with Conrad's vigorous action. Conrad raised a scratch force of Latin mercenaries and enrolled Turks and Georgians who happened to be in Constantinople for other reasons. He forced the emperor to confront the rebels. The brunt of the ensuing battle fell on the Latins commanded by Conrad, who formed the centre of the army. They swept aside the opposition. Conrad overcame the rebel leader in hand-to-hand combat. He had saved Isaac's throne for him. The success of the Latins was not to the liking of the Constantinopolitan populace. They turned on the Latin quarters hoping to plunder them in the same way as they had in 1182 under Andronicus Comnenus. However, the Latins were ready for their assault and drove them away. Nicetas Choniates has nothing but contempt for the Byzantine mob whose excesses were fuelled by wine. He admires the way the Latins dealt with the situation, down to a subterfuge which convinced the Greeks to end their violence. The Latins gathered together the Greek corpses, cut their hair to make them look like Franks, and thus convinced the mob leaders that they were the ones who had suffered the heaviest casualties. This incident did not encourage Conrad of Montferrat to stay on in Constantinople. At the first opportunity he took passage to the Holy Land. Nicetas Choniates understood that his departure fatally weakened Isaac Angelus's military capacity.[17]

Conrad arrived at Tyre in time to reinforce its defences against Saladin and to hold out until further help arrived from the West in the shape of the Third Crusade. The first western leader to set out on crusade was the German emperor Frederick Barbarossa who took the land route across the Byzantine Empire to the Holy Land. He crossed over the Byzantine frontier towards the end of August 1189. Nicetas Choniates was at the time governor of Philippopolis (the modern Plovdiv) – one of the major staging posts on the military road that led from Belgrade to Constantinople. He was directly involved in Frederick Barbarossa's passage across the Balkans. He is scathing about the measures taken by Isaac Angelus to oppose the Germans. Philippopolis was the key, but Barbarossa outmanoeuvred the Byzantine generals, who, together with its governor, were forced to evacuate the city. This was followed by a serious defeat at the hands of the Germans. Nicetas Choniates was despatched to the capital for instructions from the emperor.

Isaac Angelus comes out of Nicetas's narrative of these events even worse than he did from the latter's account of the Conrad of Montferrat episode. Nicetas was highly critical of the way Isaac wrote to Barbarossa, prophesying that the German ruler would be dead by Easter. This in Nicetas's opinion was not an action worthy of an emperor. But it was of a piece with his superstitious character. As far as Nicetas was concerned, Isaac's opposition to Barbarossa was based on nothing more concrete than the predictions of the Patriarch Dositheos. Isaac emerges as a figure of fun: there is a scene where Isaac looks out from the Blachernai Palace and takes imaginary pot-shots at non-existent Germans. This is in contrast to Frederick Barbarossa, who was anything but a figure of fun. He was the image of the ideal Christian ruler, who would abandon his homeland out of his 'burning passion for Christ . . . in order to suffer affliction with the Christians of Palestine for the name of Christ and due regard for His life-giving tomb . . . The man's zeal was apostolic, his purpose dear to God, and his achievement beyond perfection.'[18] Not for the first time in his *History*, Choniates evinces sincere empathy with the crusading ideal. It gave western kingship a spiritual and moral inspiration which Byzantine emperors lacked. But Choniates was shrewd enough an observer to realise that western kingship differed in other ways. Barbarossa's envoys to the Byzantine court were offended at the way they had been treated: they were compelled to stand before the emperor and were not offered any seats. This was the Byzantine custom, where, unless they were specially honoured, all first made obeisance to the emperor and then stood in his presence. It emphasised the gulf separating the emperor and other men. When the Byzantine emissaries reached Barbarossa, he made them sit beside him together with their servants. This shocked the Byzantine sense of decorum, which held that servants should not sit with their masters, still less with a great ruler. Choniates tells us that Barbarossa did this to mock Byzantine ceremonial which made no apparent distinction between men of different degree and status.[19] It touched a raw nerve because Byzantine court society was thoroughly hierarchical, with the top ranks graded according to relationship to the reigning emperor. However, it needed a ruler of ability and dignity to give the ordering of society meaning and purpose. This Byzantium evidently lacked.[20]

Nicetas Choniates does not show the same respect for Barbarossa's son, the Emperor Henry VI, but appreciated the threat he posed to the Byzantine Empire once he had secured control of Sicily. He laid claim to the Byzantine territories in Greece and Albania temporarily conquered by his Norman predecessors. The Byzantine Emperor Alexius III Angelus (1195–1203) decided to buy him off. He hoped to impress the German ambassadors by a display of Byzantine court ceremonial at its most magnificent. Courtiers were told to put on their most sumptuous apparel. The Germans treated the display with contempt. They dismissed all the finery with the words: 'The time has now come to take off effeminate garments and brooches and put on iron instead of gold.'[21] Nicetas Choniates made his point. The Byzantines were no match for the more virile Latins. Choniates must have been expressing a view that was widespread among the top ranks of society at Byzantium. In their dealings with the West the Byzantines were at a double disadvantage: not only had experience exposed their inferiority to the Latins, it had also underlined their reliance on the Latins. The lesson of the Conrad of Montferrat episode was plain: when in difficulty turn to a Latin for help.

It was left to the populace of Constantinople to express the resentments that this dilemma produced. The pogrom of 1182 took the Latins of Constantinople unawares. Thereafter, as the incident in 1187 demonstrated, the Latins were well able to look after themselves. The mob sought easier targets of their wrath, on one occasion indiscriminately looting Christian churches and destroying the mosque.[22] The imperial government had somehow to work out a means of nullifying the threat from the West, while at the same time retaining Latin support and placating popular sentiment. The Norman invasion of 1185 had been a nasty scare. If in the end it was contained quite easily, it demonstrated how vulnerable Byzantium was at a time of division and demoralisation. The fall of Thessalonica to the Normans was in many ways a presentiment of the fall of Constantinople to the crusaders. In the background were Byzantine aristocrats seeking foreign support for their ambitions. Thessalonica surrendered to the Normans because the imperial governor had preferred flight to organising a defence; in this he only anticipated the actions of the Byzantine emperors in 1203 and 1204.[23]

The passage of Frederick Barbarossa through the Byzantine Empire in 1189–90 was slightly different. It was not an unprovoked invasion of Byzantine territory. The German ruler had hoped for a peaceful crossing. He had to force his way through the Balkans and Thrace only because of Byzantine opposition. Nicetas Choniates ridiculed Isaac Angelus's motivation for opposing the Germans by attributing it to the prophesies of the patriarch.[24] He failed to reveal in full that underlying the Byzantine emperor's actions was a calculated attempt to distance Byzantium from the West. The key was his alliance with Saladin.[25] Initial contacts were made over the release of Alexius Angelus, Isaac's elder brother, who was held prisoner by Raymond, count of Tripoli. This hardened into an undertaking on Isaac's part to oppose the passage of the Third Crusade. The Byzantine emperor could expect in return support from Saladin against the Seljuqs of Rum. Prompted by his confidant, the Patriarch Dositheos, a former Orthodox patriarch of Jerusalem, Isaac would also have anticipated recovery of ecclesiastical jurisdiction over the churches of the Holy Land in the wake of Saladin's conquest of the crusader states.

The alliance with Saladin foundered on Isaac's uncertain handling of the passage through the Byzantine Empire of Frederick Barbarossa's forces. After the German ruler's initial victory over the Byzantines outside Philippopolis, Isaac Angelus was undecided as what to do. His first thought was to come to terms and allow Barbarossa through. Then he changed his mind, when it seemed that Barbarossa was hesitating. The truth of the matter is that Isaac Angelus found himself caught between advisers, such as Nicetas Choniates,[26] who urged peace at any price with Barbarossa, and those, such as the Patriarch Dositheos, who were opposed to any deal with the German ruler. The Byzantine establishment was split over the question. It was a predicament that a dozen or so years later would be brought into even sharper focus by the arrival of the Fourth Crusade under the walls of Constantinople.

In 1189 the voices of moderation at the Byzantine court prevailed over anti-Latin feeling, which was driven by the Patriarch Dositheos, who was forced out of office, despite the emperor's attempts to protect him.[27] The patriarch's dismissal confirmed that civil service wisdom had reasserted itself in relations with the West. It was safer to placate rather than oppose western powers. It was an attitude of mind that contributed to the outcome of the Fourth Crusade.

But before that the conquest of Sicily by the German Emperor Henry VI in 1194 was another worrying development, which Alexius III Angelus had to confront almost the moment that he had dethroned his brother Isaac. As we know, he tried to buy off the German threat. He hoped to raise the sixteen *kentenaria* of gold demanded through a special levy imposed on the provinces and the capital. So weak was his position that he had to call a general assembly consisting of the senate, representatives of synod, and members of the guilds of Constantinople, in the hope of raising a benevolence from the people of Constantinople. This general assembly was more or less unique in the history of Byzantium – certainly before 1204. It was an extraordinary measure, but it allowed opponents to express their criticism of the emperor's regime. The meeting broke up. Not only had it refused to countenance a property tax, it had also turned down the emperor's suggestion that he might avail himself of church treasure. Alexius Angelus therefore plundered the imperial tombs in the mausolea attached to the Holy Apostles.[28]

Henry VI's premature death in September 1197 seemed to solve the problem of the German threat. His heir was not quite three years old. There followed years of political uncertainty in both Sicily and Germany. The dominant figure was now the new Pope Innocent III who ascended the throne of St Peter in January 1198. His attention soon turned to Byzantium. His predecessor Celestine III had been in correspondence with Alexius III Angelus, who had hoped to use the papacy as a counterweight to Henry VI. Byzantine diplomats recognised that a situation was developing in Italy not so different from the days of Alexander III and Frederick Barbarossa. In retrospect, it looked as though Manuel I Comnenus had made effective political capital out of his support for the papacy against the German emperor.

III

With the death of Henry VI an alliance with the papacy was no longer the pressing concern that it had been for Byzantium. But for Innocent III it was another matter. He was a young man – only thirty-seven when he became pope. He was determined to press forward with the reform of Christendom, which had suffered a series of setbacks since the Third Lateran Council of 1179. The most serious was the loss of Jerusalem in 1187 and the failure of the Third Crusade to recover it. The reconquest of Jerusalem was to be Innocent III's most pressing concern. He issued his crusade bull on 15 August 1198. It was the first major act of his pontificate. At almost the same time he replied to Alexius III Angelus who had written to him to congratulate him on his elevation to the

Apostolic See. Innocent's reply does not survive, but it can be partly reconstructed from Alexius Angelus's response. The pope admonished the Byzantine emperor for failing to show proper humility before God and criticised him for his lack of interest in the condition of the Holy Land and for his refusal to support any crusade. The pope raised the question of the union of churches as a separate item. But the essential is that from the outset Innocent III attempted to involve Byzantium in his crusading plans.[29]

The emperor's reply of February 1199 was a study in prevarication.[30] He rejected the charge of lack of humility; he was full of zeal for the crusade. He would willingly lay down his life for the liberation of the Holy Sepulchre. However, he judged that this was a matter for God rather than men and that recent events had shown that God had still not forgiven the Christians those sins that had allowed the Muslims to recover the Holy Places. The emperor reminded the pope of the damage that Frederick Barbarossa had inflicted on the Byzantine Empire during the previous crusade. His unhappy fate only underlined the emperor's contention that God was not well pleased. If the pope insisted on persevering with an expedition to the Holy Land, the Byzantines would help by supplying any necessities, but Alexius would put off launching his own crusade until a more suitable occasion.

The Byzantine emperor tried to balance this snub with a more positive attitude to the question of the union of churches. He thought that the church under its shepherd Christ had always maintained its essential unity, but admitted that there were, largely for political reasons, local differences. He welcomed the pope's readiness to solve these and proposed that a general council of the church should be convened by the pope. This was a major concession on the part of a Byzantine emperor. Previous general councils had been summoned by the emperor at Constantinople.

The pope's reply is dated 13 November 1199.[31] He was writing at a time when little if any progress had been made with organising a crusade. He dismissed Alexius Angelus's position on a crusade as empty words, but would let the matter drop. He hoped that the emperor might change his mind, if only to avoid the obloquy his stance was bound to attract. As for the union of churches, the emperor should remember that Rome was 'head and mother of all churches', not so much by virtue of its recognition as such by the General Council, more by divine mandate. This meant that the patriarch of Constantinople was obliged to obey the papacy, which of course had the right to convoke a general council of the church. Innocent III suggested that such a meeting might provide an occasion where the patriarch could publicly avow the reverence and obedience he owed to the Apostolic See. Innocent ended with these ominous words which suggested a sinister purpose behind the crusade the pope was launching: 'We trust that things will not turn out differently, or we shall be compelled to proceed both against you, who can, if you so wish, carry out what we command, and against him [the patriarch] and the church of the Greeks.'

This correspondence was accompanied by another between Innocent III and the Byzantine patriarch John X Kamateros (1198–1206). This was conducted in very polite terms. In his first letter of February 1199 the patriarch was careful to spell out his solidarity with the Byzantine emperor. He emphasised that Byzantine relations with the papacy – being in his opinion primarily political in nature – were really the business of his excellent emperor Alexius Angelus. It was a way of conveying the Byzantine view that the papacy with its claim to primacy had become essentially a political power. He therefore contented himself with rejecting the papal theory of primacy, which Innocent III had spelt out all too clearly. The patriarch took issue with the notion that the Roman Church was the universal church with the pope at its head; also with the claim that Rome was the Mother Church. Properly, this was Jerusalem. The patriarch insisted that the unity of the church was not a matter of adhesion to the Church of Rome, but of belief in doctrine.[32] Innocent III replied on 12 November 1199 and restated papal primacy. God Himself had ascribed to Rome a plenitude of ecclesiastical power. The pope dismissed the patriarch's objections to Rome being considered the mother of all churches. It was not that the Church of Rome was founded by Peter before any other church, but that Peter held the highest dignity among the apostles. In his reply, which must have been drafted in the early months of 1200, the patriarch demanded chapter and verse proving that Rome was the Mother Church. In any case, Peter did not belong exclusively to Rome, but to the whole church. Historically, Rome's primacy derived from its former status as an imperial capital.[33] The patriarch did not even feel the need to point out that this had now passed to the new Rome. Against the papal claims to primacy he was content to set out the theory of the pentarchy under the presidency of Christ. It seemed to the patriarch that the pope was trying to usurp for the Roman Church the headship of the church universal. He was thus setting himself against Christ. An impasse had clearly been reached. John X Kamateros ends his letter with these words: 'If what we have written displeases your holiness, it is impossible for us to diverge from the truth, even if something a myriad times more terrible was threatened against us.'[34] The patriarch is taking up the pope's threat that he might have to proceed against the Byzantine emperor and patriarch. It is easy to detect beneath the polite surface of this correspondence between pope and patriarch impatience on the part of the former and resentment and alarm on the part of the latter. Once the crusade started to get off the ground this correspondence assumed, as we shall see, a new relevance, for the pope now seemed to have the means to proceed against the emperor and patriarch of Constantinople.

But for the moment, with the danger of a German invasion removed, the Byzantine elite could return to its political infighting. The Emperor Alexius III Angelus headed only one consortium of families, if for the moment dominant. He strengthened his position by marrying one daughter into the Palaiologos family and another into the Laskaris. His hold on power depended on such alliances. The key figure was his consort Euphrosyne Doukaina Kamatera, who brought with her the powerful Kamateros connection which at the time dominated the church and administration. She was recognised by all as the power behind the throne.[35] Malcontents congregated around the deposed Emperor Isaac, who was enjoying a comfortable exile on the shores of the Bosporus. Nicetas Choniates noted the number of Latins who visited the ex-emperor; also that he was in touch with his daughter Eirene, who was married to Philip of Swabia, now head of the Hohenstaufen family following the death of his brother, the German Emperor Henry VI. The deposed Emperor Isaac begged his daughter to use her influence on his behalf. According to Nicetas Choniates, instructions came back from the West as to what he should do.[36] The upshot was the escape to the West of Isaac's son, the 'young' Alexius Angelus.

In the spring of 1201 the Emperor Alexius Angelus took the young prince on campaign with him. It was a way of keeping an eye on him. The young Alexius repaid his uncle by evading his minders and by escaping on a Pisan ship. It must have been coordinated with supporters in the West, because Eirene was ready with a large force to escort her brother from the port of Ancona to her husband's court.[37] The consequences of this act were to be devastating. However, taking refuge in a foreign court was nothing new. Similarly, the search for foreign backing by dissident members of the ruling dynasty had plenty of precedents. There was a plot behind the Fourth Crusade, but it was a plot to rescue the young Alexius, whose life was in danger now that his uncle had designated his son-in-law, Theodore Laskaris, as his heir apparent. Between the hatching of the plot towards the end of 1200 and the arrival of the young Alexius at the court of Philip of Swabia around September 1201 much had changed, not least that a crusade was at long last taking shape. The young Alexius might well be of use to his brother-in-law Philip of Swabia. The idea of seeking help from the West for political advantage does not seem to have occasioned any revulsion at the time. Nicetas Choniates condemned it in his *History*, but this was in retrospect. He saw the Comneni, by which he meant the court aristocracy, as 'the major cause of the destruction of the Empire', especially those who had gone into exile. When they returned and seized power, they revealed how worthless they were.[38]

The politics of the Byzantine court were largely conducted by a closed circle of families. It was a selfish business played out with little reference to anything but family interest. However, in the years after Manuel Comnenus's death new factors began to make their appearance, which would not so much alter the conduct of politics, as render Byzantium increasingly fragile. The first was the growing importance of the populace of Constantinople. Nicetas Choniates testifies to their power, but, fearing and despising them, dismisses them as a rabble. He conceals that they possessed some degree of organisation and leadership. In 1182 Andronicus Comnenus had made a deal with various 'bosses' which had delivered him the support of the people of Constantinople.[39] Nicetas Choniates may just have left us a description of one of these 'bosses' in the shape of a successful businessman called Kalomodios. When he was arrested for non-payment of taxes by Alexius III Angelus's agents, the mob rose up and cornered the Patriarch John Kamateros in the Church of St Sophia. The patriarch was persuaded to intervene with the emperor on Kalomodios's behalf and obtained his release.[40] Representatives of different trades and professions were summoned to the General Assembly called in 1197 by Alexius III Angelus to consider how to buy off the German ruler Henry VI. These were the leaders of the Constantinopolitan populace. Nicetas Choniates condemns them for their mindless violence and lack of respect for traditional authority.[41] It is difficult to penetrate behind Choniates's disparaging criticism. One or two stray details suggest that their actions were better focused than Choniates allowed. They were anti-Latin, but not only for crudely materialistic reasons. There was a moral dimension to their actions, which took religious form. However misguidedly, they believed that they were defending Orthodoxy from its enemies. The people of Constantinople still retained an intense interest in religious dispute and took sides in the series of dogmatic controversies that were a feature of the second half of the twelfth century. They made their feelings felt when traditions were ignored. To take a banal example, there were complaints about a sermon of such excessive length that it threatened to curtail the festivities associated with St Xenophon's day.[42] More seriously, there were popular protests when imperial officials exceeded their authority or engaged in nefarious activities. The people of Constantinople posed as the upholders of traditional order at a time when this seemed threatened by the weakness of imperial government, the indifference of the ruling elite, and the presence of Latins in the capital.[43]

This will have struck the likes of Nicetas Choniates as sheer presumption. The moral order was none of the business of the mob. It was the preserve of men like him – well educated and public spirited – who came from families with a prominent role in the church and the civil service. Nicetas Choniates reached the position of grand logothete which placed him at the head of the civil service. His elder brother Michael was already archbishop of Athens. Nicetas married into another civil service family – the Belissariotes. A brother-in-law was prefect of Constantinople. There were far grander civil service families, such as the Kamateros, the Tornikes, and the Kastamonites, who had ties to the imperial family.[44] Theodore Kastamonites ran the civil service for his nephew Isaac II Angelus. He was succeeded in this role by Constantine Mesopotamites, who survived the coup which brought Alexius III Angelus to the throne thanks to the support he had from the Empress Euphrosyne. She preferred him to members of her own family. At the same time, he was made archbishop of Thessalonica. This was an appointment too many. The combination of administrative and episcopal office was held to be scandalous. Constantine Mesopotamites's enemies forced him out of office.[45] Nicetas Choniates outlines the infighting within the Byzantine civil service in the years leading up to the coming of the Fourth Crusade with much relish. He is careful not to reveal his own contribution nor even where his sympathies lay, despite being no stranger to controversy. His role may have been more prominent than he is willing to admit in his *History*, where he adopts a high moral stance appropriate to an incorruptible civil servant. The civil service was among the great and enduring strengths of the Byzantine Empire. However, by the end of the twelfth century it had become compromised. It was being run in the interests of various cliques. The claim made by civil servants such as Nicetas Choniates to be guardians of traditional order rang hollow.

Choniates, in the same way as many other civil servants, had the closest connections with the Patriarchal Church. He was a more than competent theologian. The Patriarchal Church was divided at the end of the twelfth century over the question of the communion elements. Were they corruptible or incorruptible? The traditional teaching was that their sanctification made them incorruptible. This had been challenged many years previously by the monk Michael Glykas, who had urged that because they were instituted by Christ as a man they remained corruptible until the moment they were consumed by the communicant, at which point they were miraculously transformed, in the same way as the Risen Christ.

It was a way of emphasising the miraculous dimension to the Eucharist, but it suggested the Real Presence a little too vividly. The main opponent of this modification was the future Patriarch John Kamateros, who accused Nicetas Choniates of being a partisan of the Glykas position. Choniates claimed that his views were scandalously misrepresented, but he was clearly an opponent of the Patriarch John Kamateros and his supporters.[46] Opposition of this kind to the Patriarch John Kamateros may explain his dependence on the emperor and his less than heroic showing in the face of the demands for submission to Rome on the part of the crusaders. He failed to give any clear lead to Byzantine society.

On the eve of the coming of the Fourth Crusade Byzantine society in the capital was deeply divided. It was also increasingly isolated from the provinces. This was something new. The Byzantine Empire was built on the domination of a circle of provinces by the capital. This had been assured by a regular system of provincial administration. The key figure was the governor appointed from Constantinople. Under Manuel I Comnenus the hold of the capital over the provinces still seemed assured. In many ways, it appeared stronger than ever. To the formal ties created by the imperial administrative system was added the increasing prestige of provincial bishops, now chosen in the main from the patriarchal clergy. The court aristocracy and the great monasteries and charitable institutions of the capital were also building up estates and other interests in provincial centres.[47]

The trouble was that the pervasiveness of Constantinopolitan interests upset the balance between capital and provinces. In the past Byzantine provincial administration worked because it made use of local figures, whether in the imperial administration or in the church. It respected local needs. Constantinople creamed off much of the surplus wealth through taxation, but equally redistributed a proportion of the proceeds in salaries and purchases. Under the Comneni, however, Constantinople benefited not only from the regular taxes levied on the provinces, but also from the rents paid to absentee landowners, of one sort or another, who were resident in the capital. It was exactly these people who were major beneficiaries of government spending. The increased exploitation of the provinces by the capital was possible because the former enjoyed a period of sustained economic and demographic growth. These were the conditions that attracted the elite based in the capital to build up its interests in the provinces and not just in the 'Home Counties' around the Sea of Marmara, as had been the case in the past. The Peloponnese can be considered as an example. According to official records the major landowners were the Branas and Cantacuzene families, Eirene, a daughter of Alexius III Angelus, who married into the Palaiologos family, and a series of monasteries, one of which was the great imperial foundation of the Pantokrator at Constantinople.[48]

On the eve of the Fourth Crusade, therefore, landholding in the Peloponnese was dominated by absentees resident in the capital. But there were also local interests. Nicetas Choniates has recorded the names of the 'tyrants', as he called them, who ruled the Peloponnese. Leo Sgouros held the Argolid; Chamateros the plain of Sparta.[49] There were also other prominent families in different parts of the Peloponnese who did not belong to the metropolitan elite but exerted considerable local influence.[50] The evidence is probably best for the Peloponnese but the existence of local ascendancies can be established for most regions of the empire. They had used the weakness of government at the centre after the death of Manuel I Comnenus to assert themselves. There was a series of rebellions throughout the Byzantine Empire. Occasionally, their leaders followed the traditional pattern of aiming to topple the reigning emperor; more often, they were content to establish their ascendancy over a region or a city. The best-documented example of this was the rebellion of Peter and Asen in 1186 which led on to the establishment of the Second Bulgarian Empire. There was an element of opportunism, obviously, but their rebellion was sparked off by the imperial government's demand for a levy to pay for the Emperor Isaac's marriage to a Hungarian princess. It was a clear example of local resentment of the capital's never-ending demands.[51]

Byzantine provincial separatism plays no part in the events that led up to the conquest of Constantinople by the Fourth Crusade. It is much more important for the consequences of 1204. In the end, it ensured that the fall of Constantinople would not be followed by the conquest of the whole empire, for the newly independent Bulgarian realm proved the crusaders' nemesis. The only region where the crusaders enjoyed permanent success was in the Greek lands, exactly the area which had been most frequented by Italian merchants in the twelfth century. The local ascendancies had built up links with Venetians and others. In some parts of the Byzantine Empire the prospect of western rule did not seem so out of place. Indeed, it was almost a guarantee of continuing prosperity, which may explain why at this juncture the port of Attaleia with its links to Cyprus and the crusader states chose the Italian Aldobrandini as its ruler.[52] This illustrates how vulnerable Byzantium was at the end of the twelfth century to any western threat.

The legacy of the Comneni and the crusades was complete ambivalence at Byzantium about westerners. It emerges from the pages of Nicetas Choniates's *History*. There is bitter hostility to the westerners: they are stupid, uncouth barbarians; there is, equally, an appreciation of their many virtues which reveal Byzantine inadequacies. Society in the capital was divided over the Latin issue: the populace was bitterly anti-Latin. This may have had something to do with competition from the Latins, but seems more rooted in the self-appointed role of the people of Constantinople as defenders of Orthodoxy. The imperial family, or perhaps better imperial aristocracy, had no qualms about using Latins in their quarrels, whatever their private thoughts might have been. The Byzantine establishment was far more exercised by the danger represented by the papacy.

IV

This was a fatal misreading of the situation. A commentary on this conflicting stance is provided by the court orator Nicephorus Chrysoberges in two speeches he delivered; the first before the Patriarch John X Kamateros in April 1202[53] and the second before Alexius IV Angelus at Epiphany (6 January) 1204.[54]

By the spring of 1202 the details of the preparations being made to launch the crusade from Venice would have become widely known in Constantinople as would the escape to the West of the young Alexius. The orator urges defiance on the patriarch. He must remain true to the spirit of his correspondence with the pope. Chrysoberges notes the arrogant tone of the pope's letters which contrasted with the humility of the patriarch's, characterised by their fidelity to the Gospels. He rehearses the content of the correspondence accurately, but he spells out its meaning, which two years earlier had not been at all clear. Innocent III is demonised. He is likened to a wild beast: 'His discourse revealed his murderous teeth.'[55] The pope's hostility to the patriarch originated with the 'Italians'. They were the people who had persuaded him to proceed against the patriarch. In other words, the spiritual authority of the papacy was being perverted by the pope's willingness to be used by these people. It is not immediately clear exactly who the Byzantine orator has in mind when he uses the term 'Italians', but it is difficult not to identify them with the crusaders who were now in league with Venice. In words reminiscent of Nicetas Choniates's famous denunciation of the Latins, the orator gives it as his opinion that the 'Italians' were a 'race characterised by a lack of breeding which is totally at variance with our noble sense of order. It is a self-evident truth that just as they are cut off from us by the sea and intervening mountains, so they are still further removed from our way of thinking.'[56] The orator closes by urging the audience to bring pressure to bear on the patriarch to adopt a forceful position in the face of this new threat from the West. The assessment of this threat in this speech may seem unrealistic, but it represents the thinking of much of the Byzantine establishment. It placed an immense responsibility on the shoulders of the patriarch to inspire resistance to the claims being made against Byzantium by the pope as the mouthpiece of these 'Italians'. John X Kamateros was not able, or perhaps even willing, to accept this responsibility. His ability to equivocate in the face of Latin demands was the despair of Nicetas Choniates.

Nicephorus Chrysoberges's second speech was addressed to Alexius IV Angelus and was delivered on 6 January 1204. Events had moved on since his previous speech. He congratulates the young emperor for the way he had succeeded in exploiting the crusaders and Venetian seapower to recover the throne of Constantinople. However, he must be aware of the dangers involved: 'Just because they conveyed you, emperor, who have come hither by God's will, let them not grow wanton, but because they, restoring the lord emperor, have fulfilled servants' roles, let them be bent to servile laws.'[57] This exactly expresses the long-held conviction at Byzantium that the Latins were there to be manipulated. The orator advocates that the emperor adopt a policy of divide and rule, taking the more amenable crusaders into his service and destroying others. The speech ends with a plea that the emperor uses the good offices of the patriarch to effect a reconciliation of the Old Rome and the New. The young emperor is in a position not unlike that of Soloman, who had to make judgement over which woman was mother of a baby. So Alexius had to choose between the claims of the Old and the New Rome. He was exhorted to pick the latter.[58] This speech must have been composed in December 1203 and probably represents a policy statement by the young emperor designed to placate Byzantine opinion. By the time it was delivered on 6 January 1204 relations with the Latins had reached a critical moment. If the sentiments expressed in the speech were by now unrealistic, they represent the conventional wisdom of the Byzantine court in its dealings with the West. It was legitimate, even laudable, for Byzantine emperors – even if originally pretenders – to exploit Latin military and naval power, but it was essential to ensure that they knew their place; that they did not 'grow wanton'.

These two speeches by Chrysoberges lay bare the naivety and lack of realism of the Byzantine elite's appreciation of the threat represented by the West. Its members continued to believe that it could be contained through negotiations with the papacy over church unity. They equally saw little harm in exploiting Latin forces for internal political advantage and believed that they still had the means to discipline them, if they got out of hand.

The outcome of the Fourth Crusade was largely determined by the decisions and actions of its leaders, but the stance adopted by the

Byzantine establishment was almost equally important. It was characterised by political division and by perfidy. The lack of solidarity typical of the Byzantine elite at this moment meant that there was no concerted resistance to the crusaders. Alexius III Angelus fled the city without putting up more than a token fight; Alexius V Doukas did little more. The efforts made to drive a wedge between the Venetians and the crusaders and then between Boniface of Montferrat and the other leaders were treated as treachery by the crusaders. The murder of the young emperor by Alexius Doukas only confirmed this. At the same time, the efforts made by Alexius IV Angelus with the help of the patriarch to work out a church settlement acceptable to the crusaders only underlined the religious differences separating the Byzantines from their allies. Stripping church treasures to pay the crusaders for their services and agreeing to submission to Rome inflamed opinion at Constantinople.[59] There were soon clashes between the Byzantine populace and Latins resident in Constantinople. The passage of the Fourth Crusade was undeniably a much greater challenge than the passage of previous crusades. Political division alone made a successful outcome for the Byzantines unlikely, but this was compounded on the part of the Byzantines by religious hatred and a tradition of contempt for the Latins, who were there to be used. The Fourth Crusade revealed the bankruptcy of Byzantium's handling of the Latin problem. The Byzantine establishment did not know how to escape its western entanglement; and perhaps did not even wish to do so.

Notes

1. P. Maas, 'Die Musen des Alexios I', *Byzantinische Zeitschrift*, 22(1913), 357–8.
2. John Cinnamus, *Epitome rerum ab Ioanne et Manuele Comnenis gestarum* (Bonn, 1836), 68–9.
3. On Comnenian foreign policy see P. Lamma, *Comneni e Staufer. Ricerche sui rapporti fra Bisanzio e l'Occidente nel secolo XII*, 2 vols (Rome, 1955–7); Magdalino, *Manuel Komnenos*, 27–108.
4. Cinnamus, *Epitome*, 220.17–24.
5. William of Tyre, *Chronicon*, ed. R. B. C. Huygens (Corpus Christianorum Cont. Med. LXIII) (Turnholt, 1986), 22, 5.19–24: II, 1012; 22, 11(10).14–25: II, 1020; Walter Map, *De Nugis Curialium*, ed. and transl. M. R. James (Oxford, 1983), 174–5.
6. Nicetas Choniates, 209.
7. Georges et Dèmètrios Tornikès, *Lettres et Discours*, ed. J. Darrouzès (Paris, 1970), 129.
8. J. Shepard and S. Franklin, *Byzantine Diplomacy* (Aldershot, 1992), 271–2.
9. See M. J. Angold, *Church and Society in Byzantium under the Comneni 1081–1261* (Cambridge, 1995), 106.

10. Ibid., 221–6.
11. D. M. Nicol, 'The Papal Scandal', *Studies in Church History*, 13(1976), 141–68.
12. See Angold, *Church and Society*, 505–14.
13. Ibid., 190–3.
14. Michael Choniates, *Tὰ Σωζόμενα* I, 183.
15. Migne *PG*, 136, c.717D.
16. Nicetas Choniates, 382.
17. Ibid., 382–95.
18. Ibid., 416–17.
19. Ibid., 410.
20. Ibid., 402–4, 406–11.
21. Ibid., 475–9.
22. Ibid., 525–6.
23. Ibid., 296–8; Eustathios, *Capture of Thessaloniki*, §49, 58–9; §68, 88–9.
24. Nicetas Choniates, 404.
25. See C. M. Brand, 'The Byzantines and Saladin, 1185–1192: opponents of the Third Crusade', *Speculum*, 37(1962), 167–81.
26. Nicetas Choniates, 410.
27. Angold, *Church and State*, 121–3.
28. Nicetas Choniates, 478–9.
29. See now G. Prinzing, 'Das Papsttum und der orthodox geprägte Südosten Europas 1180–1216', in *Das Papsttum in der Welt des 12.Jahrhunderts*, ed. E.-D. Hehl, I. H. Ringel and H. Seibert (Stuttgart, 2002), 150–62.
30. *Die Register Innocenz' III*, ed. O. Hageneder *et al.*, 8 vols (Graz-Cologne, Rome and Vienna, 1964–), II, no. 201 (210), 389–93. Cf. F. Dölger, *Regesten der Kaiserurkunden des oströmischen Reiches* (Munich and Berlin, 1924–65), 1648.
31. *Register Innocenz' III*, II, no. 202 (211), 394–7.
32. A. Papadakis and A.-M. Talbot, 'John X Camaterus confronts Innocent III', *Byzantinoslavica*, 33(1972), 33–5. Cf. J. Spiteris, *La critica bizantina del primato romano nel secolo XII* (Rome, 1979), 261–6.
33. Papadakis and Talbot, 'John X Camaterus', 40.10–12.
34. Ibid., 41.23–5.
35. Nicetas Choniates, 460–1.
36. Ibid., 536.
37. Ibid., 536–7.
38. Ibid., 529.
39. Eustathios, *Capture of Thessaloniki*, §37, 42–3.
40. Nicetas Choniates, 524.
41. Ibid., 234.
42. Angold, *Church and Society*, 131–2.
43. Cf. E. P. Thompson, 'The Moral Economy of the Crowd', in his *Customs in Common* (New York, 1991), 185–258.
44. M. J. Angold, 'The Imperial Administration and the Patriarchal Clergy in the twelfth century', *Byzantinische Forschungen*, 19(1993), 17–24.
45. Nicetas Choniates, 489–93.

46. Angold, *Church and Society*, 126–36.
47. See Magdalino, *Manuel Komnenos*, 109–79.
48. Tafel and Thomas I, 469–70.
49. Nicetas Choniates, 638.
50. See P. Magdalino, 'A neglected authority for the history of the Peloponnese in the early thirteenth century: Demetrius Chomatianos, archbishop of Bulgaria', *Byzantinische Zeitschrift*, 70(1977), 316–23.
51. J.-C. Cheynet, *Pouvoir et Contestations à Byzance (963–1210)* (Byzantina Sorbonensia 9) (Paris, 1990), 427–58.
52. Nicetas Choniates, 639–40.
53. R. Browning, 'An unpublished address of Nicephorus Chrysoberges to Patriarch John Kamateros of 1202', *Byzantine Studies/Etudes byzantines*, 5(1978), 37–68: text 48–63 (reprinted in R. Browning, *History, Language and Literature in the Byzantine world* (Northampton, 1989), no. ix).
54. C. M. Brand, 'A Byzantine plan for the Fourth Crusade', *Speculum*, 43(1968), 462–75.
55. Browning, 'An unpublished address', 61.29–30.
56. Ibid., 58.35–40.
57. Brand, 'A Byzantine plan', 467–8.
58. Ibid., 470–1.
59. Nicetas Choniates, 551–2; 555–6.

chapter 3

THE WESTERN ASSESSMENT OF BYZANTIUM

The eventual conquest of Constantinople took place as a result of a series of decisions. They were not taken mindlessly, but were reached by means of a series of debates of which some record has survived. In these debates a variety of viewpoints were put forward. They were largely based on experience of the past. It is therefore vital to reconstruct, as far as is possible, the outlook on the past of the crusaders in order to understand why their leaders arrived at the decisions that they did.

It is important at the outset to stress how different the outlook of the Venetians was from that of their Frankish allies. Whereas the crusade ideal impregnated the latter's way of thinking, it did not mean too much to the Venetians. They had not contributed very gloriously to the First Crusade, unlike the Genoese, for whom participation in the First Crusade came to be seen as the start of a new phase in the history of the commune.[1] Nor had they been closely involved in either the Second or the Third Crusades. The expedition that meant most to the Venetians was the 'crusade' of 1123–4 which resulted in the conquest of the city of Tyre. The Venetians responded to the call for aid that came from the king of Jerusalem, Baldwin II, in the aftermath of the Frankish defeat in 1120 on the Field of Blood outside Antioch. Their contribution was to defeat the Fatimid navy and help to conquer Tyre – the only major port along the Palestinian coast not yet in Frankish hands. The Venetians secured, as their reward, a third of the city, but that was not all that they gained from this expedition. It coincided with the Emperor John II Comnenus's refusal to renew their commercial privileges in the Byzantine Empire. On the outward journey the Venetian fleet had plundered Corfu and the Ionian islands. On the return journey the Venetians seized the island of Chios and systematically ravaged the shores of the Aegean. The Byzantines were made to see sense and negotiations began for the restoration of Venetian privileges, which were duly confirmed by the Byzantine emperor in his chrysobull of 1126. It was altogether a very satisfactory outcome. Venice had acquired a solid base in the crusader states and at the same time had recovered its position in the Byzantine Empire. An added bonus came in the form of the relics of St Isidore which the Venetians removed from Chios. The Venetian estimate of the possibilities of a crusade, in the end, owed much to their memory of the expedition of 1123–4.[2]

I

The Venetian attitude to Byzantium was complicated. Although Byzantium had not wielded any direct authority in the lagoon for centuries, it retained residual rights over Venice. In some sense, Venice remained a client of Byzantium. This was emphasised by the grant of imperial court titles to the doge of Venice and the patriarch of Grado in Alexius I Comnenus's chrysobull to Venice which dates to 1082. In it the Venetians are referred to as *rectis dulis Imperii mei*, in other words, 'good and faithful servants of my Empire'.[3] There was always an element of the Venetians striving not just to escape Byzantine tutelage, but also to outdo the Byzantines, who did not measure up to their 'sailor's gusto' to quote the Byzantine historian Cinnamus.[4] At the same time, they had an appreciative eye for Byzantine objets d'art, and the Byzantine way of life generally.

Venice's debt to Byzantium was enormous. The church of St Mark's provides the most obvious testimony. The original church built in the ninth century to house the relics of St Mark purloined from Alexandria was in the Byzantine style and even then seems to have been a simplified version of the church of the Holy Apostles at Constantinople. It was badly damaged by a fire in 976, but the hasty repairs cannot have been entirely satisfactory. Around the middle of the eleventh century it was rebuilt on a larger scale, but still retaining its Byzantine planning. It was then sumptuously decorated with mosaic. Initially, mosaicists were brought in from Byzantium. Very little of the original 'Byzantine' mosaic work survives. Increasingly, local artists were used who developed their own styles. St Mark's was not a 'Byzantine' church, but it owed much to Byzantine influence and taste. This was much more obvious in the twelfth century than it is now, when it still retained its shallow domes and brick façade reminiscent of the great churches built in Constantinople in the eleventh and twelfth centuries.[5] Venetian taste for Byzantine models is also apparent in the redecoration of the cathedral at Torcello.[6] The work of Byzantine mosaicists dominates in the shape of the Virgin and Child in the main apse and the Last Judgement on the west wall. More modest is the church of S. Fosca that sits in the shadow of the

cathedral. It was built around 1100 in order to house the relics of
S. Fosca, which according to tradition had been brought back in the
tenth century from Byzantium.[7] The architectural style adopted was a
version of the Greek cross octagon, which seems only to have evolved
in Byzantium in the early eleventh century and was employed in such
prestige buildings as Nea Moni, on the island of Chios, the Catholicon
of Hosios Loukas, and the monastery church of Daphni. In other words,
Venice was au fait with the latest architectural developments at Byzantium. Dating from roughly the same period is the church of S. Donato
at Murano.[8] It was designed to house the relics of the saint which had
been brought back in 1125 from Cephalonia, where they had been
acquired during the successful expedition against Byzantium. The architectural form is much less obviously Byzantine, but the mosaic floor
completed in 1140 and the mosaic of the Virgin and Child in the apse,
though of local workmanship, point to the continuing fascination with
Byzantine models.[9] Equally, the surviving palaces that go back to the
twelfth century – the Fondaco dei Turchi, for instance – appear to owe
something both in planning and architectural features to Byzantium, as
did the old Doge's Palace built by Sebastiano Ziani in the 1170s.[10] On
the eve of the Fourth Crusade Byzantine influence continued to permeate
the fabric of Venice.

The Doge Enrico Dandolo (1192–1205) seems to have been a con-
noisseur of Byzantine art. He is supposed to have sent back from the
sack of Constantinople various marbles to decorate the façade of the
palace Ca' Farsetti that his son Renier was building at Venice.[11] The
Dandolo belonged to the inner core of patrician families who dominated
Venetian politics from the middle of the twelfth century. Their origins
cannot be traced back as far as some other patrician families. They begin
to appear in the records only from the turn of the tenth century. Their
rise to prominence seems to be connected with the election in 1129 of
one of their number – Enrico Dandolo – to the patriarchal throne of
Grado. This uncle of his namesake – the future doge – remained in
office for fifty years; the family was notably long-lived. His importance
in the politics of the time is apparent from the decision taken in 1147 by
Doge Pietro Polani to expel him from Venice and to slight the property
of the family. This was only a temporary setback. On Polani's death two
years later the new Doge Domenico Morosini ordered restitution to be
made to the Dandolo family. From then on Vitale Dandolo, the future
doge's father, became increasingly powerful in ducal counsels, leaving
his sons to manage the family's affairs.

Vitale was at the centre of the events surrounding Manuel I Comnenus's coup against the Venetians on 12 March 1171. He was one of

the inner circle of advisers that the Doge Vitale Michiel consulted when news of the event reached Venice. Among the others were Sebastiano Ziani and Orio Mastropiero, who had just returned from Constantinople where they had been honorably received by Manuel Comnenus. His coup was such a reversal of policy as to be almost incomprehensible. The advice given to the doge was that he should send emissaries immediately to find out more precisely what had happened. It was overtaken by popular indignation, which demanded revenge against the Byzantine emperor. The doge responded by organising an expeditionary force which set sail in September 1171. The intention was to repeat the tactics that had worked so well in 1125. The Venetians again made Chios the centre of their operations, but this time they were struck down by plague and were forced to sail back home in the spring, having accomplished nothing at all. The Doge Vitale Michiel was blamed for the disaster. He tried to explain himself to a popular assembly, but was assassinated as he fled. He was succeeded by Sebastiano Ziani who was elected unopposed with the cry: 'Long Live the Doge and let's hope we obtain peace through him.'[12] The Venetian patriciate wanted peace with Byzantium, but not at any price.

The events of 1171–2 dominated Venetian thinking about Byzantium. They were events with which Enrico Dandolo was intimately acquainted. He had sailed with the expeditionary force. He was one of the ambassadors sent from Chios to negotiate with Manuel Comnenus, who refused to receive them. It can only be a legend that it was on this occasion that he was blinded by the Byzantines. Thereafter he and his father Vitale played an important role in the diplomatic efforts to normalise relations with the Byzantine Empire. Vitale went twice to Constantinople in 1174, dying there on his second visit. Meanwhile, Enrico had been sent first to Sicily and then on to the Sicilian expeditionary force in Egypt to see if pressure could be brought to bear on the Byzantine emperor through the king of Sicily. The Venetians followed a doggedly consistent policy of recovering their position at Constantinople by diplomatic means. Enrico Dandolo contributed to this as a diplomat and continued it as doge. He was sent as ambassador to Constantinople in 1183 to supervise the return of the Venetian quarter. He would have been deeply involved in the negotiations which eventually resulted in the issue of Isaac II Angelus's chrysobulls of February 1187. The Venetians had by patient diplomacy obtained – on paper – all that they wanted. Their commercial privileges were reconfirmed. Their quarter in Constantinople was officially returned to them. The price was the renewal of Venice's traditional alliance with Byzantium and a promise to supply the emperor with ships when called upon. The question of reparations for damage suffered in the 1171 coup was resolved in 1189. The sum of 1,500 pounds of gold was agreed, 250 pounds to be paid immediately and the rest in annual instalments over the next six years.[13]

It was left to Enrico Dandolo to implement this apparently satisfactory agreement, when in 1192 he was elected doge, despite his age and blindness. His intimate knowledge of the negotiations with Byzantium going back twenty years or more must have been one of his recommendations. Almost at once he was faced with the unwelcome news that the Byzantine emperor Isaac II Angelus had confirmed the privileges of the Genoese and Pisans. This was all too reminiscent of the events which had led up to the arrest of the Venetians resident in the Byzantine Empire in March 1171. Then the Venetians had been promised favoured status, only to find the Byzantine emperor Manuel I Comnenus turning to their rivals, the Pisans and the Genoese. The situation was complicated by the overthrow in 1195 of Isaac Angelus in favour of his brother Alexius, who failed to confirm his brother's understanding with the Venetians. Once again, Venetian interests in the Byzantine Empire were threatened, not least by the activities of Latin pirates in the Aegean, which the Byzantine emperor was unable to contain. In 1196 Dandolo despatched to the Aegean an expeditionary force to deal with the pirate menace. It is a mysterious episode. It seems that Enrico Dandolo then ordered it to return home, but the commanders of the fleet ignored his orders on the grounds that it was 'very right and necessary to stay with the fleet in Romania'.[14] If the outcome of the affair is unknown, it reveals that there were those who disagreed with Dandolo's preference for protracted negotiations with the Byzantine emperor. These, however, bore fruit in the treaty concluded in November 1198, which confirmed the old privileges enjoyed by the Venetians in the Byzantine Empire. Dandolo seems to have abandoned any claim to the balance of the reparations agreed for Venetian losses in 1171. The Byzantine emperor, for his part, made a substantial concession over judicial procedures. Cases where a Byzantine plaintiff accused a Venetian over a pecuniary matter were to go before a Venetian judge and could not be opened up again in a Byzantine court. Venetian plaintiffs would have to go before the Byzantine courts in the usual manner. Though apparently a technical matter, it did open up the way for greater Venetian autonomy within the Byzantine Empire. The old alliance between Venice and Byzantium was renewed on the terms negotiated previously with Isaac II Angelus. Through patient diplomacy the Venetians had apparently secured their position in Constantinople.[15]

The Dandolo who emerged from these negotiations was a man of caution. But that was scarcely how the Byzantine historian Nicetas Choniates presented him. He considered the doge the major threat:

his eyesight might have been impaired and he might have been bowed with age, but he was full of rancour against the Byzantines and desired revenge. He had a sharp eye for a shady deal, claiming that he was the shrewdest of the shrewd. It was his boast that failure to revenge himself on the Byzantines for their senseless treatment of his people was tantamount to a sentence of death. He kept going over in his mind, time and time again, all that the Venetians had suffered at the hands of the Angeli brothers, when they were ruling, and before them at the hands of Andronicus, and even when Manuel reigned over the Byzantines.[16]

That this was the perceived wisdom of the Byzantine civil service emerges from a clause in the 1198 treaty. The Venetians had to swear that they would not use 'the anger directed against them' by Manuel I Comnenus nor any other similar incident as a pretext for violating the treaty.[17] The story was soon circulating that Dandolo had been blinded on the orders of Manuel Comnenus. This could only have been when acting as an ambassador in 1172. The almost contemporary *Historia Ducum Veneticorum* makes the strange observation that on that occasion both Dandolo and the other envoy came back 'in good health',[18] which suggests that there were rumours that they had been ill-treated in Constantinople or that other Venetian envoys had suffered at Byzantine hands. Villehardouin attributed Dandolo's blindness to a wound he had received on the head or face, but without further comment, which suggests that it was not connected with a mission to Byzantium.[19] The fact that Dandolo continued to sign documents into the 1180s also works against any idea that his blindness was somehow connected with his 1172 embassy to Byzantium. But even if Dandolo's blindness cannot be blamed on the Byzantines, does Nicetas Choniates's judgement that Dandolo was an inveterate enemy of Byzantium still contain an essential truth? In other words, did Dandolo's past experience of Byzantium predispose him towards launching an attack upon Constantinople? As grand logothete, Nicetas Choniates would not have been directly involved in foreign affairs, but he would have been personally acquainted with Demetrius Tornikes, the logothete of the drome, who had conducted negotiations with the Venetians. Choniates also – more surprisingly – had friends in the Venetian community in Constantinople. His view of Dandolo cannot therefore be dismissed out of hand. As doge and diplomat, Dandolo had pursued Venetian interest in a single-minded fashion. He considered that it was best served by a restoration of the Venetian presence in the Byzantine Empire, backed up by legal guarantees. His experience of Byzantium is not likely to have endeared it to him. The expulsion in 1171 still rankled. It remained a running sore in the shape of the reparations Venice demanded. However, in the interests of clinching a deal with the Byzantines in 1198 the matter was allowed to drop.

Dandolo embodied the experience and wisdom of the Venetians. He was guided by what he considered the best interests of the Venetian Republic. Through his long life this had been served most effectively by dogged diplomacy. Its monument was the series of chrysobulls granted by a succession of Byzantine emperors. Dandolo would have known these backwards. He would not have been working from some sense of rancour generated by his personal experience of Byzantium, but on the basis of the rights that Venice had acquired in Constantinople and the provinces of the empire by virtue of these imperial privileges.

His actions in the course of the Fourth Crusade therefore seem to be out of keeping with his past conduct. This is all the more surprising, given that he seems to have gained all that he wanted from the treaty of 1198 with Alexius III Angelus. Was he not bound by its terms and did not the Venetians on the whole respect their treaty obligations? With the exception of the clarification of legal procedures involving Byzantines and Venetians, the treaty of 1198 was a careful restatement of Venetian rights and obligations. In a sense, it was designed as the end of a chapter: nothing was said about the question of reparations which had exercised Venetian diplomats for over twenty years. By the time the treaty was signed and sealed in November 1198 Venice was being sounded out by a papal legate about cooperation on a new crusade. The question of Venetian interests in the Byzantine Empire should now have become of subsidiary importance, as Dandolo sought to use the crusade to establish Venetian interests more solidly in the ports of the Nile Delta, which were potentially far more profitable than Constantinople and other Byzantine centres. Dandolo would have expected the treaty of 1198 to safeguard Venetian interests in Byzantium and its terms to be respected by the Byzantine emperor. There was a clause whereby the latter promised to include Venice in any truce or treaty that he might make with an erstwhile enemy.[20] The decision made by Alexius III Angelus to start negotiating with the Genoese over an extension of their quarter would seem to be a violation of this condition. The Byzantine emperor made extensive new concessions to the Genoese in the treaty of 1201, but there is no discernible reaction on the part of the Venetians. However, there was another factor that would have weighed heavily with Dandolo, best expressed by the captains of the Venetian expeditionary force of 1196: 'It is right and proper for anyone who finds himself outside his *patria* whether with an army or in some other capacity to act tirelessly in matters which pertain to the honour of his *patria*.'[21] Venetian patriotism was already a powerful force and one that meant much to Dandolo. It might be necessary to deal with the Byzantines and the Genoese as the opportunity arose.

The Venetians were notoriously coy about recording their contribution to the Fourth Crusade. By the time Martin da Canal was writing around 1267 they had got their story straight. They had been acting as the devoted servants of Mother Church. It was a line that went all the way back to the letter that Enrico Dandolo sent to Innocent III after the conquest of Constantinople in 1204: 'Your holiness should therefore know that in whatever I and the Venetian people have done, we have laboured for the honour of God and of the Holy Roman Church and for your honour.'[22]

We can follow Queller in believing that by the end of the twelfth century the Venetians had no interest in conquering Constantinople.[23] This showed in the way the doge was less than interested in a diversion to Constantinople on behalf of the young Alexius and needed considerable persuading by the crusade leaders. The expulsion of the Venetians from the Byzantine Empire in 1171 and the seizure of Venetian goods certainly rankled. It is one of the few events recorded by the continuator of the *Altinate Chronicle* – a contemporary Venetian chronicle. The most important of these chronicles was the *Historia Ducum Veneticorum*. It takes as its starting point the reign of Ordelafo Falier (1101–18) and effectively ends with the Peace of Venice in 1177. Thereafter we have to rely on a continuation of the chronicle known as 'Giustiniani', which went down to the death of Pietro Ziani who died in 1229. It has a short and thoroughly unsatisfactory account of the events of the Fourth Crusade. It is far more detailed on the events of 1171 and the failure of the Venetian expedition of 1172 led by the Doge Vitale Michiel. Thereafter, apart from short entries on the restoration of good relations under Andronicus Comnenus and the grant of a new chrysobull by Isaac Angelus, the continuation of the *Historia Ducum Veneticorum* shows little interest in Byzantium. The decisive event was the Peace of Venice in 1177 which confirmed that Venice was operating within a western context. One knows how important this event was in the developing 'Myth of Venice'. Venetian concerns were much closer to home. The chronicle reveals what amounts to an obsession with Zara. It was not so much competition from the Hungarians that was behind this, but the operations of the Pisans in the Adriatic which were becoming more and more of a threat to Venice. The fear was that they might ally with Zara. It is only after the conquest of Zara in November 1202 that the chronicler feels the need to provide a sketch of Byzantine political history since the death of Manuel I Comnenus in order to explain how it was that the crusade was then diverted to Constantinople.[24]

The Venetian chronicles reveal fears that Venice was in an increasingly exposed position. Its merchants seemed to be losing out to their rivals the Pisans and the Genoese, whose privateering practices had made much of the Aegean and eastern Mediterranean unsafe for Venetian shipping.[25] Closer to home, the southern Italian city of Brindisi had forged an alliance with the Pisans. The Venetians understood in the wake of 1171 that they needed to diversify their interests and had negotiated commercial treaties with the sultan of Cairo, the ruler of the Maghreb, and the Armenian king of Cilicia. But they were latecomers to these markets and therefore found themselves at a disadvantage. There can be little doubt that Enrico Dandolo and the Venetian leadership understood that the crusade was an opportunity that was not to be missed. It opened up the prospect of Venetian domination of the markets of both the crusader states and the ports of the Nile Delta, potentially far more profitable than Constantinople. It was one of those liminal moments that affect all great powers. It was signalled by a shift in the historical myth that sustained Venice. From being 'a good and faithful servant' of the Byzantine emperor it became the dutiful daughter of the papacy. That was the message that was read into the Peace of Venice of 1177. It signalled emancipation from the ties which still linked it to Byzantium, but which had proved less than valuable in 1171. The Venetians now sought recognition of a distinct legal status within the Byzantine Empire. This was at the centre of the negotiations that produced the chrysobull of 1198. Dandolo even threatened to break these off if on this point Venetian demands were not met. The Byzantine authorities reluctantly agreed. They were compromising imperial sovereignty by recognising the extraterritorial status of the Venetians.[26]

II

Everything suggests that in the counsels of the crusaders Dandolo was a voice of reason and caution. He was not likely to be swayed by sentimental considerations about the rights of a Byzantine prince, who had been 'disinherited'. But this would have struck a chord with the Frankish leaders, who were familiar with the plot of Chrétien of Troyes's *Cligés*. The experience and ideals that the Franks brought to the crusade were very different, far more various than those conditioning the Venetian outlook. In the first place, there was the ideal of the crusade. The history of the crusades was something that the Franks are most likely to have approached through the *chansons de la croisade*, which mythologised the deeds of the First Crusade. These watered down the church's teaching on the crusade and placed much greater emphasis on the crusade as a chivalric undertaking. Their impact is evident in the histories of the Third Crusade, where the achievements of Richard Coeur de Lion are presented in exactly this light. Either directly or indirectly the leaders of the Fourth Crusade had experience of the Third Crusade. Hugh of St-Pol, for example, had a distinguished part to play in that crusade. He set out his reasons for going on crusade once again in a conversation he had with a trusted vassal, who criticised his action, on the grounds that this time it was with young men 'who would not know how to give advice in so perilous a venture'. The count replied that he was happy to be in such company, 'because unless they performed daring feats of arms they were likely to lose their heads in God's service'.[27] This riposte perfectly expresses the spirit in which men set off on crusade. Villehardouin was another veteran of the Third Crusade. It would have coloured his view of the crusade as essentially a knightly affair, if subject to the moral supervision of the church. As far as the aims and objectives of the crusade were concerned, these were best left to the military leaders. On a practical level they would have been influenced mainly by strategic and tactical considerations. The accepted wisdom in the aftermath of the Third Crusade was that Jerusalem could only be won via Egypt.

Byzantium did not feature as prominently in the histories of the Third Crusade as it did in those of the first and second. Of the crusade leaders only Frederick Barbarossa took the traditional overland route through the Byzantine Empire. There were serious clashes with the Byzantines en route, but these were overshadowed by the emperor's death on the threshold of Syria. This did not mean that the Byzantine alliance with Saladin was allowed to go unnoticed; still less the fact that Saladin's conquest of Jerusalem in 1187 had favoured Orthodox claims to control of the church of the Holy Sepulchre. It was more that the pioneering of the sea crossing together with the conquest of Cyprus had made Byzantium less relevant to the crusading venture. This may explain why neither the massacre in 1182 of the Latins of Constantinople nor the Sicilian invasion of 1185 made much impression on western opinion. It is most unlikely that the leadership of the Fourth Crusade would have been acquainted with Odo of Deuil's account of the second crusade, *De profectione Ludovici VII in Orientem* with its anti-Greek bias. Not only did Odo accuse the Greeks of washing altars that had been used for the celebration of the Latin liturgy; not only did he accuse them of insisting that any Latin marrying a Greek must first receive Orthodox baptism, he also concluded that killing Greeks was perfectly legitimate.[28]

By the eve of the Fourth Crusade such venomous views were fading. Much more influential was the *Pilgrimage of Charlemagne* or one of its variants. In this work the main action takes place in Constantinople rather than Jerusalem. It was designed to establish the superiority of the Franks over the Byzantines. The culmination of the poem is the crown-wearing ceremony where Charlemagne overtopped his Byzantine counterpart, thus emphasising his supremacy.[29] This incident must have been a reminiscence of the French King Louis VII's reception at the Byzantine court, where he stopped on his way to the Holy Land during the Second Crusade, but with the difference that he had been placed on a lower throne than the Byzantine Emperor Manuel Comnenus. The Constantinople of the *Pilgrimage of Charlemagne* is a city of wonders. The Franks are housed in a revolving chamber which is supposed to overawe them, but thanks to the relics they have brought from Jerusalem – a source of their moral superiority – they are able to face down any Byzantine challenge. There is no marked animus against the Byzantines that can be detected in this text. They are crafty rather than treacherous. They are not enemies of Christendom, but they have to be shown their place. The tone is quite different from the bitter hatred and contempt that informs the histories of the Fourth Crusade.

In a general way, the soldiers of the Fourth Crusade were heirs to the suspicion and contempt that the Latin world had displayed towards the Greeks. This condition had a pedigree that can be traced back via Liudprand of Cremona to Juvenal and Virgil. The direct contacts between the West and Byzantium established by the crusade had had the effect of intensifying Latin distrust of the Greeks. Intertwined with the crusade were serious attempts to effect a formal reunification of the two churches. Far from effecting union these tended to underline the differences that separated them – differences that were as much of ritual and attitude as they were of dogma and church organisation. Over the last decades of the twelfth century there are indications that religious hostility was becoming more intense, but the evidence points to this as a Byzantine phenomenon rather than a Latin one. The massacre of Latins in 1182 at Constantinople had strong religious overtones. But it produced little by way of reaction in the West. The Norman occupation of Thessalonica in 1185 provided an opportunity for retaliation. Eustathius of Thessalonica indeed emphasises the brutal treatment of Orthodox priests and monks and the contemptuous interruption of church services. It is also clear that this was the work of the rank and file and that the Norman leadership quickly recovered control and provided protection for the Byzantine archbishop and his church.[30] By and large there was at the end of the twelfth century surprisingly little hostility against Byzantium on religious grounds that can be detected in the West.

The venom directed against the Greeks by Villehardouin and other chroniclers of the Fourth Crusade therefore requires some explanation.

It is missing from Count Hugh of St-Pol's letter sent in the autumn of 1203 in the aftermath of the restoration of the young Alexius. This suggests that Latin hatred of the Greeks was a product of the events that followed. There was undoubtedly a religious dimension to it, but this was more an extension of Latin contempt for Byzantine decadence, as the crusaders understood it. Orthodoxy was condemned not so much as a religious as an ethical system. The crusaders judged Byzantium by the highest standards of their own code of behaviour. 'Chivalry', as it is usual to term this code of behaviour, is, in the same way as 'feudalism', a later construct. Chivalry was never properly codified, even at the end of the Middle Ages. It consisted in a series of assumptions, which were enshrined in literature rather than in law.[31] They were stated most clearly when they were challenged, as happened when the Franks confronted the outside world. They used these assumptions to test new circumstances. This produced some surprising results. The soldiers of the Third Crusade came away deeply impressed by Saladin, who was turned into a chivalric hero. This was not going to happen with any Byzantine. Their military inferiority was evident. The count of St-Pol singles out one incident in the skirmishes that went on outside the walls of Constantinople in July 1203. The crusaders repulsed a sally made by the Byzantines. Several of them were killed including one man 'who was supposed to be among the handsomest and strongest people in Constantinople'.[32] The moral inferiority of the Byzantines was revealed by their poor performance on the battlefield. The warrior elite of the Latin West followed a harsh code, but one that gave them a sense of right and wrong, which informed their actions and their decisions.

This sense of propriety would also be applied to opponents, such as the Byzantines, who lived by a very different set of values. The military – and therefore moral – inferiority of the Byzantines was confirmed by what the West chose to remember about the Greeks and their past. Walter Map's *De Nugis Curialium* reveals a general interest in the affairs of Byzantium at the end of the twelfth century. It was a collection of stories and provides a good reflection of the topics of debate at one western court. The bulk had been compiled by the early 1180s but a few additions were made. These are of particular interest as they reveal the topics of the moment. There are only two events on which Map dwells. The first is the fall of Jerusalem to Saladin which features prominently,[33] but not the Third Crusade, apart from a late addition which mentions the assassination in 1192 of Conrad of Montferrat, who is for some reason identified as his brother Boniface.[34] The second is the usurpation of the Byzantine throne by Andronicus Comnenus.[35] The account is, as has often been noted, 'wonderfully garbled', a cross between history and romance, but the important thing is that Walter Map recognised the usurpation as an event to be placed on a par with the fall of Jerusalem to Saladin. Later in his narrative he makes plain the connection he had in mind:

> About three years before this overthrow of Jerusalem, Constantinople, which had grown old in continuous peace, was taken and held by means of many, even innumerable, intrigues by Andronicus, whose wickedness equalled, if it did not surpass, that of Nero. Thus these two overthrows were the prophetesses and harbingers of those of Jerusalem.[36]

In fact, Walter Map should not be criticised for getting things wrong, so much as congratulated on getting things so nearly right. He has Andronicus as a brother of the Emperor Manuel I Comnenus, when they were actually first cousins. He knew that Manuel had left a young son to succeed him. He gets his name wrong and calls him Manuel instead of Alexius, but knew that he was married to a daughter of Louis VII of France. He gives the title of the man who secured the reins of government as the *protosaluator*, which is not a bad stab at *protosebastos*. More important is the meaning that Walter Map attaches to the usurpation of Andronicus Comnenus and the judgements that he delivers on the Byzantines. His assessment of Manuel I Comnenus was that he was 'aware that the Greeks are soft and womanly, voluble and deceitful, of no constancy or valour against an enemy'. He therefore made good use of his treasure to keep the empire's enemies at bay. This state of affairs was upset by Andronicus's usurpation which entailed an attack upon the Franks resident in Constantinople, though nothing is said about any massacre. His line of argument is much more complicated than a mere plea for revenge. It was that the Byzantine reliance on foreigners was proof of their decadence. Walter Map goes out of his way to insist that his criticism is not directed against the piety of Byzantine monks and nuns. He insists that he is referring only to their warriors, 'for that class has degenerated in knightly practice since the destruction of the army of Troy, and nothing of soldierly honour has appeared among them since the days of Achilles, Ajax, and the son of Tydeus [i.e. Diomedes]'.[37] Walter Map's interest in Byzantine history was limited to the single episode of Andronicus Comnenus's usurpation because he understood that along with the fall of Jerusalem to Saladin it signalled an end to the relative stability that had existed in the Mediterranean sector. It allowed him to give vent to the generally low opinion of the Byzantines as warriors which had long been current in the West.

This episode also attracted the attention of a contemporary of Walter Map – somebody that he is almost certain to have come across. This was Ralph of Diceto, dean of London. He provides in his *Ymagines Historiarum* a succinct and largely accurate account of Andronicus Comnenus's usurpation. He has Andronicus swearing fealty to Alexius II Comnenus in the church of St Sophia, placing a crown on his head, and then carrying him on his shoulders – details that are more or less accurate. They only emphasised the hideousness of his murder of the young emperor and his usurpation of the throne.[38] Ralph also mentions the Norman invasion of the Byzantine Empire, but misdates it to 1182. He presents it as an act of vengeance against Andronicus for all the 'abominable and nefarious deeds he had perpetrated'.[39] Like Walter Map, Ralph of Diceto has nothing else on contemporary Byzantine history.[40] He therefore bears out the impact which Andronicus's usurpation made on western opinion. It is very possible that western opinion was alerted to the apparent importance of Andronicus Comnenus's usurpation by the patriarch of Jerusalem, Heraclius, who led a delegation to the French, German and English courts in 1184–5.[41]

Both Walter Map and Ralph of Diceto produced historical works that were very much a ragbag, but the kind of work that would reflect the stories current at a particular moment. More serious histories were likely to have had a smaller audience, but they offer the fullest information available at the time. The most accomplished contemporary history associated with the English court was that of Roger of Howden,[42] which reached its climax with the deeds of Richard I on the Third Crusade. Roger was present at the siege of Acre and was therefore an eyewitness. His participation on crusade will explain why he is relatively well informed about Byzantine affairs. The fall of Jerusalem in 1187 required an explanation, part of which was the relative weakness of the Byzantine Empire. Howden therefore includes the letter that the Emperor Manuel I Comnenus sent to Henry II which tried to explain away the defeat suffered at Myriokephalon in 1176, but in the light of subsequent events seemed only to signal to a western audience the end of Byzantine dominance.[43] It was a harbinger of the political difficulties that followed Manuel Comnenus's death in 1180. Roger of Howden provides a detailed background to the coup which overthrew Andronicus Comnenus and brought Isaac Angelus to power. It is very carefully worked. Dialogue is used to give the story greater immediacy. There is enough interesting or accurate detail to suggest that his story went back to some eyewitness of events: he has the episode of Andronicus carrying the young Alexius Comnenus on his back into the church of St Sophia for his coronation; he singles out the Patriarch Basil Kamateros as the mastermind behind Isaac Angelus's coup.[44] This is not corroborated by the Byzantine sources but has the ring of truth about it. Finally, Roger of Howden provides

the most detailed account in any western source of the coup of Isaac
Angelus, but one that is overlaid with romantic detail. In much the same
way that Chrétien of Troyes has Alexander, Cligés's father, go to the
court of King Arthur for instruction in courtesy and valour, so Roger
has – quite erroneously – Isaac Angelus 'frequenting the schools of Paris
for instruction in the Latin language and way of life'.[45] While there, he
hears that the tyrant Andronicus has blinded and exiled his father and
brothers. So he hurries back, stopping on the way at some Greek island,
where he meets a hermit – an ex-archbishop of Tyre – who has the gift
of prophesy. The hermit assures him that he will become emperor and
urges him to head straight for Constantinople, which he does. He lies
low until contacted by the patriarch and leading figures at court who
pledge their support. The tyrant is worried and calls together his magi-
cians. He wants to know who he should fear. To find out they sacrifice
the son of a poor widow. They scrutinise the entrails and are able to
inform the emperor that it is one Isaac Angelus that he needs to fear.
The chancellor is immediately despatched to arrest the young man, but
Isaac decapitates him and gallops off to St Sophia where he throws
himself on the mercy of the patriarch, who at once presents him to the
people as the new emperor. Andronicus takes refuge in the imperial
palace. Suddenly a huge crow perches on a wall next to the emperor and
croaks in his face. Andronicus takes this as an omen. He sees his rival
passing under the battlements. So he picks up his bow and takes aim,
but the bowstave snaps and Isaac is saved. Andronicus is seized and
condemned to a horrible death in the hippodrome. Isaac then has the
patriarch deposed on the grounds that he had connived in Andronicus's
usurpation. It allows him to raise the hermit with the power of prophesy
to the patriarchal throne.[46] This is not too far from the truth since Isaac
made Dositheos, Orthodox patriarch of Jerusalem, patriarch of Constantinople. He too was a monk who had predicted Isaac's accession to
the imperial dignity.

Roger of Howden may occasionally be quite close to the mark in his
version of Byzantine history, but this should not obscure the fact that it
is heavily influenced by a romantic vision of Byzantium. It is a place
where extraordinary and terrible things happen. Roger may have more
details than Walter Map, but they write in the same vein, except that
Map spells out the moral of his Byzantine stories, while Roger is more
circumspect. He was writing slightly later than Walter Map in the aftermath of the Third Crusade. He was aware of the Byzantine alliance with
Saladin. This produced complications, because he had built up Isaac
Angelus as a good emperor who was well disposed towards westerners.
But, later on in his narrative of the Third Crusade, he includes a letter

which purports to come from ambassadors sent by Philip Augustus to the Byzantine court. This shows Isaac Angelus in a rather different light. It contains not only details of his alliance with Saladin but also a claim that the latter had handed over all the churches in the Holy Land to Isaac's emissaries; further that the Byzantine emperor was about to despatch 100 galleys to aid Saladin, who had promised him all the Holy Land if he impeded the progress of the Franks. Anybody caught taking the cross in Constantinople was immediately thrown into prison, or so the letter claims. Another charge was that Saladin had despatched his idol – in reality a mihrab – to Constantinople, where Isaac agreed that it could be publicly adored. The growing tension with Byzantium is reflected in a prophesy that the letter contains to the effect that 'Latins will rule and dominate in the city of Constantinople, for it is written on the Golden Gate which has not been opened for two hundred years – "I shall open for the tawny King of the West"'. The prophesy must be connected with the passage through the Byzantine Empire of Frederick Barbarossa.[47]

Roger of Howden's *History* was completed well before the Fourth Crusade was even proclaimed. It was designed to extol the virtues and military prowess of Richard Coeur de Lion. Its immediacy and use of official documents give it a special value as a reflection of the views of the English court. It represents what it was possible to know at the end of the twelfth century about the Third Crusade and any Byzantine involvement. There was less interest in the Third Crusade on the part of Roger's French counterparts – Rigord and William the Breton – the chroniclers of the deeds of Philip Augustus. This was understandable given the latter's less than distinguished role on crusade. Rigord at least confirms that Philip Augustus despatched emissaries to the Byzantine emperor from Messina, but says nothing about the outcome of the embassy.[48] He only dwells on recent Byzantine history as part of his presentation of the events surrounding the Fourth Crusade. It was the essential background to the proposals put to the leaders of the crusade by the young Alexius Angelus. The official French chroniclers were wary of the Fourth Crusade. They connected it to the death of Richard Coeur de Lion, which had left his northern French allies and sympathisers in a vulnerable position. In the words of William the Breton 'seeing themselves deprived of aid and counsel by the death of King Richard, they took the cross'.[49]

The official French chronicles are therefore unlikely to reflect the interests of those who went on the Fourth Crusade. The kind of histories that the participants would have been familiar with, if only indirectly, were the continuators of Sigebert of Gembloux. They were not as distinguished as the great eleventh-century historian, but they pick up the currents of twelfth-century history as viewed from northern France. Needless to say, Byzantine history is not a major concern. The continuators concentrate, for the most part, on the story of Andronicus Comnenus's murder of the young Alexius Comnenus and his ultimate overthrow. There is a French connection, which would have spurred their interest. The young Alexius had married Agnes, daughter of Louis VII. After seizing the throne, Andronicus then claimed the young French empress as part of the spoils. She was only eleven years old and the marriage to an old man was a scandal.[50]

A much later continuator of Sigebert of Gembloux was Alberic of Trois-Fontaines.[51] His chronicle extends to 1241 and he himself died around the middle of the thirteenth century. For the eleventh century and earlier he relied very largely on Sigebert, but he made use of other chroniclers. He was scrupulous enough to identify his sources. It becomes clear that his account of twelfth-century history was heavily dependent on the chronicle of Guy of Bazoches. Under the year 1203 he enters an obituary of Guy, who died in that year.[52] Guy came from a noble family from the Soissons area and was born in the 1140s. He was brought up by an uncle, who happened to be the bishop of Châlons-sur-Marne. He may have been groomed to succeed his uncle. He studied at both Paris and Montpellier, as we learn from his letters with their vivid descriptions of student life.[53] For whatever reason – perhaps because his uncle died too soon; perhaps because his too obvious enjoyment of an aristocratic lifestyle was cause for comment – his career in the church of Châlons was rather modest; he only ever attained the rank of cantor. He was the kind of churchman who often found a release in crusading. He went on the Third Crusade with Henry, count of Champagne, but he came back chastened by the hardships he had experienced.[54] It is no wonder that he does not figure among the clergy who took the cross in 1199. But he is of particular interest because he belonged to exactly those noble families of northern France who provided the major recruiting ground for the Fourth Crusade. His advice was surely sought by those who did decide to take the cross. His history, which goes down to the death of Richard Coeur de Lion in 1199, was very largely a history of the crusades, culminating in the Third Crusade or, as he would call it, the Fourth Crusade, the first being, in his view, that of Charlemagne: an opinion which must have been widespread by the early thirteenth century. The crusades and the crusader states are the focus of his history. He does not stint on his account of the Third Crusade, presenting it as a triumph of French prowess. He is a partisan of Philip Augustus. He puts the blame for the failure of the crusade to recover Jerusalem on Richard I: his arrogance had forced Philip Augustus to abandon the crusade. He then proceeded to alienate the French who had been left behind under his command. Guy of Bazoches has very little interest in Byzantium, but the section which precedes his narrative of the Third Crusade is entitled 'On the Constantinopolitan tyrant'. Its starting point is the marriage of Agnes of France to Alexius II Comnenus. This leads on to an account of the death of Manuel Comnenus and the usurpation of Andronicus. This is followed by a succinct account of the latter's overthrow by Isaac Angelus with none of the later legendary accretions.[55]

Alberic would make many such additions to Guy's narrative.[56] As the account left by Roger of Howden shows, many of these details were circulating before the Fourth Crusade departed, but they assumed greater interest for a 'general' public after the conquest of Constantinople. On the eve of the departure of the Fourth Crusade it was the fall of Jerusalem and the failure of the Third Crusade to recover the Holy City from the infidel which were the centre of attention for northern French chroniclers. This does not mean that Byzantium was entirely irrelevant. The usurpation and overthrow of Andronicus Comnenus excited considerable interest. It was not only because of the way a French princess was caught up in these events. It was also because they revealed the rottenness and cruelty of Byzantine political life, which seemed to foreshadow the disaster of the fall of Jerusalem in 1187.

For those who went from northern France on the Fourth Crusade, knowledge and experience of Byzantium was available not only in histories but also in romances. The legend of Charlemagne's pilgrimage to Jerusalem and his reception at Byzantium would have been well known. But it was a different episode that caught the imagination of the courts of northern France at the end of the twelfth century. This was the story of Heraclius and his recovery of the True Cross. This had a particular resonance in the West after the defeat in 1187 of Guy of Lusignan, the king of Jerusalem, at the battle of the Horns of Hattin, where the True Cross had been carried into battle and had been lost to the infidel. As so often happens, literature anticipated history, because Walter of Arras wrote his *Eracle*[57] – his fictionalised version of the story of Heraclius – some five or six years before this disaster. He dedicated it to the young Theobald V of Champagne, who was to become one of the original leaders of the Fourth Crusade, and to Baldwin, count of Flanders and Hainault, who was the father of two other leaders of the Fourth Crusade – the future emperors of Constantinople, Baldwin IX of Flanders and his brother Henry of Hainault. The culmination of the work is the recovery of the True Cross from the Persian King of Kings Chosroes and its triumphant return to Jerusalem. It was a piece of Byzantine history that was peculiarly appropriate to the crusading era. However, Walter of Arras plays fast and loose with historical accuracy. Heraclius is now a westerner, born to a Roman senator and his pious wife. He has all the chivalric virtues: 'Eracle is a good knight – brave and true and honourable.'[58] When the emperor of Constantinople, Phokas, is treacherously killed by Chosroes, Heraclius is elected emperor at Rome. He beats a rival from Carthage in a race to reach Constantinople first. There an angel appears to him in a dream indicating the danger to Christendom from Chosroes. Walter transforms the story of Heraclius: his theme is how Constantinople is rescued by a westerner and how this is followed by the recovery of the True Cross which is returned to Jerusalem – its rightful resting place. It links Constantinople, Jerusalem and the crusading ideal.[59]

Almost exactly contemporary with Walter of Arras's *Eracle* was Chrétien of Troyes's *Cligés*.[60] It is fiction, but not historical fiction in the way that the former work is. However, it equally reflects a particular interest in Byzantium that existed in the West in the later twelfth century. It was written at the court of Champagne in the late 1170s when Count Henry the Liberal (1152–81) was preparing to make a pilgrimage to Jerusalem. As a young man he had taken part in the Second Crusade and had in all probability been knighted by Manuel I Comnenus. When returning the second time from Jerusalem in 1179 across Anatolia, he was captured by the Turks, but was ransomed by the Byzantine emperor who was negotiating to marry his son and heir Alexius to a French princess.[61] Such interconnections make Chrétien of Troyes's choice of a Byzantine background for an Arthurian romance quite understandable and appropriate for the time. The plot of *Cligés* centres on the succession to the Byzantine throne. Cligés was the son of a niece of King Arthur, but his father was the Byzantine Prince Alexander who had left Constantinople to learn chivalry at King Arthur's court and had thereby lost the Byzantine throne to his brother Alis. Alexander leads an expedition to Constantinople and extracts from his brother a promise that he would never marry and that Cligés would succeed him. The details of the story revolve around Alis breaking his oath and marrying Fenice who falls in love with Cligés. It ends with Cligés taking his complaint against his uncle to his great-uncle King Arthur, who mounts a punitive expedition 'on such a grand scale that the like neither Caesar nor Alexander ever equalled'.[62] But just as it was about to set sail messengers arrived for Cligés with news that Constantinople was his. There was no longer any need for the expedition. 'Many of those assembled were happy to hear this news, but there were many who would gladly have left their homes behind and been happy to sail with the army for Greece.'[63] Once again fiction seems to be anticipating history.

In *Cligés* immediately recognisable is the Constantinople portrayed in the *Pilgrimage of Charlemagne* – an earlier work which is most likely to date from the 1160s. There is the same accent on marvellous craftsmanship. One of the characters of *Cligés* is the craftsman John, who was in Cligés's service. It was to him that Cligés turned with his scheme to build a tomb for Fenice who would pretend to have died. It would then serve as the lovers' trysting-place. Cligés was confident that John could create any building or work of art that he put his mind to. He claimed that 'the artists in Antioch and Rome have learned all they know by imitating his work'.[64] In the *Pilgrimage of Charlemagne* Constantinople is a city of marvels. The revolving chamber in which Charlemagne and his paladins were lodged served as the focal point for much of the action that takes place in Constantinople. It was the scene of the extravagant boasts made by Charlemagne's companions. These were duly made good through divine aid. Beneath the humour of the poem it is possible to detect a statement of Frankish superiority on moral grounds – confirmed by divine aid – over the Byzantines, but it also contains a plea for cooperation between the Franks and the Byzantines. Much the same holds good for romances written in the late 1180s, such as *Partonopeus de Blois* and *Florimont*. Byzantium forms a backdrop against which to display western chivalry.[65]

On the Fourth Crusade were a number of poets and troubadours. These included one of the leaders of the crusade, if of second rank, Conon of Béthune.[66] He would play a distinguished role in the crusade and often acted as a spokesman for the crusaders. Along with Geoffrey of Villehardouin he was one of the plenipotentiaries sent to negotiate with Venice in the spring of 1201. He was a veteran of the Third Crusade. His crusade songs were the product of experiences connected with this crusade. 'Ahi! Amours, con dure departie' is a conventional lament for the way the crusade separated him from his beloved, but 'sighing with love for her' he did his duty and 'departed for Syria, for none must fail his Creator'.[67] 'Bien me deüsse targier' is more serious.[68] It was very critical of the French king Philip Augustus, who seemed to be delaying his participation in the crusade so that he could exploit moneys for the crusade in his war with the Plantagenets. It was disparaging remarks of this kind that eventually forced a reluctant king to fulfil his crusader vows. They also left Conon of Béthune open to reprisals. He was taken to task by his master in the art of poetry, Huon d'Oisi, for the way he had returned home early from the crusade: 'Don't sing any more Conon, I beg of you/ for your songs are no longer acceptable, since here you will lead a life of shame/ not willing for God's sake to die joyfully.'[69] Such stinging criticism was hard to live down, except through participation in another crusade. Conon would also have found it advisable to take such an opportunity to avoid the wrath of Philip Augustus. Another scion of a northern French family – Hugh of Berzé – celebrated experiences connected with the Fourth Crusade, but his 'S'onques nus hom por dure departie' explores the typical crusader dilemma 'to set out for God or to stay here/ for no man in the grip of love/ ought to undertake such a task'. He knew that the crusade was a calling of which those that took the cross were scarcely worthy. They were such sinners 'that it will be a great marvel, if God accords us mercy'. Just as much as Conon, Hugh assumed that he would be setting out for Syria. Byzantium does not cloud his horizons.[70] The crusade was to be a shattering experience. After his return in 1207–8 he composed his *Bible*, which was a meditation on the moral order of Christendom.[71] It has nothing of the insouciance of the songs composed before he set out on crusade. One of these was designed to encourage Boniface of Montferrat to take on the leadership of the crusade if only to honour the memory of his brother Conrad 'who had recovered Syria'.[72]

This poem was addressed to the troubadour Fouquet de Romans, one of the many poets attracted to the Montferrat court. The most interesting from the point of view of the Fourth Crusade was Raimbaut de Vaqueiras.[73] In 1194 he accompanied Boniface who was in command of the German fleet which invaded Sicily. Boniface knighted him at the end of the campaign in gratitude for the way he had saved his life. The troubadour would go with Boniface on crusade, but only with the greatest reluctance, as he makes clear in a letter written later to Boniface: 'I had no mind (may God forgive me) to cross the sea . . . and the Greeks had done me no wrong.' This catches how irrelevant Byzantium had seemed at the outset of the Fourth Crusade. Raimbaut was motivated largely by loyalty to Boniface of Montferrat: it was 'for the sake of your glory I took the cross and made confession'. Raimbaut celebrated the marquis 'as the best of all men to recover the Sepulchre'.[74] He was thinking in terms of the traditional destination of a crusade. In this letter Raimbaut was looking back on the consequences which following the marquis had had. His poetry casts a vivid light on the early desperate years of the Latin Empire.

Where the Venetians were, in modern terms, pragmatic, the crusaders were romantic, insofar as they had any real interest in Byzantium. The loss of the True Cross at the battle of the Horns of Hattin followed by the fall of Jerusalem to Saladin in 1187 was what truly exercised the crusaders. They had, it is true, a slightly hazy notion that this had some connection with the rotten state of Byzantium, revealed by the usurpation of Andronicus Comnenus. The crusaders carried with them a blurred image of Byzantium, in which there jostled marvels, tyrants and disinherited princes. The crusader leadership was disposed to be sympathetic to the appeal made to them by the young Alexius because it fitted with this image. But it in no way prepared them for the reality that they discovered. They would have to refashion and refine their understanding of Byzantium in the heat of the moment. There would be little opportunity for calm reflection. They were contemptuous of the lack of martial prowess shown by the Byzantines, which they took as emblematic of their moral turpitude. But in other respects they took their cue from their sternest critic, Pope Innocent III. Though the pope had done his best to prevent the diversion of the crusade to Constantinople, he still deplored the contumacy of the Church of Constantinople, which refused to recognise the full authority of its mother, the Church of Rome. The crusaders could justify their actions in terms of seeking to restore right order to the Christian world, which had been undermined by the insubordination of the Byzantines. By the time of the Fourth Crusade Constantinople had at one level ceased to be of consuming concern to the West, but the moment that a crusade was caught in its force field a series of submerged or half-forgotten assumptions and prejudices came into play with results that were all the more catastrophic because of Byzantine disarray and sheer pusillanimity, to put no finer point on it.

Notes

1. R. Face, 'Secular history in twelfth century Italy: Caffaro of Genoa', *Journal of Medieval History*, 6(1980), 169–84.
2. D. M. Nicol, *Byzantium, Venice and the Fourth Crusade* (Athens, 1990), 6–8; J. S. C. Riley-Smith, 'The Venetian Crusade of 1122–1124', in *I communi italiani nel regno crociato di Gerusalemme*, ed. G. Airadi and B. Z. Kedar (Genoa, 1986), 339–50.
3. Tafel and Thomas I, 54.
4. Cinnamus, *Epitome*, 280.24.
5. O. Demus, *The Church of San Marco in Venice: History, Architecture, Sculpture* (Dumbarton Oaks Studies, 6) (Washington, DC, 1960).
6. I. Andrescu, 'Torcello', *Dumbarton Oaks Papers*, 26(1972), 183–223; 29(1976), 245–341.
7. D. Howard, 'Venice and Islam in the middle ages', *Architectural History*, 34(1991), 59–74, though the Islamic influence should not be exaggerated.
8. D. Howard, *The Architectural History of Venice* (London, 1980), 22–4.
9. Ibid., 24–5.
10. R. Goy, *Venice: the City and its Architecture* (London, 1997), 111.
11. J. Schulz, 'The Houses of the Dandolo: a family compound in medieval Venice', *Journal of the Society of Architectural Historians*, 52(1993), 391–415.
12. *Historia ducum veneticorum*, ed. H. Simonsfeld (MGH, SS, 14), §8, 80–1.

13. See T. F. Madden, 'Venice and Constantinople in 1171 and 1172: Enrico Dandolo's attitudes towards Byzantium', *Mediterranean Historical Review*, 8(1993), 166–85; T. F. Madden, 'Venice's Hostage Crisis: Diplomatic Efforts to secure peace with Byzantium between 1171 and 1184', in *Medieval and Renaissance Venice*, ed. E. E. Kittell and T. F. Madden (Urbana/Chicago, 1999), 98–108.

14. Tafel and Thomas I, 213–25.

15. Ibid., I, 247–78.

16. Nicetas Choniates, 538.

17. Tafel and Thomas I, 255.

18. *Historia Ducum Veneticorum*, §8, 81.

19. Villehardouin I, §67, 69.

20. Tafel and Thomas I, 257.

21. Ibid., I, 217.

22. Ibid., I, 523; Andrea, *Contemporary Sources*, 130.

23. D. E. Queller and G. W. Day, 'Some arguments in defense of the Venetians on the Fourth Crusade', *American Historical Review*, 81(1976), 717–37; D. E. Queller and T. F. Madden, 'Some further arguments in defense of the Venetians on the Fourth Crusade', *Byzantion*, 62(1992), 433–73.

24. *Historia Ducum Veneticorum*, 76, 89–92.

25. G. Jehel, 'The struggle for hegemony in the eastern Mediterranean: an episode in the relations between Venice and Genoa according to the Chronicles of Ogerio Pane (1197–1219)', *Mediterranean Historical Review*, 11(1996), 196–207.

26. Tafel and Thomas I, 273–6. Cf. H. Ahrweiler and A. E. Laiou, *Studies on the Internal Diaspora of the Byzantine Empire* (Washington, DC, 1998), 172–7.

27. Pokorny, 203.11–17; Andrea, *Contemporary Sources*, 187.

28. Odo of Deuil, *De profectione Ludovici VII in Orientem*, ed. V. G. Berry (New York, 1948).

29. *Le voyage de Charlemagne à Jérusalem et à Constantinople*, ed. P. Aebischer (Paris, 1965), 81.816–18.

30. Eustathios, *Capture of Thessalonike*, §119–22, 130–7.

31. See M. Keen, *Chivalry* (New Haven and London, 1984), esp. 1–17.

32. Tafel and Thomas I, 308; Pokorny, 207.126–7; Andrea, *Contemporary Sources*, 195.

33. Walter Map, *De Nugis*, 40–7. Cf. 410–11, 482–3.

34. Ibid., 484–5.

35. Ibid., 174–9.

36. Ibid., 410–11. The first 'overthrow' was the Norman conquest of England.

37. Ibid., 176.

38. *The Historical Works of Master Ralph de Diceto, dean of London*, ed. W. Stubbs (Rolls Series, 68) (London, 1876), II, 11–12.

39. Ibid., 37–8.

40. Ralph of Diceto (I, 91–4, 98–9) also made use of a Latin translation of the Greek narrative (*Diegesis*) of the Building of St Sophia: K. N. Ciggaar, *Western Travellers to Constantinople. The West and Byzantium 962–1204* (Leiden, 1996), 154.

41. B. Z. Kedar, 'The Patriarch Heraclius', in *Outremer*, ed. B. Z. Kedar et al. (Jerusalem, 1982), 191–4.

42. *Chronica Magistri Rogeri de Houedene*, ed. W. Stubbs (Rolls Series, 51) (London, 1868–71); J. Gillingham, 'Roger of Howden on Crusade', in *Medieval Historical Writing in the Christian and Islamic Worlds*, ed. D. O. Morgan (London, 1982), 60–75.

43. *Chronica Magistri Rogeri de Houedene*, II, 102–4.

44. Ibid., II, 202–3.

45. Ibid., II, 204.

46. Ibid., II, 204–8.

47. Ibid., II, 355–6.

48. Rigord, *De Gestis Philippi Augusti Francorum Regis* (Recueil des historiens des Gaules et de la France, 17) (Paris, 1878), 324.

49. Guillaume le Breton, *De Gestis Philippi Augusti Francorum regis* (RHGF, 17) (Paris, 1878), 76D.

50. *Sigeberti continuato* (MGH, SS, 6), 421–3.

51. *Chronica Albrici monachi Trium Fontium*, ed. P. Scheffer-Boichorst (MGH, SS, 23).

52. Ibid., 882.26–32.

53. H. Adolfsson, *Liber epistularum Guidonis de Basochis* (Studia Latina Stock-homiensia, xvii) (Stockholm, 1969), nos IV–V; M. Bur, 'L'image de la parenté chez les comtes de Champagne', *Annales: Economies, Sociétés et Civilisations*, 38(1983), 1026–37.

54. Adolfson, *Guidonis de Basochis*, nos. XXXIV–XXXV, 145–55.

55. I have to thank Peter Edbury for his kindness and his consideration in sending me a photocopy of the original manuscript of Guy de Bazoches's *History*.

56. *Chronica Albrici monachi Trium Fontium*, 870 where there is an account of the coup of Alexius III Angelus, which does not come from Guy de Bazoches.

57. Gautier d'Arras, *Eracle*, ed. G. Raynaud de Lage (Les classiques français du moyen âge) (Paris 1976), viii–xi.

58. Ibid., ll.2915–16.

59. A. Fourrier, *Le courant réaliste dans le roman courtois en France au moyen-âge*: tome 1 – *Les débuts (XIIe siècle)* (Paris, 1960) 207–75; I. Seidel, *Byzanz im Spiegel der literarischen Entwicklung Frankreichs im 12. Jahrhundert* (Frankfurt am Main, 1977), 100–4.

60. *Les romans de Chrétien de Troyes*: II – *Cligés*, ed. A. Micha (Les classiques français du moyen âge) (Paris, 1957); see Fourrier, *Le courant réaliste*, 124–78; Seidel, *Byzanz im Spiegel*, 95–9.

61. *Roberti canonici S. Mariani Autissiodensis Chronico*, ed. O. Holder-Egger (MGH, SS, 26), 244.34–7.

62. *Cligés*, ll.6579–81.

63. Ibid., ll.6616–18.

64. Ibid., ll.5325–7.

65. See Fourrier, *Le courant réaliste*, 392–411, 471–86; Seidel, *Byzanz im Spiegel*, 105–10.

66. *Les chansons de Conon de Béthune*, ed. A. Wallensköld (Les classiques français du moyen âge) (Paris, 1924), iii–vii; J. Longnon, *Les compagnons de Villehardouin* (Geneva, 1978), 146–9.

67. J. Bédier, *Les chansons de croisade* (Paris, 1909), 25–37.

68. Ibid., 38–50.
69. Ibid., 51–64.
70. Ibid., 119–31.
71. *La Bible au Seignor de Berzé, Chastelain,* in *Fabliaux et contes des poètes françois des Xie, XIIe, XIIIe, XIVe et Xve siècles tirés des meilleurs auteurs,* ed. É. Barbazan and M. Méon, nouvelle édition (Paris, 1808), II, 394–420.
72. Bédier, *Chansons de croisade,* 153–65.
73. J. Linskill, *The Poems of the Troubadour Raimbaut de Vaqueiras* (The Hague, 1964), 1–37.
74. Ibid., 216.

chapter 4

THE EVENTS OF
THE FOURTH CRUSADE

I t must now be clear how ill-prepared the leaders of the Fourth Crusade were to face the dilemmas and the difficult decisions that awaited them. At the outset they understood their task to be the unfinished business of the Third Crusade, which had failed to recover Jerusalem. The lesson of the Third Crusade was that possession of the coastal ports of Tyre and Acre was no longer a guarantee of conquest of Jerusalem. The Holy City could only be secured on any long-term basis if first Egypt was subdued. Many of the senior crusaders had participated in the Third Crusade and were willing to be guided by that experience. They had a straightforward understanding of the crusade as a responsibility of the chivalry of western Europe, who were placing their military skills and ethos at the service of Christendom. Their sights were set on Jerusalem. Byzantium scarcely entered into their calculations. Their knowledge of past dealings with Byzantium was very limited. Their attitude to the Byzantines was contradictory. They were inclined to be contemptuous of the Byzantines' lack of fighting skills. They were aware of Byzantium's political difficulties. The religious differences do not seem to have counted for very much. The crusaders understood that they had a duty to respond to calls for aid from fellow Christians and that this duty was connected with their crusading responsibilities. Constantinople continued to have a reputation as a city of marvels.

The Venetians had a much firmer grasp on the realities of the situation. Their perspective on events was narrower and less idealistic. They understood the commercial opportunities that were opening up at the end of the twelfth century; they also saw themselves falling behind their Pisan and Genoese rivals, who had stolen a march on them by exporting western manufactures – mostly cloth – to the Levant. It was equally clear that the most lucrative markets were now in Egypt, where once again their Pisan and Genoese rivals were better established than they were. The Pisans and Genoese were also challenging the Venetians in their traditional preserve of Byzantium. At the same time, the Venetians were at last realising that their long-standing attachment to Byzantium was becoming something of a disadvantage. Their overreliance on the Byzantine market had been exposed by Manuel Comnenus's actions in 1171. Constantinople continued to be a profitable market, but the real opportunities lay elsewhere around the Mediterranean. These the Venetians had denied themselves by overconcentration on Byzantium. The long-term aim of Venetian policy was to secure its interests in Byzantium, in such a way that its merchants were free to open up other markets. This end appeared to have been achieved by the treaty eventually signed with Alexius III Angelus in November 1198.

The invitation at exactly this moment from Innocent III to supply the shipping for the crusade he was planning seemed heaven-sent. It provided them with an opportunity to consolidate their commercial operations in the ports of the Nile Delta. It also fitted with the new image that the Venetians were fashioning of their city as the loyal daughter of the Apostolic See. This signalled an awareness that Venice was an Italian power, quite distinct from Byzantium with which its destiny had for so long been bound up. These were the years when its constitution was just beginning to take on a clearer definition as it sought to come to terms with its changing situation, but the speed of change also left it peculiarly vulnerable. It was exposed to more successful rivals, while its constitution and its myth were still at an embryonic stage of development. Participation in the Fourth Crusade offered the possibility of completing the process of transformation from client of Byzantium to dominion, but the transformation that did occur as a result of participation in the crusade was far more difficult and along very different lines from anything that might have been anticipated at the outset.[1]

Byzantium was in an even more vulnerable position than Venice.[2] In the aftermath of Manuel I Comnenus's death in 1180 the central government in Constantinople lost effective control of many of its provinces. The struggle between capital and provinces was one of the permanent features of Byzantine history. It normally ended with the triumph of the central government. This time, because of the intrusion of the crusade, it would be different. The imperial government lost control not only of the provinces, but also of Constantinople in the years after 1180. The dominant force was now the populace. Rather than face up to the uncertain temper of the mob the emperor and the court aristocracy preferred to retreat into their palaces and country estates. The patriarch equally sought to escape from the hurly-burly of city life. The Patriarch John Kamateros found solace in the Church of the Holy Apostles, which gave an illusion of rural calm. It was a time of weakness for both imperial and patriarchal institutions.[3] This was a recipe for intense competition both for the imperial office and for preferment within the Patriarchal Church. By the end of the twelfth century there were few signs of that orderly government which had characterised the Byzantine Empire during the reigns of the first three Comneni emperors. Instead different groups and factions around the imperial court pursued private interests. The most notable casualty was the Emperor Isaac II Angelus, who was removed from power in 1195 by the heads of five of the most powerful court families: Branas, Palaiologos, Petraliphas, Raoul and Cantacuzene.[4] In his place they imposed his brother Alexius III Angelus, who they hoped would be more amenable to their wishes.

It was usual enough in the pursuance of political advantage to employ westerners as well as other foreigners. We have seen how earlier Isaac Angelus had retained his throne thanks to the support of Conrad of Montferrrat. Reliance on western aid left Byzantium vulnerable to the Latins. Civil servants, such as Nicetas Choniates, not only understood the institutional strengths of western society, but also realised that Latin backing in one form or another was the most effective solution to the short-term difficulties facing successive Byzantine governments. But it was more or less impossible to fashion any consistent line of policy, still less to carry it through, because of the growing hatred of the Latins, which was of course rooted in a scarcely admitted admiration for their energy and skill. The result was vacillation which was interpreted – quite rightly – by the Latins as Byzantine weakness. This lack of resolve and consistency on the part of the Byzantines irritated the Latins and contributed notably to the outcome of events.

It meant, among other things, that there was a string of miscalculations over western intentions, which stemmed from a near paranoid appraisal of the crusade. It was assumed that the crusade was an instrument for the imposition of papal authority. In some ways this was understandable, even if Innocent III tried as far as possible to maintain a clear distinction between the crusade and the reunion of churches. In his letters to Alexius III Angelus the two topics are discussed separately, but the fact that they are raised in the same letters reveals that they were interlinked. The moment that Innocent III sought to involve the Byzantine emperor in his crusade plans it became impossible to divorce the 'Byzantine question' from the crusade. It was the pope's miscalculation that he thought that he could deal with crusade and Byzantium separately. Of all the parties involved, Innocent III had the clearest vision of an ideal order and the clearest agenda.[5] He wished to recover the Holy Sepulchre; he wished to restore communion with the Orthodox Church, but on Rome's terms. It does not mean that the pope had any direct control over events. He could advise and admonish, but his greatest source of power was the authority to approve or disapprove of the course of events. The crusade leaders, even Enrico Dandolo, felt the need to explain their actions to the pope. He was a permanent point of reference. His shadow hangs over the whole enterprise.

Innocent III's understanding of a crusade was not necessarily that of the participants. The crusaders had a fairly simple-minded notion of what a crusade was about. Innocent III understood the failure of the Third Crusade to mean that there was something profoundly wrong with the crusade as an enterprise. It had become a plaything of princes. The Third Crusade failed, it was generally believed, because of the rivalry between Richard Coeur de Lion and Philip Augustus. An immediate problem that faced Innocent on his accession was the German Crusade, as it is called. This expeditionary force had been despatched by the German Emperor Henry VI to the Holy Land in 1197. It was a fulfilment of the crusading vow that the emperor had taken in 1195. It had papal approval, but it pointed to the possible appropriation of the crusade by the princes of Christendom. It emphasised the dangers of fragmentation. Innocent III was convinced that the success of the First Crusade could only be repeated if there was proper coordination from Rome. He had also to work out the implications for the crusade of the decision taken at the Third Lateran Council of 1179. That council extended the scope of the crusade by granting crusade privileges to those engaged in the routing out of heretics and highway robbers (*routiers*). In other words, crusading privileges applied not only to those fighting against the external enemies of Latin Christendom, but also to those internal enemies who disturbed its peace. Even the clearest-minded of popes will proceed by trial and error. There is no doubt that the decision of the Third Lateran Council opened the way to a transformation of the crusade and that this occurred very largely during Innocent III's pontificate. Crusade privileges were granted for wars in the Baltic against the pagans and in the Iberian peninsula against the infidels. A crusade was organised against the Albigensian heretics. But a more radical departure was Innocent III's decision to give crusading status to an expedition led by Walter of Brienne. It was ostensibly directed against the Markward of Anweiler – the de facto ruler of Sicily. Walter of Brienne never crossed over to Sicily, but used his 'crusade' to secure the county of Lecce, which had come to him in his wife's right. Innocent III justified this 'crusade' on the grounds that the Markward had made common cause with the Muslims of Sicily against the legitimate ruler Frederick II Hohenstaufen, who was the pope's ward. Innocent was careful to insist that the Markward was thus impeding the business of the crusade, but the implications were far-reaching: the crusade could be employed to defend the proper interests of a legitimate ruler, as defined, it goes without saying, by the papacy.[6]

Although Innocent III was chiefly responsible for the transformation of the crusade which occurred during his pontificate, he could not have been entirely aware of the way in which and the extent to which it would happen. He did, however, know how he wanted to shape and present events. It must look as though the papacy was in control and he insisted that papal approval was required for the way events turned out. This gave a coherence to his handling of events which was often illusory.[7] The leaders of the Fourth Crusade would have been only dimly aware of the maelstrom they were entering. The Byzantine Empire was in a state of crisis, but of the kind that had punctuated its history – a mixture of provincial separatism and aristocratic faction. In the past these crises had been resolved by decisive action by a new emperor. If not in a state of crisis, Venice found itself in an exposed position because of the success of its commercial rivals. Most worrying of all was the challenge to its mastery of the Adriatic. Finally, the crusade itself was in a state of flux. Its objectives were no longer limited to the recovery of the Holy Sepulchre. This allowed the crusade leaders greater latitude in the decisions they made, but they would not have appreciated where these might lead – nor would the doge of Venice.

I

This account of the Fourth Crusade will be one of problems faced and decisions made. It will concentrate on the decisions made by the leadership of the crusade, but there were all kinds of other decisions of a more personal kind, which will have made their peculiar contribution but which rarely left any trace in the historical record. Some opinions count for more than others, when decisions are being taken; some decisions turn out to be more important than others, though this is not apparent at the time. The two most important decisions taken by the leaders of the Fourth Crusade were, first, the decision to support the claims of the young Alexius Angelus and, second, the decision to conquer Constantinople on their own account and partition the empire between them. Other decisions can be subordinated to these.

The first step on any crusade was to take the cross. But individual reasons for taking the cross seem to have little bearing on the momentous and unexpected outcome of the crusade. There were many purely personal motives: it had become part of a family tradition to go on crusade; for some the shame of the failure of the Third Crusade needed to be erased;

for many it had been the force of Fulk of Neuilly's preaching; others felt the need to respond to their lord's decision to go on crusade. Sometimes it was convenient to be absent for a while. In the case of the barons of northern France the death of Richard I in 1199 had created, as noted above, deep uncertainties. It was most unclear how it would affect the long-standing rivalry between Capetians and Angevins. Allies of the Angevins, such as Baldwin of Flanders, feared that they would be exposed to the wrath of a triumphant Philip Augustus, but equally allies of the Capetians, such as the count of Champagne, preferred not to have their loyalty tested. In the empire the struggle between Philip of Swabia and the papacy created similar dilemmas, especially when Innocent III proceeded to the excommunication of Philip of Swabia and his supporters. Taking the cross was a way out of domestic difficulties. Byzantium was simply not a consideration. However, the decision to back the young Alexius was not taken in a vacuum. There were other decisions which contributed to the path the crusade would take. The most important were the selection of Venice to provide shipping for the crusade; the establishment of the crusader force at 4,500 knights, 9,000 esquires and 20,000 sergeants – a total of 33,500 men; the choice of Boniface of Montferrat as the leader of the crusade; and the agreement to divert the crusade to Zara in the interests of the Venetians.

The choice of Venetian shipping was in the first instance made by the pope himself. One of the papal legates – Cardinal Soffrede of S. Prassedo – was immediately despatched by Innocent III in the summer of 1198 to Venice to discuss the possibility of cooperation with the crusade that had just been proclaimed.[8] Venice was an obvious choice to make. It had not been implicated to the same extent as its rivals Pisa and Genoa in the failure of the Third Crusade, nor was it as deeply involved with the Hohenstaufen cause as they were. Ever since the Peace of Venice in 1177 the Venetian Republic had been posing as a loyal daughter of the Apostolic See. Providing the shipping for a crusade was a reward. The papal approach to Venice proved premature. Innocent III had set March 1199 as the departure date for his crusade. When the crusade eventually began to take shape in a very different form from that originally envisaged by the pope, the crusade leaders stuck with Venice. The chronicler Villehardouin was one of the emissaries despatched to obtain shipping for the crusade. He tells us that the decision was left to him and the other plenipotentiaries.[9] In normal circumstances Genoa or Pisa would have been the obvious place for crusaders coming from northern France to find shipping: it was Genoese ships that had transported Philip Augustus's force on the Third Crusade to the Holy Land. But it was only after the treaty had been signed with Venice in April 1201 that four of the emissaries went to Genoa and Pisa to discover what help they were willing to offer the Holy Land. The emissaries had already agreed among themselves 'that they would find in Venice many more vessels than in any other port'.[10] This suggests that the Venetians had already started to make preliminary preparations on the strength of Innocent III's original approach. Enrico Dandolo presented his willingness to help the crusaders as prompted by the pope himself.[11]

There are two features of the treaty of April 1201 between Venice and the crusaders that need further commentary. The first is the number of troops to be transported. It was fixed at the colossally high figure of 33,500 men. Was it a realistic figure or one plucked out of the air? Were the crusade plenipotentiaries duped by the doge? In his chronicle Villehardouin has nothing to say about how this figure was reached, though he does provide the correct figures but without comment. It can also be inferred from his account that the exact numbers were a matter of debate between the doge and the crusade emissaries. It is reasonable to suppose that they first discussed the destination of the crusade and agreed on Egypt.[12] It is equally reasonable to suppose that they then discussed the size of an expedition necessary to conquer Egypt. Their only guide was the Sicilian expedition against Alexandria in 1174, of which the doge had had first-hand experience. It was reckoned at the time that the Sicilian force numbered some 50,000 men.[13] In addition, Villehardouin will have been able to confirm that the conquest of Acre in 1192 had required a force of around 30,000.[14] The crusade envoys then had to consider whether it would be practical to raise a force of this size. If between them the French and English kings had the greatest difficulty in gathering such numbers on the Third Crusade, would it not be unrealistic to expect the barons of northern France to raise these numbers? Not necessarily. The treaty of April 1201 reckoned on a force of 20,000 sergeants, which constituted the largest element by far of the new crusading army. Experience suggested that these would be recruited from ordinary pilgrims. The success of Fulk of Neuilly's preaching gave the crusade emissaries every reason to believe that pilgrims would attach themselves to the crusade in the necessary numbers. All the same, 4,500 knights represented a very large force. Although the knights' fees of northern France had never been surveyed in the way that those of England and southern Italy had been, the crusade emissaries were perfectly capable of making a rough calculation not only of the knights available from Flanders, Champagne, Blois and Perche, but also of those who had already taken the cross. They must have been reasonably confident that 4,500 knights represented a realistic figure. They may have been less confident that each knight would be able to bring with him two esquires, because in the treaty the Venetians insisted that 'should the esquires not reach the number stated [i.e. 9,000] the money owing to us . . . should not be diminished'.[15]

We know in retrospect that the crusade emissaries seriously overestimated the numbers of crusaders who would make their way to Venice as the point of embarkation, but they could not have foreseen the turn that events would take. They could not have anticipated that Pope Innocent III would give only qualified approval to the treaty they had negotiated with the Venetians.[16] This is the second feature of the treaty that needs further consideration since it marks the beginnings of friction between the pope and his crusade. As soon as the treaty was signed both parties sent envoys to Rome to seek confirmation. Villehardouin claimed correctly that Innocent III approved it '*mult volentiers*'.[17] As the *Gesta Innocentii Papae III* made clear, the pope did indeed confirm the treaty, but with the proviso that the crusaders did not harm other Christians without good cause.[18] This was entirely acceptable to the crusade emissaries, who could not conceive at that moment of any circumstances in which they would attack other Christians without proper cause. The Venetians, however, refused to accept the papal stipulation. D. E. Queller has argued convincingly that there is no reason to question the validity of the details supplied at this point by the *Gesta Innocentii Papae III*.[19] The question therefore arises: why should the Venetians have acted in the way that they did? It can only have been because they saw the papal stipulation as an unnecessary limitation on their freedom of action. They would have foreseen circumstances in which they might well wish to attack Christian lands without a cause likely to receive papal approval. Their freedom of action would have been restricted by another stipulation made by the pope to the effect that any action against another Christian power had first to be approved by the papal legate. This meant that the Venetians might find themselves directly responsible to the papal legate, even though they had not yet taken the cross. It looks very much as if the Venetians were already contemplating some action against a Christian power. There is every reason to believe the claim made by Innocent III that Venetian emissaries had come to the papal curia to obtain papal approval for their treaty with the crusaders and that he had specifically warned them against attacking Hungarian territories.[20] Because Innocent III was then involved in the problems of the church of Zara, he would have been well aware of the tensions in the Adriatic between the Hungarians and the Venetians.[21] The pope must have found worrying the inclusion of a fleet of fifty Venetian galleys as part of the crusader force since, to reiterate, at this stage the Venetians had not taken the cross and were therefore not subject to the authority of the papal legate.

Before the Venetians could raise the question of the diversion of the crusade to Zara, there was an even more important decision to be made. The death of Theobald of Champagne on 25 May 1201 was an immense blow to the crusade. Though not technically the leader of the crusade,[22] he more than any other of the barons of northern France had been at its heart. Perhaps the largest contingent of crusaders came from Champagne.[23] His dying wish was that the crusade should go ahead. He made generous donations to those who had taken the cross, but they had to swear to fulfil their crusading vow.[24] As marshal of Champagne, Villehardouin had a special responsibility along with others to carry out his lord's wishes. Overtures to the count of Burgundy and the count of Bar-le-Duc to take the count of Champagne's place met with refusals. The barons of Champagne having failed to find a new leader for their contingent, it was left to the other leaders of the crusade to find a solution. They assembled at Soissons at the end of June 1201. Villehardouin explained the situation to them. He proposed an approach to Boniface of Montferrat. He assured the assembly that he would accept but only if he was given command of the whole crusade.[25] There is no reason to disbelieve Villehardouin. He knew the family, having shared captivity on the Third Crusade with Boniface's father. The marquises of Montferrat had the best of crusading credentials. Boniface's brother Conrad was one of the heroes of the Third Crusade and had been elected king of Jerusalem. The confidence that Villehardouin displayed about Boniface's compliance suggests that Boniface had already made known his terms for joining the crusade – nothing less than overall command. Villehardouin would have taken the opportunity to discuss matters with Boniface, as he returned in May 1201 from negotiating the treaty with Venice. His route over the Mont-Cenis pass took him through the territories of Montferrat. Though much later and more than a little garbled, the *Chronicle of the Morea* insists that the crusade emissaries turned aside to inform the marquis of Montferrat about the treaty concluded with Venice. The possibility that the chronicler had access to independent information on the matter is increased by the way the *Chronicle* specifies the exact place where in June 1201 envoys sent from Soissons by the crusade leaders found Boniface of Montferrat.[26] There does not seem to have been anything sinister about the choice of Boniface of Montferrat. Boniface had the additional merit of being related to the French king Philip Augustus, who was happy to approve the choice. It meant among other things that there was less danger of the king being eclipsed in terms of crusading reputation by one or more of his vassals. What commended Boniface of Montferrat to the crusaders were his connections with the kingdom of Jerusalem and possibly his tried and tested skills as a naval commander.

He had been admiral of the Hohenstaufen fleet in 1194 during the invasion of Sicily.[27] Family ties with Byzantium would have been of little importance; his Hohenstaufen connections of more consequence. They opened up the possibility of recruitment to the crusade from the empire.

Early in September 1201 Boniface met the assembled crusaders at Soissons where he was formally invested with the leadership of the crusade. Almost as important was his attendance a few days later at the Cistercian Chapter General held at Cîteaux: it signified the support and approval of the monastic order which ever since the days of St Bernard had been the most zealous promoter of the crusade. Boniface of Montferrat then spent the autumn and Christmas of 1201 in the company of Philip of Swabia. It was at this point that the young Alexius Angelus arrived at the Staufen court. Boniface must therefore have been involved from the very beginning in the question of whether or not to support the claims of the Byzantine prince to the throne of Constantinople. The experiences of his brothers Renier and Conrad at the Byzantine court would have inclined Boniface to caution. Very properly he insisted that it was essential to obtain papal approval for such an action. The marquis and the young prince went on separate occasions to the papal curia in the hope of securing Innocent III's approval. The *Gesta Innocentii Papae III* mentions only the marquis's visit, which can be dated to shortly before 26 March 1202. On that occasion the marquis did not raise directly the question of support for Alexius Angelus, but approached the matter tangentially.[28] Realising that the pope did not think the matter relevant, he dropped it and departed. The marquis was clearly sounding out the pope. His assessment of the pope's position must have been cautiously optimistic, because Philip of Swabia then despatched Alexius Angelus to Innocent III. Though the chronology is notoriously difficult,[29] this must have occurred in May or early June 1202. Writing some months later about this meeting, Innocent III acknowledged the sympathy that existed at the papal curia for the young prince's plight, but insisted that he had rejected the young prince's claim to the throne of Constantinople. How categorically is another matter, for Alexius apparently came away convinced that he had a degree of papal support.[30]

On the journey back to the court of his brother-in-law he passed through Verona where he fell in with crusaders making their way to Venice for embarkation.[31] We know that contingents from the empire took the route via Verona. One of the leaders, Abbot Martin of Pairis, spent two months at Verona as a guest of the bishop before making for Venice.[32] The young Alexius no doubt exaggerated the support that he had at the curia in the renewed appeal he made to Boniface of Montferrat and the other leaders of the crusade at some point in either June or July 1202. It was received favourably. The crusade leaders agreed to send envoys back with the young Alexius to the court of Philip of Swabia to discuss the matter further, but on the general understanding that in return for help in the Holy Land the crusaders would restore him to the throne of Constantinople.[33] This was the fateful moment, even if the undertaking made by the crusade leaders was only provisional. Boniface of Montferrat clearly had a leading role to play. He is the only crusade leader mentioned in Villehardouin's account by name. Who the other crusade leaders were is a matter for guesswork. However, since the date of departure had been set at 29 June, it is likely that most of the leaders were in northern Italy or Venice. Count Baldwin of Flanders was one of the first of the leaders to arrive. Others came later including Louis, count of Blois, who was in two minds whether to take ship from Venice or from one of the southern Italian ports. His defection would have been a serious blow to the crusade. The count of St-Pol and Villehardouin were sent to reason with Louis of Blois, who had reached Pavia.[34] This at least confirms the presence of crusading leaders of the first and second rank in northern Italy at approximately the right moment.

In Villehardouin's account negotiations with the Venetians are placed before the arrival of the young Alexius. These negotiations were finally completed when the doge of Venice along with many other Venetians took the cross. Villehardouin gives the date as a Sunday and a great festival. A good guess is that of Ramusio who placed it on the feast of the Nativity of the Virgin – 8 September, which in 1202 fell on a Sunday. The other possibility is the feast of St Helena – 18 August, which in 1202 also fell on a Sunday. The feast of St Helena – the discoverer of the True Cross – would have been a particularly appropiate occasion to take the cross.[35] For the purposes of the argument, whether the doge took the cross on 8 September or 18 August does not matter very much, because by whichever of these dates the crusade leaders will have been in negotiation with the young Alexius. The decision to give a qualified reply in the affirmative to his proposals makes most sense if the crusade leaders were already aware that troops assembling at Venice were insufficient to meet the demands of the Venetians. Uppermost in their minds will have been the success of the venture and a determination to keep their pledges to the Venetians. But a further consideration will have been a conviction that they had a duty as crusaders to uphold the rights of a prince who had been unjustly deprived of his rights. They needed only to be guided by the precedent of the 'crusade' of Walter of Brienne, which was intended to support the rights of the young Frederick Hohenstaufen to the kingdom of Sicily.

The crusade leaders would have worked on the understanding that the pope had shown sympathy for the plight of the young Byzantine prince, even if this had stopped short of unequivocal support for his claim to the Byzantine throne. They would have hoped that, given their difficulties, the pope might well relent in order to create conditions in Byzantium that would favour the continuation of the enterprise. At any event, the proposals of the Byzantine prince were well worth exploring. In August or September 1202 Philip of Swabia sent envoys on behalf of Alexius Angelus to the crusade leaders with agreed terms: in return for restoration to the Byzantine throne, the young Alexius pledged himself to give the crusaders 200,000 marks of silver, to accompany the crusaders in person to Egypt with an expeditionary force of 10,000 men to be supported at his expense, and to return the Church of Constantinople to Roman obedience. These were generous and advantageous terms, but the papal legate Peter Capuano had first to be consulted and papal permission obtained. The papal legate set out for the curia in September 1202 to put the crusaders' case. Innocent III was not inclined to approve any deal with Alexius Angelus, but admitted that there were those at the curia who thought that the pope 'should have looked more favourably on the former's proposal, seeing that the church of the Greeks is less than obedient and devoted to the Apostolic See'.[36] It was an admission that allowed the crusade leaders some latitiude.

We can now see that the undertaking they made to the young prince at Verona was the decisive step. His main supporter was Philip of Swabia, who made a crucial admission in the peace proposals he offered to Innocent III in May 1203. He revealed plans he had for a conquest of the 'Kingdom of the Greeks' either on his own account or in the name of his brother-in-law, the young Alexius.[37] Philip's German interests had made it impossible for him to embark on the direct pursuit of his brother-in-law's cause. Why Boniface of Montferrat allowed himself to be used by the German king does not emerge from the sources. The most likely explanation is that it was a quid pro quo for the latter's help in facilitating recruitment to the crusade from the empire. There were, in fact, strong considerations that favoured the young Alexius's cause. It appealed among other things to the chivalric instincts of the crusade leaders brought up on tales of Greek princes seeking aid in the West. But what tipped the balance was the failure of troops to assemble at Venice in sufficient numbers. It was becoming all too clear that the crusade would not be able to carry its original goal – the conquest of Egypt.

The lack of numbers meant that the crusade leaders could not meet their obligations to the Venetians. They borrowed as much as they could, but they still found that they were 34,000 marks of silver short of what they had agreed to pay the Venetians. Unwilling to abort the expedition, the crusade leaders made a deal with the Venetians: the latter would defer collecting their debts until later, if the crusaders aided them to recover Zara. The assumption seems to have been that the crusaders would be able to pay the Venetians out of the plunder obtained at Zara. The papal legate Peter Capuano brought these negotiations to the attention of the pope who refused to approve the agreement. The Venetians responded by barring the papal legate from the expedition – an action which earned them the depths of papal displeasure. Boniface of Montferrat thought it politic to stay behind, when the fleet set sail on 1 October 1202. It was a specious way of pretending that an assault on Zara did not technically count as the work of a crusade.[38]

The espousal of the cause of Alexius Angelus and the diversion to Zara were important decisions which determined the outcome of the Fourth Crusade. It is usual to assume that they were decisions taken in desperation because crusaders were arriving for embarkation at Venice in insufficient numbers. There was, however, a good chance that the crusaders would have supported Alexius Angelus and the Venetians would have insisted on the diversion to Zara, whether or not the full force turned up. The doge would have drawn up contingency plans to use the crusade in any event to strengthen Venice's position in the Adriatic. Boniface of Montferrat's initial decision to lend his support to the cause of the young Alexius was reached before March 1202. It was followed through with remarkable obstinacy, as though nothing would deflect first Boniface of Montferrat and then the other crusade leaders from honouring their undertaking to the Byzantine prince. Modern historians have often expressed surprise that the Venetians and the crusade leaders were willing to go against the pope's wishes in these matters. In the case of Alexius Angelus it was not until June 1203 that Innocent III made an unequivocal prohibition against using his cause as a pretext for conquering Byzantium,[39] by which time it was too late. Before that, he had expressed sympathy for the young prince's cause without giving any categorical opinion either way. This fed the conviction of the crusade leaders that they had a responsibility to those deprived of their legitimate rights – a conviction that the pope seemed to share. Boniface was the most deeply involved because of his family history, but this too only fed a romantic view of the crusade, which other leaders were ready to share.

Innocent III was far clearer in his dealings with the Venetians. He left them in no doubt that he would be opposed to any diversion against Hungarian-held territories in Dalmatia, which meant Zara. The Venetians preferred to be guided by the precedent of their 1123–4 'crusade'.[40] This suggested that help to the Holy Land could be combined with furthering interests closer to home. It looks as though the two crucial decisions were taken in the end because they fitted with the different preconceptions that the crusaders and Venetians had about the crusade. It has been normal, in the wake of Villehardouin's account, to treat the two sets of negotiations as quite distinct. They in fact overlapped. The crusade leaders were negotiating simultaneously with the Venetians and with Philip of Swabia and his Byzantine protégé. A bargain was struck: the crusaders would back the Venetians over Zara; the latter in return were expected to support the claims of the young Byzantine prince. It was a deal which satisfied the leaders of the crusade, but not the rank and file, who felt it went against the spirit of a crusade.

The question of honouring their undertakings to the Venetians was the cause of deep dissension in the crusader camp. Villehardouin has the majority of the crusaders gathered in Venice, both barons and rank and file, insisting that they had paid their passage and that the Venetians therefore had a duty to transport them overseas. Should the Venetians fail in this, then, it was urged, the crusaders had every right to make their own arrangements. Villehardouin put the following gloss on their stand: they wanted to return to their own lands and break up the expedition.[41] In contrast, the leaders were willing to give all they had to keep the crusade together. It is most unlikely that as a spokesman for the leadership Villehardouin accurately represented the feelings of the opposing party among the crusaders. Whereas the leadership would have reflected on the needs and goals of the crusade, the vast majority of crusaders would have remained wedded to the notion that crusading centred on pilgrimage to Jerusalem. The job of the Venetians was to transport them overseas; there was little interest in any Byzantine angle to the crusade. What came to a head in the course of the Fourth Crusade was a clash between different ideas about the purpose and ideal of the crusade. For the leadership the failure of the Third Crusade proved that the idea of the crusade as essentially an armed pilgrimage to Jerusalem was obsolescent. Jerusalem could only be recovered, on any permanent basis, if Ayyubid Egypt was neutralised. Further reflection will have underlined the importance of the Byzantine alliance to the security of the crusader states. The failure of the Byzantine Emperor Alexius III Angelus to offer any worthwhile help to the crusaders made supporting the claims of his nephew that much more attractive.[42] It is unlikely that at this stage Enrico Dandolo will have got wind of the negotiations that were in progress between Alexius III Angelus and the Genoese for an extension of the Genoese quarter at Constantinople.[43] He therefore had no quarrel with the Byzantine emperor and every reason to support him, as the guarantor of Venetian privileges in the Byzantine Empire. A diversion of the crusade to Constantinople with a view to foisting this young pretender on the Byzantines as yet made no sense to the Venetian doge, though the chances are that he was able to use it as a quid pro quo to encourage the crusade leaders to help him with his plans for Zara. This can only have increased uneasiness in the crusader camp.

The tensions intensified when the expedition reached Zara on 13 November 1202. The citizens of Zara immediately offered to surrender their city to the Venetians, but a group of crusaders encouraged them to resist, claiming that the crusaders would never attack the city. The abbot of the Cistercian monastery of Vaux then forbade the crusaders in the name of the pope to attack Zara. The citizens of Zara withdrew their offer. The doge was not to be denied and called in the promise made by the leaders of the crusade that they would help him capture the city. The leaders agreed, otherwise they would have been shamed by their failure to honour their undertaking to the doge. In addition, their authority over the crusade would have been compromised. The assault went ahead and the city fell on 18 or 19 November. It was plundered mercilessly and divided between the Venetians and the crusaders, but relations soon deteriorated. There was a very serious brawl between the Venetians and crusaders in which nearly 100 men were killed.[44] It took the doge and the leaders of the crusade the rest of the week to calm down tempers. What it was all about was never divulged. The dissatisfaction among the crusaders was evident from the way over 2,000 crusaders abandoned Zara and made their way across the Adriatic to Ancona.[45] There was disquiet because a party led by Simon de Montfort and the abbot of Vaux insisted that by their actions against Zara the crusaders had incurred the ban of excommunication. To counter this the leadership sent four envoys to Rome to seek absolution. For the time being this calmed the tensions in the crusader camp.[46]

The exact date when this delegation was despatched to Rome cannot be determined, but it was before 16 or 17 December, the likely date of the long-delayed arrival in the crusader camp of Boniface of Montferrat. Hot on his heels came an embassy sent by Philip of Swabia on behalf of his brother-in-law which arrived at Zara on 1 January 1203. The emissaries of Philip of Swabia first put their case to the leaders of the crusade, assembled in the palace requisitioned by the doge. According to Villehardouin they made their appeal with the following words: 'Because you are going for God and for right and for justice, you have a duty, if you are able, to restore the inheritances of those who have been wrongly disinherited.'[47] They then set out the terms – which have already been outlined – that the Byzantine prince offered in return for his restoration to the throne of Constantinople. As we know, these had already been accepted in principle by the leaders of the crusade. They now took the decisive step of presenting the proposal to the army. In the absence of the bishop of Soissons and the bishop-elect of Acre, the ecclesiastical spokesmen were both Cistercian abbots. The abbot of Vaux was the spokesman for those – the majority – who were against accepting the proposal. He objected that it would mean attacking Christians and would divert them from the true objective of their expedition – the Holy Land. It was another Cistercian, the abbot of Loos, who supported acceptance of the proposal. He put forward the view of the leadership that the Holy Land could be fully regained only by 'the land of Babylon' (Egypt) or by Greece.[48]

Villehardouin noted the division that existed within the Cistercians about the objective of a crusade.[49] Ever since St Bernard of Clairvaux had put his full support behind the Second Crusade the Cistercians had provided the spiritual sustenance that the crusade required. The Fourth Crusade was closely tied to Cîteaux. After being confirmed as commander of the army, Boniface of Montferrat's first action, it will be remembered, was to attend the Chapter General of the Cistercian Order. Fulk of Neuilly was also present to preach the crusade and many of the local baronage were persuaded to take the cross. The Cistercian view of the crusade was that it was essentially a spiritual undertaking inseparable from the responsibilities of knighthood. Division in the ranks of the Cistercians reflected the uncertainty there now was over the purpose of the crusade. The majority of the crusading army was with the abbot of Vaux and opposed accepting the terms offered on behalf of the Byzantine prince. At that moment the leaders intervened and declared that come what may they would accept the terms. Otherwise, they would be shamed.[50] They had used exactly the same argument a few weeks previously in order to justify aiding the Venetians with the con-quest of Zara.[51] Failure to honour their undertaking to the doge would have been a matter for shame because it would have meant that they had broken their word. It is therefore difficult to escape the conclusion that they had already made a clear undertaking to help the young Alexius.

The determination of the crusade leadership to help the Byzantine prince set in relief a dilemma at the heart of the crusading ideal: was the crusade exclusively a matter of the recovery and the defence of the Holy Sepulchre or did it possess a much more general remit as an instrument to uphold a Christian order? The rank and file thought in terms of the first alternative, while the leadership had a broader understanding of the crusade ideal. The leaders forced through acceptance of Alexius Angelus's proposal in the teeth of general opposition. They had almost no support. Only twelve came forward to sign on behalf of the crusaders when the accord was drawn up in the doge's lodgings.[52] The leaders of the opposition – the abbot of Vaux, Simon de Montfort and Enguerrand de Boves – left the crusader camp and made their way to the Hungarian court, taking many knights with them.

Enguerrand's brother Robert was one of the emissaries sent by the crusaders to the papal curia. He did not return to Zara with the other emissaries who, in the early spring of 1203, brought with them Innocent III's letters. The pope was willing to grant the crusaders absolution for their actions against Zara as long as they made restitution of all that they had taken. The crusade leaders were obliged to draw up open letters binding themselves to make satisfaction for the damage done and to refrain from attacking Christian lands in future. Innocent III held the Venetians responsible and placed them under excommunication. Boniface of Montferrat and the other crusade leaders deliberately concealed this fact from the rest of the army. Their excuse was that the army would undoubtedly have broken up if this was widely known. The return of the emissaries with papal absolution for the crusaders would have strengthened the leadership at a very difficult time, when there was widespread disquiet about the deal done with the young Alexius.[53]

The Byzantine prince had still not arrived by the middle of April when the crusading fleet began to sail out from Zara. Boniface of Montferrat and the doge waited behind at Zara for his arrival,[54] which eventually occurred on 25 April.[55] They took at least a fortnight to reach Corfu where the crusader fleet was waiting for latecomers. The exact course of events that followed is not clear. The salient point is that the three-week stay on Corfu had given the dissidents an opportunity to organise against the leadership and its decision to support the Byzantine prince. Led by some of the most prestigious figures on the crusade, including Eudes de Champlitte, Jacques d'Avesnes and Peter of Amiens, they had made arrangements to defect to Walter of Brienne, who was then at Brindisi.[56] The dissidents held their own assembly, comprising more than half the army, in a valley outside the town of Corfu. Boniface of Montferrat and the other leaders got wind of what was happening. They rode out to the valley taking with them the young prince and all the prelates attached to the crusade. They threw themselves on the mercy of the rank and file and begged that they keep the army intact. It was a scene of great emotion. In the end, the arguments put forward by the leadership were compelling. They showed that without the support of the Byzantine prince it was now impossible to mount an effective crusade. The dissidents allowed themselves to be won over, but they first demanded that the leadership make an open undertaking that they would remain at Constantinople only until 29 September 1203.[57] The young prince then made a public

THE FOURTH CRUSADE

declaration of the terms that he was offering the crusaders. A degree of harmony was restored to the crusader ranks.

This episode was very instructive. The dissidents wished above all to go to the Holy Land. They wished also to follow a leader, who, unlike Boniface of Montferrat, was not tainted by papal disapproval and by the suspicion of using the crusade to pay off old scores in the Byzantine Empire.[58] The crusade leadership now emphasised the practicalities of the situation as much as the justice of Alexius Angelus's cause. This may explain why the crusade leaders entrusted their address to the doge.[59] This signalled the growing influence of the doge in the management of the crusade. The other leaders limited themselves to an emotional appeal to the army, the importance of which should not be minimised, because it was a way of welding the expedition into a cohesive unit with an identity of its own, not just a collection of contingents recruited from various localities. This required certainty about the justice of the cause. It was at this point that the moral support given to the leaders by the prelates on the crusade was vital. Now that the abbot of Vaux was gone, the divisions within the ecclesiastical ranks disappeared. The bishop of Soissons began to emerge as a dominating force among the clergy. His prestige would surely have been enhanced by his success in obtaining papal absolution for the crusaders for what they had done at Zara. It is impossible to underestimate the importance of the unwavering support that the crusade leaders received from this quarter. At Corfu the bishops were asked whether a diversion to Constantinople would be a sin. They gave it as their opinion that it would be an act of charity, for they were helping the rightful heir to the throne of Constantinople to recover his inheritance and take vengeance on his enemies. The bishops then proceeded to administer a solemn oath whereby the Byzantine prince swore to observe his undertakings to the crusaders.[60]

II

It was one thing to support a claimant to the Byzantine throne. Quite another for the crusaders to conquer the Byzantine Empire on their own account. While the debates over the destination of the crusade revealed deep differences about the purpose of the crusade, the diversion of the crusade to Constantinople not only exposed the deep-seated divisions within Byzantium, but also reignited that combination of distrust and contempt that characterised relations between Byzantium and the West. There was still unfinished business, however much it had begun to seem that the western powers were doing their best to disengage from their Byzantine entanglements.

The crusaders assumed that, as soon as they appeared with Alexius Angelus under the walls of Constantinople, the city would open its gates to the 'rightful heir'. The hostility that greeted their arrival on 24 June 1203 was the cause of real perplexity. When they paraded the prince before the battlements of the city, he was jeered. The crusade leaders spurned the overtures made to them by the reigning emperor Alexius III Angelus.[61] It would have been the easiest course of action to do a deal with the latter, but, if the leaders abandoned the prince, they would forfeit their moral authority, which thanks to the intervention of the prelates was tied to their support for the young Alexius. With only about a fortnight's supplies left they realised that there was nothing for it but to impose the Byzantine prince by force of arms. Hugh of St-Pol admitted that on the day before the city surrendered he was in such need that he had to barter his tunic for bread, but he kept his horses and arms, good soldier that he was.[62] Despite their plight the leaders of the crusade were confident that they had God on their side, which only underlines the importance of a moral imperative.[63]

The crusade leaders remained suspicious of the doge. He had never been as committed as they were to the young Alexius. At first they accepted the doge's advice that they should make their base on the Princes' islands at a safe distance from Constantinople, but this suggested negotiation and perhaps ultimately a compromise with the existing Byzantine regime. The crusade leaders soon had a change of heart and rejected the doge's plan, preferring to make for Chalcedon, directly opposite Constantinople.[64] The Venetians do not seem to have opposed this change of plans. It is legitimate to wonder whether the doge had by now got wind of the new concessions made to the Genoese in May 1203 by Alexius III Angelus. These included a shopping arcade (*embolos*), quays, houses and an establishment at the imperial palace of the Blachernai. Such a grant to their rivals would have changed the Venetians' estimate of Alexius III Angelus. It could be construed as a breach of the treaty of 1198.[65]

Whatever, the Venetians took a leading role in the first stages of the crusader assault on Constantinople and proved their trustworthiness and prowess. They broke through the chain at the mouth of the Golden Horn and seized control of Constantinople's main anchorage. This allowed the crusaders to establish camp opposite the Blachernai Palace. The crusaders' gamble paid off. Alexius III Angelus abandoned the city during the night of 17 July 1203 after a less than determined defence of the city. He even left his Empress Euphrosyne behind. The palace officials decided that resistance was now hopeless. They restored Isaac II Angelus to the Byzantine throne. His first action was to summon his son from the crusader camp.

Naturally, the crusade leaders would only release Alexius Angelus if Isaac Angelus first confirmed his son's undertakings to the crusaders. This he did by chrysobull, though he thought the terms quite unrealistic, but he had to admit that the crusaders had done so much for him and his son that even if they 'received the whole Empire, it would be their due'.[66] To guarantee their position the crusaders also insisted that their protégé be crowned emperor. This took place in St Sophia on 1 August 1203.[67] It will be remembered that the crusade leaders had promised to depart from Constantinople by 29 September at the latest. The young Alexius did all he could to pay off his debts to the crusaders. He seems to have found the 100,000 marks of silver that he promised, but only at the price of plundering church treasures, which created great bitterness against him on the part of the people of Constantinople – high and low.[68] However, unless he retained the crusaders in his service, he was lost. He made this clear to the crusade leaders. The terms were hammered out in the course of August. Alexius Angelus would retain the crusaders in his service for a year starting on 30 September. They would be free to leave Constantinople for the Holy Land in March 1204 and they would be supported by a Byzantine expeditionary force, which Alexius might command in person. These terms were then put to a '*parlement*' of the whole army. The old divisions opened up once more. Those who had opposed the leadership at Corfu demanded that in compliance with the promise then made they be given ships there and then so that they could make their way to Syria. This demand was vetoed by those who argued that it was more practical to wait until the spring before setting out for the Holy Land. Once again the crusade leadership carried the day.[69]

Parallel to his negotiations with the crusade leaders, Alexius Angelus was conducting talks with the prelates attached to the crusade over the fulfilment of his promise to subordinate the Church of Constantinople to Rome.[70] They dictated the letter he despatched to Innocent III on 25 August 1203.[71] In it he promised to make his personal submission to the Apostolic See and to do all within his power to bring about the submission of the Church of Constantinople. Nothing is said in this letter about retaining the crusaders in his service. It was not strictly relevant to the matter in hand, but it might, in any case, have created the impression at Rome that crusaders had become Byzantine mercenaries. Alexius's promise might not have impressed Innocent III, but it was an earnest of his good faith. In all likelihood, it was the concluding piece of his negotiations with the crusaders. In the letters that Hugh of St-Pol sent back home in the late summer and early autumn of 1203, he singled out the reunion of the churches as the crusaders' major achievement, which justified the diversion of the crusade to Constantinople. He insisted that the patriarch of Constantinople had given his assent and intended to go to Rome in order to receive the *pallium*. The patriarch had apparently, along with the emperor, given the crusaders his oath on this.[72] The union of churches was coming to be regarded as the guarantee of cooperation between the crusaders and the Byzantine emperor.

Hugh of St-Pol says nothing about any difficulties between the crusaders and the people of Constantinople, but, as negotiations with the young Alexius proceeded apparently smoothly,[73] so relations with the people of Constantinople were deteriorating. A few days after the young Alexius was crowned in the church of St Sophia the city mob turned on those Latins resident in Constantinople. Choniates was dismayed. Among those who suffered were the Amalfitans, who had lived in the city for generations and were virtually indistinguishable from their Byzantine neighbours. The Pisans were also victims of the mob's anger, even though they had recently helped in the defence of Constantinople against the crusaders. The action of the Byzantine mob turned them into allies of their great enemies, the Venetians. The Latins of Constantinople abandoned the city for the safety of the crusader camp across the Golden Horn.[74] Choniates was still grand logothete and pretty much at the centre of civil service opinion. He could see that the polarisation of Greek and Latin would only drive the young Alexius more deeply into the arms of the crusaders. In retaliation for the action of the mob a group of Latins crossed over to the main city on 19 August. Their objective was apparently to plunder the city's mosque which, situated down by the quays of the Golden Horn, was an easy target. The Muslim community defended itself and soon had the support of local people, who got the better of the Latins. To cover their retreat the Latin marauders set fire to the locality. Fanned by a wind from the north the fire was soon out of control and burnt through the centre of the city, threatening the church of St Sophia.[75]

Villehardouin is adamant that by the time this happened Alexius IV Angelus had departed with a body of crusaders led by Boniface of Montferrat on a sweep through Thrace to cow opposition to his rule.[76] But Alexius, and perhaps Boniface too, must have returned to Constantinople in the wake of the events of 19 August, because Alexius's letter to Innocent III is dated 25 August and was issued in Constantinople.[77] The despatch of this letter was clearly part of the effort made by the leaders of the crusade to restore calm to the situation.[78] At first it seemed to work. With the help of Boniface of Montferrat, Alexius Angelus secured control of Thrace. When he returned in early November he was greeted as a conquering hero.[79] But he was in an impossible position, ground between the expectations of the crusaders and the dissatisfaction of all shades of Byzantine opinion. There were already signs of trouble with the crusaders. Henry of Hainault deserted Alexius Angelus in the middle of his Thracian campaign on the orders of his brother Baldwin of Flanders, who had stayed behind in the crusader camp outside Constantinople.[80] It was a way of pressurising the Emperor Isaac Angelus, who was beginning to default on his payments to the crusaders. Once back in Constantinople Alexius Angelus found himself under increasing pressure from court and church to distance himself from the crusaders. Villehardouin claims that it was then that he withdrew his favour from the crusaders.[81] Choniates, on the other hand, insists that he continued to visit the crusader camp and to demean himself by engaging in their crude horseplay. He let the crusaders remove his imperial diadem and replace it with a woollen cap.[82] One can feel Alexius's desperation, but equally the growing contempt of the crusaders.

The crusade leaders moved very quickly. By the end of November they issued Alexius Angelus with an ultimatum: either he fulfil his undertakings to them or they would cease to serve him and a state of war would exist between them.[83] This decision to defy the Byzantine emperor was an essential first step, which led on to the decision to conquer Constantinople. It was taken precipitately within a fortnight of Boniface of Montferrat's return from Thrace with Alexius Angelus. It had its roots in the deterioration of relations with the Byzantine court which had occurred while they had been away. It seems most unlikely that the leaders of the crusade were yet thinking in terms of the conquest of Constantinople. But they realised that they were losing control of Alexius Angelus now that he was back in Constantinople. This left them exposed. They were forcing Alexius Angelus to recognise his obligations to them and reminding him of how much he owed them, also of how much he depended on them. His refusal to honour his undertakings seems to have taken the crusade leaders by surprise. They agreed to send the doge to discuss matters further with Alexius, who refused to make any further payments to the crusaders. The doge is alleged to have turned on him with the words, 'Miserable youth, we dragged you out of the mire and to the mire we shall return you!'[84]

Alexius Angelus's uncompromising stance towards his allies is best explained by the recent ascendancy over the imperial court of Alexius Doukas, known as Mourtzouphlos. He became the spokesman for all-out opposition to the crusaders. Very little is known about his background. Nicetas Choniates, for some reason, fails to identify him. He was a supporter of Isaac II Angelus and had been imprisoned under Alexius III Angelus.[85] It was largely thanks to him that the decision of the crusaders to defy Alexius Angelus backfired on them. The Byzantines now had every reason to harry the crusaders. In the skirmishes that occurred from the beginning of December the crusaders probably had the worst of the encounters.[86] The most serious incident occurred on 1 January 1204. The Byzantines tried to destroy the Venetian fleet using fireships. The danger was averted thanks to the skill and the energy of the Venetian sailors, but Villehardouin realised exactly what it would have meant if the fleet had been burnt: 'They would have lost everything, not being able to go anywhere either by land or by sea.'[87]

Power at court had passed into the hands of Mourtzouphlos, whose loyalties were to Isaac II Angelus. But the old emperor was dying. Opposition to his hated son Alexius was growing. An assembly convened in the church of St Sophia on 25 January. Eventually on 27 January a new emperor was imposed by the mob. In the face of this development Alexius needed the support of the crusaders to protect himself. Nicetas Choniates reveals that Boniface agreed to bring in his troops to defend Alexius's position.[88] Villehardouin fails to mention this incident. It was more than a little embarrassing in its implications. However, it is corroborated by the letter which Baldwin of Flanders despatched to Innocent III, but with significantly different details.[89] It reveals, for instance, that Alexius used Mourtzouphlos as a go-between with Boniface of Montferrat, who was offered control of the Blachernai Palace. When the marquis arrived to take possession, he was, according to the letter, ridiculed by Alexius. Reading between the lines, this almost certainly means that Mourtzouphlos was manipulating the Byzantine emperor and was able to engineer some offer which was designed to divide the crusader leadership. Boniface rejected the overtures. Alexius was left defenceless once Mourtzouphlos revealed the former's dealings with Boniface to his fellow Byzantines. It provided Mourtzouphlos with a pretext for overthrowing Alexius on the night of 25 January and having him strangled a few days later.[90]

The overthrow of Alexius IV Angelus underlined the weakness of the crusaders' position. With Alexius gone they no longer had any hope of leverage within Constantinople. Mourtzouphlos believed that he had the crusaders at his mercy. He gave them a week to be gone.[91] At some point the doge had a meeting with the new emperor at the far end of the Golden Horn. The incident is recorded by Nicetas Choniates and corroborated by the letter of Baldwin of Flanders to Innocent III. It took place on 7 February. The doge's main demand according to Choniates was the payment of 5,000 pounds of gold for their departure. He also made certain other demands which Choniates does not specify, but included the restoration of Alexius Angelus, submission to the church of Rome, and aid to the Holy Land. Mourtzouphlos could easily have bought the crusaders off, but he thought he had them at his mercy and found their other demands insolent. Before the negotiations could be completed a detachment of Frankish cavalry charged Mourtzouphlos and scattered his party.[92] There were clearly those in the crusader camp who were deeply suspicious of any deal that the doge might make with the new Byzantine emperor. They were buoyed up by the victory won over Mourtzouphlos a few days earlier by crusader forces under Henry of Hainault. The main booty had been a precious icon of the Mother of God, which was then paraded through the crusader camp and given to the bishop of Troyes for safe keeping.[93] The leaders of the crusade, including the doge, then held a *parlement* of the whole army. The crusaders reacted with a strident denunciation of Mourtzouphlos as a traitor of the worst kind who had murdered his lord. Conveniently forgetting their act of defiance, they vowed to avenge Alexius Angelus. Their stance received moral support from the prelates with the crusade. The latter gave it as their opinion that a man guilty of such a murder had no right to remain in power. Furthermore, the Byzantines had failed to honour their promises over the union of churches. The prelates declared that 'the battle is right and just. And if you have the right intention of conquering the land and placing it in the obedience of Rome, you will obtain the pardon which the pope has granted to all of you who die having confessed.'[94] This was a momentous pronouncement because it endowed an attack on Constantinople with the sanction of a crusade.

The decision to conquer Constantinople was therefore reached early in February 1204. There is not a hint of any such intention in the letters sent back to western Europe in the immediate aftermath of Alexius IV Angelus's coronation on 1 August 1203. The crusade leaders then expected to set sail for Egypt the following March. On the surface relations with the Byzantine court were then amicable enough. However, the crusade leaders quickly learnt how volatile the situation was in Constantinople. Their guarantee of safety remained Alexius Angelus. After his coronation they arranged for Peter of Bracieux and his men to act as his palace guard.[95] The position of the crusaders deteriorated once Alexius Angelus returned from his sweep through Thrace early in November 1203. Not only did he distance himself from the crusaders, but he defaulted on his agreements with them. One of the leitmotifs of the crusade was the sanctity of contract. Failure to honour a contract was a source of the deepest shame. This aroused all the old distrust of the Greeks, which had been fanned by the bitter hostility of the people of Constantinople. The murder of Alexius IV Angelus shocked the crusaders and confirmed that regicide was a peculiarly Byzantine vice. It brought to the surface stereotypes that had been festering in Latin minds since the usurpation of the Tyrant Andronicus Comnenus. The hardening of attitudes towards the Byzantines is important, but the crusade leaders could have extricated themselves without too much difficulty from Constantinople. They seemed reluctant to take the opportunities to depart that were offered. Moral and religious grounds will certainly have played their part, but it would have dawned on the crusaders that Constantinople was a prize there for the taking. They represented the only effective military and naval power. The imperial court had little real influence on the streets of Constantinople, which were in the hands of the mob. The crusade army was now rather stronger than it had been when it first arrived under the walls of Constantinople in the summer of 1203. It had been joined by the Latins of Constantinople, estimated at about 15,000 by Villehardouin who praised their contribution.[96] In addition, some of the crusaders who had sailed directly to Syria, but had found nothing to do, arrived at Constantinople in dribs and drabs over the autumn and early winter of 1203.[97]

Robert of Clari recounts the following story, which, like all his stories, will have a kernel of truth. Soon after Mourtzouphlos seized power the crusade leaders received a delegation from Ioannitsa, the Bulgarian ruler. He offered to help them conquer Constantinople and to hold his lands from them, if they recognised him as king.[98] The leaders of the crusade considered the matter, but rejected his offer of help. The Bulgarian ruler therefore turned directly to the papacy and a cardinal was sent to crown him king.[99] The details of the story are tendentious. But the crusade leaders were well aware of Ioannitsa's existence and his power.[100] The latter had been conducting negotiations with the papacy for a crown from at least 1199. The importance of the negotiations is evident from the way he rejected counter-proposals made by the Byzantine Emperor Alexius III Angelus, who was willing to offer him both an imperial coronation and patriarchal status for the Bulgarian Church. His persistence was rewarded when on 25 February 1204 Innocent III recognised him as king of the Bulgarians and Vlachs and sent him a sceptre and crown.[101] It is therefore difficult to reject Clari's information that Ioannitsa offered to help the crusaders, who spurned it because they recognised in the Bulgarians potential competitors. Awareness of a competitor will have sharpened the crusaders' appreciation of the prize that was theirs to be won.

In March 1204 the crusade leaders concluded a new treaty with the doge Enrico Dandolo. It set out very straightforwardly how the booty and subsequently the empire would be divided and an emperor and a patriarch chosen. It was also agreed that the army would stay together for another year beginning 30 March in order to secure possession of the empire.[102] On 9 April the crusaders assaulted the city walls, but were driven off. An assembly was convoked in the evening. There were those who suggested attacking from the Marmara side of the city, but the Venetians indicated that if their fleet sailed out of the Golden Horn into the Bosporus the current would sweep them way past the city. Villehardouin remarked that there were those who would have welcomed this, because of the straits they were in.[103] There was a sense of desperation. The prelates were consulted as to the righteousness of their cause, which was troubling many crusaders. They gave it as their opinion that it was undoubtedly a just cause, because the Greeks had removed themselves from their obedience to Rome. On the morning of Sunday 11 April they preached throughout the crusader camp. Their message was the justice of their cause, not only because the Byzantines were schismatics but also because they had murdered their rightful lord and were therefore worse than the Jews. The prelates then offered the crusaders absolution in the name of God and by papal authority seeing that the Byzantines were enemies of God.[104] This appeal to the rank and file was couched in the most basic terms and was designed to stir the deepest emotions created by a belief in the sacrosanct character of loyalty to a lord. The Byzantines were enemies of God because they were traitors in the same way that the Jews were traitors to Christ. Such an idea may no longer make any sense, but on the eve of the final assault on Constantinople it strengthened the crusaders' resolve to do or die.

The next day, Monday 12 April, the crusaders attacked the walls of the city. Throughout the morning the Byzantine defenders held their own, but crusader pressure and persistence paid off. They seized a section of the sea walls near the Blachernai Palace and were then able to get into the city. They intimidated the population by burning still more of the city. Mourtzouphlos had staked all on throwing back the crusaders, but they stormed his camp below the Pantepoptes monastery, which they then occupied. Mourtzouphlos tried to rally the people of Constantinople but, panic-stricken, they refused to follow his lead. He therefore abandoned the city. A new emperor was chosen at St Sophia. With the patriarch by his side he exhorted the populace to continue resistance against the Latins. There was no response. The new emperor tried to win over the Varangian Guard, who demanded extra wages. But the moment they saw the crusader battle array they fled. The city belonged to the crusaders. Already Boniface of Montferrat was being hailed by the populace as *Hagios Basileus*. He took possession of the Buccoleon Palace while the Blachernai fell to Henry of Hainault.[105]

The city was put to the sack. It must have been a brutal affair, but the crusade leaders brought the soldiery under control within a matter of

two or three days. The approach of Easter was salutary. In 1204 Palm
Sunday fell on 18 April. The sack of Constantinople was less savage than
is often depicted. We can perhaps believe Robert of Clari, when he tells
us that 'once the city was taken, no harm was done either to the rich or
to the poor. So those who wanted to go departed thence, while those
who wanted to stay did so. It was the richest of the city who went.'[106]
This did not prevent the crusaders from collecting a vast amount of
booty, which was divided up in the aftermath of Easter Sunday (25
April).[107] This was done in conformity with the provisions of the *Partitio
Romaniae*, as was the election of an emperor. The choice fell on Baldwin
of Flanders. Although he put a brave face on it, Boniface of Montferrat,
the commander of the crusading army, felt that he had been cheated.
His precipitate marriage to Margaret of Hungary, widow of the Emperor
Isaac II Angelus, would not have commended him to the crusaders.[108] It
looked as though he was seeking to establish a right to the Byzantine
throne in his new wife's name and thus circumvent the terms of the
treaty of March 1204, which established a college of twelve electors, six
crusaders and six Venetians.[109] It pointed once again to divisions in the
crusader ranks. Villehardouin compares the tension that existed between
Baldwin of Flanders and Boniface of Montferrat over the crown of
Constantinople to that between Geoffrey of Bouillon and Raymond of
St-Gilles over the crown of Jerusalem.[110] Villehardouin has been accused
of using this comparison as a device to minimise the seriousness of the
divisions afflicting the crusading army. The very reverse. Villehardouin
employed it as an effective way of underlining the gravity of the situation.
It also reflects a mindset which was suffused with historical parallels.
In order to confront present difficulties history was enlisted as the most
effective guide. By citing the parallel with the First Crusade Villehardouin
allows us a glimpse of how the leaders of the Fourth Crusade reacted to
the momentous decisions that faced them.

III

The exact significance of the conquest of Constantinople would lie very
largely in its consequences. But without the event there would have
been no consequences. The fall of Constantinople was accidental only in
the sense that it was not the only conceivable outcome of the Fourth
Crusade's involvement in Byzantine affairs. But from the moment in the
early summer of 1202 that the leaders of the crusade made their undertaking to Alexius it can be seen in retrospect as the most likely result. The
appeal of a claimant to the Byzantine throne to the leaders of a crusade
was novel, but the involvement of Latin forces in the internal politics of

the Byzantine Empire was not. As the political situation in Byzantium deteriorated in the wake of Manuel I Comnenus's death, so Latin intervention in various forms provided an obvious solution to the empire's short-term problems. The crusade leaders' willingness to hearken to Alexius Angelus's overtures seems at first sight hopelessly naive. They were no doubt swayed by romances which had Byzantine princes restored to the throne of Constantinople by Frankish forces. But behind this Byzantium represented a serious problem. Manuel Comnenus's reign was romanticised as a time of cooperation of Byzantine and Latin which worked to the advantage of both sides. This understanding broke down under the tyrannical rule of Andronicus I Comnenus. The history and literature of the time reflected the conviction that this was connected with his murder of the rightful emperor. It was seen to have had sinister results for the Latin hold on the Holy Land. The failure of the Third Crusade seemed only to confirm this.

Innocent III's refusal to support the claims of the young Alexius might suggest that the papacy did not share this view of the Byzantine problem. This is not likely to be the case. It was more that Innocent III hoped to solve the problem by direct negotiation with the Byzantine emperor and his patriarch. He sought – not altogether successfully – to keep separate Byzantium and the crusade. He was not, however, above using the threat of the crusade as a means of bringing pressure to bear on Alexius III Angelus, which would explain why the pope waited until June 1203 to reject categorically the claims of the young Alexius. By then it was too late. The crusaders would not have received the letter until after they had put Alexius on the Byzantine throne. Innocent III had in any case already given his approval to the notion that an expedition designed to restore political order should enjoy crusading privileges. The idea of the crusade was evolving rapidly at the time. The pope himself was one of the main supporters of the idea that the crusade was not exclusively a matter of recovering and defending the Holy Sepulchre, though that remained its overriding objective. It could also be employed to maintain a proper order. The limits of the crusade were being tested in the usual way by trial and error. The soldiers of the Fourth Crusade demonstrated that it could not only be employed in support of political legitimacy, but could also be turned against schismatics.

The debates over the goal and purpose of the crusade also served another purpose. They were the painful means through which the crusade obtained a degree of unity and a sense of itself as a common enterprise. With greater cohesion, so the question of self-preservation came increasingly to the fore. Initially the leaders linked this to support for Alexius

Angelus, but the disadvantages and perils of such a course of action became all too clear. All that was left to bind the crusade together was the justice of their cause, which the prelates on the crusade had little difficulty in assimilating to the highest ideals of the crusade. Self-preservation also emphasised the practicalities of any given situation, which, taken with a belief in their cause, would explain the uncompromising position that the crusaders took up.

The Venetians were always concerned with the practical. One of the attractions of being asked by the pope to supply shipping for the crusade was the opportunity it offered for re-establishing Venice's mastery of the Adriatic, which had been challenged by the Hungarian annexation of Zara. Supporting the young Alexius Angelus was far less appealing. The doge allowed himself to be convinced by the other crusade leaders. When the crusade set out he had no quarrel with the Byzantine emperor of the day, who had recently confirmed Venetian privileges in the empire. The doge would have known exactly how shaky the young Alexius Angelus's claim to the Byzantine throne was. His sights were still fixed on securing a favourable position in the trade of the Nile Delta. The strongest argument for going to Constantinople was to pick up supplies and possibly reinforcements. What the doge might not have foreseen was that once at Constantinople he would come under pressure from the Venetians established in that city.[111] They did not regard the treaty of 1198 with the Byzantine emperor as a satisfactory solution – a view which was only confirmed by the new imperial privileges granted in May 1203 to the Genoese. The Venetians of Constantinople were also less than happy with the new turn of Venetian strategy, which suggested that trade at Constantinople would be sacrificed for new markets in the Nile Delta and elsewhere. There were differences of interest between Venice and its factory in Constantinople. Dandolo had increasingly to take into account the interests of the Venetians of Constantinople, who constituted a significant element of the Venetian force.

The participants would at best have had only an ill-defined idea of the complexities of their situation. They would have relied on a combination of the lore of history – by which is meant a simplified and often erroneous version of past events – and a sense of values derived very largely from their understanding of history, which was founded in and dominated by the Bible. On this basis they had to grapple with situations which emerged from long-term problems. In the case of Byzantium it had to do with political weakness that resulted in large measure from the encroachments into its sphere of influence in the Balkans and Levant by the West in a variety of disguises.[112] The participants were not prisoners of events; they were not controlled by the flow of history. However, long-term historical developments usually take the form of fluid and complex situations which display a surprising stability and continuity. The normal strains and pressures rarely produce much significant change, but just occasionally, as with the Fourth Crusade, the results are dramatic. This expedition fused a series of unstable and developing situations, which left to themselves might have been quite manageable. Instead, it forced a dramatic resolution, which in its turn created new situations with new problems and new dilemmas.

Notes

1. F. C. Lane, *Venice: A Maritime Republic* (Baltimore, 1973), 86–116.
2. See C. M. Brand, *Byzantium Confronts the West, 1180–1204* (Cambridge, Mass., 1968); Cheynet, *Pouvoir et Contestations à Byzance*, 427–80.
3. Angold, *Church and Society*, 126–36.
4. Nicetas Choniates, 450–1.
5. See H. Roscher, *Papst Innocenz III. und die Kreuzzüge* (Göttingen, 1969).
6. E. Kennan, 'Innocent III and the first political crusade: a comment on the limitations of papal power', *Traditio*, 27(1971), 231–49.
7. See Maleczek, *Petrus Capuanus*, 17–57.
8. Roscher, *Papst Innocenz III*, 58–63; Malaczek, *Petrus Capuanus*, 99.
9. Villehardouin I, §12–13.
10. Ibid., I, §14.
11. Tafel and Thomas I, 365.
12. Villehardouin I, §18.
13. M. C. Lyons and D. E. P. Jackson, *Saladin. The Politics of the Holy War* (Cambridge, 1982), 398–9.
14. J. Gillingham, *Richard I* (New Haven, 1999), 155–71.
15. Tafel and Thomas I, 365.
16. *Gesta Innocentii III*, §lxxxiii.
17. Villehardouin I, §31.
18. *Gesta Innocentii III*, §lxxxiii.
19. D. E. Queller, 'Innocent III and the Crusader–Venetian treaty of 1201', *Medievalia et Humanistica*, 15(1963), 31–4, reprinted in D. E. Queller, *Medieval Diplomacy and the Fourth Crusade* (London, 1980), no. IX.
20. Migne *PL* 215, 301–2; Andrea, *Contemporary Accounts*, 96–7.
21. See Maleczek, *Petrus Capuanus*, 120ff.
22. E. E. Kittell, 'Was Thibaut of Champagne leader of the fourth crusade?', *Byzantion*, 51(1981), 557–65.
23. J. Longnon, *Compagnons*, 11–77.
24. M. Bur, 'Les comtes de Champagne', 1016–26.
25. Villehardouin I, §41–3.
26. Chronicle of the Morea, 26–27.374–7.
27. Linskill, *Poems of Raimbaut de Vaqueiras*, 10–14.

28. *Gesta Innocentii III*, §cxxii: '*coepit agere a remotis*'.
29. The classic discussion is by H. Grégoire, 'The question of the diversion of the fourth crusade or an old controversy solved by a Latin adverb', *Byzantion*, 15(1940–1), 158–66, where he argued that the use of the word *olim* in a papal letter of November 1202 [Tafel and Thomas I, 404–7; Andrea, *Contemporary Sources*, 35–9] in relation to the visit of the young Alexius to the curia referred to the previous chancery year and might therefore mean that the Byzantine prince visited Innocent III as early as September 1201. It is now clear that *olim* as applied to Alexius's visit to the curia is used in contrast to a visit by the papal legate Peter Capuano, which occurred in September 1202. The only clue to the date of Alexius's visit to the papal curia is the information that he returned to the court of his brother-in-law, who without any delay sent envoys to the leaders of the Christian army. The latter then despatched the papal legate to the curia to consult the pope, datable to September 1202. This suggests very strongly that the Byzantine prince's visit to the pope took place in the early summer of 1202.
30. Tafel and Thomas I, 406: *quanquam plures assererent, quod hujusmodi postulationis* (i.e. from the young Alexius) *benignum deberemus praestare favorem pro eo, quod Graecorum Ecclesia sit apostolicae Sedi minus obediens et devota.* Cf. Andrea, *Contemporary Sources*, 37.
31. The date can be narrowed to between late May/early June, when news of the death of Fulk of Neuilly in May 1202 reached the crusaders, and the arrival of the bishop of Halberstadt on 13 August 1202 (Villehardouin I, §73–4).
32. Gunther of Pairis, 76–7. Abbot Martin of Pairis would have had no reason to draw attention to any contacts with the young Alexius, given his later stance, which was opposed to the diversion of the crusade.
33. Villehardouin I, §70–2.
34. Ibid., I, §51–3.
35. Ibid., I, §62–9. Villehardouin suggests that this event occurred as September approached (*que li setembre aprocha*), but the editor has cast doubt on the reading. For some reason the definite article is used before September – not a normal usage – which suggests to the editor that some word, such as *fins*, has been missed out, but common sense suggests that the accord with the Venetians had to be reached well before the end of September, since the expedition set sail on 1 October.
36. Tafel and Thomas I, 406.
37. *Monumenta Germaniae Historica: Constitutiones et Acta Publica Imperatorum et regum*, II, ed. L. Weiland (Hanover, 1896), 9.
38. The best account of these events is to be found in Maleczek, *Petrus Capuanus*, 117–57.
39. Andrea, *Contemporary Sources*, 62–3. The pope is likely to have been reacting to the plans of Philip of Swabia, which had recently become known to him.
40. It was considered a 'crusade' in retrospect. It was only the mid-fourteenth century chronicler Andrea Dandolo who specifies that the Venetians took the cross. Contemporaries only mention Pope Callixtus II giving the doge a banner depicting St Peter.
41. Villehardouin I, §60.

42. Innocent III's later offer to get Alexius III Angelus to provide the crusaders with provisions can be taken as a belated attempt to meet crusader criticism of the Byzantine emperor's position: Andrea, *Contemporary Sources*, 67.
43. P. Schreiner, 'Genua, Byzanz und der 4. Kreuzzug: ein neues Dokument in Staatsarchiv Genua', *Quellen und Forschungen aus italienischen Archiven und Bibliotheken*, 63(1983), 292–7.
44. *Devastatio*, 142.
45. Ibid.
46. Villehardouin I, §80–90; 105–6. They were the bishop of Soissons and the bishop-elect of Acre along with John of Friaise, who had represented Louis of Blois in the negotiations with the Venetians the previous year, and Robert of Boves, who represented the dissidents.
47. Villehardouin I, §92.
48. Ibid., I, §95–6.
49. Ibid., I, §97: *et ne vos merveillez mie se la laie genz ere en discorde, que li blanc moine de l'ordre de Cistiaus erent altresi en discorde en l'ost.*
50. Ibid., I, §98: *que il seroient **honi** se il la refusoient* (emphasis added).
51. Ibid., 1, §84: *or somes nos **honi** se nos ne l'aidons a prendre* (emphasis added).
52. Ibid., I, §99.
53. Ibid., I, §107; Clari, §XV; Tafel and Thomas I, 407–11; Andrea, *Contemporary Sources*, 39–48.
54. Villehardouin I, §111.
55. Andrea, *Contemporary Sources*, 253.
56. Villehardouin I, §113–14.
57. Ibid., I, §115–18; Tafel and Thomas I, 304–5; Pokorny, 204.45–6 ; Andrea, *Contemporary Sources*, 187–9.
58. Clari, §XXXIII.20–4.
59. Ibid., §XXXIII.2–6; §XXXIX. 6–9.
60. Ibid., §XXXIX.9–16.
61. Ibid., §XLI.5–31; Villehardouin I, §144–6; Tafel and Thomas I, 306; Pokorny, 205.61–7; Andrea, *Contemporary Sources*, 190.
62. Pokorny, 203.5–7; Andrea, *Contemporary Sources*, 186.
63. Tafel and Thomas I, 306; Pokorny, 205.71; Andrea, *Contemporary Sources*, 191.
64. Villehardouin I, §129–34.
65. Schreiner, 'Genua, Byzanz und der 4. Kreuzzug'. Cf. Tafel and Thomas I, 255.
66. Villehardouin I, §189.
67. Ibid., I, §193.
68. Nicetas Choniates, 551–2, 555–6, 559–60.
69. Villehardouin I, §194–9.
70. Tafel and Thomas I, 310–11; Pokorny, 209.182–9; Andrea, *Contemporary Sources*, 199–200.
71. *Register Innocenz' III*, VI, no. 209 (210), 355–8; Andrea, *Contemporary Sources*, 77–9.
72. See now Prinzing, 'Papsttum', 160, who thinks that St-Pol was deceiving himself.
73. Pokorny, 209.190–4; Andrea, *Contemporary Sources*, 200.

74. Nicetas Choniates, 552.
75. Ibid., 553. See T. F. Madden, 'The fires of the Fourth Crusade in Constantinople, 1203–1204: a damage assessment', *Byzantinische Zeitschrift*, 84/85(1992), 72–93.
76. Villehardouin I, §203.
77. *Register Innocenz' III*, VI, no. 209 (210), 355–8; Andrea, *Contemporary Sources*, 77–9.
78. *Devastatio*, 134.
79. Villehardouin II, §207.
80. Ibid., I, §201; *Devastatio*, 135.
81. Villehardouin II, §208.
82. Nicetas Choniates, 557.
83. Villehardouin II, §210–15.
84. Clari, §LIX.28–9.
85. Nicetas Choniates, 563–4; Clari, §LVIII.11–17; B. Hendrickx and C. Matzukis, 'Alexios V Doukas Mourtzouphlos: his life, reign and death (?–1204)', *Hellenika*, 31(1979), 108–32.
86. *Devastatio*, 135.
87. Villehardouin II, §220.
88. Nicetas Choniates, 562–3.
89. *Register Innocenz' III*, VII, no. 152, 253–62; Andrea, *Contemporary Sources*, 101–2.
90. Nicetas Choniates, 563–4; Villehardouin II, §222; Clari, §LXII.1–5.
91. Clari, §LXII.18–24.
92. Nicetas Choniates, 567–68; *Register Innocenz' III*, VII, 254–5; Andrea, *Contemporary Sources*, 104–5.
93. Clari, §LXVI.69–76.
94. Villehardouin II, §225.
95. Clari, §LV.1–4.
96. Villehardouin I, §205.
97. Gunther of Pairis, 88–9.
98. Clari, §LXIV.1–10.
99. Clari, §LXV.42–52.
100. Villehardouin I, §202.
101. Prinzing, 'Papsttum', 166–70; P. Stephenson, *Byzantium's Balkan Frontier: a political study of the northern Balkans, 900–1204* (Cambridge, 2000), 309–12.
102. Tafel and Thomas I, 444–52.
103. Villehardouin II, §239.
104. Ibid., II, §224–5; Clari, §LXXIII.
105. Villehardouin II, §241–51; Clari, §LXXIV–LXXIX; Nicetas Choniates, 569–74. The detail that Boniface of Montferrat was hailed *Hagios Basileus* comes from Gunther of Pairis, 107.
106. Clari, §LXXX.31–4.
107. Villehardouin II, §254; Clari, §LXXXI.
108. Villehardouin II, §262; Nicetas Choniates, 598. The marriage took place before 16 May 1204.
109. Tafel and Thomas I, 446–7, 450.

110. Villehardouin II, §257.

111. We owe this important observation to C. A. Maltezou, 'Venetian *habitores, burgenses* and merchants in Constantinople and its hinterland (12th–13th centuries)', in *Constantinople and its hinterland*, ed. C. Mango and G. Dagron (Aldershot, 1993), 233–41.

112. See Stephenson, *Byzantium's Balkan Frontier*, 275–315, 321–3.

Part 2

THE CONSEQUENCES OF THE FOURTH CRUSADE

chapter 5

INTRODUCTION:
REACTIONS TO 1204

The conquest of Constantinople is chiefly remembered not as a stunning feat of arms, but for the crusaders' sack of the city which has become a byword for brutality. It has been condemned as a 'crime against humanity'. Such a judgement has support in contemporary or near contemporary accounts – western, as well as Byzantine. There were reasons, as we shall see, on both sides to exaggerate the ferocity of the crusader sack of the city. It matters little in retrospect that the sack was not quite the ghastly affair it has been painted, but it is worth putting the record straight, because it illustrates that the impact that an event makes on contemporary opinion depends not so much on what happened as on how it is remembered. Nicetas Choniates's *History* is a good starting point for any reassessment of the sack of Constantinople. His narrative of the sack of Constantinople is justly famous. It contains two distinct but interwoven elements. There is his anguished denunciation of crusader excesses, which has always been accorded the respect due to an eyewitness account, but the rhetorical content is high in contrast to the factual account of his own experiences during the sack of the city. These hardly tally with his bitter condemnation of crusader actions. He suffered some inconvenience, but little harm. He was perhaps fortunate that his residence not far from St Sophia had a concealed entrance. Many of his acquaintances sought refuge with him. Nicetas had a faithful Venetian servant, who was able to keep the looters at bay until a Venetian friend of Nicetas offered him and his whole household shelter. Nicetas and his family then joined the convoy of dignitaries that left the city under a guarantee of safe-conduct on 17 April. In some ways, these were the most dangerous moments. As the column was approaching the walls a libidinous Frank snatched a young girl from Nicetas's group. With the help of his crusader escort Nicetas was able to track the man down to his lair and rescue the young girl. The crusaders were proposing to hang him if he refused to hand her over. It was in fact an example of the discipline exercised by the crusaders once the initial sack was over.[1]

Less well known is the story of John Mesarites, a recluse in one of the monasteries of Constantinople. He abandoned his cell for the greater security of the monastery of St George of the Mangana. He made his way the next morning – 13 April – to his family home, which had been burnt out in one of the earlier fires. He found his brother Nicholas who told him that he was going to seek refuge in the imperial palace, while their mother was making for St Sophia. John Mesarites returned to St George of the Mangana. When the crusaders broke into the monastery, he showed no fear, simply indifference to their threats. His behaviour made a great impression on the crusader leader: almost certainly the count of St-Pol, who took over the monastery. He called John Mesarites into his presence and stood up as a sign of respect. He told him through an interpreter, 'If the people of Byzantium are obedient to a man of God like you, so should we be obedient and express our subservience.'[2] This was not said sarcastically. This incident occurred two days after the crusaders broke into the city, in other words 14 April. We owe this story to Nicholas Mesarites, who came through the sack unscathed, as did his mother. We cannot put too much weight on anecdotes of this sort, but the common thread that links the experiences of the Mesarites and Choniates families is that the crusade leadership acted quickly to rein in the worst excesses of the rank and file.

The author of the *Devastatio* asserts that there was a tremendous slaughter as the crusaders entered the city, but the next day – 13 April – the Greeks surrendered.[3] This put an end to the danger that there would be a prolonged massacre of the population. Instead there was the seizure of houses and property and treasure. None of the sources make clear how long this lasted, but order had certainly been restored by 17 April and probably before. The sack of Constantinople was, as these things go, less savage than might be expected. This is not to discount the horror of the sack, but it does seem to have been over relatively quickly. The nearest thing we have to a neutral source is the Novgorod chronicle. It gives a detailed description of the plundering of St Sophia. It reveals that monks and nuns were stopped in the streets and robbed, but very few were killed. Nothing is said about the rape of nuns, which is a standard charge in the more lurid accounts.[4]

There are reasons to suppose that more damage was done by the fire that devastated Constantinople in August 1203 than by the crusader sack.[5] Were the crusaders, in fact, any worse than the agents of Alexius IV Angelus, who 'not only cut down the holy icons of Christ with axes and mercilessly ripped out their precious frames, which they consigned to the flames, but also without compunction stripped the churches of their hallowed furnishings, which they melted down into base silver and gold . . .'?[6] Just the residue of their spoils excited the wonder of the crusade leaders when it fell into their hands along with other treasures from the Boucoleon and Blachernai palaces.[7] The division of booty was going to turn into a source of bitter contention. The rank and file suspected that the leadership had kept back all the most precious objects from the common pool of booty, which was divided among the troops. These suspicions were forcefully voiced by Robert of Clari. They were rejected with equal vigour by Villehardouin on behalf of the leadership.

The division of the booty created a great deal of bad feeling and contributed to the decision of many of the rank and file to return to the West at the earliest opportunity. It coloured contemporary assessments of the conquest of Constantinople, which were inclined as a result to exaggerate the savagery of the sack and the amount of booty seized.

I

The Latin Empire of Constantinople existed under a shadow of disapproval. Its history was in many ways a matter of great hopes disappointed. News of the conquest of Constantinople had initially been the cause of exultation in the West. The official letters despatched by the new Emperor Baldwin I soon after his coronation on 16 May 1204 provided the solidest information. It presented the conquest as a miraculous solution to Byzantine intransigence, which had for so long harmed the interests of the Holy Land. The Greeks had now suffered condign punishment at the hands of the crusaders, acting as agents of divine justice. All that remained was for the pope to come to Constantinople in order to reconcile the Greeks to Rome.[8]

The news was at first taken at face value. Innocent III's reaction was euphoric. God had indeed worked His miracles through the crusaders and had humbled the schismatic Greeks. The pope immediately took Baldwin's land and people under the protection of St Peter.[9] Then, quite suddenly, in the summer of 1205 the tone of his letters to the crusade leaders changed. He took them to task for the brutality of the sack of Constantinople. The most serious consequence was that it deterred the Greek Church from returning to union with Rome.[10] The pope's change of heart occurred before he received news of the Latin defeat at the battle of Adrianople. Innocent III never abandoned his belief that the conquest of Constantinople was divinely ordained to mend 'the seamless garment of Christ'. But it was a prize endangered by base humanity. By the summer of 1205 reports of the sack of Constantinople will have filtered back to the West, along with more precise information about the establishment of the Latin Empire. Taken together the pope would have found them doubly worrying, for they made clear how little control he had over the situation. This was brought home to the pope as he examined the crusaders' partition treaty with a view to confirming it: something that he never did because he realised that it had been drawn up with little regard for ecclesiastical interests, while the unilateral decision to create a Latin patriarchate of Constantinople struck at the heart of papal authority.[11] Still worse, the conquest of Constantinople appeared to have compromised the security of the Holy Land by enticing away its natural defenders. The papal legate Peter Capuano was held responsible. He had disobeyed papal instructions to remain in the Holy Land and had instead made his way to Constantinople. His example was followed by many magnates and even prelates from the kingdom of Jerusalem together with large numbers of commoners.[12] Innocent III wrote to Philip Augustus in July 1205 urging him to send help to the Holy Land 'which had been left almost devoid of men and resources' because so many had departed for Constantinople.[13] To recover the situation Innocent III had to assert his moral authority. A way of doing this was to take the crusade leaders to task for the sack of Constantinople, which Innocent III had hitherto chosen to ignore.

Papal condemnation cast a shadow over the moral standing of the Latin Empire of Constantinople. There were those in the West who had an interest in disparaging the Latin Empire. A good example is Peter of Vaux-de-Cernay, the historian of the Albigensian crusade. As a young man he had gone on the Fourth Crusade with his uncle Guy, the abbot of Vaux-de-Cernay, who together with Simon de Montfort led the opposition to the diversion of the crusade. They abandoned the crusader camp at Zara and eventually made their way to Syria. According to Peter they 'returned with honour to their country', whereas the leaders they had left at Zara had, with a few exceptions, perished ignominiously. Simon de Montfort went on to lead the Albigensian crusade, while Abbot Guy was one of the early preachers of that crusade. It was in the interests of those involved in the Albigensian crusade to stress the ignoble character and lack of success of the Fourth Crusade.[14] The historical compilation, emanating originally from the crusader states, known as *Heracles* is equally hostile to the Latin Empire. It is also rather well informed about its early history. It gives considerable prominence to the sack of Constantinople, which proved that the crusaders had rejected God's 'shilling' and had taken the Devil's.[15] This was then confirmed by the bitter struggle over the division of the booty. But more revealing is the compiler's dismay at the departure of so many from the Holy Land to seek their fortune in

Constantinople. He gives a figure – no doubt something of an exaggeration – of 100 knights and 10,000 commoners. It looked as though the crusader states might have in the Latin Empire a serious competitor for manpower and resources.[16]

The disquiet occasioned by the circumstances of the creation of the Latin Empire had one serious consequence. It never engaged the interest and the sympathies of the West in the way that the crusader states did. Surprisingly few contemporary Latin chronicles contain sustained and enthusiastic accounts of the Fourth Crusade. The Premonstratensian Robert of Auxerre, for example, has more than most on the events of the Fourth Crusade. He was the compiler of a world chronicle, which he took down to 1211, the year of his death. His account of the conquest of Constantinople is quite detailed and makes full use of the Emperor Baldwin's letter.[17] He began brightly describing the event as a 'stupendous and quite unexpected change of fortunes',[18] but then the doubts set in. The chronicler was disturbed at the way the Holy Land had been left as a result 'more or less destitute of men and resources',[19] a phrase that echoed Innocent III's letter to Philip Augustus. He recorded the defeat suffered at Adrianople and concluded that 'the joy of our enemies and our own confusion increased',[20] a remark that reflected a general pessimism about the Latin Empire. Another contemporary witness to the confused reaction to the conquest of Constantinople is Arnold of Lübeck. He had been abbot of the monastery of St John at Lübeck since 1177. He died in 1211 or shortly thereafter. His interest in the East was sparked off by Henry the Lion's pilgrimage to Jerusalem in 1172, which is the event with which he begins his chronicle. His account of the Fourth Crusade is largely a matter of reproducing the letters of the count of St-Pol and of the Emperor Baldwin, but it is prefaced by a series of remarks which reflected the questions that were being asked about the Fourth Crusade. He began by saluting the Latin achievements, but concluded that 'whether they were the deeds of God or of men, a fitting outcome is not yet in sight'. He compared the Latins to Job. Though God was on their side, their faith was being tested by the Devil. They needed to repeat after Job: 'the Lord giveth and the Lord taketh away'.[21] Arnold and Robert of Auxerre died within a few years of the conquest of Constantinople. Their accounts reflect the interest of contemporaries in the event, but also their uncertainty about its morality. These doubts inhibited other chroniclers of their generation.

Alfred J. Andrea has recently drawn attention to two slightly later Cistercian chroniclers who provide accounts of the Fourth Crusade. They were Ralph of Coggeshall from England and Alberic of Trois Fontaines from Champagne; Ralph was completing his chronicle in the

1220s and Alberic in the 1250s.[22] In much the same way as his contemporary Caesarius of Heisterbach, Ralph was celebrating the Cistercian
achievement. He begins with the preaching of Fulk of Neuilly, which he
presents as the main inspiration for the Fourth Crusade. The climax
comes with Fulk's arrival in September 1198 at the Chapter General of
the Cistercians. It was there that he assumed the cross. Quite inaccurately
Ralph is presenting this meeting as the true beginning of the Fourth
Crusade, which he turned into a Cistercian enterprise. By comparison
Ralph's account of the conquest of Constantinople is quite flat and
perfunctory. He has little to say about the defeat at Adrianople, although
it provides him with the opportunity to relate how a relic of the True
Cross came to the priory of Bromholm in Norfolk. Under cover of the
defeat an English priest serving in the Latin emperor's chapel was able
to filch the relic and bring it back home with him. In other words,
Ralph's treatment of the Fourth Crusade is thoroughly misleading. The
highpoint is the preaching of the crusade, ultimately under Cistercian
auspices. The outcome is of much less interest to the chronicler. Alberic
provides a rather better balanced narrative and has little to say about
Cistercian involvement in the crusade. He pays due attention to Fulk's
preaching, but does not connect it to Cîteaux and, unlike Ralph, relays
some of the criticism there was of Fulk. Again unlike Ralph, he makes
good use of the Emperor Baldwin's letter as the core of his narrative of
the conquest of Constantinople. The defeat at Adrianople is treated in
sombre fashion. It allowed Laskaris in Asia Minor and Michael Doukas
in Epiros to seize the initiative against the Latins. It was God's wish that
'through them a trial might be made for Israel'.[23] The comparison with
Israel is striking, but it provided the chronicler with a neat way out of
his dilemma. He could suspend judgement on the outcome of the
Fourth Crusade, because the fate of the Latins was still in the balance.
On the whole, those western chroniclers who do pay attention to the
Fourth Crusade only underline what a problem it presented to contemporaries. This explains its comparative neglect in western chronicles. It
reflected an ambivalence about the Latin Empire, which had practical
consequences: after Adrianople there were difficulties in attracting settlers
to the Latin Empire, while as a crusading goal Latin Constantinople never
aroused the same enthusiasm in the West as there was for Jerusalem.[24]

II

As 'a crime against humanity' the conquest of Constantinople hardly
rates beside the crusader sack of Jerusalem in 1099 or the excesses of the
Albigensian crusade, but these were forgotten while the reputation of

the Latin Empire suffered. Exaggeration of the horrors of the sack of Constantinople coloured how the Latin Empire was regarded and how the Fourth Crusade was remembered in the West. The reaction of contemporaries is one way of measuring the impact of an event. But how an event was remembered and judged must be reckoned of lesser importance than its direct historical consequences. But this is the historian's dilemma: the realisation that we remain dependent on the way an event was remembered or recorded, but that this will be at some distance from the truth. It is easier to assess contemporary reactions than to discern the truth of the matter. More than that: the way the sources have survived is to an extent a matter of chance, but it may also point to some basic truth about an event. The interest generated by the Fourth Crusade meant that the narrative sources for the early history of the Latin Empire are comparatively rich; thereafter they are patchy in the extreme. Whereas the conquest of Constantinople and its immediate aftermath attracted intense attention, the Latin Empire, as such, found no contemporary historian – a judgement in itself. The modern historian has to cobble together a narrative from chance remarks in western chronicles, such as Matthew Paris and Philip Mousket. The Byzantine historian of the period of exile, George Akropolites, has surprisingly little on the Latin Empire. He was writing after the Byzantine recovery of Constantinople in 1261. By then the Latin Empire seemed an aberration.[25] The documentary sources follow much the same pattern. Innocent III's *Letters* are a capital source for the establishment of the Latin Church of Constantinople. His immediate successor, Honorius III (1216–27), maintained an interest in the affairs of the Latin Church, but thereafter the papal archives have relatively little on the Latin Empire.[26] The Venetian archives are a rich source of documentation for the activities of the Venetians in the Latin Empire, a great deal of it relating to the conquest and settlement of Crete.[27] They are less helpful as a source for the Latin Empire. The survival of these documentary sources means that we are more precisely informed about the establishment of the Latin Church and the creation of a Venetian 'Empire' than we are about the Latin Empire itself, which can boast next to no surviving documentation. It may be indicative that the Latin emperors failed to issue their own coinage.[28] This tends to confirm that the neglect of the Latin Empire by the narrative sources is no accident; more an index of its failure, as western opinion became increasingly indifferent to its fate.

The comparative lack of documentation after 1216 for the history of the Latin Empire forces us to concentrate on the direct consequences of 1204. This has one major advantage. The sorry fate of the Latin Empire was unknown to those writing in the immediate aftermath of the conquest of Constantinople. They had no reason to shape their story in a way that reflected the ultimate failure of the Latin Empire. We are dealing with material that was itself the product of the creation of a new set of circumstances triggered off by the conquest of Constantinople. In some ways, we are fortunate that the main narrative sources for the Fourth Crusade follow through the early stages of the conquest. Nicetas Choniates carries his *History* down to the end of 1206; Geoffrey of Villehardouin down to the death of Boniface of Montferrat in September 1207; Robert of Clari only to the battle of Adrianople in April 1205.

Nicetas Choniates provides a full and accurate narrative of events following the fall of the city, which he was in a good position to chronicle. He first found refuge at Selymbria on the Sea of Marmara and witnessed at first-hand the turmoil in Thrace produced by the Bulgarian invasions. He returned to Constantinople for some months before finally reaching the safety of Nicaea at the end of 1206. His account of events is unsurprisingly informed by a strong moral sense that the Byzantines were being punished by God, but he took heart from the defeat at Adrianople and the Bulgarian depredations in Thrace: the lesson was that the crusaders no longer enjoyed the special favour of God, now that they had fulfilled their allotted role – to punish the Byzantines for their sins. Once at Nicaea Nicetas helped to frame an ideology of exile, which insisted that the Byzantines, like the Israelites of old, might have been condemned to exile for their sins, but in the fullness of time they would recover their Jerusalem.[29]

The Frankish perspective was different, if informed by the same desire to understand the meaning of the conquest of Constantinople. Geoffrey of Villehardouin has also left a sustained narrative. As marshal of the Latin Empire he was at the centre of events and therefore in an even better position than Nicetas Choniates to know what was happening. In contrast, Robert of Clari's narrative of events post-1204 has little of substance; he is likely to have been among those who left for home in April 1205, their obligation to serve the Latin Empire having come to an end on 31 March. But his treatment is symptomatic. He seeks to find meaning in the unravelling of events. He presents the defeat at Adrianople as divine vengeance on the leaders of the crusade: 'for their pride and the bad faith which they had shown to the poor people of the host and for the horrific sins which they had committed in the City after they had taken it'.[30] Robert of Clari was incensed by the way the greater part of the booty taken had, as he saw it, gone to the leaders of the crusade.

Villehardouin equally seeks the meaning of 1204, but not so obviously. The stupendous feat of arms which had brought the crusaders Constantinople shed lustre on the participants. He wished to preserve their reputations. He notes the deaths of his companions-in-arms. Hugh of St-Pol died early in 1205 from natural causes: '[T]his was a very great loss and very bitter blow and he was much mourned by his men and by his friends.'[31] Villehardouin concludes his *History* with the death of Boniface. His ending is elegaic: 'Alas! What a bitter blow it was for the Emperor Henry and for all the Latins of the land of Romania to lose by misadventure such a man, the best and most generous of leaders and one of the best knights to be found anywhere in the world.'[32] It was a suitable place to stop. With the exception of the Emperor Henry all the major leaders of the Fourth Crusade were dead, but the fate of the Latin Empire still hung in the balance. Like Robert of Clari he understands that the defeat at Adrianople was in some sense a divine judgement on the crusaders, but he is more matter of fact: he concludes, 'Finally, they were defeated, since God permits changes of fortune.'[33] Villehardouin was not willing to explain himself further. His aim was to preserve the good name of the crusade leaders in the face of criticism, such as that which came from the pen of Robert of Clari. If anybody was blameworthy in Villehardouin's opinion, it was those members of the rank and file who kept back part of their booty, 'for avarice which is the root of all evils is ever present . . . and Our Lord began to love them less'.[34] Villehardouin remained convinced that 'if God had not loved this host, it could not have remained united, when so many wished it evil'.[35] He was thinking in particular of those who had abandoned the crusade at Zara and had made their way to Syria.

Geoffrey of Villehardouin found a continuator in Henry of Valenciennes, a cleric in the service of the Emperor Henry. His narrative is limited to little more than a year of the latter's reign. It covers the period from Pentecost (25 May) 1208 to July 1209. This was very roughly the time that a leading Flemish nobleman, Peter of Douai, was in the Emperor Henry's service. Of all the emperor's intimates, Peter was the one singled out for special prominence by Henry of Valenciennes. There is therefore a strong possibility that the chronicle was commissioned by Peter as a record of the events in the Latin Empire while he was there.[36] That it was intended for a Flemish audience is apparent from the way that Henry of Valenciennes was careful to name names, as a way of reporting on the prowess displayed by men of Flanders and the Low Countries. Describing the assault on the castle of Thebes by the Emperor Henry's forces Henry notes that four squires from Valenciennes distinguished themselves and gives their names.[37] Henry finally brings his narrative to an end quite suddenly in the middle of some negotiations, in which Peter of Douai had had a part to play.[38] The abrupt ending is best explained by the latter's imminent departure from the Latin Empire, which took place in September 1209. He wanted to take Henry's narrative back with him to Flanders. It was designed to counteract the poor press that the Latin Empire had received in the West and to attract new recruits into the service of the Latin emperor, who remained desperately short of followers. Henry himself remained behind – perhaps as a canon of St Sophia.

There is a high moral content to Henry of Valenciennes's *History*, as there is with the other narratives, for the good reason that the interpretation of history was largely a matter of making moral judgements. The problem for modern historians is to know how to convert moral judgements into a more objective assessment of the consequences of an event. The fact that the fall of Constantinople sparked off a debate about its moral value is a consequence in itself. It helps to explain why, as we have argued, there was a comparative lack of interest in Latin Constantinople in the West. It alerts us to an unease about the Latin Empire, even during that brief period when the Emperor Henry of Hainault (1206–16) succeeded in imposing his authority over much of the former Byzantine Empire. This meant disciplining the recalcitrant Lombards of Thessalonica, as well as a series of Slav and Greek leaders.

Western chronicles more or less ignore his considerable achievements. This comes as a surprise because they had at their disposal the circular letters sent by the leaders of the Fourth Crusade back home to inform, offer reassurance, impress, and ask for aid. No less than ten letters from the Emperor Henry have survived.[39] Most are addressed to specific recipients, but this does not preclude a wide audience. One letter sent in 1212 was addressed to 'all his friends'. Henry used it to broadcast his crushing victory over the forces of the Greek Emperor Theodore Laskaris.[40] The intention was to underline the recovery from the disaster at the battle of Adrianople in April 1205 and the establishment of the Latin Empire of Constantinople on a firm basis.

A different impression was left by 'La Bible au seignor de Berzé, chastelain' which contains a sombre evaluation of the Fourth Crusade: 'And who has seen what I have seen [knows] how little love of riches is worth, for in Constantinople which is so beautiful and rich and noble I saw four emperors within the space of a year and a half and then I saw [each of] them die within so short a term an evil death . . .'[41] It was the defeat at Adrianople which left a more lasting impression on him than the conquest of Constantinople.

Rather different is the poetry of the troubadours Raimbaut of Vaqueiras and Elias of Cairel, who were drawn from the ranks of the Lombards, as Boniface of Montferrat's followers were known. Their verses provide a commentary on the heroic early period of the Latin Empire. Writing soon after the conquest of Constantinople, Raimbaut reflects a current of opinion still strong among the rank and file that only the 'succour the Holy Sepulchre' could justify 'the burning of the churches and the palaces'.[42] But the slightly later 'Epic Letter' addressed to the marquis of Montferrat celebrated the conquest of Constantinople as the culmination of a chivalric career, which required that his prowess and loyalty be properly rewarded.[43] His final offering – *No m'agrad iverns ni pascors* ('Neither winter nor spring delights me') – is more sombre. The theme was the futility of conquest and prowess without love, but this did not prevent Raimbaut taking pride in what the Latins had achieved in Romania: 'Never did Alexander or Charlemagne or King Louis lead such a glorious expedition, nor could the valiant lord Aimeri or Roland with his warriors win by might, in such noble fashion, such a powerful empire as we have won, whereby our Faith is in the ascendant.'[44] Raimbaut did not leave a lament for the death of Boniface of Montferrat, which suggests the possibility that he may have died with his lord in September 1207 when caught in an ambush by the Bulgarians. Elias of Cairel, another troubador in Boniface's service survived his lord. His bitterness fuels his *sirventes* – *Pus chai la fuelha del jaric*: 'Now that the oak leaves fall'. It was addressed to Boniface's son, William of Montferrat, who had failed to come to the aid of the Lombards of Thessalonica after the death of his father: it would be better if he had become abbot of Cluny or Cîteaux rather than pretend to be his father's son. He was no Bohemond. Elias also voiced the rancour felt by the Lombards at their treatment by the Emperor Henry.[45] The contrast in tone between the troubadours and the lord of Berzé is instructive. The former stayed on and gave voice to the defiant and disruptive pride of the veterans of the Fourth Crusade, while the latter returned home to Burgundy and reflected pessimistically about his experiences.

In some ways we are fortunate that sources are most abundant for exactly that period when the fate of the Latin Empire was in the balance, but it does mean that it is that much harder to decide why that balance went one way rather than another. When Henry of Hainault died in 1216 the condition of the Latin Empire of Constantinople looked on the surface far from hopeless. But we know that the balance would soon turn against it, whereas in the Greek lands the opposite was happening. There westerners were putting down deep roots. Athens remained in Latin hands until 1456 when Mehmed the Conqueror marched in, and there was a Latin presence in the western Peloponnese almost as long. This was the last remnant of the principality of Achaea established in the Peloponnese in the aftermath of the conquest of Constantinople in 1204. The history of the Frankish conquest and the establishment of the principality of Achaea is contained in the *Chronicle of the Morea*, which is the principal literary monument to the Latin colonisation in the former Byzantine Empire. It survives in a series of versions: French, Greek, Aragonese and – much later – Italian.[46] They date from the mid-fourteenth century or later and represent abridgements of an original that was compiled at the beginning of the fourteenth century. There has been a long debate as to whether the original was written in French or Greek. At the moment the balance of opinion favours David Jacoby's arguments for the precedence of a French version.[47] Whereas the sources for the Latin Empire of Constantinople that we have been considering were aimed as much at an audience in western Europe as they were at one in Romania, the *Chronicle of the Morea* seems to have been produced for the courts of Frankish Greece. The surviving French version was an abridgement of a master copy kept in the early fourteenth century in the castle at Thebes, which incidentally was decorated with scenes from the Trojan War. It was compiled in the aftermath of the death in 1278 of William – the last Villehardouin prince of Achaea. He was the younger son of the founder of the principality. His death cut almost the last direct link to the period of conquest. The *Chronicle of the Morea* celebrated the conquest and exalted the regime that the Franks established, with the accent placed firmly on prowess and due process of law. The Franks of the Peloponnese also elaborated their own code of laws – the *Assises of Romania* – which existed in some form by 1276, when reference was made to the 'usages and customs of the country' by the *Chronicle of the Morea*.[48] In the form that they have come down to us the *Assises of Romania* were compiled between 1333 and 1346.[49]

The *Chronicle of the Morea* and the *Assises of Romania* are therefore difficult to compare with the sources for the early history of the Latin Empire. The latter represent an immediate response to situations which were to lead who knows where. But by the early fourteenth century the outcome of the Fourth Crusade was only too clear. The Latin Empire led nowhere and the great days of the principality of Achaea were over. However, the *Chronicle of the Morea* and the *Assises of Romania* preserve in however exaggerated a form something of the crusader ideal that inspired the first generation of the Latins of Constantinople. The *Chronicle* is prefaced by an account of the First Crusade and the conquest of Jerusalem; the preface to the *Assises* insists that the first Latin Emperor Baldwin requested the king and patriarch of Jerusalem 'to send their usages and assises, for they wished to be ruled by them since they were usages of conquest'.[50] This cannot be literally true, but the usages of the kingdom of Jerusalem certainly had some influence on the development of feudal law in the Latin Empire. For example, Geoffrey of Villehardouin the Younger cited a Jerusalem custom to bar another claimant to the principality of Achaea.[51] The leaders of the Fourth Crusade used the crusading ideal to justify their conquest of the Byzantine Empire. Their battle cry was 'Holy Sepulchre', while a relic of the True Cross was borne before the Latin emperor when on campaign in imitation of the practice of the kingdom of Jerusalem.[52] Though late, the *Chronicle of the Morea* and the *Assises of Romania* are best used for our purposes to give perspective to the events immediately following the fall of Constantinople.

The establishment of the Latin Empire was not just the work of the crusaders. The Venetians played just as important a role. The lack of a Venetian account of the Fourth Crusade deprives us of a contemporary Venetian view of the conquest of Constantinople. The first substantial Venetian history to deal in detail with the events of the Fourth Crusade and the subsequent conquests was, as we know, the *Cronique des Veniciens* of Martin da Canal.[53] It was compiled between 1267 and 1275, in other words, after Constantinople had been recovered by the Greeks. Significantly, it was written in French and for an audience in the Frankish Levant. At a difficult time for the Latin Orient the *Cronique des Veniciens* was designed to justify the actions of Venice, which might otherwise have appeared motivated by little more than self-interest. Martin da Canal presents the Venetians as loyal servants of the papacy and faithful supporters of the crusade ideal. Venetian success in the East, to his way of thinking, was in the interests of Christendom and the Venetians' public-spirited conduct contrasted with the self-interest of their Genoese opponents.[54] It was a self-serving interpretation that was refined by the Doge Andreas Dandolo (1343–54) in his *Chronica per extensum descripta*, which took the history of Venice down to 1280.[55] It represents an official standpoint which gave historical buttressing to the 'Myth of Venice'. This had its roots in the translation of St Mark to Venice. But two historical events in particular would be twisted to support the idea of Venice's imperial destiny: the Peace of Venice in 1177 and the conquest of Constantinople in 1204. The former allowed Venice to pose as the loyal servant of the papacy; the latter gave it a share in imperial dignity. This took on increased importance with the failure of the Latin Empire of Constantinople.

The relationship between the fallen Latin Empire and Venice was at the heart of the *Istoria del regno di Romania* by Marino Sanudo Torsello. Sanudo was a Venetian crusade propagandist who knew the Levant well. He was related to the dukes of Naxos and had spent time in the Peloponnese. His *Istoria del regno di Romania* was an offshoot of his crusade propaganda.[56] It was written in the late 1320s, by which time it was clear that the Latin Empire would never be restored and that without

Venetian support it would be impossible to maintain a Latin presence in the Peloponnese. He looked back with regret. He remembered the reputation the principality of Achaea had as a school of chivalry; the prince was famed for his retinue of eighty gold-spurred knights and such was his 'courtoisie and friendship that not only knights but also merchants arrived there without money and were lodged with the *Baili* who with a simple writ gave them money and abundant expenses'. Sanudo's history is written not only out of a sense of nostalgia but also from a distinctively Venetian point of view. Sanudo conceived his history as a continuation of what he calls the *Book of the conquest of the Empire of Romania*. This is almost certainly Villehardouin's *History*, with which variants of Sanudo's *History* are associated in the manuscript tradition.[57] Sanudo aimed to provide a Venetian perspective to the history of the Latin Empire. To his way of thinking it was the efforts of the Venetian Republic which lay at the heart of the history of the 'Latins in the Levant'. The greater part of his history is therefore devoted to the role of the Venetians in the politics of the Levant, culminating in the struggle with Michael VIII Palaiologos after 1261.

The narrative sources establish the parameters within which we can investigate the consequences of 1204. They alert us to the very different perspectives that we have to juggle. So we can follow the immediate response of the crusade leaders to the problems that they confronted following their conquest of Constantinople. By the death of Henry of Hainault in 1216 they appeared to have surmounted their initial political and military problems. Looked at in this way the defeat at Adrianople seems to have been only a temporary setback, but in the light of the collapse of the fortunes of the Latin Empire in the wake of Henry's death it has always appeared more sinister, as a portent of the Latin Empire's basic weaknesses. The comparative lack of sources for the period after 1216 is in itself a reflection of failure, but renders explanation problematical. The sources for the Latin Empire provide contemporary information about the establishment of the Franks in the Greek lands in the immediate aftermath of 1204. The *Chronicle of the Morea* and the *Assises of Romania* allow a more nuanced assessment of their contribution to the changes occurring after 1204, even though they were both texts which presented an idealised version of events. They were probably less concerned with myth-making than were the Venetian histories, which aimed long after the event to glorify Venice's imperial destiny. Thanks to the survival of documents from the Venetian archives the underlying reality of the Venetian presence in the Levant can be followed in a way that is more or less impossible for the Latin Empire. They allow us not just to reconstruct in some detail the Venetian conquests made in the aftermath of 1204, but also to trace the development of Venetian policy towards the Latin Empire. Generally speaking, the role of the Latin Empire of Constantinople was negative. It led nowhere and this is an impression that is only intensified by the nature of the evidence. In contrast, Venice played a positive part in the reshaping of the 'Levant' in the aftermath of the fall of Constantinople. The archival documents bring this out in sharp relief.

III

The consequences of the fall of Constantinople to the crusaders in April 1204 revolve around the failure of the Latin Empire. At first sight, this suggests that a spectacular event changed nothing, in the sense that the Latin Empire inherited all the weakness of the defunct Byzantine Empire and was in its turn overwhelmed by them. It was certainly the case that the Latin Empire was heir to all the main problems that confronted its predecessor. There was a crisis of authority at the centre; there was provincial dissidence, of which the emergence of a new Bulgarian Empire was the most obvious manifestation before 1204; finally, there was a struggle for control of the seas of Byzantium between various Italian powers – the Genoese and Sicilians to the fore. On the face of it, the conquerors seemed to be in a good position to deal with these problems. They brought with them a new vigour and a new outlook which should have cut to the heart of the difficulties that had threatened the old Byzantine regime. While Henry of Hainault reigned, it looked as though the Latin Empire had a good chance of establishing itself as a permanent feature of the political landscape of the Levant.

But it is important to make a distinction between the Latin Empire based on Constantinople and a Latin presence in the lands of the old Byzantine Empire. The city of Constantinople was too great a burden for the Latin Empire. The Latins allowed it to decay in a way that was quite inconceivable under a Byzantine regime. The decline of Constantinople was at the heart of the transformation of the Byzantine lands in the aftermath of 1204 – a transformation paradoxically that ensured a Latin presence down to the end of the Middle Ages and in some parts even longer. The Byzantine Empire had always been held together by the political and ecclesiastical authority exercised from Constantinople. Its dramatic decline after 1204 meant that power passed to the provinces where new political structures took shape. The Franks of the Peloponnese and mainland Greece were beneficiaries, but they were not the only beneficiaries; Greek leaders too were able to establish local power bases in Asia Minor and in Epiros. The roots of this fragmentation of political power can in some places be traced back before 1204. But its intensification and development into a new political system was only possible because of what happened after 1204; because of the deliberate dismantling of an imperial structure of government by the conquerors, which in its turn entailed the decay of the capital.

Its failure had economic implications.[58] Constantinople ceased to be a major centre of consumption and the dominating economic force. This made possible a restructuring of the commerce of the region. This was largely the work of the Venetians. Their energies were at first engaged in the reduction of the island of Crete. This became the hub of a commercial 'empire' built on control of the trade routes linking Venice to the eastern Mediterranean. Whereas Venetian trade in the twelfth century was largely built on supplying the needs of Constantinople, in the thirteenth century it was founded on control of lands and routes, which made possible the subsequent domination of international trade. By the early fourteenth century Constantinople had in commercial terms been transformed from a great imperial capital into nothing much more than an Italian entrepôt.

The linking theme will be the transformation of the Byzantine lands in the aftermath of the Latin conquest. The starting point will be the Latin-held territories, but we must not forget that those most deeply affected were the Orthodox inhabitants of these lands. The fall of Constantinople in 1204 was a more traumatic event than the final fall in 1453. It challenged the very core of the Byzantine identity. There was for a time a real danger that Byzantium might be recreated in a Latin image. However, this passed. The Byzantine elite was able to regroup around a variety of leaders, who set themselves up as heirs to the old Byzantine emperors. Its members pondered the Byzantine legacy and the nature of the Byzantine identity. It was a salutary process from which Byzantium emerged in many respects revitalised, but also decisively changed. All this will be considered later.

Notes

1. Nicetas Choniates, 587–91.
2. Mesarites I, §31.
3. *Devastatio*, 137.
4. Chronicle of Novgorod, 309–10.
5. T. F. Madden, 'The fires of the Fourth Crusade'.
6. Nicetas Choniates, 552.67–71.
7. Villehardouin II, §249–50.
8. *Register Innocenz' III*, VII, no. 152, 253ff.; Andrea, *Contemporary Sources*, 100–12.

9. *Register Innocenz' III*, VII, no. 153, 262ff.; ed. Haluscynski, no. 64, 276–77; Andrea, *Contemporary Sources*, 113–15.

10. *Reg.* VIII, cxxvi: Migne *PL* 215, 699–702; ed. Haluscynski, no. 84, 307–8; *Reg.* VIII, cxxxiii: Migne *PL* 215, 710–14; ed. Haluscynski, no. 87, 311–13; Andrea, *Contemporary Sources*, 162–76.

11. *Reg.* VII, ccvi: Migne *PL* 215, 519–21; ed. Haluscynski, no. 69, 290; Andrea, *Contemporary Sources*, 146–8; *Reg.* VII, ccviii: Migne *PL* 521–3; ed. Haluscynski, no. 70, 291–2; Andrea, *Contemporary Sources*, 150–1.

12. Migne *PL* 215, 700A; ed. Haluscynski, 308.

13. *Reg.* VIII, cxxv: Migne *PL* 215, 698–9; ed. Haluscynski, no. 90, 315–17.

14. *The History of the Albigensian Crusade. Peter of les Vaux-de-Cernay's Historia Albigensis*, transl. W. A. and M. D. Sibly (Woodbridge, 1998), §106, 57–9; M. Zerner-Chardavoine and H. Piéchon-Palloc, 'La croisade albigeoise, un revanche. Des rapports entre la quatrième croisade et la croisade albigeoise', *Revue historique*, 267(1982), 3–18.

15. '... avoient l'escu de Dame Deu embracé. Et tant tost come il furent dedens il le geterent jus et embracerent l'escu au Deable.'

16. *Estoire d'Heracles* in *Receuil des historiens de la croisade: Historiens Occidentaux* II, xxix, i, 274–5. On the complicated composition of this text, see J. H. Pryor, 'The *Eracles* and William of Tyre. An interim report', in *The Horns of Hattin*, ed. B. Z. Kedar (Aldershot, 1992), 270–93; P. Edbury, 'The Lyon *Eracles* and the Old French continuations', in *Montjoie*, ed. B. Z. Kedar *et al.* (Aldershot, 1997), 139–52.

17. Robert of Auxerre, *Chronicon*, ed. O. Holder-Egger (MGH, SS, 26), 265–70.

18. Ibid., 265.

19. Ibid., 269.

20. Ibid., 270.

21. Arnold of Lübeck, *Chronica Slavorum*, ed. G. H. Pertz (MGH, SS, 21), 223–4. Cf. *Chronica Regia Coloniensis*, 203–15.

22. Andrea, *Contemporary Sources*, 265–309.

23. Ibid., 309.

24. M. Barber, 'Western attitudes to Frankish Greece in the thirteenth century', in *Latins and Greeks in the eastern Mediterranean after 1204* (London, 1989), 111–28.

25. *Oxford Dictionary of Byzantium* I – sub. AKROPOLITES, GEORGE.

26. L. Santifaller, *Beiträge zur Geschichte des Lateinischen Patriarchats von Konstantinopel (1204–1261). und der venezianischen Urkunde* (Weimar, 1938), 167–216.

27. Tafel and Thomas, I–III.

28. A. M. Stahl, 'Coinage and Money in the Latin Empire of Constantinople', *Dumbarton Oaks Papers*, 55(2001), 197–206.

29. J.-L. van Dieten, *Niketas Choniates: Erläuterungen zu den Reden und Briefen nebst einer Biographie* (Berlin/New York, 1971), 41–51.

30. Clari, §cxii.

31. Villehardouin II, §334.

32. Ibid., II, §500.

33. Ibid., II, §360.

34. Ibid., II, §253.
35. Ibid., I, §104.
36. Henri de Valenciennes, 7–13; J. Longnon, 'Le chroniqueur Henri de Valenciennes', *Journal des Savants* 1945, 134–43; J. Longnon, 'Sur l'histoire de l'empereur Henri de Constantinople par Henri de Valenciennes', *Romania*, 69(1946–7), 198–241.
37. Henri de Valenciennes, §676, 112.
38. Ibid., §692–4, 120–1.
39. Ph. Lauer, 'Une lettre inédite d'Henri 1er d'Angre, empereur de Constantinople, aux prélats italiens (1213?)', in *Mélanges offerts à M. Gustave Schlumberger*, I (Paris, 1924), 191–201.
40. G. Prinzing, 'Der Brief Kaiser Heinrichs von Konstantinopel vom 13. Januar 1212', *Byzantion*, 43(1973), 395–431.
41. *La Bible au Seignor de Berzé, Chastelain*, II, 406–9. See G. Paris, 'Hugues de Berzé', *Romania*, 18(1889), 553–70.
42. Linskill, *Poems of Raimbaut de Vaqueiras*, 228.
43. Ibid., 309–12.
44. Ibid., 246.
45. V. de Bartholomaeis, 'Un Sirventés historique d'Élias Cairel', *Annales du Midi*, 16(1904), 468–94; V. de Bartholomaeis, *Poesie provenzali storiche relative all'Italia* (Fonti per la storia d'Italia, 71) (Rome, 1931), I, 171–80.
46. Chronicle of the Morea; *Libro de los fechos*, ed. A. Morel-Fatio (Geneva, 1885). See P. Lock, *The Franks in the Aegean, 1204–1500* (Harlow, 1995), 21–4.
47. D. Jacoby, 'Quelques considérations sur les versions de la Chronique de Morée', *Journal des Savants* 1968, 133–89. Cf. M. J. Jeffreys, 'The Chronicle of the Morea: priority of the Greek version', *Byzantinische Zeitschrift*, 68(1975), 304–50.
48. Chronicle of the Morea, ll.7567–76; ll.7587–640, Esp. 7638–40.
49. D. Jacoby, *La féodalité en Grèce médiévale. Les <<assisses de Romanie>>* (Paris, 1971), 75–91.
50. *Les Assises de Romanie*, ed. G. Recoura (Paris, 1930), 149–50.
51. Jacoby, *Féodalité*, 38–44.
52. Henri de Valenciennes, §539.
53. Martin da Canal.
54. Fasoli, '*Cronique des Veniciens* di Martino da Canale'; Pertusi, 'Maistre Martino da Canal'; Carile, *Chronachistica veneziana*, 172–93.
55. Andrea Dandolo, *Chronica*, ed. Pastorello.
56. Marino Sanudo Torsello, *Istoria del regno di Romania*, in *Chroniques gréco-romanes*, ed. Ch. Hopf (Berlin, 1873), 99–170.
57. R. L. Wolff, 'Hopf's so-called "Fragmentum" of Marino Sanudo Torsello', in *The Joshua Starr Memorial Volume* (New York, 1953), 149–59 (reprinted in R. L. Wolff, *Studies in the Latin Empire of Constantinople* (London, 1976), no. X).
58. See, in general, M. F. Hendy, *Alexius I to Michael VIII 1081–1261 [Catalogue of the Byzantine Coins in the Dumbarton Oaks Collection and in the Whittemore Collection*, IV] (Washington, DC, 1999), 1–9.

chapter 6

THE LATIN EMPIRE OF CONSTANTINOPLE

The failure of the Latin Empire was a judgement on the crusader conquest of Constantinople. But was it also a forgone conclusion? Were the Latin emperors heirs to those weaknesses which had made their conquest of Constantinople possible? Though this explanation contains more than a grain of truth, it is not quite as simple as this seems. It assumes that the Latin emperors stepped straight into the shoes of their Byzantine predecessors, whereas the conquerors attempted to impose their own organisation on the old Byzantine Empire. This, it is true, was done while wrestling with a legacy of unresolved problems inherited from their Byzantine predecessors. The combination may explain the failure of the Latin Empire to put down roots outside the Greek lands.

I

The blueprint for the Latin Empire comes in the shape of the *Partitio Romaniae* of March 1204, which would be supplemented by other undertakings entered into between the crusade leaders and the Venetians.[1] It was only a blueprint, but the early history of the Latin Empire is largely a matter of how well or how badly it was implemented. The first question that has to be asked is this: was this blueprint for the Latin Empire flawed? In other words, can the ultimate failure of the Latin Empire be traced back to an ill-considered or unrealistic constitution?

Every blueprint is flawed. It is easy at this distance to give the crusaders advice about what they should have done. They should have been nicer to the Greeks! They should have made it a priority to include the Greek elite as part of the new structures of power they were imposing. They should have left the Church of Constantinople in the hands of the Greeks, but this is simply unrealistic. The main justification for the crusader conquest of Constantinople had become the reunion of churches. As a plan of conquest the partition treaty of March 1204 had the virtues of clarity and simplicity. It dealt with the immediate problems with admirable common sense. First the booty had to be divided in a way that honoured the crusaders' debts to the Venetians. Then an emperor was to be elected, with six electors chosen from each side. The emperor was to have the palaces of Blachernai and Boucoleon. To balance this it was agreed that the clergy of the party that did not provide the emperor should have the church of St Sophia and the right to elect the patriarch. But the clergy of each party would take possession of the churches that fell within their allotted areas. The clergy were to retain property and revenues sufficient to maintain themselves in a proper state, but the remaining church property was to be divided up along with other property. This went against the spirit of the reformed papacy and did not commend itself to Innocent III.

The partition of the Byzantine Empire was to be the work of a commission consisting of twelve or more men for each party. It was to divide the empire into a series of fiefs, which were to be the holders' full property, saving their obligations to the emperor and empire. The crusaders were far-sighted enough to realise that it might be necessary to make alterations to the partition treaty. In such an eventuality these had to have the approval of both parties. The doge was exempted from taking any oath to whoever became emperor for any fiefs or honours that were allotted to him, but those acting for him would have to do so. Finally, it was agreed that the whole army would remain in the service of the emperor and empire until the end of March 1205. It would not have been realistic to insist that men who had been away from home since early in 1202 should stay any longer, but, as it turned out, April 1205 was not an opportune moment to return home.

Modern historians have detected in these eminently sensible provisions two main flaws. The most serious was apparently the division between the crusaders and the Venetians. The exemption of the doge from paying homage to the Latin emperor is seen as symptomatic of a difference of interests. The Venetians, it is urged, had no stake in the continued existence of a Latin Empire, only in securing strategic points that would assure their commercial ascendancy. It is certainly true that Venetian energies went into securing control of Crete, but this did not preclude honouring their obligations to the Latin Empire. In the end, the survival of the Latin Empire depended upon Venetian seapower. The Venetians continued to support the defence of Constantinople, long after it had become clear that it had proved less than a commercial success. As late as May 1260 the doge was trying to organise a permanent garrison of 1,000 men for Latin Constantinople, recruited from the Latin territories in the Levant.[2] Less attention has been paid to a more serious difference of interests separating the Venetians and the crusaders. This centred on the Patriarchal Church which by the terms of the partition treaty fell to the Venetians. They made a determined effort to monopolise it for their own clergy and sought to exclude others. As we shall see, membership of the patriarchal chapter became an issue that divided the Venetians and the Franks and contributed to the weakness of the Latin Church of Constantinople.

Another flaw in the provisions of the partition treaty has been singled out. They set limitations on the authority of the Latin emperor, in the sense that he did not enjoy the absolute power of a Byzantine emperor. But where had Byzantine absolutism lead? To the chaos which was characteristic of Byzantium at the end of the twelfth century. In many ways the limitations on the authority of a feudal monarch pointed to a greater flexibility capable of dealing with the strains imposed on any system of government. The Emperor Henry showed that the powers granted to the Latin emperor were quite sufficient to allow him to assert his authority over the lands of the old Byzantine Empire, whether they were held by vassals or by local dynasts.

What were the immediate problems arising from the conquest of Constantinople and the partition of the empire? The most pressing was undoubtedly the division of booty, which, as we know, created much ill feeling on the part of the rank and file. Then there was the election of an emperor which opened up a bitter rivalry between Boniface of Montferrat and Baldwin of Flanders, so much so that it was thought advisable to alter the partition treaty and allot the losing candidate territories in Asia Minor and the Peloponnese as some kind of compensation.[3] The ensuing quarrel between Boniface and Baldwin can thus be traced back to the provisions contained in the partition treaty for the election of a Latin emperor. Again it is difficult to know what other – or fairer – method there was for the election of a Latin emperor. In fact, the quarrel between Boniface and Baldwin was quickly resolved. It scarcely slowed down the pace of the Latin occupation of Byzantine territories. Its main effect was on public opinion in the West where it suggested that all was not well in the newly-created Latin Empire. The question of the division of booty pointed in the same direction. Resentments of the kind expressed by Robert of Clari may have been a factor in encouraging the rank and file to return home rather than stay and conquer. It also contributed to something more serious: the reluctance of westerners to take service with the Latin emperor. The Latin Empire always suffered from a shortage of soldiers. But, all in all, the failure of the Latin Empire can scarcely be laid at the door of the partition treaty.

II

Was it, then, the problems inherited from the defunct Byzantine Empire? The Bulgarians were a major threat. Antagonising them was on any reckoning a bad miscalculation. According to Robert of Clari, Ioannitsa, the Bulgarian tsar, made overtures to the crusaders in February or March 1204 offering his help against the Byzantines.[4] This is corroborated in its general outlines by Nicetas Choniates, but he does not give any indications as to the date.[5] The *Gesta Innocentii Papae III* is clear that Ioannitsa sent an embassy to the Emperor Baldwin after the crusader conquest of Constantinople, but 'the latter replied to it in the haughtiest of fashions to the effect that they would not consider making peace with him unless he returned the land that belonged to the Empire of Con-stantinople, which he had taken by force'.[6] Confident in new-found papal favour, Ioannitsa questioned the legitimacy of the crusader conquest of Constantinople and labelled the Latin emperor a usurper. A clash between the Bulgarians and whoever held Constantinople was more or less inevitable, but it would have been wise for the Latins to delay confronting the Bulgarians until they were well and truly established in their conquests. The crusader leadership seems even before the conquest – if Clari's information is correct – to have singled out the Bulgarians as their most dangerous opponents.[7] During their sweep through Thrace in the autumn of 1203 in the company of the young Alexius the crusaders would have learnt something about the Bulgarians and their Cuman auxiliaries. But the fundamental cause of the hostility of the crusade leadership to the Bulgarians lay in the assumption that the Latin Empire was the heir to all lands to which their Byzantine predecessors had laid claim. The defeat of the Latin Emperor Baldwin I at Adrianople in April 1205 by the Bulgarians was treated as a catastrophe, but it provided Innocent III with an opportunity to act as arbiter of the situation by intervening with Ioannitsa on behalf of the Emperor Baldwin.[8] The defeat at Adrianople was far more of a blow than the quarrels over the division of booty or the election of an emperor, but the Latin Empire recovered from it surprisingly quickly. The greatest harm, as with the other incidents, was to its reputation.

The emergence of a new Bulgarian Empire in the last years of the twelfth century was symptomatic of provincial dissidence, which was among the most serious of the problems facing the Byzantine Empire. As we shall see, the conquerors were able in many cases to turn provincial unrest to their advantage. Another major problem before 1204 was the struggle for control of the waters of the Aegean between Latin pirates, the imperial fleet and the Venetians. This had been a source of political weakness, but in the aftermath of 1204 the Venetians were able to impose a large degree of order and drive the pirates from the Aegean. The pirate menace and provincial dissidence were symptomatic of the crisis of authority which existed before 1204 at the heart of imperial government. The secret of the success of the Byzantine Empire had always been the concentration of power and resources in Constantinople. It was only after the death of Manuel I Comnenus that it started to become clear how weakly-founded imperial control had become. The growth of fiscal immunities meant that a smaller proportion of the tax revenue was making its way to the imperial treasury at Constantinople. The customs concessions made to the Italians meant that a smaller proportion of the customs revenue was reaching the imperial government. But these developments were much less important than the failure of the emperors at the end of the twelfth century to impose themselves upon and give direction to the machinery of government. The emperor became little more than the head of one faction, while the city of Constantinople ran out of control.

The Latin conquest of the city cut into this downward spiral. The sack of Constantinople left its people thoroughly chastened, while the Byzantine elite either abandoned the city or was neutralised, a few entering Latin service. Under the Emperor Henry it did seem possible that the Latins would be able to cut through the problems that had undermined the Byzantine Empire. The strength of the Latin Empire was apparent in the way it was able to overcome very serious setbacks, such as the defeat at Adrianople and then the death of Boniface of Montferrat in a Bulgarian ambush two years later. Henry of Hainault's achievements were immensely impressive. He asserted his authority over the Latins in the Greek lands and Thessalonica. He secured effective control over Thrace and north-western Asia Minor. In the southern Balkans he was also able to secure recognition from local rulers, be they Greek, Slav or Bulgarian, which gave a degree of protection to the Latin territories. He was even able to impose terms on Theodore Laskaris, the Greek 'emperor' in Asia Minor.[9]

The first question to ask is why this impetus was so quickly lost. What was the underlying weakness of the Latin Empire? The Emperor Henry diagnosed it as a lack of manpower. He ends his circular letter sent after his comprehensive victory over Theodore Laskaris in 1212 with a plea for reinforcements.[10] Otherwise there was a serious danger that the conquests he had made would be lost. The numbers required were not that great. Take, for example, the first plantation of military settlers made by the Venetians in Crete in 1211. It consisted of 94 knights and 26 sergeants, subsequently raised to 132 knights and 408 sergeants.[11] As we shall see, the struggle for Crete was hard and prolonged and other batches of military settlers had to be sent out, but we are dealing with hundreds rather than thousands at any given time. In the Peloponnese and in the duchy of Thebes this order of settlement – perhaps less – sufficed to provide a basis for effective Frankish occupation. Even so, by the early thirteenth century Frankish settlers were in short supply. There were too many other distractions. There was the Albigensian crusade, which offered much richer pickings. For reasons that have already been outlined, the leaders of that crusade had their own grounds for belittling the achievements of the Fourth Crusade. At much the same time there was the Spanish crusade of 1212, which also recruited heavily from northern France. Add to this Innocent III's plans for a new crusade to the Holy Land and it is easy to see why the Latin Empire was overlooked by the northern French. An altogether more promising recruiting ground for colonists was northern Italy. The Lombards, as the people of the region were known, were a distinct group among the settlers in the Latin Empire. However, the Emperor Henry's repression of the Lombards in 1209 discouraged Italian settlement at a crucial juncture. Their bitterness was given full expression by the troubadour Elias of Cairel, who describes the Emperor Henry as another Darius 'who chased his barons from their homes'. Elias himself returned to Italy a few years later.[12]

III

If the defence and settlement of the crusader states are anything to go by, just as important as Frankish settlers were the military orders. The Templars and Hospitallers were established in the Latin Empire from early on. The Hospitallers had a pilgrim hostel in Constantinople before 1204. The Emperor Baldwin I gave them Pergamon to conquer and to the Templars, Attaleia.[13] He obviously intended that the military orders should have a significant role in the conquest of Asia Minor. These plans failed to materialise, but the two orders were prominent in the conquest of mainland Greece under the auspices of Boniface of Montferrat. The Templars acquired the castles of Ravenikka and Lamia in Thessaly and the Hospitallers seized neighbouring Gardiki from its Latin bishop. However, after Boniface's death the Templars sided with the Lombards against Henry of Hainault. The latter brushed aside the resistance offered by their castles of Ravennika and Lamia which he then proceeded to confiscate. Thereafter the Templars ceased to play much part in the affairs of the Latin Empire. Their unpopularity is evident from an incident that occurred in Greece in September 1210. The Latin bishop of Kitros knocked the chalice out of the hands of a Templar chaplain when he was administering the last rites to a brother of the order.[14] The long list of complaints that the order made to Innocent III about their treatment in Greece reflects the pressure they were under. In the Peloponnese Geoffrey of Villehardouin granted them territories equivalent to four knights' fees, as he did to the Hospitallers and the Teutonic Knights, but this was a token gesture and did not lead at this stage to any serious involvement in the affairs of the principality of Achaea. Whereas the defence of the crusader states in the Holy Land came to depend increasingly heavily upon the military orders, they do not play any prominent role in the history of the Latin Empire. Henry of Hainault's actions against the Templars appear to have been decisive. He clearly treated them as a challenge to his authority as Latin emperor. The local Latin hierarchy in Greece also regarded them as an intrusive element.

There was an attempt to create a new military order for the Latin Empire around the hospital of St Sampson at Constantinople. Its statutes were drawn up on instructions from the papal legate, Benedict of Santa Susanna, and confirmed by Pope Innocent III, who took the order under the protection of the Holy See.[15] The Emperor Henry granted it the fortress of Garella, near Apros in Thrace, with surrounding properties.[16] The order maintained a presence in and around Constantinople down to 1261. A list of properties dating from 1244 shows it to have been quite a substantial landowner. Its properties were concentrated in Constantinople and its environs, but it had interests in Hungary and a house at Douai, which it had received from a Latin archbishop of Thessalonica.[17] For all that it failed to make its mark. This may have been because the charitable responsibilities of the order took precedence over their military duties: it was only in 1222 that the master and brothers first received papal dispensation to make personal use of the horses and weapons gifted to the order. The reason given was the threat now posed by the Greeks to the Latin Empire.[18] The failure of the military orders to develop on any scale in the Latin Empire was perceived at the time as a source of weakness; hence Baldwin II's desperate and unsuccessful attempt in 1246 to secure the services of the Castilian Order of Santiago.[19]

IV

In his letter of 1212 the Emperor Henry provides information about the size of the forces with which he took on the Greek 'Emperor' Theodore Laskaris. He had 14 squadrons of 15 knights each, which makes a force of 210, and his own squadron of 50 knights. It was in his interest to exaggerate the discrepancy in the size of the opposing armies, in order to make his victory the more stunning.[20] The interesting thing about Theodore Laskaris's army is that in it were 8 squadrons of Latins and this was after he had lost most of his force of 800 Latin mercenaries the previous year in a battle against the Seljuq Turks.[21] In other words, Theodore I Laskaris and for that matter Michael Doukas in Epiros had no difficulty in recruiting Latin mercenaries at a time when the manpower of the Latin Empire was seriously depleted. Innocent III specifically forbade Latins to serve in Greek armies on pain of excommunication, but it made no difference.[22] There was a pool of Latin mercenaries floating around the Levant, taking service with any ruler that would pay them. Later on the Seljuqs of Rum recruited Latins on a large scale into their armies which faced the Mongols. Why did the Latin Empire not monopolise the services of such men? Leaving aside the question of distaste – mercenaries had fallen foul of the Third Lateran Council (1179) – the most obvious reason is that the Latin emperors could not afford their rates of pay. As the Emperor Henry made clear, what he could offer was the prospect of lands to be conquered. He needed settlers not rootless adventurers. But it is most unlikely that he would have been able to pay for a mercenary force. Ready cash was always a problem for Latin emperors, because the logic of the division of the empire was the division of fiscal rights. The Byzantine land tax or *akrostichon*, as the Latins called it, remained in force, but now served very largely as the basis of feudal revenues. The Latin emperor would have benefited, but only as the largest landholder.

In other words, the Latin Empire aggravated some of the trends that were already apparent before 1204, for example the decline of Constantinople as a centre of trade and consumption. Before 1204 this was still not clearly visible. The growth of piracy in the Aegean will have interrupted the smooth working of the commercial networks – local and long distance – which centred on Constantinople. But more serious was the political instability that characterised the history of the city in the late twelfth century. Constantinople's commercial role was a function of its position as a capital city. Merchants were attracted by the wealth that was concentrated there, which made it a great consumer. A by-product was its role as a centre of international exchanges and re-export, but these were scarcely significant beside consumption and imports. Constantinople was a producer of luxury goods, but most of these were consumed on the spot. By the fourteenth century the situation had become very different: Constantinople had ceased to be primarily a consumer and had become largely a staging post for international trade. This change was prepared by its history under the Latin Empire of Constantinople.

The sack of Constantinople is not an explanation in itself for the city's rapid decline. It in any case caused less damage to the fabric of the city than the fires that had already devastated the city centre. In the normal course of events, the damage done would have been made good once a degree of stability returned. Byzantine Constantinople, like its Ottoman successor, was periodically ravaged by fires but the necessary repairs were soon effected. But this time it did not recover. The population continued to fall. There is no reason to suppose that the slaughter of the inhabitants of Constantinople by the crusaders was on any very great scale. There was no mass exodus; only members of the elite of Church and State – and by no means all of them – evacuated the city. However, the economic and social rationale of Constantinople as a capital was servicing the needs of this elite. The Latin conquerors failed to fill the shoes of the old elite. The administrative and ecclesiastical machinery of the Latin Empire was on a markedly reduced scale when compared with that of the old Byzantine Empire. Even more serious was the disintegration of the fiscal system, which meant that Constantinople now drew its revenues from its immediate hinterland. This was at first masked by the booty, but once it had run out Latin Constantinople lost its role as a major consumer. One of the consequences was a decline in economic activity and a corresponding decline of population. The presence of the Venetians in Constantinople did not bring any upsurge in economic activity. They were undoubtedly there and their quarter was the most prosperous area of the city, but their main business activity involved property deals and lending money to the impoverished Latin emperors; trade pure and simple is less in evidence. As Louise Robbert has urged, there was a marked decline in turnover compared with the years before 1204 and particularly before 1171.[23]

By the end of the Latin Empire Constantinople resembled Rome in the Dark Ages – a great city that had lost its original purpose and had been allowed to decay. Constantinople still had its magnificent churches and palaces, but the Latins were able to occupy and maintain only a fraction of them. Large areas of the city were abandoned. Latin occupation has left almost no traces in Constantinople beyond a cycle of St Francis in the Kalenderhane Cami and signs of liturgical alterations in St Sophia. It is therefore ironic that despite the best efforts of the Byzantines after 1261 the Latins bequeathed Constantinople the general appearance that it would maintain to 1453: a densely populated strip along the Golden Horn, where foreign traders had their concesssions; then there were centres of ceremonial importance such as St Sophia, the hippodrome and the Blachernai complex, but otherwise a scattering of monasteries and palaces set in orchards and gardens.

It has always been recognised that the decay of Constantinople was the most lasting and sinister legacy of Latin rule, but it was only part of the transformation of the old Byzantine world that occurred under Latin auspices. From a Latin perspective the decay of Constantinople was not necessarily a bad thing. A great capital, such as Constantinople, was still alien to western styles of royal government. Effective government was personal, with power concentrated not in some fixed centre but in the person of the ruler and in a devotion to a dynasty. There is no need to repeat the refrain that the Byzantine tradition of centralised government had not been a success either in theory or in practice in the closing years of the twelfth century. A man such as Nicetas Choniates understood the virtues of the more devolved and personal system of government that he observed among westerners. It stood to reason that a looser form of government might be better suited to the provincial dissidence which was a feature of the history of the Byzantine Empire in the last years of the twelfth century. Despite the crusader defeat at Adrianople at the hands of the Bulgarians, the Emperor Henry seems to have been able to deal with the Bulgarians more effectively than his Byzantine predecessors. In any case, the emergence of a new Bulgarian Empire at the end of the twelfth century was not typical of provincial dissidence, which before 1204 was far more localised, limited to a city and its *contado*.[24] The Bulgarian uprising was different, because its leaders, the Vlach chieftains Peter and Asen and subsequently their younger brother Ioannitsa, were able to appeal to memories of the empire of Tsar Symeon in the tenth century to weld together the population of the eastern Balkans and turn it into a movement of more than local importance. No other provincial revolt before 1204 had the potential to create an independent state.

V

This changed with the Latin conquest. The Latins were able to exploit provincial dissidence. It left the Greek lands peculiarly vulnerable. The region split up into its component parts, as each district threw up a leader or 'dynast' as he might be called. Nicetas Choniates describes what happened:

> Servile men – turned by utter ambition against their native land having been corrupted by dissipation and other senseless actions – seized precipitous fortifications and fortresses or made themselves masters of well-walled cities. There they established ill-starred tyrannies. Rather than do their duty and take up arms against the Latins, they did the unthinkable and made peace with them, while wrangling among themselves.[25]

In the Peloponnese the main figure was Leo Sgouras, who before 1204 had made himself ruler of Nauplion and the Argolid. In all fairness, he tried and failed to organise resistance to the Latins in continental Greece. He fell back on Corinth, which he held until his death in 1210. A Leo Chamaretos held Lakedaimonia and the vale of Sparta. He was at odds with other local leaders based on Monemvasia.[26] Another, unnamed, Byzantine aristocrat held the south-western corner of the Peloponnese. His cooperation with a small band of crusaders under Geoffrey of Villehardouin, the nephew of the historian, opened the way for the crusader conquest of this region. Geoffrey was one of those crusaders who abandoned the main body and went off to Syria. Very little was happening out there, so he made for home, but on the return journey his ship put in at Methoni on the south-western tip of the Peloponnese. Here he and his company fell in with the local leader, who recruited them into his service. With their help the latter soon made himself the dominant force in the western Peloponnese. The trouble came when he died and his son tried to dispense with the Franks who were beginning to outlive their usefulness. By this time Boniface of Montferrat and his followers were encamped under the Acrocorinth. Geoffrey of Villehardouin made his way there and did a deal with William of Champlitte – a neighbour of his from Champagne. He would enter the latter's service and together they would conquer the rich lands of the western Peloponnese. They set off with 100 knights and a large body of mounted sergeants, which in the circumstances constituted a formidable force. They made Methoni their base. They were almost immediately attacked by Michael Doukas, a Byzantine aristocrat who had established himself across the Gulf of Corinth at Arta. Their victory at the battle of Kountoura ensured control of the south-western Peloponnese. The Franks then had little difficulty in securing the rest of the western Peloponnese as far north as Patras.[27] The conquest of the eastern Peloponnese took rather longer. It was only effectively subdued under William II Villehardouin (1246–78), who built fortresses at Mistra and Maina and secured control over Monemvasia.

The story of the Frankish conquest of the Peloponnese has often been told and there is no need to rehearse it in detail. On the face of it, the Franks should have expected more resistance. Their advance up the western coast of the Peloponnese was barred by the powerful fortress of Arcadia (modern Kyparissia). Their final conquest, Monemvasia, was virtually impregnable. But it was the same in both places. The local ascendancy or *archontes* surrendered on the understanding that they retained their lands and their Orthodox faith.[28] A modicum of respect for their Greek subjects and their faith was the foundation of Frankish rule in the Peloponnese.

At first sight, the organisation of the Frankish Peloponnese owed very little to Byzantine practice. It conformed more or less to western feudal norms. The conquered territories were divided up into fiefs. The Villehardouin princes of Achaea kept much of the most fertile land in Elis and in Messenia, leaving their tenants-in-chief to establish their lordships in less favoured parts of the Peloponnese. Here they built their castles from which they could survey the land and command the lines of communication. The Frankish fortresses were in most instances built from scratch, usually above an existing Byzantine settlement, as happened at Mistra above the ancient Sparta, or for that matter at Karytaina and Geraki. It left the Greek *archontes* more or less undisturbed, though there is no denying that in terms of the feudal hierarchy they came at the bottom of the heap. They were incorporated at the same level as minor Frankish feudatories – those of simple homage, as they were called. But they were allowed to keep their laws and customs, so partible inheritance continued to apply to Greek estates.[29]

Religion does not seem to have been the divide in the Peloponnese that it was in other parts of the Latin Empire; this despite the expulsion of the Greek bishops and the establishment of a new episcopal order by the Latins. As we shall see, an understanding between Greeks and Franks was made all the easier by the papal interdict imposed on the prince of Achaea for his failure to respect the property of the Latin Church. In 1223 he finally accepted with some modifications the compromise that had earlier been worked out under the Emperor Henry. The contentious issues affected the property of the Latin Church, but the status of the Greek clergy was also settled. In terms of retaining the loyalty of the local population this was of the greatest importance, because at the village level the Greek clergy formed perhaps the most influential group. Their material position had improved markedly from the middle of the twelfth century. Thanks to an ill-considered measure on the part of the Emperor Manuel I Comnenus priests were granted exemption from the payment of the land tax. In next to no time the imperial government became aware of the large numbers claiming tax exemptions as priests. It was a problem that faced the Frankish conquerors. The number of priests per village was fixed according to the number of households. They were to be free from lay jurisdiction and their property had to pay the land tax only if it had paid it before 1204. A powerful section of local Greek society had reason to be grateful to the Frankish conquerors.[30]

The intention is not to idealise the condition of the Greeks under Frankish rule. They were still a subject people. But there seems to have been surprisingly little friction between the Greeks of the Peloponnese and their conquerors. This was to some extent because large parts of the

Peloponnese had been held before 1204 by absentee landowners from Constantinople. The Frankish conquest also brought greater order as well as greater protection for the agricultural population from the pastoralists who dominated the mountainous interior of the Peloponnese. William Villehardouin built the fortresses of Mistra, Beaufort and Grande Magne (Maina) to protect the southern Peloponnese from the depredations of the Melings – a Slav tribe which roamed the Taygetus. This receives considerable support from J. M. Wagstaff's plausible identification of the site of Grande Magne with the castle of Kelepha, which dominates the pass of Milolangada in the same way that to the north Mistra dominates the pass of Langada. These were the main points of exit used by the Melings from their mountain lairs.[31] Another indication of the benefits of Frankish rule was the rapid growth of the port of Clarentza, close to the prince of Achaea's chief residence at Andravida. It testifies to the commercial advantages which Frankish conquest brought. It was an entirely new foundation, but well positioned for the trade of the region. However, the best proof of the success of the Frankish regime was the support it later enjoyed from its Greek subjects, in the face of the Byzantine reconquest of the late thirteenth and fourteenth centuries.

Paradoxically, the events which allowed the Byzantines to establish a toehold in the south-east of the Peloponnese in the 1260s were the product of the Franks' integration into local Greek politics. The prince of Achaea, William II Villehardouin, married a daughter of the Greek ruler of Epiros. It was part of an alliance designed to oppose the Laskarids of Nicaea – the most powerful of the Byzantine successor states which from its European base at Thessalonica was a threat to the various powers (Greek and Latin) of the Greek lands. In 1259 the prince of Achaea led the chivalry of the Peloponnese to support his father-in-law's efforts to hold back the Nicaean forces who were pushing westwards along the Via Egnatia. For his pains he was completely defeated by the Nicaeans at the battle of Pelagonia. He was captured along with most of his vassals and thrown into a Nicaean jail. The Nicaean victory at Pelagonia was a prelude to their recovery of Constantinople in 1261. Once that had happened it became increasingly difficult for William Villehardouin to resist the terms demanded by the new Byzantine Emperor Michael VIII Palaiologos for his release. He was asked to cede the south-eastern corner of the Peloponnese, to which he finally agreed in 1262.[32]

The Byzantine expeditionary force came ashore at Monemvasia, which was one of the places that William Villehardouin had ceded. But for the next half-century the Byzantines had the greatest difficulty in breaking out of the south-eastern Peloponnese. There was no mass defection of the Greeks of the Peloponnese to the Byzantines. They remained loyal to their Frankish overlords, who by this time were far less foreign than the Byzantine armies which were recruited in the main from Anatolia. The native population of the Peloponnese resisted reincorporation in a Byzantine state. This was a measure of the change that had come about in the aftermath of the Latin conquest of 1204. In the Peloponnese the Frankish conquerors had given shape to the endemic dissidence that had characterised the Byzantine provinces at the end of the twelfth century. They had shown how well they could protect local interests. It meant that over the period of exile localised structures of power took root. These defied the efforts made by a succession of Byzantine emperors to restore a centralised system of government.

VI

In the Frankish Peloponnese local organisation was largely western and feudal. In other parts of the old Byzantine Empire Greek resistance leaders equally took advantage of local dissidence and exploited it as the basis for the development of localised power structures. Epiros provides an excellent example. It would last in one form or another until the final Turkish conquest in 1430.[33] Its foundations were laid in the aftermath of the fall of Constantinople in 1204 by Michael Doukas (often called Angelus). He was a high born bastard, the son of John Doukas, who was uncle of both Isaac II and Alexius III Angelus.[34] Even before 1204 Michael Doukas had mounted a rebellion against Alexius III Angelus in the south-western corner of Asia Minor, where he had been sent as provincial governor. He fled to the Seljuq court at Konya. With the backing of the sultan he ravaged the Maiander frontier. He returned to Constantinople when he heard of Isaac II's restoration by the crusaders. At some stage Michael Doukas joined the entourage of Boniface of Montferrat and campaigned with him in Greece. However, he abandoned Boniface and made his way to Arta where he allied with the Byzantine governor and began to organise resistance to the Latins.[35] Initially, this was directed against the Franks in the Peloponnese,[36] but after his defeat at Koundoura in 1205 by Geoffrey of Villehardouin – the nephew of the chronicler – he returned to Epiros and made Arta his centre of operations.

He enhanced his prestige among the Greeks by ransoming the former Byzantine Emperor Alexius III Angelus, who had been sent for safe keeping to Genoa. Alexius arrived at Arta with his Empress Euphrosyne in 1209 or 1210. For whatever reason, Alexius left Arta as soon as he was able in order to make his way to the Seljuq court of Konya. He hoped to use his friendship with the Seljuq sultan Kaykhusraw to supplant

Theodore I Laskaris in western Asia Minor. The old emperor's ambitions soon came to grief. He was defeated and captured by Laskaris in 1211.[37] Who knows exactly what game Michael Doukas was playing. He kept the Empress Euphrosyne with him at Arta. She may have been a hostage, but it is more probable that she was interested in recovering the estates in southern Thessaly that she had held before 1203.[38] If Michael Doukas had ever contemplated setting up a Byzantine successor state under the auspices or with the blessing of Alexius III Angelus, it came to nothing. Willingly or not, he had to operate within a political framework created by the Latin Empire; all the more so once the Emperor Henry restored the situation in Thessalonica and mainland Greece in 1208–9. Michael Doukas sent emissaries seeking the Latin Emperor's friendship. The latter set out his terms: he would recognise him as ruler of Epiros but only on condition that he became his vassal. Michael Doukas accepted and the agreement was sealed by the marriage of one of his daughters to Eustace, the emperor's younger brother.[39] He followed this up by offering his submission to the papacy.[40]

His adhesion to the new order seemed confirmed by the treaty he concluded in June 1210 with Venice. Michael Doukas recognised the Doge Pietro Ziani as his feudal overlord for all the territories from the Gulf of Corinth to the approaches to Dyrrachion – Venice's main base in Albania. These had originally been allotted to Venice in the partition of the Byzantine Empire, but had subsequently been occupied by Michael Doukas.[41] This double allegiance to both the doge and to the emperor of Constantinople replicated the position adopted at the same time by Geoffrey of Villehardouin, the prince of Achaea. Michael Doukas did not prove to be the most reliable of vassals. In alliance with the Bulgarians he raided the region around Thessalonica, but was quickly brought to heel by the Emperor Henry. He remained loyal long enough to help the latter's brother Eustace win a great victory in 1212 on the plains of Pelagonia over the Bulgarians who remained quiescent for more than a decade. Michael lost no time in securing appropriate rewards for his part in this victory. He immediately seized Larissa, along with much of southern Thessaly. The next year he drove the Venetians out of Dyrrachion and followed this up by occupying the island of Corfu.[42] He died in mysterious circumstances a year or two later. The exact date cannot be established. But by the time of his death he was one of the most powerful rulers of the region. He was theoretically a vassal of the Latin Empire, but seemed more a law unto himself. Emperor Henry had warned that Michael was never to be trusted. He complained that the latter had taken an oath of allegiance to the Latin emperor on no less than three occasions and each time he had broken it.

Modern historians have always portrayed Michael Doukas as a doughty champion of Greek independence, but there are no signs that Michael Doukas entertained imperial ambitions of the kind harboured by Theodore I Laskaris in Anatolia. He did not attempt to create a Byzantine Empire in exile. It is always assumed that he had the interests of the Orthodox Church at heart, even that he promoted religious war against the Latins. It is true that his followers systematically murdered Latin priests who fell into their hands. This culminated in the crucifixion of Amé Pofey, constable of Romania, along with his chaplain.[43] The Latins blamed Michael, but it may have been more a question of his being unable to control his followers, who included ferocious Vlach and Albanian tribesmen. A more commendable, but not strictly speaking lawful, sign of his devotion to the Orthodox Church was his concern to appoint to vacant sees. Among his first actions on securing Larissa and then Dyrrachion was to appoint Orthodox incumbents. Against this has to be set his willingness to submit to Rome. This may not be quite as contradictory as it seems at first sight. Michael was looking for political advantage, perhaps even the grant of a crown.[44] The religious side of things was a matter for churchmen, but some kind of accommodation with the Latin Church was not yet out of the question.

Michael Doukas's achievement was to lay the foundations of what has come to be called in modern times the despotate of Epiros, though he himself never laid claim to the title of despot.[45] He had been forced to adapt to a political framework dominated by the Latin conquerors. Epiros was strong enough as a political unit to survive bewildering changes of fortune. It was a region which had a long tradition of provincial dissidence, but it is most unlikely that this could have been transformed into political autonomy without the intervention of the Latin conquest. The establishment of Epiros demonstrates how few difficulties there were in accommodating autonomous political units, be they Frankish, Greek or Slav, within the structures that were coming into being as a result of the establishment of the Latin Empire.[46] These were loose enough to accommodate the continued existence of Byzantine institutions. So Michael Doukas was able to work through the theme system which continued to operate in Epiros.[47] He also preserved the fabric of the Orthodox Church in his territories, but this was strictly in line with Innocent III's ruling that in areas with a majority of Orthodox the church should remain in Orthodox hands. Michael Doukas anticipated the forms that government would take in the later Byzantine Empire, where power was exercised from a series of princely courts loosely united under the hegemony of an emperor at Constantinople.

Michael Doukas left a bastard son, also called Michael, who would later do much to complete his father's work. He was only eight or nine when his father was murdered and he was sent into exile in the Peloponnese by his uncle Theodore Angelus, who had secured the succession after the murder of Michael Doukas.[48] Theodore had earlier been in the service of Theodore I Laskaris and was clearly influenced by the latter's assumption of the imperial title. Whereas Michael Doukas seemed content with establishing himself as a local ruler, if needs be with Latin approval, Theodore was far more ambitious and more openly anti-Latin. He had the good fortune at the beginning of his reign to seize the Latin Emperor Peter of Courtenay. This was almost certainly the result of treachery, but Greek propaganda had no difficulty in presenting it as a feat of arms and Theodore as a champion against the hated Latin. This 'victory' was a prelude to a sustained campaign against Thessalonica, which brought Theodore the city in the autumn of 1224. His imperial claims were confirmed by a meeting of Epirot bishops. The task of performing the coronation eventually fell in 1227 to Demetrius Chomatianos, the archbishop of Ohrid.[49] Theodore now controlled Epiros, Thessaly and the southern Balkans as far as Adrianople. His sights were set on Latin Constantinople. But there was a competitor in the shape of the Bulgarian Tsar John Asen II (1218–41). The Bulgarian was nominally a Catholic and in the wake of the death of the Latin Emperor Robert he hoped that he might be acceptable to the barons of Constantinople as regent. His offer was spurned, which Theodore took as a sign of weakness. He invaded Bulgaria, but was defeated and captured in 1230 at the battle of Klokotnitsa.

His territories broke up into their component parts with different members of his family ruling Epiros, Thessaly and Thessalonica. These remained surprisingly durable political units in contrast to Theodore's 'empire' which proved evanescent. Each area shows different ways in which a regional identity was created during the period of exile. Thessaly is the least known.[50] It seems to have been run as a loose alliance of landowning families under the nominal authority of a member of the Angelus dynasty. Of these families the Maliasenoi are the best documented. Their centre of power appears to have been the monastery of Makrinitissa on Mount Pelion. Although there were urban centres in Thessaly, such as Larissa and Trikalla, monasteries seem to have been more important for the aristocracy. This may account for the looser political structures in the region.

In Epiros Michael Doukas used Arta as his centre of operations. It was left to his bastard son Michael II Angelus (1230–67) to turn it into a dynastic capital. Arta had previously been of little importance, only

emerging in the course of the twelfth century with the decline of neighbouring Nikopolis, the old theme capital. Its defences were largely provided by the walls of classical Ambrakia, which girdled the akropolis.
Below it a town spread out. Arta is still renowned for its Byzantine
churches; some of these may go back to the twelfth century, but to a
very large extent they are the product of the thirteenth century. The
dynastic activity is evident in the church of St Theodora (originally
dedicated to St George). This was founded by Michael II's consort
Theodora Petraliphina. She became a nun and was buried in the narthex.
Her piety was such that she was revered as a saint. Her cult would have
done much to perpetuate dynastic loyalties. Outside Arta was the nunnery
of the Blachernai. It was substantially enlarged by Michael II Angelus,
who transformed it into a dynastic shrine where he along with other
members of his family were buried.[51] The creation of dynastic centres,
such as Arta, was of the greatest importance for the development of
regional loyalties. Arta owed its emergence from provincial obscurity to
the Angelus dynasty. Much the same is true of Ioannina to the north. It
had been of some strategic importance at the end of the eleventh century,
when it was occupied and fortified by the Norman Bohemond. However,
Michael Doukas was remembered with gratitude by its inhabitants as a
new founder. Its adoption of the Archangel Michael as its patron saint
reflected this. It was in memory of Michael Doukas that Theodore Angelus
exempted its inhabitants from the payment of tax on house property.
This presupposes a privilege of some kind.[52] All we know is that when in
1319 Ioannina recognised the authority of the Byzantine Emperor
Andronicus II it received an imperial chrysobull conceding a large degree
of self-government.[53] Such a grant was in no way exceptional by the
early fourteenth century, but municipal autonomy was not part of the
Byzantine tradition. It is not until after 1204 that we find towns being
granted privileges which endow them with a distinct legal status.

VII

By the twelfth century the European provinces of the Byzantine Empire
were dotted with prosperous provincial towns. Power was in the hands
of local ascendancies, who are referred to as *archontes* or *kastrenoi*. They
tended to be property owners and rentiers rather than engaged in trade
or handicrafts. The more important towns were the residence of an
imperial governor, who was usually treated with due deference. Almost
all provincial towns were the seat of a bishopric. The relationship between
the bishop and the local ascendancies was altogether more complicated.
There had been a time when the bishop was the dominant force, but as

Byzantine towns grew in the eleventh and twelfth centuries bishops found their position under threat from elements within the town, who sometimes combined with the local clergy. Friction of this kind was inherent in the growth of urban centres. Bishops protected their position by obtaining imperial chrysobulls, which defined their rights over their clergy and itemised their properties. The towns themselves do not appear to have possessed any privileges; they do not appear even to have had a clear legal status.[54]

The first evidence for the grant of urban privileges comes with the Latin conquest. Villehardouin informs us that Thessalonica surrendered to Baldwin of Flanders on condition that 'he would respect the usages and customs as the Greek emperors had done'.[55] Exactly what these usages and customs were is another matter, for there is no record of the grant of imperial privileges to a city before 1204. The so-called *Pactum Adrianopolitanum* of 1206 is more revealing. It was a convention made by the Venetian *podestà*, which regularised the position of the city of Adrianople. It was in the first instance a grant of Adrianople and its dependencies to the citizens of Adrianople, but under the authority of Theodore Branas, who was to rule *secundum usum Grecorum*. In other words, there were to be no Latin innovations. It was almost certainly on these terms that the citizens of Thessalonica made their submission to Baldwin I. The Latin conquerors understood that allowing the citizens of provincial towns to run their own affairs was a small price to pay for their submission.[56] Before 1204 there were town meetings, where the leading citizens thrashed out local problems, but they were not held on any regular basis. Byzantine cities enjoyed a degree of autonomy, but it had never been formalised in any legal sense. Now it was. To the Latins it was the obvious thing to do, but in Byzantine terms it was a radical step.

It allowed the leading citizens of towns that came under Latin rule to define their rights and privileges more precisely, so that they were well placed to make demands on other conquerors as the price of a quick submission. In 1246 the Nicaean ruler John Vatatzes took advantage of Bulgarian difficulties to annexe much of Macedonia and to secure the submission of Thessalonica, which along with other towns received an imperial chrysobull confirming their customs and rights and guaranteeing their freedom. Only brief summaries of these privileges have survived. Later chrysobulls suggest that as the price of loyalty towns were granted freedom from taxation and customs duties together with freedom from the interference of imperial officials. In other words, privileged towns became immunities. In legal terms, they enjoyed a status hardly different from the immunities accorded to aristocratic and monastic estates. The towns were turned into corporations with a measure of self-government.

The leading citizens were mainly interested in preserving this privileged status. After 1261 they remained loyal to the imperial regime at Constantinople, as long as their rights were confirmed and respected.[57]

In many ways, the restored Byzantine Empire became a confederation of city states around Constantinople. It was a far looser and fragmented political system than had existed before 1204. This was the lasting legacy of the Latin Empire. The Bulgarian Empire excepted, it is very difficult to see the provincial dissidence that existed before 1204 leading in normal circumstances to the creation of autonomous political units. By normal circumstances I mean the continuation of the Byzantine Empire or at the very least Constantinople's survival as an imperial capital where power and administration was concentrated, as a *megalopolis* with a population and resources that dwarfed the surrounding circle of lands and seas. The collapse of Constantinople was only conceivable under the conditions of Latin rule because it was connected with the devolution of power as a necessary function of conquest. Its impact was the greater for the swiftness of Constantinople's impoverishment. It is well known that the last Latin Emperor Baldwin II had to sell the lead from the roof of the imperial palace out of sheer poverty,[58] but this was in the last desperate years of the Latin Empire. It is more surprising to find Pope Honorius III reprimanding the Latin patriarch as early as 1222 for stripping the churches of Constantinople of their copper and lead.[59] At the bottom of the failure of the Latin Empire was the impoverishment of Constantinople and the rapid decline of its population. But this opened up new possibilities in the provinces so long dominated by the City. These were taken in the first instance by the Latin conquerors, but to more lasting effect by local ascendancies. Potentially, the power likely to be most deeply affected by the decline of Constantinople was Venice, since its commercial prosperity was initially founded on the wealth of Constantinople.

Notes

1. Tafel and Thomas I, cxix–cxxi, 444–501, clx, 571–4; II, ccxlix, 193–5, cclx, 227–30, cclxxix, 290–7; Andrea, *Contemporary Sources*, 140–4.
2. W. Norden, *Das Papstum und Byzanz. Die Trennung der beiden Mächte und das Problem ihrer Wiedervereinigung bis zum Untergang des byzantinischen Reichs (1453)* (Berlin, 1903), 759–60; S. Borsari, *Studi sulle colonie veneziane in Romania nel XIII secolo* (Naples, 1966), 62.
3. Villehardouin II, §258, 65.
4. Clari, §lxiv.
5. Nicetas Choniates, 613.58–63.

6. *Gesta Innocentii III*, 214, 147–8.

7. Clari, §lxiv–lxv.

8. *Reg.* VIII, cxxix: Migne *PL* 215, 705–6; ed. Haluscynski, no. 89, 314–15. See Prinzing, 'Papsttum', 170–4.

9. F. van Tricht, ' "La Gloire de l'Empire". L'idée impériale de Henri de Flandre-Hainaut, deuxième empereur latin de Constantinople (1206–1216)', *Byzantion*, 70(2000), 211–41.

10. Prinzing, 'Der Brief Kaiser Heinrichs', 417–18.

11. Tafel and Thomas II, ccxxix–ccxxx, 129–42; S. Borsari, *Il dominio veneziano a Creta nel XIII secolo* (Naples, 1963), 28–9.

12. De Bartholomaeis, *Poesie provenzali storiche relative all'Italia*, I, 171–80.

13. *Reg.* IX, clxxx: Migne *PL* 215, 1019–20. See P. Lock, 'The military orders in mainland Greece', in *The Military Orders: Fighting for the Faith and Caring for the Sick*, ed. M. Barber (Aldershot, 1994), 333–9.

14. *Reg.* XIII, cli: Migne *PL* 216, 330.

15. *Reg.* XI, cxxiii: Migne *PL* 215, 1435; ed. Haluscynski, no. 117, 349–50.

16. *Reg.* XIII, xvii: Migne *PL* 216, 217; ed. Haluscynski, no. 140, 377.

17. *Registres d'Innocent IV*, ed. E. Berger (Paris, 1884–1921), 4 vols: I, 124, no. 730; T. S. Miller, 'The Sampson Hospital of Constantinople', *Byzantinische Forschungen*, 15(1990), 101–35, at 128–9.

18. *Regesta Honorii Papae III*, ed. P. Pressutti (Rome, 1888–95), 2 vols: no. 4088.

19. R. L. Wolff, 'Mortgage and Redemption of an Emperor's son: Castile and the Latin Empire of Constantinople', *Speculum*, 29(1954), 82–4.

20. G. Prinzing, 'Der Brief Kaiser Heinrichs', 416.131–4.

21. Acropolites I, 16.7–8, 16.18–20.

22. *Reg.* XIII, clxxiv: Migne *PL* 216, 353–4; ed. Haluscynski, no. 173, 402–3.

23. L. B. Robbert, 'Rialto business men and Constantinople, 1204–61', *Dumbarton Oaks Papers*, 49(1995), 43–58. D. Jacoby, 'Venetian settlers in Latin Constantinople', in Πλούσιοι καὶ Φτωχοί (Venice, 1998), 181–204, does produce evidence of a Venetian community in Constantinople, but does not overturn Robbert's conclusions.

24. J.-C. Cheynet, *Pouvoir et contestations à Byzance*, 427–58, who quite rightly insists (464) that the disintegration of the Empire, Bulgaria excepted, only started after April 1204.

25. Nicetas Choniates, 637.34–40.

26. Ibid., 611.26–35 + app.; 638.42–4.

27. Villehardouin II, §325–30.

28. Chronicle of the Morea, l.2094.

29. For the organisation of Frankish Achaea see A. Bon, *La Morée franque* (Paris, 1969), 82–115; P. Lock, *The Franks in the Aegean*, 68–92; and esp. D. Jacoby, 'The encounter of two societies: western conquerors and Byzantines in the Peloponnesus after the fourth crusade', *American Historical Review*, 78(1973), 873–906; D. Jacoby, 'Les archontes grecs et la féodalité en Morée franque', *Travaux et Mémoires*, 2(1967), 421–81.

30. Migne *PL* 216, 969.

31. J. M. Wagstaff, 'Further observations on the location of Grande Magne', *Dumbarton Oaks Papers*, 45(1991), 141–8.

32. D. Geanakoplos, 'Greco-Latin relations on the eve of the Byzantine restoration: the battle of Pelagonia, 1259', *Dumbarton Oaks Papers*, 7(1953), 101–41; D. Geanakoplos, *Emperor Michael Palaeologus and the West* (Cambridge, Mass., 1959), 47–74, 154–60.

33. D. M. Nicol, *The Despotate of Epiros 1267–1479* (Cambridge, 1984).

34. R.-J. Loenertz, 'Aux origines du despotat d'Epire et de la principauté d'Achaie', *Byzantion*, 43(1973), 360–94; K. Varzos, Ἡ γενεαλογία τῶν Κομνηνῶν (Thessalonica, 1984), II, no. 174, 669–89.

35. Villehardouin II, §301.

36. Ibid., II, §328–9.

37. Acropolites I, 14–17.

38. D. I. Polemis, *The Doukai. A Contribution to Byzantine Prosopography* (London, 1968), no. 101.

39. Henri de Valenciennes, §688–94.

40. *Reg.* XII, xcvi: Migne *PL* 216, 106–7.

41. Tafel and Thomas II, 120–3.

42. Nicol, *Epiros*, 37–8.

43. *Reg.* XIII, clxxxiv: Migne *PL* 216, 353–4; ed. Haluscynski, no. 173, 402–3. Cf. Longnon, *Compagnons*, 217–19.

44. '*Qui servos suos adoptat in filios et coronat in reges*': Migne *PL* 216, 106; ed. Haluscynski, no. 132, 369.

45. On his title see Varzos, Γενεαλογιά τῶν Κομνηνῶν, II, 688.

46. Cf. P. Magdalino, 'Between Romaniae: Thessaly and Epirus in the later Middle Ages', in *Latins and Greeks in the Eastern Mediterranean after 1204*, ed. B. Arbel, B. Hamilton and D. Jacoby (London, 1989), 87–8.

47. G. Prinzing, 'Studien zur Provinz- und Zentralverwaltung im Machtbereich der Epirotischen Herrscher Michael I. und Theodoros Doukas', Ἠπειρωτικὰ Χρονικά, 24(1982), 73–120; 25(1983), 37–112.

48. Varzos, Γενεαλογία τῶν Κομνηνῶν, II, no. 168, 548–637.

49. A. Stauridou-Zaphraka, 'Συμβολὴ στὸ ζήτημα τῆς ἀναγόρευσης τοῦ Θεοδώρου Δουκᾶ', in Ἀφιέρωμα στὸν Ἐμμανουὴλ Κριαρᾶ (Thessalonica, 1988), 37–62.

50. B. Ferjancic, *Tesalija u XIII i XIV veku* (Belgrade, 1974).

51. *Oxford Dictionary of Byzantium*, I – sub. ARTA.

52. A. Papadopoulos-Kerameus, 'Περὶ συνοικισμοῦ τῶν Ιωαννίνων', Δελτίον τῆς ἱστορικῆς καὶ ἐθνολογικῆς ἑταιρείας τῆς Ἑλλάδος, 3(1890–1), 451–5.

53. F. Miklosich and J. Müller, *Acta et diplomata graeca medii aevi sacra et profana* (Vienna, 1860–90), 6 vols: V, 77–84.

54. M. J. Angold, 'The shaping of the medieval Byzantine "city"', *Byzantinische Forschungen*, 10(1985), 1–37.

55. Villehardouin II, §280: *il les tendroit as us et as costumes que li empereur Grieu les avoient tenuz.*

56. Tafel and Thomas II, 18–19.

57. M. J. Angold, *The Byzantine Aristocracy IX to XIII Centuries* (Oxford, 1984), 242–9.

58. Wolff, 'Hopf's Fragmentum', 150.

59. R. L. Wolff, 'Politics in the Latin Patriarchate of Constantinople, 1204–1261', *Dumbarton Oaks Papers*, 8(1954), 278.

chapter 7

THE VENETIAN *DOMINIO*

❧ ━━━━━━━━━━━━━━━━━━━━━━━━━━━ ❧

The discussion of the Venetian contribution to the Latin Empire has usually started from the assumption that Venice's interests were so different from those of the Latin Empire that there was bound to be friction. It is also assumed that the task of establishing Venetian control over areas of strategic and commercial importance, such as Crete, detracted from the help that the Venetians might have brought to the Latin Empire. But should the failure of the Latin Empire be traced back to the selfish ambitions of the Venetians? This is a line of thought that is founded in the belief that the Venetians were the instigators and the major beneficiaries of the conquest of the Byzantine Empire. This is a view which has lately come in for severe and justified criticism. Far from neglecting their obligations to the Latin Empire the Venetians fulfilled them to the letter. Enrico Dandolo played a notable role in the desperate days that followed the defeat at Adrianople. Without Venetian seapower Constantinople would not have remained in Latin hands as long as it did. By the last days of the Latin Empire the Venetians had to all intents and purposes taken over responsibility for the defence of Constantinople. Marino Torsello Sanudo regarded the recovery of the city by Michael Palaiologos in 1261 as a severe blow to Venetian pride and interests. The time has come to discard the conventional view that sees Venice selfishly pursuing its own political and commercial interests to the detriment of the Latin Empire of Constantinople. As we shall see in the next chapter, there was a real difference of interests, but this was over control of the church of St Sophia. It was to have ramifications that did more damage to the Latin Empire than more obvious political rivalry might have done.

I

The Venetians may have been less enthusiastic than the Franks in their support for the claims of the young Alexius to the Byzantine throne, but by January 1204 the Doge Enrico Dandolo had become the main proponent of decisive action. He must have formed a reasonably clear idea of what Venice stood to gain from the conquest of Constantinople. There was every reason to suppose that Venice would regain or even improve upon the very favourable terms it had enjoyed in the trade of Constantinople before Manuel I Comnenus's 1171 coup against them. Their trade in the Byzantine Empire had latterly suffered not so much from the direct competition of the Genoese and Pisans, as from the piracy which was rife in Byzantine waters and which the Byzantine emperors did very little to suppress. The way that Pisan, Genoese and Sicilian pirates were beginning to infiltrate Byzantine territory and establish more or less permanent bases was extremely worrying to the Venetians. The most immediate benefit of the conquest of Constantinople was the opportunity to deal with piracy, which the Venetians took.

It is natural to assume that, when it came to the parcelling out of the Byzantine Empire, the Venetians gave a great deal of thought as to exactly which territories best suited their commercial interests. A glance at the territories assigned to the Venetians reveals two guiding principles at work: first, to secure regions and centres where they had developed their trading interests before 1204 and, second, and probably the more important, to secure command of the sea lanes linking the Adriatic to Constantinople. So, around Constantinople Venice took the major market centres of Thrace along with a string of ports leading from Gallipoli to Constantinople. Of areas still to be conquered Venice reserved for itself the Peloponnese, Epiros and Albania, along with the Ionian islands and some of the Aegean islands. These territories controlled the sea lanes. However, nothing made the Venetian intentions clearer than the treaty concluded on 12 August 1204 between the doge and Boniface of Montferrat. By it the latter surrendered all his claims to territory in the old Byzantine Empire in return for 1,000 marks of silver and – more vaguely – lands from Venice's portion of provinces capable of producing a revenue of 10,000 gold *hyperpyra*. Boniface agreed to hold these lands from the doge and the Venetians *in perpetuo*. Much of this would remain a dead letter, but not the provisions relating to the island of Crete, which had been granted personally to Boniface by Alexius IV Angelus and had thus been excluded from the partition treaty. Effectively, Boniface surrendered his claims to the island in return for 1,000 marks of silver. Boniface's quittance for this sum has survived.[1] Crete was, of course, essential to the control of Byzantine waters and – more to the point – was already in danger of falling into the hands of the Genoese in the shape of Enrico Pescatore, count of Malta.

It was one thing to have acquired claims to these Byzantine lands. It was quite another to conquer them. Enrico Dandolo despatched his nephew Marco Sanudo with a fleet of eight galleys to the Aegean. His most likely task was to counter any danger from the Genoese, which will explain why he seized the island of Naxos when it was not part of the Venetian share of the lands to be conquered. Sanudo returned to Constantinople around the time of Enrico Dandolo's death at the end of May 1205. He played a major role in the election of Marino Zeno as *podestà* of the Venetians at Constantinople. This action has been mis-interpreted as a demand for autonomy on the part of the Venetian community at Constantinople. Marco Sanudo has been singled out as a leader of this movement. When in 1207 he returned to the Aegean and finally established control over Naxos, he did homage for the duchy of the Archipelago, as it came to be called, to the Latin Emperor Henry. This was not directed against Venetian control. It was determined by the niceties of the partition treaty, which gave most of the Aegean to the emperor. After the election of Marino Zeno as *podestà* Marco Sanudo was one of those sent back to Venice to explain the situation. A later tradition records that the new doge Pietro Ziani proposed that he should move the seat of government from Venice to Constantinople. It is not a story to be taken seriously. At best, it reflects the enormity of the challenge that now faced the Venetians. In fact, the relationship between Venice and the Venetian community in Constantinople was quickly regu-lated. By the beginning of September 1205 Venetian legates despatched by Renier Dandolo, son of the dead doge, had arrived at Constantinople. They approved of the election of Marino Zeno, but made it clear that in future the *podestà* of Constantinople would be appointed in Venice. At the same time they coordinated a strategy of conquest with the *podestà*. Venice was to deal with western Greece, while the Venetians of Con-stantinople secured control of their territories around the Sea of Marmara. Nothing was said at this stage about Crete, but this became the respons-ibility of Venice. It was a sensible division of labour. Managing the complicated relationship with the Latin Empire was left to the *podestà*, which meant that he had considerable freedom of action. He was able to conclude treaties with foreign powers, but this must not be mistaken for a desire for greater autonomy or independence on the part of the Venetian community in Constantinople.[2]

The great worry at Venice was that the Genoese would take advantage of the situation created by the conquest of Constantinople to seize strategic points. Already one Genoese freebooter, Leone Vetrano, had established a base on the island of Corfu. He was driven out in the summer of 1205 by a fleet despatched from Venice, but he was soon back again. A second expedition failed to dislodge him, but a third succeeded in capturing him. It then moved on to seize the ports of Methoni and Koroni. The Venetians were following a sensible strategy of securing the key points along the route leading from the Adriatic to Constantinople. Corfu was singled out as of special importance. In July 1207 the doge and people of Venice ceded the island to a consortium of ten Venetian nobles, who agreed to raise at their own expense a force necessary to conquer the island.[3] They never established effective control over the island and by 1213 had been driven out by Michael Doukas, the Greek ruler of Epiros, who had already benefited from the Venetian decision to abandon the idea of conquering any mainland territories. In 1210 the doge granted him, as we have seen, the lands between the Gulf of Corinth and the approaches to Dyrrachion.[4] It was of a piece with the grant made around the same time of the Peloponnese to Geoffrey Villehardouin, Methoni and Koroni always excepted. Venice equally recognised Ravano delle Carceri as the ruler of the island of Euboea, which had fallen to Venice by the terms of the partition treaty.

These treaties with local rulers left Venice free to concentrate on the subjection of the island of Crete, where the Genoese were already establishing themselves under Enrico Pescatore, count of Malta, who had support from other Genoese. At his side were Guiglielmo Porco, admiral of Sicily, and Alamano da Costa, count of Syracuse. In 1206 they drove off the first attempt made by the Venetians to dislodge them, but a second Venetian expedition in 1207 succeeded in securing the key base of Candia. Pescatore was then defeated off Rhodes in 1212 by the Venetians and abandoned his designs on Crete. His comrade-in-arms Alamano Costa returned to the island, but without any substantial support among the Cretans he was driven out of Crete in 1217. This prepared the way for a peace treaty of 1218. In return for recognising Venice's possession of the island, the Genoese recovered the trading rights they had enjoyed before 1204.[5]

By 1218 the Venetians were more or less firmly established on the island. They divided Crete into 200 knights' fees and 48 sergeantries. This would provide a rather more formidable force than at first appears because each knight was obliged to serve with a retinue of four men, two of whom were mounted. This feudal framework was given a Venetian coating, because the island was divided into *sestieri*, like Venice itself. This helped in the recruiting of military colonists, which was done by *sestiere*. The first batch was sent out in 1211. It consisted of 94 knights and 26 sergeants, which fell short of the 132 knights and 48 sergeants that had been hoped for. But this initial plantation must have worked reasonably well, for by 1222 there were Venetians clamouring to go to

Crete as colonists and Venice was able to augment the original number of fees by another sixty. More colonists were despatched in 1233. Venice retained the region around Candia, which became the seat of the duke or governor of Crete. The feudatories were obliged to keep a house in the city and to attend the great council. In other words, there was an attempt to organise Crete along much the same lines as Venice itself. It was a remarkable effort on the part of Venice. It had not hitherto been a military power and a feudal organisation was alien to it. On the whole, the Venetian colonisation of Crete is testimony to the flexibility of a feudal organisation which could be adapted to all kinds of political and administrative structures.[6]

The people with most to lose were the native Cretan aristocracy, who found themselves pushed to the margins of the island by Italian colonists. The Venetian government of the island refused to recognise that the Cretans had any rights unless they first submitted to the new order. It is therefore hardly a surprise that the despatch of the first batch of military colonists produced an uprising in 1212 led by the Hagiostephanites family. The Cretans pinned down the Venetian governor Giacomo Tiepolo in Candia. Only the intervention of Marco Sanudo, the duke of the Archipelago, saved him. However, Tiepolo failed to honour the promise he had made to Sanudo of thirty knights' fees, as the price of the latter's help. Sanudo therefore joined forces with another Greek *archon* and forced Tiepolo out of Candia. His success was short-lived. The Venetian feudatories rallied to their duke and recovered control of Candia. Marco Sanudo evacuated the island taking some of his Greek allies with him.[7]

Elements among the Cretan *archontes* remained disaffected. In 1217 there was a new uprising. Its leaders, Constantine Skordyles and Theodore Melissenos, came to terms in September 1219. They were granted sixty-seven-and-a-half knights' fees against an annual payment to the duke of Crete of 1,000 *hyperpyra*. They were to serve on exactly the same terms as Venetian feudatories.[8] The Melissenos family acquired another two fees in 1224.[9] A pattern was being set whereby Greek archontic families were integrated into the feudal structure created by the Venetians. But part of the dynamic was rebellion, since this was a way of extracting further concessions from the Venetians. As Sally McKee argues, the Cretan *archontes* were not motivated by any sense of national solidarity. They wanted to safeguard their status which was threatened by the Venetian settlement.[10] The Venetians became adept at playing off one aristocratic clan against another. This became clear when in 1230 and again in 1233 the Nicaean Emperor John Vatatzes despatched expeditions against Crete. The Venetians were able to limit the amount of local support the invaders received by making a series of grants to the Cretan *archontes*, who were the real gainers.[11] The pattern of rebellion and concession continued after the Nicaeans recovered Constantinople in 1261. It more or less came to an end in 1299 when Alexius Kalergis, the Cretan leader, finally made peace with the Venetians. It confirmed that the Cretan aristocracy had been drawn into the framework of Venetian government and society. There was a pattern of marriage alliances between the archontic families and the Venetian feudatories. Venice reluctantly accepted the place of the archontic families.[12]

The Venetians were even willing to make concessions over ecclesiastical organisation. Kalergis requested that the bishopric of Ario should be conceded to a Greek incumbent on a permanent basis, while the bishoprics of Mylopotamos and Kalamos should be held by Greeks on a temporary basis. As part of a policy of divide and rule the Venetian government was fairly accommodating over the question of ecclesiastical organisation; the Venetian authorities in Crete rather less so. In 1224 the Greek bishop of Knossos sketched the state of the Orthodox Church in a petition sent to the Doge Pietro Ziani. He complained that 'what they had suffered had never happened in any other Venetian territory'. Most of the Greek bishops were now either dead or in exile; only two were still in possession of their sees, while two others were homeless, reduced to living off charity. The bishop of Knossos had turned to the doge because he could expect no justice from the duke of Crete who referred to the native inhabitants as 'dogs and devils'.[13]

The doge did his best to protect the interests of the Orthodox Church. He showed particular favour to the monastery of Sinai. As early as March 1212 he confirmed it in its Cretan possessions.[14] This did not prevent the first Venetian archbishop of Crete, Giacomo Viadro, mounting a long campaign of harrassment against the monks of Sinai on the island. Injunctions from the doge and from the pope apparently had no effect. In December 1223 the papacy commissioned the bishops of Ario and Mylopotamos to intervene on behalf of the monks. There is a strong possibility that both bishops were Greeks who had made their submission. The Venetians allowed the Orthodox incumbent of the see of Chiron to remain in office until his death in the 1230s when he was succeeded again by a Greek from a prominent archontic family. In the same way another archontic family seems to have controlled the bishopric of Ario at least to the middle of the century.[15] Even Giacomo Viadro seems to have established a working relationship with the Greeks, if not of the most reputable kind. His conduct was such that in 1232 Pope Gregory IX set up a commission to investigate him. Among the string of charges brought against him were those of conspiring with Greeks against Latins and allowing a Greek to marry a nun.[16] The Venetian regime was realistic enough to understand the importance of accepting the role of the Orthodox Church. The district of Candia was served by 130 Greek priests. The numbers for the rest of the island were not regulated in the same way. Their organisation was, however, the responsibility of a *protopappas* and a *protopsaltes*, both of whom were chosen by the Greek clergy. It meant a fair degree of autonomy.[17] The importance attached by the Venetians to placating their Cretan subjects is evident from one detail of the peace made in 1219 with the Cretan rebels: the Cretan estates of the monastery of St John on the island of Patmos were specifically exempted from any reprisals.[18] Protection and patronage of Orthodox monasteries was one way of reconciling the Cretans to Venetian rule; another was to accept the continuing presence of Orthodox bishops.

II

The length of time and the expenditure required to hold down Crete testify to the strength and resilience of the Venetian Republic. It is highly unlikely that Enrico Dandolo could have had the remotest idea of how costly his deal with Boniface of Montferrat over Crete would prove to be. Crete was the keystone of Venice's 'empire', which took shape in the aftermath of 1204. In retrospect, it looks as though these developments had their roots in Venetian commercial expansion into the eastern Mediterranean during the twelfth century. It was then that Venetian merchants established permanent quarters in a series of provincial centres, notably Halmyros in Thessaly and Adrianople in Thrace. These were organised around churches acquired by the Venetians. However, there was not much continuity between Venetian activities in the twelfth century and those after the conquest of Constantinople. The places frequented by the Venetians in the twelfth century, such as Halmyros and Adrianople, were quickly abandoned as new possibilities opened up. Constantinople apart, the major Venetian centres after 1204 were Candia, Negroponte on the island of Euboea, Methoni and Koroni, places that had not been of much interest to Venetian merchants at an earlier period. It is most unlikely that before 1204 the Venetians had contemplated bringing any part of the Byzantine Empire under their direct control. To that extent, the fall of Constantinople in 1204 pointed to a radical transformation of Venice's position in the old Byzantine Empire. The opportunities seized were rather different from any that might have been anticipated. It was an experience that turned the Venetian Republic into an 'empire'. This was the most enduring consequence of 1204.

After all, it lasted as a serious concern until 1669, when Crete finally fell to the Ottomans.

There is no need to assume that the Latin Empire was sacrificed to the creation of this 'empire'. Venetian involvement in the conquest of Crete did not mean neglect of obligations to the Latin Empire. The struggle for Crete was, in any case, largely over by 1218. Though rebellions continued throughout the thirteenth century, Venice had the situation under control. It is difficult to see that the settlement of Crete diverted manpower and resources that might otherwise have gone to shore up the Latin Empire. Relations with the Latin Empire were primarily the responsibility of the Venetians of Constantinople. They occupied key positions around the Sea of Marmara and, what is more, created an effective military organisation.[19] The Venetian *podestà* Giacomo Tiepolo cooperated with the Latin regime after the death of Peter of Courtenay in 1217. He negotiated treaties with the Greek ruler of Anatolia, Theodore Laskaris, and with the Seljuq Sultan of Konya. These provided the Latin Empire with some protection at a difficult moment.

Nor should it be forgotten that until 1216 and the death of Henry of Hainault the Latin Empire was relatively successful. The rapid decline of the Latin Empire only set in later and it had very little to do with Venice directly. Indirectly it is another matter. As suggested earlier, the root cause of the failure of the Latin Empire was Constantinople's failure to prosper. Around the year 1200 Constantinople was by the standards of the time an enormous city – a *megalopolis*. When the Greeks of Nicaea recovered the city in 1261, it was a shell. The population had declined disastrously. Almost all the great buildings of the city had been allowed to deteriorate. Too poor to maintain their palaces and churches, the emperor and patriarch preferred to strip their roofs of lead and copper. Under the Latins Constantinople suffered not only depopulation but also poverty. By the 1240s the Latin clergy of Constantinople were seeking refuge in Italy out of poverty. The financial straits of the last Latin Emperor Baldwin II are almost too well known. He sold off relics of the Passion that had belonged to the Byzantine emperors. He even mortgaged his own son.[20]

The impoverishment of Constantinople was one of the major consequences of the Latin conquest. How far were the Venetians responsible? Why did they so singularly fail to exploit their near monopoly of the trade of Constantinople? It was only to be expected that there might at first be a hiatus, as the Latins established a new regime, but this should have been followed by a recovery of trade. The pattern is more or less the reverse. In the early years of the Latin Empire Venetian merchants strove to maintain their trading contacts with Constantinople, much as they had before 1200. The falling off of Venetian trade comes from the 1220s, at exactly the time when Venice had secured much of what it wanted in terms of lands and conditions from the conquest of Constantinople.

It is not that hard to see why Constantinople declined under the Latins. The Venetians and other Italian merchants played an important role in the city's economy before 1204. Their contribution was twofold: they supplied Constantinople with the commodities it required, but they also stimulated a market economy. Before 1204 the former was more important, but by the 1300s it was the latter. Constantinople before 1204 was a consumer economy. The dominant elements were the imperial government and the aristocracy, the patriarchate and the monks and clergy. A large proportion of the population of the Byzantine capital in the end depended on these for their livelihood. Constantinople's role as an entrepôt of international trade was dependent upon and subordinated to its role as a consumer, in the sense that a tiny proportion of the commodities shipped to Constantinople was then re-exported. This is in contrast to the situation existing in the fourteenth century.

Constantinople was a centre of consumption on a vast scale before 1204 because of the revenues which poured in from the provinces, whether in the shape of taxation or incomes from landed estates. Some historians have detected a falling off of economic and commercial activity at Constantinople in the decades before 1204 and have attributed it to shifts in international trade routes, but this explanation scarcely makes sense. It is too early to blame the Mongols for disruption of the trade routes. If there was a decline in Constantinople's trade it was much more likely to be the result of provincial disaffection, which would have meant that a smaller proportion of the empire's disposable wealth was reaching the capital. This was a situation that was magnified out of all proportion by the Latin conquest. The structure of the Latin Empire meant that the emperor could effectively expect revenues to come in from the territories that he controlled around the Sea of Marmara. He might expect service from the Frankish states established in Greece, but nothing in the way of revenues. As long as the Latin Empire controlled the shores of the Sea of Marmara – Constantinople's 'Home Counties' – it was more or less viable because these were some of the richest agricultural lands in the whole Mediterranean region. The recovery of the Asiatic shores of the Sea of Marmara in 1224 by the Greeks of Nicaea was therefore a disaster for the Latin Empire. It was soon followed by the loss of Adrianople, the capital of Thrace. It is no surprise that it was during the Emperor Robert's reign from 1221 to 1228 that the weakness of the Latin Empire became crystal clear. There was no longer the minimum economic base to support Constantinople.

The major consequence of the Latin conquest of Constantinople was that an economic system was irrevocably destroyed. It was a system that in the past the Venetians had adapted to and had benefited by. Its collapse hardly worked to Venice's immediate advantage. The old system had depended on an effective central government, which could maintain law and order, discipline foreign merchants, patrol the Byzantine waters, and ensure that trading privileges enjoyed the necessary respect. As the largest carriers of goods to Constantinople the Venetians suffered most heavily from the breakdown of effective central control. A rationalisation of the diversion of the Fourth Crusade to Constantinople would be that it was designed to shore up imperial government in the interests of Venetian trade. Instead the Venetians contributed to a permanent weakening of the centre. It seems nigh impossible that even they could have foreseen these particular consequences of the conquest of Constantinople. But their reaction to these unforeseen circumstances was to build on another – hitherto less important – side of their activities in the twelfth century. This was their infiltration of the local trade of the Greek lands. They established themselves in the twelfth century in centres such as Halmyros, the outlet for the goods of Thessaly and Boeotia, and Corinth, the entrepôt of the Peloponnese and Attica. While the bulk of their transactions were designed with Constantinople in mind, there were other deals involving the export of Greek products to other Mediterranean destinations. The presence of Venetian merchants in the Greek lands stimulated the local economy. This side of their activities did not suffer after 1204 to the same extent as trade at Constantinople. Even in the difficult early years of conquest and settlement Venetian merchants developed their local interests. They were to be found trading at Candia in Crete even before the final expulsion of the Genoese. There was inevitably a degree of disruption as the important centres of local trade changed. Halmyros was abandoned for the greater security of Negroponte, as it was known to the Latins, on the island of Euboea. The Venetian quarter expanded rapidly and by the end of the period of exile the whole town was in Venetian possession. In Crete Candia, the seat of the Venetian duke of Crete, quickly became an important commercial centre, irrespective of conditions on the island. Even Methoni and Koroni on the south-western tip of the Peloponnese prospered under Venetian rule. The Venetians took advantage of their strong political position in the years after 1204 to lay the foundations of a new trading system, which was based on local exchanges.[21] Preferably these were to be concentrated in centres under Venetian control.

The concomitant of this new trading system was political fragmentation, which suited Venetian interests very well. Maintaining this state of affairs became a cornerstone of Venetian policy. Later on, it explains Venice's dogged opposition to the Ottomans. Another consequence of Venetian success was to be the long-drawn-out struggle with the Genoese, who reacted to the conquest and plundering of Constantinople with undisguised envy.[22] The Genoese failed to dislodge the Venetians from Crete or to establish any effective base of their own. They were forced to come to terms. This meant that despite the periodical renewal of the treaty of 1218 their presence in the Latin Empire was very much on sufferance. They had a factory of sorts under a consul at Negroponte. Another at Constantinople under consuls and viscounts and rectors was certainly envisaged, but it seems never to have been established under the Latin Empire. The Genoese targeted the island of Rhodes, in its way as important a route centre as Crete. They seized the island in 1249 but were driven out by Nicaean forces from the mainland. This setback was followed in 1251 with a renewal of their treaty with Venice and by despatch of an expedition to the Latin Empire, which was organised by the Gattilusio family on behalf of Boniface, marquis of Carreto. The expedition was not primarily a trading venture, but seems to have had some military purpose. The marquis had been a supporter of Frederick II, so it is possible that he was taking service with John Vatatzes, who had been Frederick's ally.[23]

This was an isolated Genoese enterprise and seems quite unconnected with the new opportunities that were being opened up by the advance of the Mongols into southern Russia and Anatolia. Venetian merchants were just beginning to explore these possibilities on the eve of the recovery of Constantinople in 1261 by the Greeks of Nicaea under Michael VIII Palaiologos (1259–82), who at the time was allied to the Genoese. Thanks to the favour of the Byzantine emperor the latter were initially in a better position than the Venetians to seize the new opportunities opening up in the Black Sea region. While Michael VIII Palaiologos lived there was a possibility that the currents of international trade created through Mongol intervention would come under Byzantine control. But it was not to be. After his death they passed into the hands of the Venetians and Genoese. Constantinople – the Genoese colony at Pera included – became one of the most important staging posts along the trade route linking western Europe with markets of Asia, but it was the Venetians and Genoese, not the Byzantine emperor, who were the beneficiaries. This was the culmination of the transformation begun in 1204 with the conquest of Constantinople. The Venetians and the Genoese learnt that it was not in their interests to have a powerful political force in control of Constantinople.

Notes

1. Borsari, *Dominio*, 11–13; Borsari, *Colonie veneziane*, 21.
2. F. Thiriet, *La Romanie vénitienne au moyen âge* (Paris, 1959), 74–101; Borsari, *Colonie veneziane*, 15–48.
3. Tafel and Thomas II, 54.
4. Ibid., II, 119–22.
5. Borsari, *Dominio*, 21–5, 37–8; D. Abulafia, 'Henry Count of Malta and his Mediterranean activities: 1203–1230', in *Medieval Malta. Studies on Malta before the Knights*, ed. A. T. Luttrell (London, 1975), 104–25, esp. 114–19; Jehel, 'The struggle for hegemony'.
6. Thiriet, *La Romanie vénitienne*, 88–101, 105–39; Borsari, *Dominio*, 28–30, 45–6; S. McKee, *Uncommon Dominion. Venetian Crete and the Myth of Ethnic Purity* (Philadelphia, 2000), 32–9.
7. Borsari, *Dominio*, 32–6; J. K. Fotheringham, *Marco Sanudo* (Oxford, 1915), 81–103.
8. Tafel and Thomas II, 210–13.
9. Ibid., II, 252.
10. McKee, *Uncommon Dominion*, 68–70.
11. Borsari, *Dominio*, 40–5.
12. McKee, *Uncommon Dominion*, 71–4; Borsari, *Dominio*, 55–6.
13. G. B. Cervellini, *Documento inedito veneto-cretese del dugento* (Padua, 1906), quoted in G. Fedalto, *La chiesa latina in Oriente*, I (Verona, 1973), 318–19.
14. Tafel and Thomas II, 146–50; Borsari, *Dominio*, 117–21.
15. Borsari, *Dominio*, 75, n. 37, 105–8; Fedalto, *Chiesa latina*, 320–8.
16. *Registres de Grégoire IX*, ed. L. Auvray, no. 1013.
17. McKee, *Uncommon Dominion*, 106.
18. Tafel and Thomas II, 213.
19. D. Jacoby, 'The Venetian presence in the Latin Empire of Constantinople (1204–1261): the challenge of feudalism and the Byzantine inheritance', *Jahrbuch des österreichischen Byzantinistik*, 43(1993), 141–201, esp. 189–96.
20. R. L. Wolff, 'Mortgage and Redemption', 45–84.
21. Borsari, *Dominio*, 68–73.
22. *Annales Ianuenses*, II, ed. L. T. Belgrano (Fonti per la storia d'Italia, 12) (Rome, 1901), 88–9.
23. M. Balard, 'Les génois en Romanie entre 1204 et 1261. Recherches dans les minutiers notariaux génois', *Mélanges d'archéologie et d'histoire*, 78(1966), 467–502, esp. 484–6.

chapter 8

THE LATIN CHURCH OF CONSTANTINOPLE

I

As Marino Sanudo Torsello admitted many years later, the Venetians 'took possession of much of the [Byzantine] Empire, but were never able to win the people's hearts [and lead them] to the Roman obedience'.[1] This was an essential weakness of the Latin Empire of Constantinople. The Venetians must bear a great deal of the blame, for their selfish exploitation of the Patriarchal Church, which fell to their lot in the partition of the empire. The three-cornered rivalry over St Sophia between the Venetians, the Franks and the papacy is at the heart of the failure – if we leave aside the Greek lands for the moment – to establish a viable Latin Church in the newly-conquered territories. This left a hollow at the heart of the Latin Empire. Because of the existence of papal records it is an aspect of the empire's history about which we are well informed. It allows us to follow in some detail how the Latin settlement began to go wrong.[2]

St Sophia had fallen to the Venetians as a consolation prize after they failed to obtain the imperial throne. This conformed with the terms of the partition treaty drawn up in March 1204. The relevant clause goes on:

> Clergy of both parties should administer those churches, which fall to their share; from the property of the churches sufficient should be alloted to the clergy and the churches, so that they can with due honour [*honorifice*] live and support themselves. The remaining property of the churches should be divided and partitioned in the manner indicated above.[3]

Lip-service may have been paid to the honour of the Roman Church and to the honour of the clergy, but the meaning was clear: church property was to be treated like any other property. It went entirely against the spirit of Gregorian reform, but accorded with the Venetian view, that the church should serve the interests of state.[4] It must have been obvious that it would not meet with the approval of Pope Innocent III, but the crusade leaders would surely have consulted the prelates who accompanied the crusade, if only because at this critical stage they were a powerful voice in crusader counsels. It goes without saying that not a word was said about the Orthodox Church and clergy. By the time the partition treaty was drawn up in March 1204 feeling in the crusader camp against the schismatic Greeks was at its height. Perhaps this is an explanation for the clergy's willingness to accept the envisaged division of ecclesiastical property. It represented part of that transfer of wealth, as Innocent III would later put it, 'from the proud to the humble, from the disobedient to the obedient, from schismatics to Catholics'.[5]

The arrangements made in the partition treaty over the church proved a liability in so many different ways. They produced friction between the Latin patriarch and the pope; between the Latin Church and the secular authorities over ecclesiastical property; and between the Venetians and the Franks. As serious was the way they intensified the distrust and outright hatred of Greeks for Latins. The result was that the Latin Empire of Constantinople was never underpinned by an effective ecclesiastical organisation. This contrasted with experience in the Holy Land, in southern Italy and Sicily, even in the kingdom of Cyprus, where the Western Church was successfully implanted. In all these areas there was a significant Orthodox presence, which was tolerated, and a modus vivendi worked out. Admittedly, the task facing the Western Church in the Latin Empire was more formidable, but what might have been accomplished is evident from the achievements of the Franciscans and Dominicans once they began to establish themselves in Latin Constantinople from the 1220s, but by then it was too late.[6]

We have seen how powerful a voice the prelates had in the counsels of the crusade leadership. They gave to the conquest of Constantinople meaning and purpose. Pre-eminent among them was Nivelon, bishop of Soissons.[7] He had the task of announcing the election of Baldwin of Flanders as emperor and then of carrying out his coronation. After the defeat at Adrianople he headed a delegation to the West designed to recruit help for the Latin Empire, but he died in 1207 at Bari on the return journey. He was never able to take up his appointment to the see of Thessalonica. His successor was another of the spiritual leaders of the Fourth Crusade, Peter, abbot of Lucedio. He too was unable to take up the position because he was then promoted to the troubled patriarchate of Antioch. Thus, the Latin Church of Constantinople soon found itself deprived of its original leaders, who were trusted and respected.

The first patriarch, Thomas Morosini, seems to have deserved the unflattering description of him that we have from the pen of Nicetas Choniates.[8] His main concerns were to protect Venetian interests and to ensure the finances of the patriarchate. He was faced with constant interference on the part of Pope Innocent III, for whom the news of the election of a Latin patriarch came as a shock. His initial instructions to the crusader clergy simply envisaged their election of a *rector* to act as their interim head.[9] Nothing is said about any patriarch, but faced with a fait accompli the pope was determined to ensure that the patriarchate of Constantinople came under direct papal supervision. He was far from happy with the arrangements of the partition treaty as they affected the church. In the end, he refused to confirm the treaty because of its provisions about the division of ecclesiastical property.[10] He reluctantly agreed to the appointment of Thomas Morosini as patriarch, but only after quashing the initial election as uncanonical and then using the papal *plenitudo potestas* to reinstate him.[11] Morosini was a scion of a great Venetian family, but at the time of his election he was a papal subdeacon. In the course of March 1205 Innocent III first ordained him into the orders of priesthood before consecrating him bishop and bestowing the pallium on him.[12]

Innocent III must have hoped that his personal involvement in the new patriarch's elevation would guarantee the latter's loyalty to the Holy See and counteract Venetian influence. He was determined that the church of St Sophia should not become a Venetian dependency. He had, however, counted without the pressure that the Venetians brought to bear on Morosini, when he reached Venice in May 1205 intending to take ship to Constantinople. The Venetian authorities exploited the patriarch's troubles with his creditors to bar his departure, unless he was willing to take the oath – already sworn by the Venetian canons of St Sophia – that only Venetians were to be admitted to the clergy of the patriarchal church. In addition, Morosini was to ensure that Venetians were put into all the sees of the patriarchate. To strengthen their hold on St Sophia another seventeen canons were appointed there and then in Venice, each taking the same oath as the patriarch. These appointments were also designed to bind Morosini more closely to his obligations to Venice. Before he departed, he was pressurised by his canons into exempting from patriarchal jurisdiction all those churches that the Venetians had controlled in the Byzantine Empire before 1204.[13] Rather later, in 1208, Morosini made a public declaration in Constantinople regretting the concessions he had made to the Venetians but, whether this was the case or not, he was from the very beginning caught between the demands of the pope and those of the Venetians. This helps to explain the difficulties that he encountered.

The journey out to Constantinople gave him a chance to display his Venetian loyalties, as he enthusiastically participated in the subjugation of both Ragusa and Dyrrachion. His arrival in Constantinople was consequently delayed until the end of 1205. His peremptory demand that he be received with due honour so infuriated the Frankish clergy of Constantinople that they refused to acknowledge him or obey him, giving as their grounds the deceptions he had used to obtain office. With the support of the papal legate Peter Capuano they appealed to the pope against Morosini's appointment. There followed a short-lived schism between the patriarch and the Frankish clergy which the newly-arrived papal legate Benedict of Santa Susanna was able to bring to an end some six months later.[14]

However, relations remained cool. The Frankish clergy objected to the Venetian monopoly of the Patriarchal Church. This was guaranteed by the oath taken by the patriarch and canons that they would only admit Venetians to the offices and prebends of St Sophia. These oaths were repeated word for word in November 1207 and April 1208 when additional canons of St Sophia were appointed.[15] It meant among other things that the patriarch had reneged on his undertaking to the papal legate Benedict of Santa Susanna that he was prepared to accept canons appointed both by Benedict and by his predecessor Peter Capuano. Once again the Frankish clergy withdrew their obedience and appealed to the pope against the action of the patriarch with further charges added: that he had embezzled 100,000 marks of silver from the treasury of St Sophia; that he had pocketed 600 *hyperpyra* which should have gone to meet the expenses of the papal legate; that he had seized precious marbles from the church of the Anastasis to help with the reconstruction of the altar of St Sophia. Innocent III was deeply concerned by the state of schism within the Church of Constantinople. He thought that the patriarch was mostly to blame. The root cause was the oath excluding all but Venetians from the church of St Sophia. The pope demanded that the patriarch and canons publicly abjure that oath. If they failed to, the legate who had just been appointed would investigate his conduct of office.[16] Faced with the threat of humiliation the patriarch was forced to comply. He agreed to a meeting of all the clergy of Constantinople which gathered on 15 December 1208. There he publicly abjured the oath he had taken at Venice and along with him the canons of St Sophia. As proof of his sincerity he admitted to the chapter of St Sophia a canon from Piacenza. This done he defended himself from the other charges that had been brought against him.[17] Just as the state of schism was coming to an end, Morosini's relations with the Emperor Henry began to deteriorate. The latter complained to the pope that the patriarch had imposed his own nominees to prebends in the various churches of Constantinople, presentation to which rightly belonged to the emperor. It was a quarrel that remained unresolved when Thomas Morosini died at Thessalonica in June or July 1211.

Innocent III wrote to the chapter of St Sophia outlining the procedures to be followed for the election of a new patriarch. In order to counter Venetian influence the pope insisted that the heads of the conventual churches set up in Constantinople under Frankish auspices should participate in the election of a new patriarch.[18] It is little wonder that there ensued a disputed election, which was finally sent to Innocent III for resolution. He deposed both candidates, but then reinstated the French one, who happened to be a Venetian. The new patriarch, Gervasius (1215–19), was no more inspiring than Morosini and was overwhelmed by the same problems that had beset his predecessor. He was criticised by the papacy for his use of legates, as though he was guilty of usurping papal privileges. It was clear that Rome had no desire for the Latin patriarchs of Constantinople to develop any degree of independence. Innocent III ensured that appointment to the patriarchate of Constantinople remained in the hands of the papacy, so much so that the longest-serving Latin patriarch, Nicholas of Castro Arquato (1234–51), spent most of his time at the papal curia.[19]

What was at issue between the Venetian chapter of St Sophia and the Frankish clergy of Constantinople that produced such a bitter and debilitating struggle? At its most basic it was a matter of exploitation and control. The clergy, whether Venetian or Frankish, understood and treated the conquest as an opportunity for profit. Their possession of St Sophia gave the Venetians decided advantages. These were only underlined by the sheer exclusivity of their position. This would have come as a surprise to the Franks, but was in keeping with the Venetian view that the main function of the church was to serve the interests of the regime. The insistence by the Venetian authorities that the patriarch took an oath limiting membership of the chapter of St Sophia to Venetians was directly related to their fear that otherwise they would lose contol of the Patriarchal Church.[20] Looking at it from a strictly practical point of view, it would have struck the Franks that the subordination of the Patriarchal Church to Venetian political interests was, at the least, inappropriate and likely to be detrimental to the Latin Empire. They therefore sought to circumvent the authority of the patriarch by turning to the papacy and by seeking the intervention of the Latin emperor.

The effect of the struggle between the Venetian chapter of St Sophia and the Frankish clergy of Constantinople was to impede the orderly establishment of a Latin Church. The patriarch found himself caught in the middle and unable to act decisively. His scope for initiative was further limited by the presence of papal legates. Virtually all decisions were in the end referred to the pope. The result was that the Latin patriarchate was never an effective organisation. It was not capable of providing the moral and spiritual support that the Latin Empire required. Even in Constantinople the Latins never had an impressive ecclesiastical presence. They quickly took over some of the most important of the Byzantine shrines, such as the church of the Blachernai, the Holy Apostles, the Chalkoprateia and St George of the Mangana.[21] Secular canons were appointed in each. These were not the only churches occupied by the Latins, but the remainder are hard to identify because the Latin presence only generated stray references in the sources – almost always from the period immediately after the conquest – but no continuous history. The straitened circumstances of the Latin clergy are revealed by a plan to dismantle the churches of the Blachernai and of the Archangel Michael at Anaplous, as well as the monastery of Rouphinianai near Chalcedon, and use the materials to alleviate their poverty. To prevent this happening the Nicaean Emperor John Vatatzes bought them up. He also paid for repairs to the church of the Holy Apostles which suffered earthquake damage.[22]

If it can safely be said that Morosini saw no further than the prerogatives and profits of his office, this was not true of Innocent III, who had a very clear idea of the shape that the Latin Church should take. His idealism was, however, undermined by its failure to establish an effective and appropriate presence. The disreputable reality of the Latin Church – personified in the shape of the patriarch – did not incline Greeks to accept the new order. It dashed papal hopes of the establishment of an episcopal hierarchy, which combined both Greek and Latin. From the outset Innocent III appears to have envisaged a solution similar to that arrived at in southern Italy, where there was a single hierarchy which included both Latin and Orthodox bishops. In the end, the history of the Latin Church of Constantinople owed far more to Morosini's avarice than to Innocent III's idealism. The results were depressing; the Latin Church came to have no purpose other than serving the relatively few westerners established in the territories of the Latin Empire.[23]

This was in distinct contrast to the joy with which Innocent III received the news that Constantinople had been conquered by the soldiers of the Fourth Crusade. By an act of God – or so it seemed – the Church of Constantinople had returned in obedience to its mother, Rome. Innocent III understood that, if God had provided the opportunity, it would take tact and forbearance on his part to reconcile the Greeks to the ultimate authority of Rome. He was angered by the brutality of the crusaders' sack of Constantinople, but mostly because it gave the Greeks reason not to return in obedience to the Apostolic See. Innocent had hoped to make this as painless as possible.[24] But he never wavered in his belief that the fall of Constantinople was an act of God designed to repair 'the seamless garment of Jesus Christ'. Whatever the Greeks might have suffered, their refusal to recognise this only underlined their obtuseness. They had to be shown the light.

II

At first, Innocent III had high hopes that the Greeks could be won over by the evident superiority of the Latin faith. He turned to France for help. In 1205 he wrote to the archbishops of France asking for help in planting the Catholic faith in the newly-conquered territories.[25] He also approached the masters of the schools of Paris, hoping that they would despatch teachers to Constantinople who could instruct in the Christian faith.[26] Neither of these initiatives had any obvious success, though the Latin archbishop and chapter of Athens sought to model the organisation of their church on that of the Church of Paris.[27] Berard, the first Latin archbishop of Athens, was the chaplain of Otto de la Roche, the lord of Athens and Thebes. He was therefore presumably a Burgundian, like Antelm, the first Latin archbishop of Patras, who had been a monk at Cluny.[28]

There is much more information about the Latin Church in the Peloponnese and the Greek mainland around Athens and Thebes than there is about the Latin Church in other provinces of the Latin Empire.[29] The reason is obvious: in the Greek lands the Latin Church was a partial success, in the sense that it endured – it is true with little distinction – for many generations. This was some reward for the great efforts made by Innocent III. But it also raises a fundamental problem: why should the Latin Church have proved so durable in this region and so ephemeral in other parts of the Latin Empire? It was not as though the behaviour of the Latin clergy was any better in the Greek lands than elsewhere. If anything it was more scandalous. There was a surprisingly high quotient of violence. The Hospitallers seized the fortress of Gardiki, along with other property, from the Latin bishop, reducing him to poverty and forcing him to beg on the streets. When he protested the Hospitallers threatened to kill him.[30] The Templars were equally guilty of encroaching on episcopal rights and properties. But the military orders did not have a monopoly of violence. If they had, then it could easily be discounted, since clashes between the military orders and local bishops were common throughout Latin Christendom. Violence seems to have been endemic in the Greek lands in the aftermath of the Frankish conquest. The dean and chapter of Thebes engaged in a vendetta with a suffragan bishop who, they alleged, had burnt their crops. They responded by organising a posse under the castellan of Thebes, which broke into the bishop's residence and hauled off to jail the one man who had tried to defend the bishop.[31]

This kind of incident recurs over and over again in Innocent III's register. It will be sufficient to look at the travails of Archbishop Antelm of Patras, in order to understand the difficulties that confronted the Latin episcopate in Greece. Antelm, in the same way as other Latin bishops in Greece, had his problems with the Templars, though it is not clear that right was entirely on his side. He was, for example, prepared to disregard the adverse decision of the bishops commissioned by the pope to investigate the matter.[32] His struggle with his chapter was more unusual. As with all other Latin bishoprics established in Greece, his chapter was initially made up of secular canons. However, they abandoned the cathedral because it was situated outside the city of Patras and was exposed to pirate attacks.[33] Antelm therefore decided to replace them with Augustinian canons from the abbey of St Ruff near Valence.[34] The secular canons reacted by driving out the new arrivals by force.[35] An earlier incident reveals the lack of respect for the archbishop. Traditionally, the archbishops of Patras had their residence in the akropolis in the church of St Theodore, but this was commandeered to help strengthen the fortifications.[36] In the process a knight and several companions broke into the archbishop's residence, cut off the nose of his bailiff who tried to defend him, and then held the archbishop prisoner for five days.[37]

It was not as though the Latin churches in Greece were richer than their counterparts elsewhere in the Latin Empire. Poverty was a problem everywhere. It was inherited from the Greek Church. Its bishoprics were notoriously more poverty-stricken than those of western Christendom. Part of the problem was Innocent III's initial insistence on preserving the existing diocesan organisation, which meant that he condemned most of the Latin hierarchy to poverty, but he quickly reversed this policy and agreed to the amalgamation of sees.[38] A case in point was the see of Domoko in Thessaly, where the pope agreed to amalgamation with a neighbouring see as a way to solve its financial problems. It seems to have made no difference because Walon of Dampierre, the next Latin bishop of Domoko, was so appalled at the state of his church that he abandoned it three days after consecration, leaving its lands in the hands of the most powerful local lord. As a result the see could scarcely support three members of the clergy.[39] When the Latin bishop of Lamia – quite illegally – turned the cathedral of a neighbouring see into a grange,[40] he was only presuming on similar measures already taken by Innocent III. Honorius III proceeded in 1222 to give his approval to a series of mergers of the sees of the Latin Church of Constantinople as the only practical solution to its diocesan organisation. This was an admission that there was no need for any highly developed diocesan organisation, whether in the Greek lands or in other parts of the Latin Empire.

There seems no reason to suppose that the standard of the Latin clergy was any higher in Greece than elsewhere. The archbishop of Athens complained to Innocent III about the absenteeism rife among his cathedral chapter.[41] Much the same was happening elsewhere in Greece.[42] Innocent III was especially worried about the Latin priests appearing in the Peloponnese without the necessary credentials. The fear was that the new conquests would attract the wrong kind of clergy – imposters and defrocked priests – looking for a quick profit, which is exactly what happened.[43]

Innocent III realised that it would be easy to alienate the local Greek population, which is why he counselled tolerance. The Latin archbishop of Patras consulted him as to what steps he should take to effect a reconciliation with the Greek bishops of his province who had abandoned their sees. The pope advised that the latter should be invited not once, not twice, but three times to return to their sees. If they persisted in their contumacy then others should be appointed in their place, but compassion required that they were not defrocked.[44] The pope was prepared to be flexible, but the same could not be said of the Latin hierarchy in Greece. Theodore, bishop of Euripos on the island of Euboea, made his submission to the papal legate, Benedict of Santa Susanna, and despite being a Greek was confirmed in office. His superior, the Latin archbishop of Athens, refused to accept that his submission had been genuine. Trusting in his own authority he dismissed Theodore from office and appointed another in his place. Only the intervention of Innocent himself saved Theodore.[45] The pope also took under his protection the Greek clergy of the island of Euboea, known to the Latins as Negroponte.[46] Theodore was not the only Greek bishop to make his submission to Rome. John of Rhaidestos is another example.[47] The archbishop of Neopatras is almost certainly another. But he was elected by the Latin chapter, who then accused him of having originally been in the service of Leo Sgouros and of having killed a number of Latins.[48] We never learn the outcome of the case, but the archbishop did make his sworn submission to the Latin patriarch and was confirmed in office. The Greek bishop of Zakynthos also stayed on, but was to be investigated. Again we do not know what the outcome was.[49]

This brief catalogue provides a commentary on the failure of Innocent III's hopes to retain Greek bishops. His hopes had not been entirely illusory. Michael Choniates, the archbishop of Athens, went in good faith to Thessalonica in the summer of 1206 to negotiate with the papal legate, Benedict of Santa Susanna, but he found the terms demanded for his submission too stringent. He preferred to abandon his see and go into exile. There were other Greek bishops who were prepared to submit, but a combination of the strict conditions for submission and harassment by the Latin hierarchy dissuaded them. Innocent III's counsels of moderation fell on deaf ears. The Latin clergy in the conquered territories had a different agenda. Their moral and spiritual duty to put an end to schism counted for little beside the opportunities there were for gain, whence the violence that characterised the establishment of a Latin Church in the Greek lands. Though we hear mostly about the quarrels among the conquerors, the ordinary people must have suffered. Occasionally there was a reaction, as when a Frankish archdeacon was beaten up near Athens by local Greeks.[50] In other parts of the Latin Empire the Orthodox may have fared slightly better at the hands of the Latin hierarchy. At Thessalonica they found a champion in Margaret of Hungary, who ruled for her infant son Demetrius after the death of her husband Boniface of Montferrat in September 1207. She had, it must be remembered, previously been a Byzantine Empress, the consort of Isaac II Angelus. She was even accused of favouring Greek bishops at the expense of the archbishop of Larissa and his suffragans.[51] At Constantinople the Emperor Henry equally offered his protection and support to the Orthodox. In other words, the Latin Church was established in the Greek lands in much the same way as it was in the rest of the Latin Empire.

It differed in two respects that would be decisive. The first was luck: the Greek lands were not a target of the armies of Theodore Angelus in the way that Thessalonica was to become. This gave the Frankish rulers time to establish themselves. The second was the greater involvement of the papacy in the affairs of the Latin Church in Greece. Innocent III's initial inclination was to leave the organisation and running of the church in Greece to the Latin Patriarch Thomas Morosini. The earliest appointment to a Greek see was to the church of Patras in 1205. The Frankish prince of Achaea despatched Antelm, the elect of Patras, to Innocent III for ordination. As was right and proper, the pope considered that this would be an infringement of the prerogatives of the Latin patriarch and insisted that Antelm proceed to Constantinople for consecration.[52] Antelm later claimed that it had been too dangerous for him to make the journey to Constantinople. In any case, the new patriarch would not have been able to consecrate him for want of suitable colleagues. He had heard what had happened to the newly-elected archbishops of Athens and Thebes: they had been forced to travel to Syria in order to obtain consecration, because the patriarch was not yet in a position to officiate.

Antelm had therefore returned to Rome, where this time Innocent III consented to consecrate him.[53] Antelm would later use this to argue that his church was directly dependent on the Holy See, a claim which Innocent III refused to countenance, but which was later accepted by his successor Honorius III.[54]

These particulars underline two important facts about the establishment of the Latin Church in Greece. The first is that the patriarch was more or less powerless to act; the second is that the Latin settlers, rulers and clergy alike, preferred to take their business to Rome. Innocent III was forced to take responsibility. As a Latin hierarchy began to be established in the Greek lands, so the number of disputes referred to Innocent III increased, reaching a peak in 1210, but declining at the very end of his pontificate, when organising the Fourth Lateran Council monopolised his energies.[55] It would be unrealistic to expect the establishment of a Latin Church in new territories to have been a tidy operation. Much of the violence and chaos revealed by Innocent III's letters can be explained as teething troubles. They were inseparable from the business of conquest, though the level of violence still comes as a surprise, because other sources present the Frankish conquest of the Greek lands as a straightforward affair. The *Chronicle of the Morea*, for example, suggests that the Greeks quickly came to terms with the conquerors, who then proceeded to divide up the territories into fiefs, but in such a way that the rights of the Greek *archontes* were safeguarded. If that was the case, then church lands and rights will have become a tempting target for the greed of laity and clergy alike.

This was the background to the long-running quarrel between Antelm, archbishop of Patras, and Geoffrey of Villehardouin, the prince of Achaea. In 1210 the former went directly to Rome to protest at the way the latter treated the church in his territories. He had allowed the seizure of ecclesiastical property; he had kept sees vacant; he had distributed ecclesiastical benefices to clergy and laity alike; he had intruded excommunicates into cathedral chapters; he had forced members of the clergy to appear before secular courts. Perhaps still worse was his failure to keep his solemn promise that he would ensure that all, Franks and Greeks alike, would pay tithes to the church.[56] The pope delegated the matter to a commission of local bishops, which excommunicated Geoffrey of Villehardouin and placed his territories under an interdict. The archbishop of Patras wanted this sentence confirmed by the pope himself. Innocent III was not willing to do this, preferring to leave the matter for further investigation by a papal legate.[57] There matters rested until 21 January 1219, when at long last Pope Honorius III confirmed the sentence.[58] Hoist with his own petard, Antelm then found himself under investigation at Rome for breaking the interdict. The matter was, however, dropped, which prepared the way for the lifting of the interdict in 1223 and much better relations thereafter between Geoffrey of Villehardouin and the church. The *Chronicle of the Morea* provides the prince's side of the story. He claimed that he had only appropriated church lands for three years. He had used the revenues to pay for the construction of the fortress of Chlemoutsi at a time when the church had refused him help in a project that was vital to the security of his territories. The pope apparently sympathised with the prince's dilemma.[59] The prince was using the construction of a castle as a screen to patch up his relations with the church. Chlemoutsi was designed to protect the prince's capital at Andravida. Defence against the Greeks of Epiros was just a convenient excuse.

Antelm continued on in office for another twenty years. Controversy still dogged him. He was accused in 1238 of misappropriating the funds of his church to ease his retirement to France.[60] Antelm enjoyed a very long term of office. He lived to see the bones of a diocesan organisation in place. He had done enough to ensure the survival of his own church, which lasted until 1429. It helped that the Church of Patras took over the lordship of Patras with its twenty-four knights' fees, because it meant that the church was integrated into the feudal structure of the principality of Achaea.

This was part of the way that Geoffrey of Villehardouin was able to create new structures of government and society in the conquered lands, which included not just the chivalry of Achaea, but also the Latin Church hierarchy and local Greek leaders. As we have seen, the native population of the Peloponnese was quickly reconciled to Frankish rule. But a first reaction might be to ask how such a thing was possible. Surely the actions of the Latin Church would have alienated the Greeks? Not necessarily so, for their impact on the Greeks of the Peloponnese was tempered by a number of factors. In the first place, it was blunted by the way so many Orthodox bishops preferred refuge in Epiros or even Asia Minor rather than remaining with their flocks. This deprived the people of Greece and the Peloponnese of their spiritual leaders. This apparent passivity on the part of the Greek population does not fit with the notion that the successes of the Epirots and the Nicaeans were underpinned by a surge of Orthodox fervour produced by indignation at Latin atrocities. This fervour is not entirely imaginary, but it originated with the Byzantine elite. The Greeks of the Peloponnese, Boeotia, Attica and Euboea found themselves pretty much leaderless. The Frankish conquerors filled the vacuum. They offered local Greek society certain advantages. At their crudest, there were the chances for plundering ecclesiastical and monastic property, which Greeks took along with the conquerors. What seems most to have disturbed the Greeks about the establishment of the Latin Church was its demand for tithes. These were quite unknown to Orthodox practice. The Greeks turned for protection to their conquerors, who in many instances were just as reluctant to pay tithes to the Latin Church as the Greeks were. Of the complaints made to Innocent III by the Latin Church in Greece, one of the most frequent was about the way Frankish lords encouraged the Greeks to withhold the payment of tithes. But according to the archbishop of Patras there was another side to this. Frankish lords demanded labour services from Greek monks and priests and made sure that they did not show 'due obedience and reverence' to Latin prelates.[61] Reading between the lines it is easy to see that the interests of the conquerors were served by offering the Greeks protection against the direct interference of the Latin hierarchy. The problem of the Greek clergy was treated more or less in passing in the convention regulating the status of the Latin Church in Greece, which was reached at Ravenikka in May 1210 under the auspices of the Latin Emperor Henry. It was agreed that there should be no baronial interference in the inheritance of Greek priests and their families.

This convention was to provide the basis for the peace made between Geoffrey of Villehardouin and the papacy in 1223. It is striking how much space is now devoted to the exact status of the Greek clergy, which underlines the importance that the problem had assumed. The number of Greek clergy per village was precisely established according to the number of households a village had. These 'regular' priests had to pay the *akrostichon* to whoever was the lord of the village, but were otherwise exempt from dues and services. This left a mass of 'unbeneficed' rural priests who did not enjoy the same protection. It was laid down that 'their temporal lords . . . were not to allow [them] to celebrate the liturgy on their lands against the wish of the Latin clergy. [*Quod ipsorum domini temporales . . . nec permittent quod in terra contra Latinorum clericorum celebretur voluntatem.*]' This suggests that they were often encouraged by their Frankish lords to do exactly that. There was also a class of *papates* described as 'the Greek clergy of the cathedral churches'. They were to enjoy the same privileges as the 'regular' priests in the villages. But they were distinguished from other 'unbeneficed' Greek priests established in the towns.[62] It is therefore clear that under Frankish auspices a clerical elite had emerged among the Greeks of the Peloponnese: it consisted of the beneficed clergy in the villages and of the Orthodox clergy attached to the Latin bishoprics of the Peloponnese. One wonders whether they were organised under a *protopappas* as happened in Crete and Negroponte, where the Greek clergy was able to retain a degree of autonomy under Latin rule. There still remains the puzzle of how the Greek clergy was ordained. Leaving aside the distinct possibility that some may have accepted Latin ordination, the most likely solution is that they turned to the Orthodox bishop of Koroni. It is known that in the fourteenth century the Venetians tolerated the presence of Orthodox bishops at Methoni and Koroni, though the latter was forced to reside in a monastery at some distance from the town. They allowed these bishops to ordain Orthodox priests for the island of Crete.[63] About the year 1210 the Orthodox bishop of Koroni was the recipient of a fierce letter from John Apokaukos, the metropolitan bishop of Naupaktos, warning of the perils of cooperation with the Latins. There is a strong presumption that this bishop was engaged in ordaining Orthodox priests for Frankish-held territories in the early decades of the thirteenth century.[64] The absence of other Greek bishops worked to the advantage of the Orthodox clergy in the Frankish Peloponnese, giving them higher status and greater influence.

The principality of Achaea along with the Frankish lordships around Thebes and Athens show what might have been accomplished. Geoffrey of Villehardouin was allowed the time to create structures, which consolidated the initial conquest. At one level, his struggle with the Latin Church gave him the opportunity to work out a settlement with his Greek subjects, which safeguarded their rights and their faith. At another level, the Latin diocesan organisation was better developed than elsewhere in the Latin Empire, which can be explained in part by the closer supervision by the papacy of ecclesiastical affairs in Greece. There is, however, no disguising the refractory, divisive and downright mercenary character of the Latin Church in its initial stages. It opened up all kinds of divisions among the conquerors: between the Franks and the Venetians, between the emperor and the patriarch, between the patriarch and the papacy. It tilted the balance against the establishment of the Latin Empire on any long-term basis, but the possibilities were there. Outside the Greek lands the crusaders failed to grasp them.

III

One of the keys to Frankish success in the Peloponnese was the ability to come to terms with the native inhabitants in circumstances where outside forces – whether in the shape of the Latin Church or in the form of Orthodox revanchism – impinged less than they did in other parts of the Latin Empire. There was time enough to discover that local Greek society could flourish under Frankish rule. Signs of this were the continued foundation and construction under Frankish rule of Greek churches and monasteries. There is a series of churches in the Peloponnese in a late twelfth-century Byzantine style which show additional Latin features. The two best examples are the monastery of the Blachernai in Elis and the church of the Pantanassa at Geroumana. The former may have been converted to the Latin rite; the latter is unlikely to have been. The point is that the Frankish occupation did not break the continuity of ecclesiastical building. Of particular interest is the church of the Holy Trinity at Kranidion in the Argolid. It was founded in 1244–5 by a local Greek *archon* Manuel Mourmouras and his wife. It was always used to celebrate the Orthodox rite. It was decorated by a painter from Athens called John, who was also responsible around the same time for the decoration on an Orthodox church on the island of Euboea.[65] This example suggests that in some parts of the Peloponnese the Frankish occupation did not change very much where religious observance was concerned.

The same seems to be true of monastic life. Although there are occasional references to monasteries in the Peloponnese being transferred to Latin authority, most seemed to have remained in Orthodox hands. The refusal of the Greek abbots to show due obedience and reverence to the Latin archbishop of Corinth was exceptional and relates to the disturbed conditions that followed the end of the long-drawn-out siege of Corinth.[66] The Greek monasteries provided the Orthodox Church under Frankish rule with an alternative framework. Innocent III had realised the importance of monasticism to the Orthodox Church and set great store by winning over Greek monasteries. He professed real admiration for Greek monasticism: 'Because . . . of St John, who was the source of the religious life of perfect monks, the Greek Church well portrays the character of the Spirit, who seeks and loves spiritual men.'[67] He had a special affection for the monasteries of Athos, which he described as 'the house of the lord and in a sense heaven's gate'. Their welfare was entrusted to the bishop of Sebastea in the Holy Land, but he committed such 'enormities' – too heinous to specify – that in March 1209 he was removed from office.[68] This only made things worse, because a robber baron built a castle on Athos and began to plunder the monasteries. The Emperor Henry put a stop to his activities. In 1213 at the request of the abbots of the Holy Mountain, the *hegoumenos* of the Lavra at their head, Innocent III took the monasteries of Athos under the protection of the Holy See and confirmed all their privileges.[69] This presumably meant that they recovered their autonomy, but now under papal auspices. The Greek monks of Iveron would later complain about Latin oppression, but they were reacting to the ease with which their Georgian brethren accepted the Latin regime.[70] The monasteries of Athos may have suffered under Latin rule, but out of sheer respect Innocent III did what he could to protect them.

Innocent III handed over the responsibility for drawing Greek monasticism within the Catholic fold to the Cistercians. He had hopes that
their piety would be an instrument for reconciling the Greeks to the
new Latin dispensation.[71] The Cistercians were far and away the most
prominent monastic order in the Latin Empire of Constantinople, but
their presence was still not very impressive. There were two Cistercian
abbeys at Constantinople and one nunnery. The monastery of the
Theotokos Chortaiton, outside Thessalonica, was given to the Cistercians,
as was Daphni outside Athens. Daughter houses included, there were in
all perhaps twelve houses in the whole of the Latin Empire. In 1225 the
Chapter General of the Cistercians were asked to found a new abbey in
the Peloponnese. The result was the monastery established on the shores
of Lake Stymphalia known as Saracez. There was another new Cistercian
foundation in the Peloponnese at Isova which was destroyed by Byzantine
forces in 1263. The remoteness of its site suggests that it was specially
targeted.[72] The Cistercian involvement in the Latin Empire was a natural
outcome of the order's long-standing connection with the crusade.
Innocent III turned to the Cistercians for the preaching of the crusade.
He also turned to them when faced with the problem of the Albigensian
heresy in the south of France. They disappointed Innocent III's expectations in both areas. Neither in the south of France nor in the Latin
Empire were they able to make a decisive contribution. It was not just
that the great period of expansion was over. It was more that the
Cistercians were not suited to the tasks that Innocent III was imposing
on them. They were not a missionary order.

Despite Caesarius of Heisterbach's declaration that 'the vine of Cîteaux
has been planted in Greece' there was very little enthusiasm for new
plantations in the Latin Empire. The Cistercians had reluctantly allowed
themselves to be used to preach the Fourth Crusade. When the Chapter
General was originally approached by Fulk of Neuilly in 1198 they
turned down his request to provide preachers. They only acquiesced in
1201 because it was on the orders of Innocent III himself. By the turn
of the twelfth century the order was beginning to lose its original impetus,
but earlier successes meant that it was the obvious place to turn to when
Innocent III needed preachers and missionaries. The disarray within the
order is obvious from the differences of opinion among the Cistercians
who accompanied the crusade or, in the case of Adam of Perseigne,
failed to join up with the main body of crusaders at Venice, going
instead directly to Syria.[73] Three of the Cistercian abbots who had been
commissioned to preach the crusade left the crusader camp at Zara; only
Simon, abbot of Loos, and Peter, abbot of Lucedio, remained with the
crusade to Constantinople. Their decision was determined by the fact

that the former was in the entourage of Baldwin of Flanders, while the latter was in that of Boniface of Montferrat. Their secular ties counted for more than any common allegiance to their order. In turn, it reflected the fact that the Cistercians' thinking on the crusade had not evolved beyond the idea of the penitential pilgrimage espoused by St Bernard. It was quite insufficient to meet the problems thrown up by the rapid evolution of crusade theory in the early thirteenth century. The importance of secular ties for the Cistercians is equally reflected in the foundations that were made in the Latin Empire. Peter, abbot of Lucedio, was given the monastery of the Theotokos Chortaiton for his abbey by a grateful Boniface of Montferrat. Otto de la Roche, the lord of Thebes and Athens, gave Daphni to the Cistercian abbey of Bellevaux in his native Burgundy. These grants demonstrate that they were intended to serve as a means by which the conquerors could maintain links with home, rather than as a way of winning over the Orthodox. To judge by the example of the monastery of the Theotokos Chortaiton, the Cistercians did not find any means of relating to Greek monasticism. Innocent III's hope had been that they would prove an inspiration to Greek monks. Instead, like so many other churchmen, they saw acquisition of Greek monasteries as a chance for gain.

Byzantium boasted rich monasteries, not just in the capital but scattered through the provinces. These were the monasteries by and large that were taken over by westerners. If the monasteries of Chortaiton and of Daphni went to the Cistericians, Hosios Loukas was granted to the canons of the Holy Sepulchre at Jerusalem. There was, on the other hand, no general dispossession of Greek monasteries in favour of the conquerors, but they still suffered. The realities of the takeover of monastic property at the time of the Latin conquest appear most vividly in the correspondence of Michael Choniates, the exiled Orthodox archbishop of Athens. Brought to his attention was the fate of the monastery of St George in the Kerameikos. It had been closed, not because of pressure from the Franks, who respected its abbot, but because of the depredations of local people. The monasteries of Hosios Meletios and of the Holy Confessors were in equal danger and for the same reasons. The threat did not come from the laity alone. Michael Choniates took the abbot of Kaisariani to task for the way in which he had gobbled up property belonging to other monasteries. This state of affairs underlines the opportunities there were for the Latin monastic orders to give a lead in the turmoil that followed the fall of Constantinople, but they failed to make anything of them. Once again, it is worth emphasising what might have been by recalling the successes of the Dominicans and Franciscans in more difficult circumstances.[74]

Given the dynamism of the Western Church in the early thirteenth century its chequered showing in Romania requires an explanation. It can, for example, take little credit for the relative success in Greece, which was owed to the restraint and common sense of the prince of Achaea and his barons rather than to the actions of the Latin clergy. Essentially, the Latin Empire never acquired a purpose beyond conquest. Innocent III's optimism was misplaced and was based largely on the hope that it would provide increased support for the Holy Land. He was equally mistaken when he assumed that the creation of a Latin Empire had solved the problem of the schism with the Orthodox Church. To his way of thinking it only needed clear explanation for the Greeks to be convinced of the evident superiority of Latin Christianity. As it became plain that this was not the case, the pope's forbearance began to wear thin. Before 1204 Constantinople had been a place of pilgrimage renowned for its precious relics. In the aftermath of 1204 these were shipped back in increasing numbers to the West. This only underlined the mentality of conquest. Romania was a place where clergy could get rich quick. Innocent III was appalled at the standard of the clergy attracted to Romania. The truth was that at the start there were rich pickings in the way of booty, but these soon dried up. Clerics discovered that the bishoprics of the Orthodox Church were rarely well endowed. It meant that it was necessary to proceed even before Innocent III's death to a wholesale amalgamation of sees to provide a reasonable income for the incumbents. Even in the early years of the Latin Empire there are examples of western bishops returning home, exasperated by the poverty of their sees. Equally, those appointed to cathedral prebends often refused to serve in person.[75]

IV

There are many explanations for the failure of the Latin Church in Romania, but the major factor was the alienation – outside the Peloponnese – of the Greek population. It is in no way clear that this was the inevitable consequence of the conquest of Constantinople. In the provinces the initial reaction of the Greeks to their Latin conquerors was moderate, sometimes even welcoming. Greek provincials were happy that for the time being they were released from the yoke of Constantinople. They were not deeply shocked by the sack of the capital, which is what, in the opinion of many, its haughty denizens deserved. The sack of Constantinople in 1204 is now remembered as a crime against humanity. As we have argued earlier, the sack was not as brutal as it was later made out to be. It suited the papacy and other interested parties in the Latin West to dwell on its horrors. Byzantine writers would soon demonise it as a deliberate insult to Orthodoxy, but this was to counter the apparent willingness of the many to come to an understanding with their conquerors in the immediate aftermath of the fall of Constantinople. The citizens of Constantinople were chastened, but not yet alienated by the prospect of Latin rule. They had, in the recent past, shown scant respect for their natural leaders. They had little reason to regret the expulsion of the patriarch and members of the Byzantine elite from Constantinople. Leadership, such as it was, passed into the hands of those who remained behind: men like Nicholas Mesarites, a middle-ranking official of St Sophia. These were men disposed to compromise with the conquerors; they were interested above all in negotiating a settlement that preserved the essentials of Orthodoxy. This required freedom of worship and respect for the Orthodox rite and pious practices, but it inevitably involved the question of ecclesiastical organisation. The creation of a Latin patriarchate had implications that remained to be worked out. The Greeks were soon aware of the reservations that Innocent III had about the manner in which the Latin patriarchate had come into being and hoped that the pope would accept the continued existence of the Orthodox patriarchate. It was the failure to find such a compromise, far more than the sack of the city, that alienated the Greeks from Latin rule, because it made clear how little true respect the Latin church had for the essentials of Orthodoxy.

Here the incident of the Hodegetria icon is instructive.[76] Far from being a footnote it revealed the tensions that had already built up by the summer of 1206. The Hodegetria icon was an image of the Mother of God claimed to have been the work of St Luke. By the eleventh century it was kept in the monastery of the Hodegoi, which was situated on the seashore adjacent to the imperial palace. Every Tuesday it was paraded through the streets of Constantinople, attracting a great throng of men and women.[77] Its importance was underlined when the Emperor John II Comnenus obtained permission for the icon to be lodged in the imperial foundation of the Pantokrator, but only on those days when either he or his empress were commemorated. The Emperor Isaac II Angelus had it paraded around the walls of Constantinople in the hope of warding off an opponent. In 1200 Antony of Novgorod venerated the icon in the palace church of St Michael.[78] The custom of parading it through the streets of the capital still continued. It remained a focus of popular piety. The Novgorod chronicler – who may have been Antony – records that good men ensured that it survived the conquest of the city.[79] All we know is that along with other relics from the imperial palace it passed into the safe keeping of the Latin Emperor. It was then given by the

Emperor Henry to the Latin Patriarch Thomas Morosini on the occasion
of his coronation on 20 August 1206. The Greeks reacted to the news
that the icon was now deposited in St Sophia by immediately requesting
the revival of the old ceremonies surrounding the icon. The Latin patriarch
would allow this only on condition that he was remembered in their
prayers. The timing of this apparently innocuous demand was embarrassing for the Greeks because their patriarch, John X Kamateros, had only
just died. Remembering the Latin patriarch in their prayers amounted to
recognition of the latter's authority over the Orthodox Church. It was
too high a price for the Greeks to pay. Faced with this refusal on the
part of the Greeks the Latin patriarch banned the celebration of the
Eucharist in the Orthodox churches of Constantinople. Patriarchal agents
were sent to close them down. When they tried to break up the celebration
of the liturgy in the church of St Nicholas near St Sophia, they were
driven out by the infuriated congregation, but more significant was the
reaction of one of the patriarchal officers – certainly a Venetian. He protested that the patriarch's action was contrary to the spirit of Christianity
and encouraged the Greeks of the capital to resist.[80]

There was far more to this incident than a clash between the Latin
patriarch and the Greeks of Constantinople. Leaving aside for the moment
any papal interest in the matter there was a Venetian connection. The
Venetian *podestà* Marino Zeno claimed that the Emperor Henry had
already promised the icon to his community. He therefore proceeded
with the help of a Greek to burgle the sacristy of St Sophia from which
the icon was removed and transferred to the monastery of the Pantokrator,
which now lay at the centre of the Venetian quarter. There may be
something to a Greek claim that behind the theft of the icon was
the patriarch's refusal to share the proceeds from the icon with the
Venetian community.[81] But it was more than an opportunist attempt to
appropriate a local cult. It showed a willingness to assimilate Greek
habits of icon veneration which was serious enough to alarm Innocent
III.[82] There was a search for reconciliation with the Greeks which was
evident in the Venetian *podestà*'s mediation with the Latin patriarch on
behalf of the Greeks.

This resulted in a meeting between the patriarch and Greek representatives which took place on 30 August 1206. The point at issue was
whether the Greeks should recognise the Latin patriarch's authority, now
that the Orthodox patriarch was dead. They were unwilling to do so, in
the first instance because the Latin patriarch did not speak or understand
their language and therefore was unable to carry out his duties, most
obviously so when it came to hearing confessions. The patriarch was
forced to half concede that this created a problem. Discussion then

passed to the question of differences of dogma and finally to the nature of the authority that Rome had inherited from St Peter. The disputation ended inconclusively with the Latin patriarch insisting that before he could go any further he must consult his books.[83] This was a diplomatic way of indicating that he needed to take counsel with the papal legate Benedict of Santa Susanna, for the most telling charge made by the Greeks was: 'Who has appointed you teacher and ruler over us?'[84] The patriarch could hardly use an act of violence to justify the creation of a Latin patriarchate of Constantinople. He had to resort to papal authority to defend his legitimacy.

Benedict of Santa Susanna had been conducting negotiations over the union of churches since the spring of 1206. The details of his mission to the Orthodox Church are set out in a report by an important member of his entourage, his interpreter Nektarios, who came from the Greek monastery of Casole in southern Italy. Such a choice can only have been designed to show the more tolerant face of Latin Christianity. Nektarios was proof that Orthodox monasticism could flourish under a Latin regime.[85] This may help to explain why Benedict was anxious to negotiate at Constantinople with monastic leaders. There was a meeting on 29 September 1206, from which it emerged that what the Greeks now wanted was the right to elect their own patriarch. For this they had the backing of the Emperor Henry. A letter to this effect was drafted by John Mesarites. It asked that the pope give his assent to the election of a new Orthodox patriarch under the supervision of the Emperor Henry. It was further suggested that once this had been done the next step should be a church council at Constantinople which could resolve the differences between the two churches. The letter ended with the assertion that Christ was the one head of the church: unobjectionable in itself, but so phrased to alert anybody to the reservations that a good Orthodox had about extreme claims for papal primacy.[86] This letter is of the greatest importance. It shows that the Emperor Henry was favourably disposed to the election of an Orthodox patriarch. It also meant that the pope was directly involved in the question. It was the critical moment, but what happened next is far from clear.

The whole question is made far more difficult by the existence of another letter from the Greeks of Constantinople to Pope Innocent III. It is quite impossible to determine with any certainty when it was drafted.[87] It was a rather different document from the one drawn up by John Mesarites. The Greek is in a more popular register. It is more conciliatory. The theme was the imminence of union. But the union of churches could not be forced. A general council was needed to debate the issues that continued to separate the two churches. The Greeks would go wherever the pope thought best suited, but they urged the advantages of Constantinople. Before this could take place they needed their own patriarch. They noted the precedent set by both the churches of Jerusalem and Antioch where there were a Latin and an Orthodox patriarch. The letter concludes with the instructions that they have received from the Emperor Henry to give the pope due honour and to acclaim him. This would be a token not just of the obedience of the Greeks, but of that of all those many peoples who followed the Orthodox rite. One of the leitmotifs of the letter is the loyalty of the Greeks to the Emperor Henry. There can be little doubt that this letter to Innocent III was drawn up with the emperor's express approval.[88]

But were either of these letters ever sent to the pope? There is no direct acknowledgement of any such letter by Innocent III, which is not in itself surprising, since the pope would not have recognised the Greeks of Constantinople as a properly constituted community. However, he did take the problems of the Latin Church seriously. There is almost nothing in the many letters he sent dealing with the problems of the Latin Church in the years 1207 and 1208 to indicate that the election of an Orthodox patriarch was being considered. The one possible exception is a papal letter dated 7 March 1208, reprimanding the Emperor Henry for the support he had given to the Greeks. The pope reminded the emperor of his responsibility for the proper implementation of the interdict which the patriarch had imposed on the Greeks.[89] A few days later Innocent III wrote a long letter to the Greek ruler of Nicaea, Theodore Laskaris. Again it contains nothing to suggest that the election of an Orthodox patriarch was in the air.[90] The conclusion has to be that the Greeks were not allowed to forward their request to the pope. There were reasons why Henry may have thought better of the project. They were connected with events in Antioch, on which he had the latest information.[91] In 1206 Bohemund IV, prince of Antioch, deposed the Latin patriarch of the city and imposed the Orthodox patriarch. This produced a civil war, which was only ended when, under pressure from Innocent III, the prince of Antioch accepted a new Latin patriarch. The pope made it abundantly clear what he thought of Latin princes who intruded an Orthodox patriarch.[92] The chastened tone of the letter in which Henry announced to the pope his great victory over the Bulgarians at Philippopolis on 1 August 1208 suggests that he had no intention of forfeiting papal favour.[93]

The emperor's encouragement of, but ultimate failure to support, his Greek subjects' desire for their own patriarchate can be seen as playing a decisive part in their progressive alienation. The Greeks looked to him as a protector of their interests. They also regarded the pope as sufficiently sympathetic to their cause to counterbalance the excesses of the patriarch and the Latin clergy. The aftermath of the negotiations of September 1206 will have punctured any such illusions. Henry understood the importance of the support of his Greek subjects, but was unwilling at this stage to take any action that might deprive him of papal favour. Innocent III, for his part, had made up his mind about Orthodoxy. He was under the impression that the Greeks had accepted union on Latin terms. As it became clear that this was not the case, his attitude towards the Greeks hardened. He abandoned his conciliatory stance towards the Orthodox Church. His letter to the Latin patriarch of 7 December 1210 is full of foreboding. He foresees the possibility that the Greeks might recover Constantinople, in which case he would launch a crusade against them. He includes horror stories of Michael Doukas crucifying the constable of Thessalonica and decapitating Latin priests, and of Theodore Laskaris having a distinguished Latin flayed alive. These details were designed to emphasise Greek contumacy. In the pope's opinion, any success on the part of these resistance leaders would only strengthen the Greeks 'in their vice of apostasy'.[94] He may have been thinking of Theodore Laskaris's role in the election of a new Orthodox patriarch in exile at Nicaea. He would certainly have been in possession of the details by the end of 1210, even if he chose to ignore them. His concern is evident in his decision in August 1213 to appoint a new papal legate to Constantinople with special responsibility for the union of churches.[95] Such an appointment had become still more urgent because of the death of the Latin patriarch Thomas Morosini in 1211 and the subsequent vacancy.

The new legate was Pelagius, cardinal bishop of Albano.[96] He arrived in Constantinople towards the end of 1213. Initially, it was the affairs of the Latin patriarchate which took up his time. His attention then turned to the Orthodox Church. As a first step on the path of reform he demanded recognition of papal supremacy from the people of Constantinople. Those who refused were thrown in prison and the churches were closed. He resorted to persecution to enforce union on Latin terms. The Greeks of Constantinople turned for help to the Emperor Henry. On his own authority he reopened the churches and freed those who had been imprisoned.[97] This won him the gratitude of the Greeks and he was long remembered as a ruler who had the interests of his Greek subjects at heart. Henry's actions were not entirely altruistic: the creation of a Byzantine Empire in exile at Nicaea meant that he had to vie with Theodore Laskaris for the loyalty of the Greeks of the capital.

Monks from Constantinople and the surrounding region had gone to the latter in the hope of finding protection against the persecution unleashed by Pelagius. Laskaris was in a difficult situation. He had been badly beaten by the Latin armies in the previous year and had lost the north-western corner of Asia Minor – the Troad – to the Latins, along with the Marmara coastlands. Nikomedeia was in Latin hands, leaving Nicaea and Prousa dangerously exposed. Laskaris was trying to make peace with Henry, so that he could exploit David Comnenus's death in December 1212 to seize his Paphlagonian territories. These would be some compensation for the lands lost to the Latins. On top of this there was a vacancy following the death of Michael Autoreianos, the Orthodox patriarch, on 13 November 1213.[98] A new patriarch, Theodore Eirenikos, was not elected until 28 September 1214. It seems to have been Pelagius who recognised the possibilities of the situation. He sent emissaries to Theodore Laskaris, who responded by despatching a delegation to negotiate with the papal legate. Nicholas Mesarites, now bishop of Ephesus, was one of its members, but is reluctant to give any hard details of the negotiations. He seeks rather to put himself in a good light by making much of his protest against Pelagius's persecution of Orthodox monks. Pelagius informed him that only the intervention of Theodore Laskaris had prevented him from proceeding to a much more severe persecution. He assured Mesarites that, if he was able to turn Theodore Laskaris 'into a true son of Rome', then not only would the monks be free to go about their business but the Orthodox churches would be reopened. In other words, Pelagius thought that there was still a point in continuing negotiations with Laskaris. Mesarites returned in late November with the papal envoys and together they made their way to Pontic Heraclea, where Theodore Laskaris was encamped. There a debate took place between Nicholas Mesarites and the papal envoys over the question of Roman primacy and the procession of the Holy Spirit. In the interests of good relations the two sides agreed to differ. The papal envoys returned to Constantinople well rewarded by Theodore Laskaris, while Nicholas Mesarites made his way to Nicaea, where he had to face the anger of the new patriarch, Theodore Eirenikos. The patriarch had not been a party to the negotiations. He felt that he was being disparaged. He took Mesarites to task for allowing Pelagius to refer to him as the 'Archbishop of the Greeks', which called in question his patriarchal status.[99]

Theodore Eirenikos clearly disapproved of the emperor's willingness to reach an accommodation with the Latins. Instead of intervening with Pelagius on behalf of the Orthodox of Constantinople, in the manner of the emperor, he despatched an encyclical to them, urging them to remain strong in the faith in the face of Latin persecution. He was not willing to make any compromises with the Latins. This was the start of a period of bad relations between the emperor and the patriarchate over rapprochement with the Latins of Constantinople. It culminated in Theodore Laskaris's decision to take as his third wife the sister of the Latin Emperor Robert of Courtenay. To make matters still worse he tried to arrange a marriage between one of his daughters and the Latin emperor. To quell opposition from the church Theodore Laskaris imposed his confessor as patriarch in succession to Theodore Eirenikos. The reign lasted no more than six months, but in that time the new patriarch had caused trouble between the emperor and the people of Nicaea. To cap it all, Laskaris proposed to hold a council of the Orthodox Church to approve a reunion of churches. This provoked bitter opposition from Orthodox bishops in Epiros, notably John Apokaukos, bishop of Naupaktos.[100]

This was the last chapter in the efforts made since the fall of Constantinople to find common ground between the two churches. There were those on the Orthodox side who were willing within reason to accept the Latin conditions. They became fewer and fewer once the Orthodox patriarchate was re-established in exile at Nicaea in March 1208. This produced a hardening of attitudes towards the Latins, which had not previously been so pronounced. It was matched by a similar trend on the Latin side. This was all too evident when Innocent III came to consider the problem of the Greek Church at the Fourth Lateran Council. The tone is defensive. The Apostolic See had done its best to honour and empathise with the Greek Church and had gone out of its way to tolerate its rites and customs, but this forbearance had not been enough to eradicate the ancient hatred that the Greeks had for the Latins. They still refused to allow Latin priests to celebrate at their altars and still insisted on the rebaptism of those who had been baptised into the Latin Church. Those who continued in their contumacy were to be excommunicated and deprived of ecclesiastical office.[101] It was more or less an admission that the union of churches was a sham.

Innocent III had already spent ten years trying to find ways of implementing the union of the churches. He did not want union to be forced. He showed his forbearance and goodwill by taking Greek prelates and ecclesiastical institutions under his protection.[102] He had a high regard for Byzantine monasticism. He expected Greek bishops to remain in office, admittedly having first recognised the authority of Rome, but to make this step easier he was willing to waive consecration in the Latin manner.[103] The impulse for discussions on church union came from the pope. The voluntary submission of the Greek Church always figured at the head of his instructions to the legates he sent one after the other to Constantinople. All to no avail. Innocent III had little control over the realities of the establishment of the Latin Church, which increasingly served to alienate the Greek population. He himself began to doubt the good faith of the Greeks. He invited Basil Pediadites, the Orthodox metropolitan bishop of Corfu, to attend the Fourth Lateran Council. Pediadites had already revealed his views on papal primacy to the prelates of the Fourth Crusade during their brief stay at Corfu in May 1203, when he invited them to lunch. He suggested partly in jest that the only reason he could adduce for Roman claims to primacy was that Christ had been crucified by Roman soldiers.[104] It is therefore no surprise that he turned down Innocent III's invitation to participate in the forth-coming council, but he did it in a way that revealed only too clearly the differences that existed between the two churches. He began with the specious argument that a vacancy of the Orthodox patriarchate of Con-stantinople made it impossible for him to attend, but it allowed him to set out Orthodox conciliar theory, which emphasised that a general council was organised as a pentarchy of patriarchates. This contradicted the monarchical views of the papacy. Pediadites then raised the sore issue of Orthodox prelates, such as those of Athens, Thessalonica, Ohrid and Patras, who had been driven from their sees by the Latins. He was highlighting the way the establishment of the Latin Church in Romania had only intensified the schism between the two churches.[105]

The Fourth Lateran Council was a turning point. Its provisions reflected a closing of minds; they left little room for the voluntary submission of the Greek Church. Innocent III assumed that the Greek Church had been reunited with Rome by an act of God. In any case, the matter was of little relevance beside the recovery of Jerusalem, which became Innocent III's main concern at the end of his pontificate. It was not quite that he had washed his hands of the Greek Church, but no longer would the initiative for the union of churches come from the papacy. Instead, it was left to the various Greek rulers to make their approaches to Rome.[106]

The crusader conquest of Constantinople intensified the hatred existing between Byzantium and the Latin West, but the example of the Frankish Peloponnese shows that this was not the foregone conclusion that it is normally assumed to have been. For a number of years there was a distinct possibility that the Greeks might accept a settlement with the Latin Church. In the short term the sack of Constantinople did not make that much of an impact. It was not the utterly barbarous act that it is often made out to be. What alienated the Greeks far more was the manner in which the Latin Church was implanted. It showed a lack of tolerance for Orthodoxy. Here despite his apparently good intentions Innocent III was at fault. He may have given a degree of protection to Greek monasteries, but he was peculiarly blind to the needs of the Orthodox hierarchy. While he showed some leniency towards Greek bishops already in office, he was adamant that any new bishops must be consecrated according to Latin custom.[107] He was determined that the Greeks should accept a Latin patriarch. He was, in the end, more interested in absorbing the Orthodox Church within a Latin framework than in allowing it a proper degree of autonomy. He was convinced that the Greeks would learn the advantages of the Latin faith and acknowledge its manifest superiority. When they failed to do so, the pope's patience began to wear thin.

Sir Steven Runciman has argued that the conquest of Constantinople produced a clarification of the relations between the two churches, whereby potential schism became an enduring reality. He insists that the schism was not a matter of precedence or authority: 'It went deeper: it was based on mutual dislike between the peoples of Eastern and Western Christendom.'[108] The events of 1204 may well have created that state of enforced proximity of the two churches which intensified mutual prejudices. The Latins believed that the conquest vindicated their position, while the Greeks came to see it as an insult to Orthodoxy. This did not prevent sincere efforts being made on both sides to resolve their differences, but they foundered on the intransigence of papal legates and the cupidity of the Latin clergy.

Notes

1. Cited by Thiriet, *Romanie vénitienne*, 144: '*Et ponamus quod haberemus terram imperii pro magna parte, non tamen haberemus cor populi ad obedietiam ecclesiae romanae*'.
2. The fundamental studies are: R. L. Wolff, 'The Organization of the Latin Patriarchate of Constantinople, 1204–61', *Traditio*, 6(1948), 33–60; Wolff, 'Politics in the Latin Patriarchate', 228–303; J. Richard, 'The Establishment of the Latin Church in the Empire of Constantinople (1204–1227)', in *Latins and Greeks in the Eastern Mediterranean after 1204*, 45–62; Santifaller, *Beiträge*; Fedalto, *Chiesa latina*, I.
3. Tafel and Thomas I, 447, 451.
4. Lane, *Venice*, 88, 98.
5. *Reg.* VII, cliv: Migne *PL* 215, 456; ed. Haluscynski, no. 65, 277–8; Andrea, *Contemporary Sources*, 116.
6. R. L. Wolff, 'The Latin Empire of Constantinople and the Franciscans', *Traditio*, 2(1944), 213–37.
7. Andrea, *Contemporary Sources*, 223–5.
8. Nicetas Choniates, 623.74–9, 647.5–18.
9. *Reg.* VII, clxiv: Migne *PL* 215, 471–2; ed. Haluscynski, no. 66, 283–4; Tafel and Thomas I, 519–20.
10. Andrea, *Contemporary Sources*, 150–1.
11. Ibid., 138–9.

12. *Gesta Innocentii III*, §xcviii, c.CXLIII.
13. Tafel and Thomas I, 547–53; II, 105–6; Fedalto, *Chiesa latina*, 183–91; Santifaller, *Beiträge*, 118–21.
14. *Gesta Innocentii III*, §xcix, c.CXLIII–CXLIV; *Reg.* XI, lxxvi: Migne *PL* 215, 1388; *Devastatio*, 137.
15. Tafel and Thomas II, 61–2, 75–6.
16. *Reg.* XI, lxxvi: Migne *PL* 215, 1387–92.
17. Tafel and Thomas II, ccix, 101–9; *Reg.* XII, cv: Migne *PL* 216, 118–24.
18. Tafel and Thomas II, ccxxviii, 127–8; *Reg.* XIV, xcvii: Migne *PL* 216, 459–60.
19. Santifaller, *Beiträge*, 17–45.
20. Tafel and Thomas II, 105.
21. R. Janin, 'Les sanctuaires de Byzance sous la domination latine (1204–1261)', *Etudes byzantines*, 2(1944), 134–84.
22. Acropolites I, 287.20–8.
23. *Reg.* XIII, xvi: Migne *PL* 216, 216; ed. Haluscynski, no. 140, 377.
24. *Reg.* VIII, cxxxiii: Migne *PL* 215, 712; ed. Haluscynski, no. 87, 312; Andrea, *Contemporary Sources*, 173.
25. *Reg.* VIII, lxx: Migne *PL* 215, 636–7; ed. Haluscynski, no. 81, 303–4.
26. *Reg.* VIII, lxxi: Migne *PL* 215, 637–8.
27. *Reg.* XI, cxiii: Migne *PL* 215, 1433.
28. Fedalto, *Chiesa latina*, 250.
29. See J. Longnon, 'L'organisation de l'Eglise d'Athènes par Innocent III', in *Mémorial Louis Petit* (Bucarest, 1948), 336–46; Fedalto, *Chiesa latina*, 232–73; P. Lock, 'The Latin Secular Church in Mainland Greece, 1204–1220', *Medieval History*, 1(1991), 93–105.
30. *Reg.* XIII, ci: Migne *PL* 216, 297–8; ed. Haluscynski, no. 154, 387; *Reg.* XIII, cxvii: Migne *PL* 216, 304; ed. Haluscynski, no. 161, 392; *Reg.* XIII, cxx: Migne *PL* 216, 307–8.
31. *Reg.* XV, xxx: Migne *PL* 216, 565–6.
32. *Reg.* XIII, clv–clvi: Migne *PL* 216, 331–2.
33. *Reg.* XIII, clxix: Migne *PL* 216, 342.
34. *Reg.* XIII, clix–clx: Migne *PL* 216, 336–8. For St Ruff, *Reg.* IX, lxvii: Migne *PL* 215, 885–8.
35. *Reg.* XV, xxxi: Migne *PL* 216, 559–60.
36. *Reg.* XIII, clxiv: Migne *PL* 216, 340; ed. Haluscynski, no. 170, 400.
37. *Reg.* XIII, clxxi: Migne *PL* 216, 343; ed. Haluscynski, no. 172, 401–2.
38. *Reg.* XI, cxiv–cxv: Migne *PL* 215, 1433–4.
39. *Reg.* XIII, civ: Migne *PL* 216, 299–300. See Longnon, *Compagnons*, 219.
40. *Reg.* XVI, xcvii: Migne *PL* 216, 897.
41. *Reg.* XI, ccxlvi: Migne *PL* 215, 1551; ed. Haluscynski, no. 124, 356.
42. *Reg.* X, l: Migne *PL* 215, 1142.
43. *Reg.* X, li: Migne *PL* 215, 1143; ed. Haluscynski, no. 100, 328–9.
44. *Reg.* X, li: Migne *PL* 215, 1142; ed. Haluscynski, no. 100, 328–9.
45. *Reg.* XI, clxxix: Migne *PL* 215, 1492–3; ed. Haluscynski, no. 122, 353–4.
46. *Reg.* IX, cxciii: Migne *PL* 215, 1030.
47. *Reg.* XV, cxxxiv–cxxxv: Migne *PL* 216, 647; ed. Haluscynski, nos 198–9, 432–3.

48. *Reg.* XIV, xcviii: Migne *PL* 216, 460–1; ed. Haluscynski, no. 177, 407–8.
49. *Reg.* X, cxxviii: Migne *PL* 215, 1235. Benedict of Cephalonia was not a Greek.
50. *Reg.* XV, xxvii: Migne *PL* 216, 564; ed. Haluscynski, no. 186, 419.
51. *Reg.* XI, clii: Migne *PL* 215, 1167.
52. *Reg.* VIII, cliii: Migne *PL* 215, 727–9; ed. Haluscynski, no. 86, 310–11.
53. *Reg.* X, lvi: Migne *PL* 215, 1151–2; ed. Haluscynski, no. 101, 329–30.
54. *Reg.* XII, cxliii: Migne *PL* 216, 163; ed. Haluscynski, no. 136, 373; Santifaller, *Beiträge*, 196, no. 63.
55. In 1206 only three papal letters addressed the problems of the Latin Church in Greece; in 1207 it was five; in 1208 it jumped to thirty-two; in 1209 there were only two; in 1210 there were seventy; in 1211 only four; in 1212 forty-two; in 1213 five.
56. *Reg.* XIII, clxi: Migne *PL* 216, 338–9; ed. Haluscynski, no. 171, 400–1.
57. *Reg.* XVI, xcviii: Migne *PL* 216, 898–9; ed. Haluscynski, no. 209, 448–9.
58. Fedalto, *Chiesa latina*, 262.
59. Chronicle of the Morea, ll.2650–720.
60. Fedalto, *Chiesa latina*, 266–7.
61. *Reg.* XIII, clxxii: Migne *PL* 216, 343; ed. Haluscynski, no. 172, 401–2.
62. Migne *PL* 216, 968–72.
63. D. A. Zakythinos, *Le despotat grec de Morée*, II (Athens, 1953), 275–6.
64. Angold, *Church and Society*, 531.
65. S. Kalopissi-Verti, *Die Kirche der Hagia Triada bei Kranidi in der Argolis (1244)* (Munich, 1975); D. Feissel and A. Philippidis-Brat, 'Inscriptions du Peloponnèse', *Travaux et Mémoires*, 9(1985), no. 54, 311.
66. *Reg.* XV, liii: Migne *PL* 216, 582; ed. Haluscynski, no. 189, 421.
67. *Reg.* VII, cliv: Migne *PL* 215, 458D.
68. *Reg.* IX, cxcii: Migne *PL* 215, 1030; ed. Haluscynski, no. 95, 323; *Reg.* XIII, xl: Migne *PL* 216, 229; ed. Haluscynski, no. 147, 381–2.
69. *Reg.* XVI, clxviii: Migne *PL* 216, 956–8; ed. Haluscynski, no. 214, 454–5. See Prinzing, 'Papsttum', 178–80.
70. Demetrius Chomatianus, in J. B. Pitra, *Analecta sacra et classica spicelegio Solesmensi Parata*, VII (VI) (Rome, 1891, repr. Farnborough, 1967), no. 54, 245–50.
71. *Reg.* XV, lxx: Migne *PL* 216, 594–5; ed. Haluscynski, no. 195, 429–30.
72. E. A. R. Brown, 'The Cistercians in the Latin Empire of Constantinople and Greece 1204–1276', *Traditio*, 14(1958), 63–120; B. M. Bolton, 'A Mission to the Orthodox? The Cistercians in Romania', *Studies in Church History*, 13(1976), 169–81.
73. A. J. Andrea, 'Adam of Perseigne and the Fourth Crusade', *Cîteaux*, 36(1985), 21–37.
74. M. J. Angold, *Church and Society*, 207–8.
75. *Reg.* XI, ccxlv: Migne *PL* 215, 1551i; ed. Haluscynski, no. 124, 356.
76. Wolff, 'Footnote'.
77. K. N. Ciggaar, 'Une description de Constantinople traduite par un pèlerin anglais du XIIe siècle', *Revue des études byzantines*, 34(1976), 249, §4.1–9.
78. B. de Khitrowo, *Itinéraires russes en Orient* (Geneva, 1889), 99.
79. Chronicle of Novgorod, 310.

80. Mesarites II, 16–17.
81. Ibid., II, 16.14–16.
82. *Reg.* IX, ccxliii: Migne *PL* 215, 1078; ed. Haluscynski, no. 97, 325.
83. Mesarites II, 18–25.
84. Ibid., II, 18.14–15.
85. J. M. Hoeck and R. J. Loenertz, *Nikolaos-Nektarios von Otranto, Abt von Casole. Beiträge zur Geschichte der ost-westlichen Beziehungen unter Innozenz III. und Friederich II.* (Studia Patristica et Byzantina, 11) (Ettal, 1965), 25–54.
86. Mesarites I, 63–6.
87. It is attached to a document that relates to Cardinal Pelagius's mission to Constantinople of 1213–14. It may therefore be connected with the joint vacancy to the Latin and the Greek patriarchates that existed in the summer of 1214.
88. J. B. Cotelerius, *Ecclesiae Graecae Monumenta*, III (Paris, 1686), 514–20.
89. *Reg.* XI, xxi: Migne *PL* 215, 1352; ed. Haluscynski, no. 109, 341.
90. *Reg.* XI, xlvii: Migne *PL* 215, 1372–5; ed. Haluscynski, no. 114, 345–8.
91. Bohemund IV, prince of Antioch, transferred his allegiance from the King of Jerusalem to the Latin Emperor of Constantinople. Cf. B. Hamilton, *The Latin Church in the Crusader States. The Secular Church* (London, 1980), 216–21, 313–15.
92. *Reg.* XI, ix: Migne *PL* 215, 1345.
93. *Reg.* XI, ccvii: Migne *PL* 215, 1522–3.
94. *Reg.* XIII, clxxxiv: Migne *PL* 216, 353–4; ed. Haluscynski, no. 173, 402–3.
95. *Reg.* XVI, civ–cvi: Migne *PL* 216, 901–4; ed. Haluscynski, nos 210–12, 449–52.
96. J. P. Donovan, *Pelagius and the Fifth Crusade* (Philadelphia, 1950), 1–24.
97. Acropolites I, 30.4–17.
98. K. A. Manaphes, Ἐπιστολὴ Βασιλείου Πεδιαδίτου, μητροπολίτου Κέρκυρας, πρὸς τὸν πάπαν Ἰννοκέντιον Γ' καὶ ὁ χρόνος πατρειαρχείας Μιχαὴλ Δ' τοῦ Αὐτορειανοῦ', Ἐπετερὶς Ἑταιρείας Βυζαντινῶν Σπουδῶν, 42(1976–7), 435.24.
99. Mesarites III, §21, 26; §32–3, 33–4; §50–1, 46–7.
100. Angold, *Church and Society*, 531.
101. Lateran IV, §4: published in *Conciliorum Oecumenicorum Decreta*, 3rd edn (Bologna, 1973), 235–6; R. Foreville, *Latran I, II, III et Latran IV* (Histoire des conciles oecuméniques, 6) (Paris, 1965), 347–8.
102. J. Gill, 'Innocent III and the Greeks: Aggressor or Apostle?' in *Relations between East and West in the Middle Ages*, ed. D. Baker (Edinburgh, 1973), 95–108.
103. *Reg.* XI, xxiii: Migne *PL* 215, 1353; ed. Haluscynski, no. 109, 341.
104. Andrea, *Contemporary Sources*, 254.
105. H. J. Sieben, 'Basileios Pediadites und Innozenz III.', *Annuarium Historiae Conciliorum*, 27/28 (1995–6), 249–74.
106. Fedalto, *Chiesa latina*, 213–14.
107. *Reg.* XI, xxiii: Migne *PL* 215, 1353; ed. Haluscynski, no. 109, 341.
108. S. Runciman, *Eastern Schism* (Oxford, 1955), 188.

chapter 9

THE ORTHODOX REVIVAL

For elements of the Constantinopolitan elite the fall of the city to the crusaders was an overwhelming catastrophe – a 'cosmic cataclysm'.[1] Other sections of Byzantine society were more sanguine. Some members of the imperial aristocracy attached themselves to crusade leaders. Provincials seem to have positively welcomed the overthrow of Constantinople. There was a scramble to find a place in the new order. We have already examined the career of Michael Doukas, which may not be typical but is instructive. He was determined to establish himself as a local ruler and happy to work within a framework provided by the Latin Empire. His counterpart in Asia Minor was Theodore Laskaris, but his position was rather different, if only because he was the son-in-law of the Emperor Alexius III Angelus. He had been raised to the rank of despot which marked him out as the emperor's heir apparent. In the summer of 1203 he escaped from Constantinople – now dominated by the supporters of Isaac II Angelus and the young Alexius – and made his way to Prousa, which he turned into a centre of opposition, first to Isaac and Alexius and then to the Latins. Once news reached him that his father-in-law had been captured by the Latins, he took steps to have himself proclaimed emperor at Nicaea in the summer of 1205.[2] This was a defiant attempt to preserve Byzantium's imperial traditions in the face of the Latin advance. But, as we have seen, even Theodore Laskaris was willing to temporise with the new regime.

I

Concerted opposition to the Latin conquest would be the work of members of the Constantinopolitan elite, which over many centuries provided Byzantium with its ruling class. But it would take some years before they regained a voice, for the elite's very existence was threatened by the Latin conquest and with it the Byzantine identity which its members defined and articulated. Their influence had if anything grown in the course of the twelfth century, particularly after the death of Manuel I Comnenus in 1180. Their function was to run the patriarchal and imperial administrations. The essential qualification was ability and education. At the core of the elite was a handful of families who had provided servants of Church and State over many generations, but birth was no absolute criterion for entry.[3] Many came from quite obscure families. The Choniates – among the more prominent members of the elite on the eve of the fall of Constantinople – came from a relatively humble provincial background. Whether provincial or metropolitan by origin the members of the elite were bound by a common devotion to Constantinople, where it would be safe to say they had all received their higher education. Their influence had grown over the twelfth century for two main reasons. Official culture became still more rhetorical. There was a constant round of speeches designed to mark occasions of the imperial and liturgical calendars. Rhetoric was designed to complement ceremonial, but in the course of the twelfth century began to overshadow it. The purpose of speechmaking was not so much to justify policy as to extol the ideology of Orthodoxy, personified by the emperor and the patriarch. It was a task that fell to members of the elite, who have been dubbed the 'Guardians of Orthodoxy'.[4]

The second reason why these 'Guardians of Orthodoxy' became more prominent in the twelfth century relates to changes taking place in the organisation of the patriarchal church, which for the first time provided for the teaching of theology. Three new teaching positions were created: those of the *didaskalos* of the Gospel (sometimes referred to as the oecumenical *didaskalos*); of the *didaskalos* of the Apostles and of the *didaskalos* of the Psalter. These positions were held by deacons of St Sophia, a group which suddenly comes into prominence in the twelfth century. They provided not only the officers of the Patriarchal Church, but also many of the most important bishops.

The patriarchal clergy came to exercise an increasingly powerful influence within the elite.[5] In the eleventh century there still existed a clear distinction between the imperial administration and the Patriarchal Church. By the end of the twelfth century members of the same families would serve in either. A small number of families came to have a dominant role in both: the Tornikes, the Kamateros, the Kastamonites, the Choniates. But the focus of their interests had shifted away from the imperial court to the Patriarchal Church, which by the end of the twelfth century they dominated. The Kamateros, for example, provided two patriarchs in the last two decades of the century. These elite families had a very high conceit of their moral standing, which they contrasted with the scandalous behaviour of the imperial court. When Nicetas Choniates came to apportion blame, he singled out members of the imperial family for the calamities that overcame the Byzantine Empire at the turn of the twelfth century.[6] It was a way of absolving members of the elite who ran the organs of Church and State, but they were just as responsible for the rotten state of the Empire.

The popular pleasure taken in the discomfiture of the elite in the immediate aftermath of the conquest of Constantinople underlined how vulnerable traditional values and even a sense of identity had become, now that the fallibility of the 'Guardians of Orthodoxy' had been exposed. A general disillusionment with the old ideology made acceptance of a new Latin order that much easier. The Constantinopolitan elite followed the patriarch John X Kamateros into exile in Thrace. The patriarch's refusal to give any kind of a lead for the time being deprived the members of the elite of a role in the creation of the new order.[7] Their sense of disorientation is apparent in the movements of Nicetas Choniates. He escaped with the patriarch to Thrace, where he stayed until the latter's death in the spring of 1206. He then returned to Constantinople, where he spent the next six months. It was a stay that coincided with the protracted negotiations between the Greeks, the Latin patriarch and the papal legate Benedict of Santa Susanna. By the end of the year he had had enough 'of the Latins and their drivelling' and left for Nicaea.[8] It probably meant that there was no place for him in the Greek community in Constantinople. The leadership had passed to others, who were endeavouring to come to terms with the Latins.

Nicetas was not the only prominent Byzantine who found this willingness to deal with the conqueror alarming and who decided to move to Nicaea, but we have to rely very heavily on the writings of Nicholas Mesarites, who became an intermediary between the Greeks in Constantinople and Nicaea. He was the joint leader of the Greek deputation which met with the Latin patriarch, Thomas Morosini, on 30 August 1206.[9] His elder brother John was the head of the monastic delegation that entered into discussions with the papal legate Benedict on 29 September 1206, and which continued into another session on 2 October. John Mesarites was adamant that it was impossible for the Greeks to accept Morosini as their patriarch, whether he was sent from Rome or not. Equally, he was willing to submit the election of an Orthodox patriarch to the pope for approval. We have seen how with the support of the Emperor Henry he drafted a letter to Innocent III to this effect.[10] John Mesarites died six months later without this initiative making any progress. His brother Nicholas delivered a funeral oration over his tomb. He used the occasion to present him as a dauntless champion of

Orthodoxy, who had 'fought valiantly against the whole motley crew of Italians and stood firm against the deviant faith that prevails among them, displaying a divinely inspired zeal for his religion'.[11] It was a way of obscuring how close his contacts with the Latins had been. He had come under the protection of the count of St-Pol during the sack of the city. Nicholas Mesarites balances this by dwelling on the horrors perpetrated at the time by the Latins.[12] These were presented as a deliberate insult to Orthodoxy. Mesarites concluded: 'Such was the reverence that those bearing the cross of our Lord on their shoulders showed to the things of God; thus were they taught to behave by their bishops. What should we call them? Bishops posing as soldiers or warriors posing as bishops?'[13]

The role played by bishops in the storming of Constantinople was a recurring theme of Orthodox polemic. However, only one Latin cleric was singled out as a hate figure. This was the Latin Patriarch Thomas Morosini. He, of course, did not participate in the Fourth Crusade. He arrived at Constantinople only late in 1205. But he was hated by the Greeks with good reason because he was at the head of the Latin Church at Constantinople, which the spokesmen of the Orthodox Church understood quite correctly to be the main threat to Orthodoxy. Their task was in the first instance to uphold Orthodoxy in the capital. As John Mesarites observed, they could all have escaped from Constantinople to a variety of refuges in the provinces, but they preferred the Latin yoke. They rejoiced in the opportunity that God had thought fit to provide to wipe away their sins.[14]

Incidents that occurred during the sack of the city provided the necessary ammunition to serve the Orthodox cause. Greek propagandists went out of their way to exaggerate the horrors of the taking of the city. They put particular emphasis on the disrespect of the Latins for icons. Their precious frames will have excited the cupidity of the crusaders. But this did not mean that westerners were incapable of appreciating Byzantine icons. Two precious icons were despatched from the booty collected at Constantinople to the Templars.[15] Though less prized as religious objects than relics, westerners understood the spiritual worth of icons, so much so that Innocent III was anxious that the Latins of Constantinople would not pick up bad habits in this respect from the Greeks. He made clear that he could not approve of the Greek conviction that the spirit of the Virgin Mary resided in her image.[16] Accusing westerners of disdain for icons allowed Greek polemicists to condemn them as iconoclasts. But this has to be seen for what it was – polemic. The stuff of this polemic might well be the horrors of the sack of Constantinople, but the occasion was the imposition of a Latin patriarch, the full implications of which only began to become apparent some two years after the fall of the city. The group that had most to lose was the Byzantine elite, whose interests and very existence had come to be increasingly closely attached to the Patriarchal Church. One of the subplots of the fall of Constantinople was the elite's struggle for survival. On it rested the continuity of Byzantine culture and identity.

By the time of the death of John Mesarites in March 1207 the Greek community in Constantinople was uncertain how to proceed. There were those who saw the Emperor Henry as a patron and protector, but a degree of disenchantment followed his failure to make any progress with the creation of an Orthodox patriarchate under papal auspices. Another possibility was to turn to Nicaea, where Theodore Laskaris had established a Byzantine regime in exile by having had himself proclaimed emperor. Increasing numbers of the elite, for example the historian Nicetas Choniates, gravitated there, but they were not necessarily welcome. Choniates was deeply disappointed by his initial reception.[17] The local people, in the same way as other provincials, had little affection for the Constantinopolitan elite. As for Theodore Laskaris, he was trying to secure his hold over western Asia Minor and was not above putting out feelers to Pope Innocent III, to whom he wrote in the aftermath of Boniface of Montferrat's death on 4 September 1207. The letter does not survive, but it can be partly reconstructed from the pope's reply which is dated March 1208.[18]

Theodore had written the pope a letter of some prolixity, which Innocent tried to reduce to its essentials. Theodore began by accusing the Latins of apostasy because they had turned a crusade against a Christian people; of sacrilege because of the sack of Constantinople; of perjury because of their failure to observe truces. He requested that the pope send a legate to mediate on his behalf with the Emperor Henry. He hoped to obtain recognition as ruler over western Asia Minor, which would have involved a Latin withdrawal from strongpoints on the Marmara shores. He also proposed an alliance with the Latin Empire against the Seljuqs. Otherwise, he threatened to ally with the Bulgarian ruler against the Latins. In other words, at a time when Constantinople was under renewed threat from the Bulgarians, Theodore was offering an alliance with the Latins in return for recognition as independent ruler of western Asia Minor.

The pope assured Theodore that he had reprimanded the Latins of Constantinople for the brutality of their sack of Constantinople, but went on to defend the conquest as an act of God through which the Greek Church returned in obedience to Rome. Through them the Greeks had been punished 'by the just judgement of God' for rending the seamless garment of Christ. It was God who had transferred the empire of Constantinople to the Latins. The pope advised Theodore to submit to the authority of the Emperor Henry and to show due devotion to St Peter's lieutenant, the pope. In a later letter to the Latin patriarch of Constantinople, Innocent III refers to Theodore's claims to imperial status,[19] but not in the letter under consideration, which is addressed to the nobleman Theodore Laskaris. There is good reason to suppose that the pope had no intention of giving Theodore even the satisfaction of discussing and then dismissing his claims to the imperial title. His insistence on Henry as emperor suggests that Theodore had raised the question in the original letter. There is, however, no hint in Innocent's reply that Theodore may also have broached the matter of the election of a new Orthodox patriarch now that John X Kamateros was dead. It was certainly a matter that concerned the court at Nicaea. However, this much is clear: at this juncture Theodore Laskaris along with other Greek leaders was willing to consider the reconstitution of Byzantine political and ecclesiastical institutions under papal auspices. Innocent III's reply revealed that such a possibility was no part of his plans. He maintained his insistence that the Greeks must submit to the Latin Empire and the Latin patriarchate.

By the time Theodore Laskaris received the pope's reply – this would not have been before the early summer of 1208 – events had moved on. An Orthodox patriarch of Constantinople had been elected at Nicaea on 20 March 1208. His first significant action was to crown Theodore Laskaris emperor on Easter Sunday. The importance of the event can hardly be exaggerated. It meant the recreation in exile of the Byzantine Empire. However, the initiative for electing a new Orthodox patriarch did not come from the Nicaean court, but from the Orthodox clergy of Constantinople. In the autumn of 1207 Nicholas Mesarites was sent to Nicaea with a plea to Theodore Laskaris that he would gather together the bishops of his territories and any others, so that they could proceed to the election of a new patriarch.[20] What induced the clergy of Constantinople to approach Theodore Laskaris is never revealed. It may have become clear by then that the Emperor Henry had withdrawn his support for any initiative over the election of a new Orthodox patriarch. Equally, Theodore Laskaris's assumption of the imperial title may have begun to seem less presumptuous than it had. The over-lavish praises heaped on Theodore Laskaris by Nicolas Mesarites suggest that the Orthodox clergy of Constantinople had previously been very suspicious of Laskaris. Again, why Theodore should have responded positively to the approach made by the Constantinopolitan clergy is unclear, given that shortly before he had despatched a letter to Innocent III, which suggested quite different priorities. The competing imperatives were, on the one hand, survival – this was especially true of the Constantinopolitan elite – and, on the other, the need to find acceptance within the new order. The election of a new Orthodox patriarch was the most effective way of ensuring the former, while offering a negotiating counter for the latter. Theodore Laskaris sent orders to the bishops of Anatolia to meet in the third week of Lent (2–8 March 1208) so that they could proceed to the election of a new Orthodox patriarch, while Nicholas Mesarites returned to Constantinople with invitations to the different members of the Orthodox clergy of Constantinople to attend, if at all possible. Once back in Constantinople Mesarites discovered that a Latin spy had got wind of his mission and had informed the Venetian *podestà*.[21] Afraid that he might be arrested and deeply suspicious that he might be betrayed by other Greeks, he slipped away from Constantinople and made his way once again to Nicaea.[22]

The assembly chose Michael Autoreianos as patriarch. He had previously been grand *sakellarios* of St Sophia and was therefore one of the highest ranking officers of St Sophia. After the fall of Constantinople he had accompanied the old patriarch into exile, but had then found refuge in a monastery on Mount Olympos above Prousa.[23] One of the consequences of his election as patriarch was the migration of members of the higher ranks of the Orthodox clergy of Constantinople to Nicaea. Nicholas Mesarites, for instance, would become bishop of Ephesus. Another example is Theodore Eirenikos, who had been chief minister under Alexius III Angelus. He would succeed Michael Autoreianos as patriarch, but when Nicetas Choniates wrote to him from Nicaea in 1208 they were separated by water, which must mean that he was still resident at Constantinople.[24] The gravitation of the Byzantine elite to Nicaea in the wake of the election of a new Orthodox patriarch was an important change because before this, despite their loyalty to their faith, the leaders of the Greek community in Constantinople sought to come to terms with the new Latin dispensation. They were suspicious of the leaders of resistance who had established themselves in the provinces. Theodore Laskaris's original assumption of the imperial title marked him out as a usurper. This all changed once a patriarch had been installed at Nicaea. His first significant action was to crown Theodore Laskaris emperor. It meant that Laskaris had at last won recognition from the Constantinopolitan elite. This had important consequences. The new patriarch backed Theodore's struggle against the Latins. He granted absolution to all those dying in battle against Theodore's enemies. This went directly against the teaching of the Orthodox Church about war, which enjoined that it was always evil, if sometimes a necessity.

The patriarch's action turned the fight against the Latins into a holy war.[25]

The restoration of the Orthodox patriarchate in exile at Nicaea allowed the Constantinopolitan elite to regroup and to recover its voice. It ensured its survival and with it Byzantine high culture. But it had been a close-run thing and produced a significant refashioning of the Byzantine thought-world. The old certainties depended on the inviolability of Constantinople. It was the New Sion and the New Rome. As such, it was central to Byzantine ideology and identity. Its loss had to be explained. This was to be the work of the historian Nicetas Choniates. He may have been disappointed by his initial reception at Nicaea, but he soon found that his gifts as an orator were in demand at the Laskarid court. His speeches may have played some part in persuading Theodore Laskaris to act upon the request made by the Constantinopolitan clergy that he organise the election of an Orthodox patriarch. Nicetas composed the Lenten addresses given by Theodore I Laskaris in February 1207 and then again in February 1208.[26] They were calls for support for Theodore Laskaris. In 1207 there was only the hope that prayer and fasting would bring success over his enemies. By 1208 there was a confidence that Theodore would be able to recover Constantinople now that the Greeks had atoned for their sins, which were seen as the cause of the loss of the city to the Latins who had been sent by God to punish them.

In these speeches Nicetas Choniates developed an ideology of exile. His starting point was the parallel with the children of Israel who had equally known exile. For Choniates the limpid waters of Lake Ascania were his 'Waters of Babylon'. Like the Israelites the Byzantines had been exiled from their Jerusalem because of their sins. The conquest of Constantinople was divinely sanctioned punishment for their transgressions. This was another reason to exaggerate the horrors of the sack of Constantinople: it was a way of emphasising the loathsome state into which the Byzantines had fallen. Exile was a continuation of this trial, but it provided an opportunity for the Byzantines to atone for their sins and to recover divine favour. Their reward would be to reconquer the New Jerusalem – Constantinople – from the hated Latins. This ideology of exile contained the germs of a reworking of the Byzantine identity, which had always revolved around the notion that the Byzantines were the new Israelites and their capital was the New Sion. Before 1204 it produced a sense of identity that was constructed against the Jews, who were deemed to have lost their status as the chosen people. In the aftermath of the fall of Constantinople it was the Latins who became the 'adversary'. Again there was good reason to exaggerate the savagery of their conquest of Constantinople, for it revealed that they were not only enemies of the true faith – Orthodoxy – but they were also barbarians and opposed to all the civilised values that the Byzantine elite held dear.[27] Nicetas Choniates added an excursus to his *History* in which he itemised the classical statuary destroyed by the Latins. How closely he linked such uncivilised behaviour with the Latin attack upon Orthodoxy is revealed by the way the excursus is prefaced by his character assassination of the Latin Patriarch Thomas Morosini.[28]

As we shall see, the defence of Byzantine civilisation became an element in the definition of the elite. For cultural purposes members of the Byzantine elite increasingly identified themselves with the Hellenes and presented themselves as defenders of Hellenic civilisation against the barbarians. The roots of this development can be traced back before 1204, but the critical changes occurred during the period of exile.[29] However, in the aftermath of the crusader conquest of Constantinople it was the defence of Orthodoxy which was vital. It was necessary to ensure that the intellectual foundations of Orthodoxy were preserved in exile. Nicetas Choniates sought to contribute to this by compiling a treatise on heresy, entitled the *Treasury of Orthodoxy* (also known as the *Dogmatic Panoply*). He completed it soon after his arrival at Nicaea.[30] His interest in heresy had been aroused before 1204 by his involvement in the controversy over the Eucharist, but the relevance of his tract to the moment lay in the charge brought against the Orthodox Church by the Latins that it was a nursery of heresies. The purpose was to demonstrate the success the Orthodox Church had always had in dealing with heresies.

The key document was not drafted by Nicetas Choniates, but by another Constantinopolitan exile, Constantine Stilbes, who before 1204 had held one of the professorial chairs at the patriarchal school. In the same way as many of his colleagues, he eventually made his way to Nicaea where he obtained the see of Kyzikos.[31] He penned an anti-Latin tract known as the *Aitiamata* or *Griefs*. There is a note which refers to Cardinal Pelagius's mission to Constantinople in 1214. This suggests as a strong possibility that the treatise was drawn up in response.[32] Pelagius's mission posed a double-edged threat to the exiled Constantinopolitan elite. The Greeks of Constantinople were once again looking towards the Latin Emperor Henry as their natural protector, while, as we have already seen, Theodore Laskaris was seeking to use Pelagius to obtain terms from the Latin emperor. The new Orthodox patriarch, Theodore Eirenikos, sent an encyclical to the Greeks of Constantinople urging them to remain firm in their Orthodoxy.[33] It was essential to remind the Orthodox, both in exile and in Constantinople, of the dangers of compromising with the Latins.

Constantine Stilbes's tract did exactly this. It underlined the gulf that separated the Greeks from the Latins and it brought out the true meaning of the sack of Constantinople. The work of a skilled rhetorician, it was nevertheless couched in simple language and was directed to a popular audience. It paid relatively little attention to the abstruse points of doctrine that separated the two churches. It concentrated on differences of practice. Its originality lay in the way that it was the first piece of Byzantine polemic that demonstrated how the crusades had distorted the Latin Church and transformed it into a machine for war. Stilbes was the first Byzantine to single out indulgences as an abuse: 'The pope and the bishops pardon murders, perjury, and other sins to be committed in the future and in the time to come . . . This charade also applies to the past, for they pardon past sins for a set number of years, months, or days. They are unable to cite any ecclesiastical laws in justification . . .'[34] There is very little pretence at accuracy in the presentation of Latin customs. Stilbes alleged that 'their bishops and especially the Pope approve of the slaughter of Christians and proclaim that they are a path to salvation for those who commit such actions'.[35] The Latins apparently believed 'that those of them who are killed in war are saved and proclaimed that they go straight to paradise, even if they died fighting for gain, or bloodlust, or some other excess of evil'.[36] Stilbes has picked up on popular distortions of Latin practice, but they gained currency from the sack of Constantinople which seemed ample proof of the way addiction to war had perverted the Latin faith. Stilbes's account of the sack of Constantinople weaves together and amplifies a whole series of horror stories. No doubt there was some kernel of truth, though the crusaders were not the iconoclasts that Stilbes suggests. We have already seen that they valued icons. Stilbes's charge that 'they tore relics out of their reliquaries and deposited them on dung heaps as something vile'[37] does not ring true, given the value attached by the Latins to relics. There is nothing to support the accusation that the crusaders slaughtered clergy and laity alike in the sanctuaries of churches where they had sought refuge.[38] Stilbes's description of the bishop who led the assault on the walls of Constantinople is suspiciously similar to Nicetas Choniates's description of Thomas Morosini. Stilbes's tract has to be seen as a piece of polemic addressed to the Orthodox of Constantinople at a dangerous moment, which saw memories of the sack beginning to fade while an accommodation with the Latins remained a distinct possibility.

One of the most important consequences of the crusader conquest of Constantinople was the reshaping of the Byzantine identity along anti-Latin lines. The Latins were now singled out as the great enemy of

Orthodoxy. This reshaping of the Byzantine identity was not, as is often supposed, the automatic result of the sack of Constantinople. It was more that the Constantinopolitan elite found itself sidelined by the Latin conquest, as other sections of Byzantine society, including its military leaders, were disposed to accept the Latin order. The elite countered by trying to preserve its own existence along with that of Byzantium. Its members strove to drive home what Latin rule would mean. The most effective means to achieve this end was to exaggerate Latin atrocities and to present the sack of Constantinople as a deliberate humiliation of Orthodoxy. Stilbes's tract was the culmination of this work of propaganda, which was designed to ensure the survival of Byzantine culture and identity, but equally to provide the Constantinopolitan elite with a role and a justification in the new dispensation as the defender of Orthodoxy against the Latins. Among other things it provided religious grounds for war against the Latins, which became a struggle to recover the New Jerusalem. It also represented a desperate attempt on the part of the old Constantinopolitan elite to remain the focus of Orthodox society and to retain its loyalties.

The view of the Latins set out in Stilbes's tract was the one that by and large was going to prevail among the Byzantines. But even in 1214 it did not command universal respect: neither among the Greeks of Constantinople nor even at the Laskarid court, which increasingly felt that a compromise with the Latins offered more than outright opposition and despaired of recovering Constantinople in the immediate future. The last years of Theodore Laskaris's reign were marked by deteriorating relations with the Patriarchal Church. Laskaris was at odds with the Patriarch Theodore Eirenikos over how to proceed in the face of Pelagius's mission. The emperor then withdrew from Nicaea to Nymphaion near Smyrna. When the patriarch died in January 1216 there were two elections, one at Nicaea and the other at the imperial camp near Nymphaion. The emperor succeeded in imposing his nominee, his confessor Maximus, on the patriarchal throne. But the latter was an object of scorn because of his lack of education and succeeded in making trouble between the emperor and the citizens of Nicaea. We do not know the exact details, but it looks as though Theodore Laskaris was at loggerheads with the Constantinopolitan elite at Nicaea. It was at exactly this juncture that Nicetas Choniates once again found himself out of imperial favour.[39] The likeliest explanation is opposition on the part of the Constantinopolitan elite not just to the imposition of an imperial nominee as patriarch but also to Laskaris's insistence on rapprochement with the Latin regime at Constantinople.

II

Writing after the reconquest of Constantinople in 1261 George Akropolites presented Theodore I Laskaris as the saviour of Orthodoxy. He had certainly laid the foundations of Byzantine recovery, but at the time of his death – late in 1221 – it was still far from clear what form Byzantium would take. George Akropolites can find almost nothing to say about the last ten years of Theodore Laskaris's reign. He has to admit that the emperor was at loggerheads with his patriarch, by now Manuel I Sarantenos (1215–22), over his marriage to a Latin princess.[40] Theodore's death appears to have been followed by an interregnum of about a month. He left one son by his second wife, an Armenian princess. His rights were brushed aside and the succession passed to the *proto-vestiarites* John Vatatzes, who at some stage married one of Theodore's daughters.

Despite a distinguished surname John Vatatzes's background is extremely obscure and his rank at court was decidedly modest. His accession therefore has all the marks of a *coup d'état*. It was immediately opposed by Theodore Laskaris's brothers who went to Constantinople to seek Latin help to unseat him. They returned in 1224 with a Latin army, which John Vatatzes defeated at the battle of Poimanenon. He followed this up by driving the Latins out of north-western Asia Minor and confining them to a few places around Nikomedia.[41] It was an important victory not only because it put an end to any conceivable Latin threat to the Laskarid territories in Asia Minor, but also because it marked the ascendancy of the anti-Latin party at the Nicaean court. It vindicated the stance taken by the Constantinopolitan elite, which had opposed Theodore Laskaris's policy of rapprochement with the Latins. The new patriarch Germanos II (1223–40) congratulated John Vatatzes on his victory in exactly these terms. He also thanked him for his generous donations to the patriarchate which until then had had to share the revenues of the diocese of Nicaea.[42] Vatatzes took the opportunity of his victory over the Latins to reach a definitive church settlement. To avoid the friction that existed under Theodore Laskaris, John Vatatzes withdrew to Nymphaion which became the imperial headquarters. Nicaea was left to the patriarch, his clergy and the Constantinopolitan elite.

As George Akropolites noted, Theodore Laskaris 'made a beginning'.[43] It was left to John Vatatzes and the Patriarch Germanos II to build on this. The fall of Constantinople meant the loss of the central organs of government. Theodore Laskaris's government was makeshift. He must have worked through the machinery of provincial government which was still in place. Otherwise, his rule was personal. He relied heavily on his relatives to carry out essential missions. By the end of his reign there was some kind of household government coordinated by Demetrius Tornikes, who then became John Vatatzes's chief minister. Such was the trust that Vatatzes had in him that he adopted him as a brother. Tornikes operated as the emperor's deputy and presided over a small but effective central government. It was capable of carrying out near the beginning of John Vatatzes's reign a fiscal survey of his territories, which provided the basis for a revision of the tax burden. Whatever advantages the bureaucratic system brought the imperial government before 1204 in terms of control, it was cumbersome and oppressive, run largely in the interest of the Constantinopolitan elite. The fall of Constantinople brought a simplification of administrative procedures and a drastic reduction in personnel.[44] To Nicephorus Gregoras (c.1290–c.1360), looking back nearly a century later, the Nicaean Empire under John Vatatzes appeared a model of prosperity and effective government. He tried to explain it in terms of self-sufficiency. The Nicaean emperor's main source of revenue was provided by the imperial estates, so much so that he was able to give his empress a crown paid for out of the proceeds of the sale of eggs from the home farms. Vatatzes also fostered local manufactures through a sumptuary law that required all his subjects to wear home-produced cloth. This was directed against the import of Latin cloth.[45] It was from the early thirteenth century that western cloth was exported in ever-growing quantities to the eastern Mediterranean. So it is more than likely that Vatatzes took a measure of this kind, not that it would have had anything but a short-term effect.

The prosperity of the Nicaean Empire is best explained by the restoration of stability to one of the richest agricultural areas of the Mediterranean. The emperor was among the major beneficiaries because he had appropriated some of the most productive lands around Smyrna, which is the region for which we have the best evidence. There was a redistribution of property in this region, which favoured families of Thracian origin who, like Vatatzes himself, had been forced by the Latin conquest to seek refuge in Anatolia. Their estates enjoyed extensive privileges, including exemption from taxes. Before 1204 there is very little evidence for exempt property in the region. The period of exile played a critical role in its development. One feature is of the greatest importance. This was the creation of exempt military holdings or *pronoiai*. The origins of this system go back at least to the reign of Manuel I Comnenus, who supported cavalrymen in the standing army with the grant of taxes and dues from the peasants of a particular village. It seems to have been in the nature of an experiment and not very widely employed. Its extension was the work of John Vatatzes, who used it as a means of financing his army. It entailed establishing the rights that the holder of a *pronoia* had over the peasants and their holdings. It emerged that it was not merely a fiscal device, but entitled the holder to real, if temporary, rights of lordship. It meant that the peasants settled on such grants were reduced to dependant status, which produced considerable discontent. It was a Latin holder of a *pronoia* – Syrgares – who was most persistent in asserting these rights. Such grants must have done much to assure the loyalty of the members of the Latin corps which was at the heart of the Nicaean military organisation. The success of the *pronoia*-system, as it is sometimes called, was evident from the size of the armies that John Vatatzes was able to keep in the field. By the end of his reign he had turned the Nicaean Empire into the dominant military power of the region.[46]

It used to be almost an article of faith with some modern Byzantine historians that the decline of the Byzantine Empire could be linked to the advance of privileged property, which not only undermined central authority but destroyed a free peasantry, the backbone of the empire in the days of its greatness. It would certainly be true that before 1204 the central bureaux of government at Constantinople did something to check the growth of privileged property. The Latin conquest removed this barrier and the example of the Nicaean Empire reveals how quickly immunities and *pronoiai* spread. They became an integral part of the system of government. A reason why the Nicaean Empire could function so effectively with so restricted a central government was exactly this: much of the burden of government passed to landowners. In essence, it was reminiscent of the system of government that prevailed in the medieval West. It was not copied directly from the Latin example, for its roots can be traced well before 1204. But it is difficult to imagine that there could have been so radical a transformation of Byzantine government and society without the intervention of the Latin conquest of Constantinople.

The reduction in the machinery of imperial government meant that there was less scope for the talents of the old Constantinopolitan elite, which came increasingly to be identified with the Patriarchal Church. Just as John Vatatzes must take the credit for creating a viable imperial regime in exile, so Germanos II was responsible for restoring the standing of the patriarchate. The new patriarch had been a deacon of St Sophia before 1204. Although he managed to remain on good terms with John Vatatzes, his views were surprisingly radical under a pretence of traditionalism. Though born at Anaplous on the Bosporus he is bitter in his denunciation of the people of Constantinople, attributing the fall of the city to their racial impurity. They were *mixobarbaroi*. Exile offered an opportunity for the Byzantines to cleanse themselves. He realised that the Latin conquest had been deeply damaging to Byzantine prestige, not least to the patriarchate. Germanos II sought from the beginning to minister to a much wider community than just the churches in the territories under John Vatatzes's control. He insisted on his position as oecumenical patriarch. He encouraged the Greeks of Constantinople and of Cyprus in their struggle against the Latin Church. He made contact with the Orthodox churches in the Caucasus, Balkans and Russian lands.

The major challenge came from the Orthodox bishops loyal to Theodore Angelus, who had himself proclaimed emperor after his conquest of Thessalonica in the autumn of 1224. He was later crowned emperor by the archbishop of Ohrid, Demetrios Chomatianos. This was an act challenged by the Patriarch Germanos II on the grounds that there could be only a single Orthodox Empire. Germanos insisted in traditional fashion that the existence of two emperors threatened the unity of Orthodoxy. George Bardanes, the bishop of Kerkyra, riposted by calling in question the legitimacy of the patriarchate established at Nicaea. His argument went to the heart of the problem. The Latin conquest of Constantinople had not destroyed Byzantium. Instead, it had left it fragmented. Bardanes proposed acceptance of political fragmentation, 'each enjoying his own Sparta' but on the understanding that Orthodoxy provided a unifying force. Germanos II supplied the official Nicaean response, which was to claim that the Nicaean Empire represented the continuation of Byzantium and its traditions. However, aspects of his view of the patriarchal office were at odds with this official response. He compared himself to Gideon. Just as the latter was the fifth judge of Israel, so he was the fifth patriarch since the fall of Constantinople. This parallel suggested that the patriarch was the leader of the Orthodox community. In many ways, this was the case. If Germanos II was unwilling to state this explicitly, one of his protégés was happy to do so. This was Nicephorus Blemmydes – the polymath of his time. In the same way as George Bardanes he subscribed to the view that the old order – which he dismissed as hopelessly corrupt – had been destroyed in 1204. The Latin conquest offered a chance to build afresh. He did not like the idea that the imperial regime set up in exile in Asia Minor was the continuation of the old order. He blamed the moral failings of the emperors and their court for the loss of Constantinople. He preferred the state of affairs that had arisen after 1204: a collection of separate territories ruled over by Orthodox princes, but given meaning and unity by the Orthodox faith. He was offered the patriarchal throne, but turned it down because he knew among other things that the Nicaean emperor of the day expected him to impose an interdict on the lands of his Epirot rival. He refused to allow patriarchal authority to be exploited for political ends.[47]

The debate over the unity of the Byzantine world produced a radical reassessment of the nature of the Byzantine order. It was one that stressed the self-sufficiency of Orthodoxy. An imperial regime was its appendage; it was not an integral part. After the recovery of Constantinople in August 1261 there were few who dared to be as outspoken as Nicephorus Blemmydes, but the views he articulated in exile were those that gave the truest account of the new situation created by the Latin conquest. Blemmydes never held high office, but he was an influential figure at the Nicaean court. He was even able to take the Emperor John Vatatzes to task for keeping a Latin mistress – the infamous Marchesina. His power derived from his reputation for sanctity and from his learning. He was born in 1197 in Constantinople, the son of a doctor. His family fled to Asia Minor, where he obtained his education. After he had completed his secondary education at Nicaea he was unable to go on to higher studies. This was for a variety of reasons, but one of them, he claimed, was a lack of teachers at this level. In the end, he heard of a scholar who had retired to the mountains in the then Latin-held Troad. He made the difficult journey there and sat at the man's feet imbibing the disciplines of the quadrivium – mathematics, geometry, astronomy and perhaps music. His teacher was almost certainly a product of the patriarchal school who had fled to the safety of Asia Minor.

Blemmydes's need to travel to so remote a spot in order to obtain a higher education may not mean that after 1204 Byzantine learning hung by a thread. Blemmydes could almost certainly have studied with suitably qualified teachers either at the imperial court – now established near Smyrna – or at Nicaea, but this was ruled out by a clash he had had with the official that John Vatatzes placed in charge of education. In fact, at this time there was a considerable effort made to ensure the transfer of educational traditions from Constantinople to Nicaea. One of the early appointments made by Michael Autoreianos after becoming patriarch was of a *didaskalos* of the Psalter.[48] Before succeeding Michael as patriarch, Theodore Eirenikos held the post of consul of the philosophers, which gave him responsibility for education. It was not as difficult as Blemmydes liked to make out to obtain an education at Nicaea, but it was nevertheless a major achievement to have preserved as much of the Byzantine heritage of learning and scholarship as occurred in the Nicaean Empire. In this Nicephorus Blemmydes had an important role, but perhaps not quite as important as he claimed. The Emperor John Vatatzes entrusted to him the education of young men from the imperial court. It was a kind of a court school, though he never had more than a handful of pupils at any one time. The emperor then engaged him as a tutor to his son, the future Theodore II Laskaris. In this capacity he compiled a series of textbooks – on logic, physics, geography. In no way original, their value was educational. However, Blemmydes's criticism of John Vatatzes's affair with the Marchesina made his position at court untenable. He withdrew to the monastery that he was founding. There he established a school which soon became famous. Its reputation was such that Gregory of Cyprus left his native island in the hope of studying there. Before being summoned to the imperial court Blemmydes had run a school at Nicaea, which was always more important as an educational centre. Blemmydes's pupil, the Emperor Theodore II Laskaris created a school attached to the church of St Tryphon at Nicaea, which he refounded.[49]

Another contribution made by Nicephorus Blemmydes was his work in collecting manuscripts. With the backing of the emperor he made a long journey to the West, visiting Athos, Ohrid, Thessalonica and Larissa in his search for manuscripts, which he studied and copied. The 'Paris Demosthenes' – a manuscript dating from the late ninth century – may well have been part of his haul, for it passed into the possession of one of John Vatatzes's foundations, the monastery of Sosandra, close to the imperial residence at Nymphaion.[50] The richness of Nicaean libraries is illustrated by the way William of Moerbeke, the famous Dominican translator, came as a comparatively young man to Nicaea in the search for Aristotelian texts.[51] He was one of the beneficiaries of the concerted effort made at Nicaea in the aftermath of the fall of Constantinople to preserve Byzantium's literary heritage. The earliest examples of many classical texts are to be found in manuscripts copied in the thirteenth century. Just as important were texts of the more recent past. We owe the survival of so many twelfth-century rhetorical pieces to the labours of Nicaean copyists. But it is difficult to find much in the way of original work. The Patriarch Germanos II delivered a series of powerful sermons, which thanks to their arresting imagery still make an impact.[52] The one work of real originality was Nicephorus Blemmydes's autobiography.[53] It enlarged the scope of Byzantine literature, but it produced no imitators.[54] Blemmydes also wrote a *Mirror of Princes* – which is a model of its kind – for his charge, the future Emperor Theodore II Laskaris, who was far and away the most prolific author from the period of exile. His works covered a very wide range: from philosophy to theology, from satire to rhetoric. His encomium of the city of Nicaea maintains the highest standards of Byzantine rhetoric.[55] He was also a talented letter-writer. One of his letters is devoted to a description of the ruins of

Pergamon and is justly famous. His treatment of the ruined city displays a new sense of the 'Hellenic' achievement. The classical remains excited his wonder and admiration, even if they left him with a sense of the inadequacy of the present. He took the view that his own generation had a cultural mission to preserve the classical legacy; that as guardians of Hellenic wisdom the Byzantines still retained their superiority over others, the Latins above all. Theodore II Laskaris was able to articulate a different – a cultural – dimension to the Byzantine identity.

The period of exile reinvigorated the Byzantine polity and its culture. It removed the burden of an overbearing capital. This allowed the localisation of political power, which was reflected in the continuing growth of provincial centres. More practically, the disappearance of the central departments of state made for more effective and efficient government, which in the case of the Nicaean Empire was reflected in its impressive military establishment and achievements. In the absence of any overarching imperial administrative system Orthodoxy became the main unifying force. Among the elite, this was reinforced by a devotion to Byzantium's Hellenic heritage. There was an intense awareness of how close Byzantium had come to being destroyed in the aftermath of the Latin conquest. This produced a much deeper appreciation of its fundamentals, which was intensified by the belief that the fall of Constantinople offered the chance of renewal.

III

The surprise is how long delayed the recovery of Constantinople was. John Vatatzes had laid siege to Constantinople in 1235 but achieved next to nothing. His efforts to prevent reinforcements coming to the help of the Latins were to no avail, once the Venetians sent his fleet to the bottom. There was nothing for it, but to leave Constantinople in the hands of the Latins. Thereafter John Vatatzes deployed his military strength in extending his control over the southern Balkans. It was only in 1259 that the Nicaean hold on the region was finally secured with the victory at Pelagonia (Monastir) on the Via Egnatia. The recovery of Constantinople had by now become all the more pressing because the new emperor, Michael VIII Palaiologos, was a usurper. He had set aside the rights of John Laskaris, Theodore II Laskaris's son and heir. Michael Palaiologos was at the centre of a network of aristocratic families that had found themselves excluded from power by Theodore II Laskaris. The conquest of Constantinople would set the seal on his usurpation. Already he was having difficulties with the Patriarch Arsenius Autoreianos who had resigned office rather than condone his usurpation.[56] Michael

Palaiologos did not underestimate the task in front of him. He thought that the key to the conquest of Constantinople was seapower. He therefore engaged the services of the Genoese fleet. These careful preparations turned out to be unnecessary, because in July 1261 a small reconnaissance force was able to seize Constantinople while the Latin garrison was absent securing a small Black Sea island close to the mouth of the Bosporus. It was so unexpected that, when the news came, Michael Palaiologos asked his favourite sister to pinch his toes, so that he could be sure he was not dreaming.[57]

Michael Palaiologos re-entered Constantinople in triumph on 15 August 1261. For a time he carried everything before him. He recovered the Black Sea coastlands up to the Danube mouths. He negotiated the return of the eastern Peloponnese from William of Villehardouin, the prince of Achaea. Michael II Angelus, the ruler of Epiros, submitted to his authority, as did the petty dynasts of Thessaly. Under Michael Palaiologos the restored empire was for the last time a great power, capable of coordinating a network of diplomatic contacts stretching from southern Russia to Egypt and from Iran to the Iberian peninsula. Michael Palaiologos was more than able to defend his gains against a formidable enemy in the shape of Charles of Anjou – the Capetian prince who had conquered southern Italy and Sicily at the behest of the papacy. Even before Charles of Anjou was securely in possession of his new territories, he made clear that he saw the restoration of the Latin Empire of Constantinople as his major task. By a mixture of opportunism and diplomacy Michael Palaiologos was able to contain this threat, which was the more serious because of the Venetian stance. Potentially, Venice had more to lose from the Byzantine recovery of Constantinople than any other power. The Venetians at first preferred to come to terms and were relieved in 1265 when they recovered the privileges and quarters they had enjoyed at Constantinople before 1204. But it soon became apparent that their position had deteriorated to the point of being nearly untenable. Favoured at their expense were the Genoese, who received a trading enclave at Galata, across the Golden Horn, which they quickly turned into one of the major trading centres of the Mediterranean. At the same time, Michael Palaiologos unleashed a swarm of privateers on the waters of the Aegean; their prime target was Venetian shipping. One by one the Aegean islands were recovered from their Venetian lords. But the major Byzantine objective was to drive the Venetians out of their bases on the islands of Crete and Euboea. It was only by the skin of their teeth that the Venetians held on to Candia and Negroponte. For the last time, the Byzantines controlled the waters of the Aegean.[58]

Michael Palaiologos's achievements were sustained over twenty years and are testimony to the new vigour of the Byzantine Empire, which was something more than just the recovery of military and naval strength. It was also apparent in the rebuilding and embellishment of Constantinople;[59] in the creation of an imperial academy under George Akropolites which safeguarded the educational work done during the period of exile;[60] and in an intellectual vitality, capable of producing a scholar of the stature of Maximus Planoudes.[61] While giving Michael Palaiologos his due, the usual judgement is that his reign was just an interlude before those weaknesses apparent before 1204 reasserted themselves. In other words, by this reckoning the fall of Constantinople and its recovery changed nothing. They were just part of a steady decline, which some might trace back to the Comnenian settlement and others even earlier. However, Byzantium famously took an unconscionably long time dying, which suggests not only that it had reserves of strength, but also that it was capable of refashioning itself. I would contend that this is what occurred during the period of exile. The localisation of power; the ascendancy of the church; the allegiance to a common Hellenic culture, all separate late Byzantium from its earlier manifestations. These helped to compensate for the decline in imperial authority that followed the death of Michael Palaiologos.

Michael Palaiologos's greatest misjudgement was to assume that nothing had been changed by the Latin conquest of Constantinople. His tragedy was that too much had changed. It was no longer possible for an emperor to bully the church into submission. In the absence of Constantinople the Orthodox Church had, during the period of exile, become the main unifying factor. Its authority remained ecumenical while that of the so-called Nicaean emperors was strictly local. Michael Palaiologos assumed that the recovery of Constantinople restored an ecumenical dimension to imperial authority. He tried to impose his will on the Orthodox Church, which produced continuing friction. Faced with the threat from Charles of Anjou, Michael Palaiologos turned to the papacy with the offer of union of churches. It was a diplomatic ploy, but Pope Gregory X called his bluff at the Second Council of Lyons (1274) and his representatives had to accept reunification on Latin terms. Even if Michael Palaiologos was able to impose a pro-unionist patriarch he was unable to carry his people. He was condemned for the way in which he was prepared to sacrifice Orthodoxy for short-term political gains. It gave the Greek rulers of Epiros and Thessaly a pretext to throw off his authority. Opposition to Michael Palaiologos's unionist strategy only embedded more deeply in the Byzantine psyche the stereotype that emerged in the aftermath of 1204: of the Latins as the enemies of

Orthodoxy. The autobiographical pieces that Michael Palaiologos drafted shortly before his death in December 1282 bear witness to his bitterness and bewilderment. He had spent his life struggling for his church and people. He had recovered Constantinople; he had defended it against its enemies. He had restored the patriarchate, which its detractors had laughingly referred to as the bishopric of Bithynia. And still he received no thanks![62] Michael Palaiologos's bafflement stemmed from his unwillingness to accept the changed position of the monarchy in relation to the Orthodox Church and society which had taken place during the period of exile. The reign of Michael Palaiologos demonstrated that the changes set in train by the events of 1204 were a source not only of renewed vitality but also of dispute and division.

When Michael Palaiologos recovered Constantinople in 1261, all seemed set fair for the restoration of the Byzantine Empire on sounder foundations than those existing before the Latin conquest. But the process would take place against a quite new historical backdrop. The Mongol presence loomed over Michael Palaiologos's reign. Among his most spectacular but deceiving successes was his reception of the Seljuq Sultan 'Izz al-Din just before the return to Constantinople. The sultan was fleeing from the Mongols who had turned the Seljuq territories into a protectorate and in doing so created the conditions which eventually produced the Ottoman emirate. Michael Palaiologos's far-flung diplomacy involved missions to the courts of the Ilkhans of Persia, of the Golden Horde, and of the Mamluks of Cairo. Its purpose was to try to hold the balance of power in the Near East in order to protect Byzantine interests and frontiers from the Mongol threat that was felt on all sides. The commercial opportunities that the Mongol presence on the shores of the Black Sea offered were not of much interest to the Byzantine emperor. He was perfectly content to allow his Genoese allies to exploit them. After his death the Venetians would follow their rivals into the Black Sea. The combination of Italian commerce and Mongol power created a new scale of activity, which left the restored Byzantine Empire much reduced by comparison. This has overshadowed the true extent of the changes that followed from the fall of Constantinople to the Latins. Its most profound effect was to liberate Byzantine society and culture from the oppressive weight of a domineering capital. The results were far-reaching. Late Byzantium was more broadly based than its earlier manifestations. Its real influence in the so-called 'Byzantine Commonwealth' was far greater. The transfer of the Byzantine model to Serbia, Bulgaria and Russia was accomplished at this time largely through the agency of Orthodoxy, which had also been a beneficiary of the fall of Constantinople.[63]

However, in terms of imperial power and influence the fall of Constantinople in 1204 was a disaster. Byzantine dominance depended on the concentration of power and resources in the capital, even if it was at the expense of the provinces. It required a ruling elite that understood the use of power. As with all autocratic and overcentralised regimes, from time to time the system broke down. The centre looked as though it could not hold, but it always did. This was a recurrent pattern of Byzantine history: that is, until 1204. The period of exile saw the complete dismantling of a centralised system of government. The ruling elite may have ensured the survival of Byzantine traditions and ideology, but it emerged from the period of exile not only much reduced, but also with different allegiances. Its members were scattered in different courts and centres. Their allegiance was given as much to the church as it was to the emperor. The elite's cultural role began to take precedence over its political role. This may explain the apparent vitality of late Byzantium. But it also explains why it was unable to put up very much resistance to the advancing Ottomans, who would eventually bring peace and stability to the lands formerly occupied by the Byzantine Empire. To do so they created a centralised system of government which in principle, if not in detail, was very similar to that of the Byzantine Empire before 1204.[64] The political and military success of the Ottomans only underlined the practical advantages of an effective system of centralised government.

'The Last Centuries of Byzantium' therefore present themselves as something rather different: an interlude between two imperial traditions of power. The structures were much looser, hence the adverse judgements passed on this phase of Byzantine history. A series of regional powers competing for influence on more or less equal terms was a recipe for petty wars and endemic disorder. It also meant an enhanced role for monastic confederations, such as Athos and Meteora, which acted as independent powers. In this they were not that different from the major towns. But in both monasteries and towns greater autonomy produced new tensions, which left them prey to factionalism, whether religious or social in origin. The two currents often combined. Such conflicts coexisted with commercial opportunities, in which Greek traders, aristocrats and businessmen had an increasingly important role. It was also a time of artistic and intellectual achievements, some of which would feed into the Italian Renaissance. These were 'interesting times'. They were made possible in the first instance by the crusader conquest of Constantinople in 1204, which opened up a new set of possibilities. These took on clearer shape during the period of exile, when the foundations for the last phase of Byzantine history were laid.

Notes

1. J. Darrouzès, 'Les discours d'Euthyme Tornikès (1200–1205)', *Revue des études byzantines*, 26(1968), 82–3.
2. J.-L. van Dieten, *Niketas Choniates... nebst einer Biographie*, 151–2.
3. Angold, 'Imperial Administration'.
4. See Magdalino, *Empire of Manuel Komnenos*, 316–412.
5. Angold, *Church and Society*, 89–98.
6. Nicetas Choniates, 529.25–31.
7. J. Draeseke, 'Ein unbekannter Gegner der Lateiner', *Zeitschrift für Kirchengeschichte*, 18(1898), 546–71; P. Wirth, 'Zur Frage eines politischen Engagements Patriarch Johannes' X Kamateros nach dem vierten Kreuzzug', *Byzantinische Forschungen*, 4(1972), 239–52.
8. Nicetas Choniates, 635.3–4 app.; Van Dieten, *Niketas Choniates... nebst einer Biographie*, 43–6.
9. Mesarites II, 15.3–4.
10. Mesarites I, 61.22–34, 63–6.
11. Ibid., I, 68.13–16.
12. Ibid., I, 46–7.
13. Ibid., I, 47.1–4.
14. Ibid., I, 62.27–32.
15. *Reg.* VII, cxlvii: Migne *PL* 215, 434A.
16. Tafel and Thomas II, 47.
17. Nicetas Choniates, 635.90–16; Van Dieten, *Niketas Choniates... nebst einer Biographie*, 46–7.
18. *Reg.* XI, xlvii: Migne *PL* 215, 1372–5; ed. Haluscynski, no. 114, 345–8.
19. *Reg.* XIII, clxxxiv: Migne *PL* 216, 353–4; ed. Haluscynski, no. 173, 402–3.
20. Mesarites II, 8–11. Gounarides in *ΣΥΜΜΕΙΚΤΑ*, 6(1985), 65–71 argues that Michael Autoreianos was elected patriarch at Nicaea in March 1207. One of the major difficulties in accepting such a date is that on 17 March 1207 Nicholas Mesarites was delivering an *epitaphios* over the grave of his brother John who had died in Constantinople. Gounarides's solution is that Nicholas Mesarites will have delivered the speech *in absentio* at Nicaea. He also notes the emphasis on imperial unction in a speech praising Theodore I Laskaris, drafted by Nicetas Choniates and dated by Van Dieten to the late summer of 1206, whereas this imagery is absent from the *Selention* delivered by Theodore I Laskaris in March 1208. There are considerable difficulties surrounding Choniates's first speech, not least that he had yet to reach Nicaea and was still stuck in Constantinople. The main reason for not accepting Gounarides's ingenious presentation of his case is that the initiative for the creation of an Orthodox patriarchate at Nicaea came from Constantinople. The intermediary was Nicholas Mesarites who made two journeys from Constantinople to Nicaea – one in the autumn and the other in the spring. In the autumn of 1206 the approach to Innocent III with the support of the Emperor Henry was still going ahead. This makes it unlikely that Nicholas Mesarites would be travelling to Nicaea in the autumn of 1206 to discuss the possibility of the election of an Orthodox patriarch at Nicaea. Combine this with the date of Mesarites's funeral oration for his brother in

March 1207 and it suggests that the autumn of 1207 must therefore be the date of his first journey to Nicaea, which in turn means that the election of Autoreianos as patriarch has to be in March 1208.

21. Mesarites II, 43–4.
22. Ibid., II, 44–6.
23. M. Loukaki, 'Première didaskalie de Serge le diacre: éloge du patriarche Michel Autôreianos', *Revue des études byzantines*, 52(1994), 165.55–7, 64–70.
24. *Nicetae Choniatae orationes et epistulae*, ed. J.-L. van Dieten (Berlin/New York, 1972), 211–14.
25. N. Oikonomidès, 'Cinq actes inédits du patriarche Michel Autôreianos', *Revue des études byzantines*, 25(1967), 117–19.
26. *Nicetae Choniatae orationes et epistulae*, 120–8, 176–85. For dating: Van Dieten, *Niketas Choniates... nebst eine Biographie*, 140–3, 162–5.
27. Cf. Mesarites I, 25.23–26.1.
28. Nicetas Choniates, 647–55.
29. M. J. Angold, 'Byzantine "nationalism" and the Nicaean Empire', *Byzantine and Modern Greek Studies*, 1(1975), 49–70.
30. Van Dieten, *Niketas Choniates... nebst eine Biographie*, 46–7.
31. *Oxford Dictionary of Byzantium* III – sub. STILBES, CONSTANTINE.
32. J. Darrouzès, 'Le mémoire de Constantin Stilbès contre les Latins', *REB* 21(1963), 85.403.
33. A. I. Papadopoulos-Kerameus, 'Θεόδωρος Εἰρηνικὸς πατριάρχης οἰκουμενικός', *Byzantinische Zeitschrift*, 10(1901), 187–92.
34. Darrouzès, 'Constantin Stilbès', §33.
35. Ibid., §60.
36. Ibid., §61.
37. Ibid., §88.
38. Ibid., §93.
39. Van Dieten, *Niketas Choniates... nebst eine Biographie*, 49.
40. Acropolites I, 31.7–9.
41. Acropolites I, 34–6.
42. J. Nicole, 'Bref inédit de Germain II, patriarche de Constantinople (Année 1230)', *Revue des études grecques*, 7(1894), 74–9.
43. Acropolites I, 32.6–7.
44. M. J. Angold, *A Byzantine Government in Exile: Government and Society under the Laskarids of Nicaea, 1204–1261* (Oxford, 1975), 147–81.
45. Nicephorus Gregoras, ed. L. Schopen, I (Bonn, 1829), 42–4.
46. Angold, *A Byzantine Government in Exile*, 122–32.
47. Angold, *Church and Society*, 530–54.
48. Loukaki, 'Première didaskalie de Serge le diacre', 159.
49. J. A. Munitiz, *Nikephoros Blemmydes: a partial account* (Louvain, 1988), 1–42; C. N. Constantinides, *Higher Education in Byzantium in the thirteenth and early fourteenth centuries (1204–ca.1310)* (Nicosia, 1982), 5–27.
50. N. G. Wilson, *Scholars of Byzantium* (London, 1983), 219–20, where, however, the monastery of Sosandra is badly mislocated.
51. *Oxford Dictionary of Byzantium* III – sub. WILLIAM OF MOERBEKE.
52. Angold, *Church and Society*, 547–54.

53. *Nicephori Blemmydae Autobiographia sive curriculum vitae* (Corpus Christianorum, series graeca, 13), ed. J. A. Munitiz (Brepols/Turnhout, 1984).
54. See M. J. Angold, 'The autobiographical impulse in Byzantium', *Dumbarton Oaks Papers*, 52(1998), 246–51.
55. Theodorus II Ducas Lascaris, *Opuscula rhetorica*, ed. A. Tartaglia (Munich/Leipzig, 2000); C. Foss, *Nicaea: A Byzantine Capital and Its Praises* (Brookline, 1996), 133–53.
56. Angold, *Church and Society*, 560–3.
57. Georges Pachymérès, *Relations historiques*, ed. A. Failler, I (Paris, 1984).
58. D. J. Geanakoplos, *Emperor Michael Palaeologus and the West.*
59. R. Macrides, 'The New Constantine and the New Constantinople – 1261?', *Byzantine and Modern Greek Studies*, 6(1980), 13–41; A.-M. Talbot, 'The Restoration of Constantinople under Michael VIII', *Dumbarton Oaks Papers*, 47(1993), 243–61.
60. Constantinides, *Higher Education in Byzantium*, 33–49.
61. Ibid., 66–89; Wilson, *Scholars of Byzantium*, 230–4.
62. M. J. Angold, 'Autobiography and Identity: the case of the late Byzantine Empire', *Byzantinoslavica*, 60(1999), 53–4.
63. D. Obolensky, *The Byzantine Commonwealth. Eastern Europe 500–1453* (London, 1971), 237–90; J. Meyendorff, *Byzantium and the Rise of Russia* (Cambridge, 1981), 119–44.
64. G. Necipoglu, *Architecture, Ceremonial, and Power. The Topkapi Palace in the fifteenth and sixteenth centuries* (Cambridge, Mass., 1991), 12–13, 249–51.

Part 3

THE MYTH OF BYZANTIUM:
DESTRUCTION AND
RECONSTRUCTION

THE MYTH OF BYZANTIUM:
DESTRUCTION AND
RECONSTRUCTION

I

The meaning ascribed to an event may not be the same as the sum of its consequences. The crusader conquest of Constantinople was no ordinary conquest. It entailed the shattering of a civilisation. It was one of those events that force societies to decide where they stand. For the Byzantines it was devastating. It called in question the validity of the empire, which had always been identified with the city of Constantinople. The Byzantine capital was not only identical with the Byzantine Empire, it was also the heart of a civilisation. This gave Byzantium its peculiar character. In the past, it had been a source of immense strength, but in 1204 it was left pitifully vulnerable to a thrust that went straight to its heart. The elucidation of the full meaning of the fall of Constantinople to the Fourth Crusade requires an examination of the kaleidoscopic patterns created by the destruction of a civilisation. One side of this we have already touched on: the reaction of the Byzantine elite. Their existence came under threat because they were the guardians of the Byzantine myth which was anchored in the capital: Constantinople was the New Sion and its people were the New Israelites. Its loss was un-thinkable. However, in the face of the unthinkable the parallel with Israel gave hope. In exile at Nicaea the Byzantines took heart that they had preserved their divine law. They were thus more favoured than Ancient Israel, which in exile did not even have a place to make sacri-fice.[1] The Old Testament provided the parallel out of which the myth and with it the Byzantine identity could be sustained in the face of catastrophe. Just as the Israelites had suffered exile and had returned to Jerusalem, so the Byzantines were now enduring exile with the hope that in the fullness of time they would in their turn re-enter their Sion.

The experience of exile meant that there would be significant shifts in the Byzantine sense of identity. Orthodoxy and Hellenic culture came into their own as independent forces, rather than linked to Constantinople. The notion was advanced that there was no longer a single empire, but a series of political units of roughly equivalent status united under the umbrella of Orthodoxy, in which the dominant figure was the patriarch. This was to create problems when in 1261 the Byzantines returned to their capital. The Emperor Michael VIII Palaiologos assumed that he was entering into the inheritance of the Byzantine emperors of old and that exile had changed nothing. He believed that the emperor would return unchallenged to the centre of the Orthodox stage. Instead, he was to be throughout his reign at loggerheads with the patriarch or other elements of the church. There was little sympathy for his western diplomacy which entailed negotiations with the papacy. His subsequent willingness to implement church union earned him the hatred of society at large and left him isolated. His difficulties revealed the impossibility of resurrecting the Byzantine myth in its entirety. He failed to restore the full integrity of imperial authority, which left a hollow at the centre of the Byzantine polity. The consequences became apparent under his heir Andronicus II Palaiologos (1282–1328), whose long reign saw the disintegration of the restored Byzantine Empire.

In political terms the Byzantine recovery stalled. Much the same is true of the so-called Palaeologan Renaissance, which had its roots in Michael Palaiologos's impressive programme for the reconstitution of the educational, cultural and artistic foundations of Byzantine public life. With the help of the Grand Logothete George Akropolites he set about restoring higher education, without which there would be no effective civil service. This was accompanied by the collection and copying of manuscripts which continued on a larger scale the work of scholars during the period of exile. With the help of the aristocracy Michael Palaiologos undertook the colossal task of restoring the major buildings of Constantinople, which had been left in a disgusting state by the departing Latins; so much so that Michael Palaiologos was unable to take up immediate residence in the Blachernai Palace, because it was judged unfit for human habitation.[2] The Latin legacy of neglect meant that after 1261 Constantinople saw relatively little new building, but a great deal in the way of restoration.

One of the first tasks was to restore the church of St Sophia after its occupation by Latin clergy. Art historians are now agreed more or less unanimously that the Deësis in the south gallery dates to the restoration of the Great Church undertaken at this time.[3] There is no documentary evidence and the lettering suggests a rather earlier date, but this may have been done deliberately to suggest continuity. The grounds for attributing this composition – the most breathtakingly beautiful to have survived from Byzantium – to the reign of Michael Palaiologos are entirely stylistic and technical. The use of very small tesserae for the face and hands is a technique most often employed in Palaeologan work. The sublimated humanity of the figures is most closely approached in the decoration of the church of St Saviour in Chora (Kariye Cami), which dates to the first quarter of the fourteenth century. Dating the St Sophia Deësis to the period of the restoration of the empire poses many problems, not least that there is nothing either in the art of the late twelfth century or in that of the period of exile that prepared the way for such an exceptional achievement. But just as scholars are allowed to recover the past, so can artists and mosaicists. It is art and architecture that gives substance to Renovatio. More or less all that was required of the Byzantine architects and masons was the renovation of the fabric of the capital's churches and other monuments. But for artists and their patrons it was a different matter: they had to decide what styles were most fitting for the celebration of the restoration of Constantinople as a seat of empire. They wished to evoke the splendour which characterised the imperial court in its heyday in the tenth century under the Macedonian dynasty. More often than not, they went back to the so-called Macedonian Renaissance for their models. This is best seen in early Palaeologan illuminated manuscripts. The most arresting is Vatican Palat.gr. 381, where the illustrations of the Paris Psalter (Bibl. nat. gr. 139) – a master-piece of the Macedonian Renaissance – are reproduced with astonishing accuracy.[4]

The recovery of an imperial legacy lies at the roots of the Palaeologan Renaissance. It produced works of great virtuosity, but as with all revivals there was a large element of artificiality. There was also a loss of creativity. Hans Belting notes apropos of icon painting how 'restricted . . . its creative vigour' had become and concludes that 'its proverbial immobility is characteristic only of its history in late Byzantium'.[5] Byzantine art no longer displayed to the same degree that ability – so evident in the eleventh and twelfth centuries – to produce new iconographies and to evolve new styles. Otto Demus even detected the onset of declining powers in the art of St Saviour in Chora (Kariye Djami), the most impressive surviving monument of the Palaeologan Renaissance.[6]

But recovery of an artistic tradition was only part of the reconstitution of a shattered civilisation. The prestige of Constantinople and its emperors depended on ceremonial, which enacted the myth of Byzantium. During the period of exile the ceremonial of the imperial court was simplified. This was made that much easier by changes that had taken place under Manuel I Comnenus. St Sophia, the Hippodrome and the Great Palace still functioned as ceremonial centres in the twelfth century, but increasingly the life of the emperors shifted away from these traditional venues to the Palace of the Blachernai, which was situated close to the city walls beside the Golden Horn. For this new stage Manuel Comnenus contrived an alternative imperial ceremonial. It was far less elaborate than the traditional ceremonial. At its heart was the *prokypsis*, which originally meant a saluting stand and came to be applied to the ceremonial. It has been described as a *tableau vivant*. It consisted of the emperor either alone or with his consort hidden behind a curtain. This was then raised to reveal the emperor in all his majesty to the assembled court, which responded with appropriate acclamations. It came to be associated with the Christmas festivities and with imperial marriages. In this form, it was retained by the Nicaean emperors and passed on to their Palaeologan successors.[7]

The importance attached to ceremonial permeates the triumphal entry of Michael Palaiologos into Constantinople on the feast of the Dormition (15 August) 1261. It harks back to the rituals of the Macedonian dynasty. The procession entered the city through the Golden Gate and wound its way along the Imperial Avenue to the church of St Sophia. In a display of humility the emperor went on foot, but in other respects he followed the example set by the triumphal entry of the Emperor John Tzimiskes (969–76). He too was proceeded by an icon of the Mother of God – the Hodegetria – and was accompanied by hymns of thanksgiving to the Mother of God.[8] It was an earnest of Michael Palaiologos's intention to restore the imperial state to its previous splendour. But his successors increasingly neglected the importance of ceremonial. A ceremonial book dating to the middle of the fourteenth century reveals how rudimentary the ceremonial of the late Palaeologan court had become. The only detailed stipulations are for the Christmas festivities, where the procession and the *prokypsis* lay at the heart of the ceremonial. There were less elaborate celebrations on the other major festivals.[9]

This contrasted with a passionate interest in Constantinople's past which according to George Pachymeres animated Michael Palaiologos's restoration of Constantinople. The historian singled out in support of this contention the emperor's re-establishment of imperial clergies at the churches of the Holy Apostles and of the Blachernai together with the refoundation of the secondary school attached to the St Paul's orphanage.[10] At the same time Patriarch Germanos III (1265–6) was able to revive the ceremonial and order of the Patriarchal Church of St Sophia. He had the advantage of the instruction he had received as a young man from the Patriarch Germanos II, who had been a deacon of St Sophia before 1204.[11] In other words, the restoration of the ecclesiastical order was an integral part of the restoration of Constantinople as an imperial capital. The churches and monasteries of Constantinople had suffered during the period of Latin rule and had to be refurbished. They had also lost the greater part of their treasures and relics, which would have to be replaced. The reappearance of many of the precious relics in the course of the late thirteenth and fourteenth centuries might lead one to suppose that the sack of Constantinople in 1204 was not as systematic as is often suggested. The problem is at its clearest with the relics of the Passion. Most of these were on display in St Sophia by the mid-fourteenth century, but equally they were known to be elsewhere, notably in the Sainte-Chapelle at Paris. In *Sir John Mandeville's Travels* the narrator lists the relics of the Passion he saw in St Sophia. These included the Crown of Thorns. He had to confess that he had also seen this relic in the Sainte-Chapelle.[12] He offers a partial explanation by hinting that the relic had been divided. Synecdoche, along with deliberate fraud, best explains how Constantinople was within two or three generations of the recovery of the city once again the 'treasure house' of relics that it had been before 1204. Alice-Mary Talbot has a fascinating sidelight on the process of the recovery of relics at Constantinople. She wonders why from the turn of the thirteenth century there was so much rewriting of traditional and often very obscure saints' lives. She is able to show convincingly that in several cases they had acquired a new relevance: their cults were being renewed thanks to the miraculous reappearance of their relics.[13]

It is difficult not to be impressed by the restoration of Byzantium that was carried out after the recovery of the city in 1261. It underpinned the cultural achievements of the so-called Palaeologan Renaissance, which had its roots in the work of Michael VIII Palaiologos and a close circle of advisers, notably George Akropolites. Its flowering came in the early fourteenth century, by which time it owed more to aristocratic patrons than it did to the emperor. Nor was it just confined to Constantinople. It also diffused to other centres, above all Thessalonica. However notable the achievements of the Palaeologan Renaissance, they nevertheless remained essentially backward looking – an attempt to recover an idea of Byzantium as it had existed at the height of its power under the Macedonians and the Comneni. Interwoven with this was a deep pessimism created by the contrast of past and present. Byzantine scholars could not hope to match the achievements of classical antiquity. There had also been hopes of a restoration of Byzantine political ascendancy in the wake of the recovery of Constantinople. Once these had begun to fade the damage done by 1204 was only too clear.

II

The fall of Constantinople produced a desperate need among the Byzantine elite to recover the most important elements of their civilisation which was shattered by the loss of the capital. It is possible to imagine a different scenario where Byzantine traditions of government, court life and culture were taken over by the conquerors and transformed into something new. It is clear that the Latin emperors of Constantinople adopted some of the imperial trappings of Byzantium, but as Peter Lock has shown, that was all it was.[14] After the death of Peter of Courtenay in 1217 the Latin emperors counted for very little. There was no danger of an imperial tradition being forged in Latin Constantinople. The Latins in the Levant failed to evolve any clear identity. Increasingly, they saw themselves as an offshoot of France. In 1258 a quarrel between William of Villehardouin, the prince of Achaea, and Guy de la Roche, the lord of Athens, was eventually taken before the French King Louis IX for arbitration. Twenty years earlier Louis IX secured the relics of the Passion which the Latin emperor Baldwin II had pawned to a Venetian merchant to cover his debts. It was an action that underlined the Latin Empire's subservience to the French king.

It brought next to nothing in terms of concrete help. Only the papacy continued to offer worthwhile support. Pope Gregory IX (1227–41) made strenuous efforts to direct crusading energies towards the defence of the Latin Empire, which was in crisis following the expulsion and subsequent death of the Emperor Robert of Courtenay in 1228. The heir to the throne of Constantinople was his young brother Baldwin II, who was only ten years old. The pope therefore helped to mediate the succession of John of Brienne, formerly king of Jerusalem, who would hold the Latin Empire in trust for the young emperor. He arrived in 1231 at Constantinople with an impressive force of 500 knights, 5,000 sergeants and, just as important, 1,200 horses. His achievement was to hold off the combined Nicaean-Bulgarian assault on Constantinople in 1235–6. After John of Brienne's death in 1237 Gregory IX organised the expedition overland which brought Baldwin II to Constantinople. The pope sought Hungarian aid to bolster the fortunes of Latin Constantinople, offering the inducements of crusade privileges. Baldwin II soon returned to the West and was given a place of honour at the First Council of Lyons (1245).[15]

The defence of the Latin Empire of Constantinople was placed near the top of the council's agenda, but this more or less marked the end of the active involvement of the papacy in organising military aid for the Latin Empire. The Latin Empire was sidelined by Louis IX's Egyptian crusade of 1249–50. Despite the papacy's efforts its cause never generated much enthusiasm in western Christendom. There was a suspicion of the Latin Empire. This had been fanned by the propaganda for the western Emperor Frederick II who was locked in a struggle with the papacy. The scandal of a crusade against a Christian power was used to discredit the actions being taken against him by the papacy. The clearest expression of the reservations about the Latin Empire of Constantinople came from papal envoys sent in 1234 to the Nicaean court. They were forced to admit that the Latin Empire was the product of an unholy crusade, which had been the work of men who had defied papal orders. These envoys were Dominicans and Franciscans. They were missionaries, who put their trust in preaching and reasoned argument as the most effective means of bringing about understanding between the two churches. From this perspective the conquest of Constantinople now seemed a serious mistake because it was clear that it had deepened and widened the gulf separating the two churches.[16]

The Nicaean court welcomed the overtures of the friars. Their demeanour impressed Byzantines, because the ideals of St Francis and of St Dominic appealed to their understanding of monasticism. It became increasingly clear to Pope Innocent IV (1243–54) that their irenic approach was more likely to provide a solution to the problem of the Latin Empire than looking to the crusade alone to prop it up. Just as pilgrimage had provided the spiritual support for the crusade in its early stages, so mission increasingly contributed an underpinning to the crusade in the thirteenth century.[17] It was very unclear that Constantinople was a fitting goal for traditional crusading activity. The West never regarded it as another Jerusalem, as a focus for Christian piety. At the end of his pontificate Innocent IV engaged in a series of protracted negotiations with the Nicaean Emperor John Vatatzes with the aim of settling the question of the Latin Empire. The understanding was that the pope would withdraw his support for the Latin Empire in return for recognition by the Orthodox Church of papal supremacy. It was not to be, because the moment that agreement was in sight both pope and emperor died. These negotiations were, all the same, proof that even the papacy now understood the Latin Empire to be a hopeless case. Unsurprisingly, it ended 'not with a bang, but a whimper'. This is the fate of empires that lose their purpose and identity, or never develop them in the first place, as happened with the Latin Empire.

III

The Fourth Crusade shattered a civilisation, but the Latin Empire was quite incapable of putting it back together again. Constantinople became a quarry to be plundered. Much was just melted down. This is what happened – with one famous exception to be considered later – to the classical statuary, which adorned Constantinople's public spaces. There was little or no appreciation of its aesthetic worth among the crusaders, but then this was also the case for the majority of Byzantines, who invested classical statues with demonic powers.[18] In fact, the plundering of Constantinople was anything but indiscriminate. There was much that westerners appreciated for spiritual, moral and artistic reasons. They had long been aware of Constantinople as a storehouse of many of the most prized relics. They knew that the relics of the Passion were kept in a chapel in the Great Palace of the Emperors. This does not mean that the acquisition of relics was a motivation for the conquest of Constantinople by the crusaders in 1204, let alone behind the diversion of the crusade to Constantinople. However, the mass seizure of the relics and works of religious art was a corollary of what became the major justification for the conquest of the City – the need to end the schism between the two churches. As schismatics the Greeks had no right to the spiritual riches stored in their city. It was in exactly these terms that Abbot Martin of Pairis justified the acquisition of relics by the crusaders.[19] He was fortunate enough to visit the imperial monastery of the Pantokrator, where he persuaded a Greek interpreter to show him where the relics were kept. A chest was opened up and the relics displayed. They were more precious to Abbot Martin 'than all the riches of Greece'. Hurriedly the abbot and his chaplain 'filled the folds of their habits with sacred sacrilege'. He thought it wisest to conceal all the relics that he thus obtained aboard a ship.[20] It was some haul, which is lovingly listed by the abbot's biographer Gunther of Pairis.[21] The purpose of the biography was to explain the transfer of these relics to the safety of the abbey of Pairis.

A surprising number of the minor narratives of the conquest of Constantinople were written as testimony to the acquisition of relics from Constantinople. This is true of Gunther of Pairis's *Hystoria Constantinopolitana* and equally of the section of the *Deeds of the bishops of Halberstadt (Gesta episcoporum Halberstadensium)*[22] devoted to Bishop Conrad's participation on the Fourth Crusade and of *Concerning the land of Jerusalem and how the relics were brought from the City of Constantinople to this church [of Soissons] (De terra Iherosolimitana et quodmodo ab urbe Constantinopolitana ad hanc ecclesiam [Suessionensem] allate sunt reliquie)*[23] which dealt with the relics brought or sent back by Nivelon, bishop of Soissons. As perhaps the most prominent prelate on the crusade – he not only announced the election of Baldwin of Flanders as emperor but was also entrusted with his coronation – Nivelon was in an excellent position to acquire relics quite openly. The abbot of Pairis by contrast obtained his cache of relics surreptitiously. We have seen how he stowed them away on board his ship. This was done in anticipation of a swift departure to the Holy Land. It was in part to counter such behaviour that the crusade leadership entrusted relics to the safekeeping of Garnier, bishop of Troyes, who was responsible for their allotment to worthy homes. His reputation did something to remove the stain of sacrilege that hung over the acquistion of relics. He kept for his own church a fragment of the Cross, the dish of the Last Supper, an arm of St James the Greater, the head of St Philip, and the body of St Helena of Athyra, about which more later. He sent the head of St Victor to the cathedral of Sens. He also intended to make a gift of the head of St Mamas to the cathedral of Langres in Burgundy, which had long been a centre of the saint's cult, but he died in April 1205 before he could carry out this wish. A priest from Langres, Walon of Dampierre – somebody we have already met in a different context – then requested the relic from the papal legate, Peter Capuano, who had assumed responsibility for the distribution of relics. Priest and legate went together to the bishop of Troyes's lodgings, where the relics were stored, and the priest was allowed to take away the head. He went to great trouble to have the relic authenticated, even calling on the abbot and monks of the monastery of St Mamas to obtain confirmation of its authenticity. Almost immediately he was made bishop of Domoko in Thessaly, for Walon of Dampierre is none other than the runaway bishop of Domoko, who sold off his bishopric to the constable of Romania. He returned home, taking with him the head of St Mamas, which he gave in 1209 to the cathedral of Langres.[24]

This tale of the translation of a relic is not perhaps as edifying as the canon of Langres who tells it would like, nor was Walon of Dampierre quite 'the honest man of good repute' that he remembered. But the story underlines two important considerations about the wholesale transfer of relics from Constantinople to the West. The first was that the element of sacrilege was minimised; the second was that the relics had to be properly authenticated. This emerges from the contemporary narrative of Rostang, a monk of Cluny, about the abbey's acquisition of the head of St Clement from two Burgundian knights, who had taken part in the conquest of Constantinople and had then set off to fulfil their vows by making a pilgrimage to Jerusalem. They were frustrated by contrary winds which drove them back to Constantinople. They wanted some memento of their endeavour and turned to the papal legates Peter Capuano and Benedict of Santa Susanna, who authorised their acquisition of relics as long as it was not tarnished by the use of money. They heard that the monastery of the Peribleptos possessed the head of St Clement. While one knight distracted the attention of the sacristan, the other walked off with the head. Since no money exchanged hands, they had fulfilled their pledge to the papal legates! After making sure of the authenticity of the relic they set off home.[25]

Official authorisation was not always forthcoming as the story of Walon of Sarton reveals. He was a canon of Picquigny, just outside Amiens, who went on the Fourth Crusade and became a canon of the church of St George of the Mangana. In the aftermath of Adrianople he decided that it was time to return home, but did not want to go empty-handed. He claimed to have found not only reliquaries containing an arm and a finger of St George, which had been carefully hidden in the church precincts, but also two larger silver reliquaries identified by Greek inscriptions. Not wishing to alert anybody to his discovery, he went round the churches of Constantinople comparing inscriptions until he could be sure that one reliquary contained the head of St George and the other the head of John the Baptist. Back at Amiens he gave the head of John the Baptist to the cathedral while the head of St George went to the abbey of Marestmontiers. His reward was not long in coming. Six months later he was made a canon of Amiens, but on the understanding that he would endow a chapel within the cathedral. This was by way of atonement for selling off the silver reliquaries which contained the two heads. It strongly suggests that there were some misgivings about how the relics were obtained.[26] The same is true of the Holy Rood of Bromholm, a fragment of the True Cross which was supposed to have been carried into battle by the Byzantine emperors. It reached the East Anglian house long after the conquest of Constantinople, as a result of a deal with an English priest who had been on pilgrimage to Jerusalem at the time of the Fourth Crusade. Like so many others, he decided to try his luck at Constantinople, where he became a chaplain of the Emperor Baldwin I. He found himself in charge of the relics from the imperial palace that had passed into the safe keeping of the Latin emperor. On the eve of the battle of Adrianople he was sent back to Constantinople to fetch the relic of the True Cross which the Byzantine emperors had used as a battle standard. The outcome of the battle prompted him to return home taking the Holy Rood with him. He originally wanted it to go to the Augustinian house of Weybourne, but the canons turned down the offer as suspicious.[27]

The transfer of relics from Constantinople to the West in the immediate aftermath of the fall of the city played an important role in the way contemporaries understood the meaning of the event. The crusade leadership sought to regulate the traffic in relics by placing their distribution in the hands of reputable figures, first the bishop of Troyes and then the papal legates. But there were still worries about the traffic in relics, which surfaced at the Fourth Lateran Council in 1215. It was felt that the buying and selling of relics was bringing Christianity into disrepute. Too often relics were put on display or hawked around for the sake of profit. The influx of relics from Constantinople evidently produced something of a crisis of authority, which the council sought to defuse by bringing the traffic in relics more closely under papal supervision. The display of relics to attract alms now required papal authorisation. Particularly worrying were the cults that grew up around newly-acquired relics. These too needed papal approval. How otherwise was it possible to know whether they were genuine? This was a question addressed by the council. It decided that relics must be displayed in reliquaries, which provided some proof of identity.[28] This measure seems to have satisfied the doubts there were about the influx of relics, because thereafter there were few, if any, voices raised in the West questioning the acquisition of relics from Constantinople, which was seen as a happy – if unlooked for – consequence of a flawed undertaking.

It made it possible to appropriate elements from Byzantium without paying too much attention to the rights and wrongs of the conquest of Constantinople. Of the presents that Abbot Martin made to the German King Philip of Swabia, Gunther of Pairis singles out a single item: an *enkolpion* containing precious relics with a lid in the form of a large jasper. Engraved on it was the Lord's Passion. Gunther claimed that it was worn by the Byzantine emperor on solemn occasions, as an 'indisputable token of his imperial power'.[29] The meaning of this gift did not have to be spelt out. It represented to however small a degree the appropriation by the German king of Byzantine imperial claims. In more general terms, the transfer of relics from Constantinople to the West was hailed as a sign of divine favour. Gunther of Pairis makes much of this:

> None of the faithful ought, therefore, to believe or even imagine anything other than that this was done under the shelter of divine grace, in order that so many important, deeply venerated relics would arrive at our church by the agency of a man who retained his great modesty in the face of numerous obstacles.

Gunther believed that the acquisition of these relics was for the benefit of 'all of Germany [which] began to be adjudged happier in its own eyes, more famous before humanity, and more blessed before God'.[30] His conclusion was that the relics provided proof that the conquest of Constantinople was not a mere accident, but the will of God. Scarcely less enthusiastic was the Halberstadt chronicler when he described Bishop Conrad's return with the relics he acquired at Constantinople. He ascribed to their arrival the peace and prosperity which reigned in Germany now that the schism between empire and papacy had ended. The occasion was one of great rejoicing as the whole town flocked to greet the relics which were paraded on a cart.[31] It was the same when Abbot Martin entered the city of Basel, whence he had set out on crusade,[32] or when the relics sent back by Bishop Nivelon reached Soissons. But on this occasion a blind man was healed.[33] Over and over again, miraculous cures revealed the efficacy of relics brought back from Constantinople. They helped to overcome popular objections to any innovations that the acquisition of new relics produced. To enhance his gift of the head of St Thomas to the church of Soissons, Bishop Nivelon enjoined that throughout the diocese the feast of the translation of St Thomas should be celebrated with due solemnity as a holiday. This produced widespread opposition because it interrupted work. There was general resentment at the loss of a day's wages. The wave of discontent was defused when the leader of the protest – described as a deranged old woman – was led into the cathedral and emerged in a calmer state of mind. The church's propaganda succeeded and the festival was thereafter celebrated to popular acclaim.[34]

The lists of the relics acquired after the conquest of Constantinople suggest at first sight a complete lack of discrimination. On closer inspection, it is clear that some relics were more highly prized than others. At the top of the list of relics brought back by Abbot Martin of Pairis comes 'a trace of the Blood of our Lord Jesus Christ, which was shed for the redemption of the entire human race'.[35] Next there was 'wood from our Lord's Cross, on which the Son of the Father was sacrificed for us, the new Adam who paid the debt of the old Adam'. There followed 'a not inconsiderable piece' of St John the Baptist and the arm of St James the Apostle. The larger the relic the more it was appreciated: heads and arms in particular. In Gunther of Pairis's list of relics a foot of St Cosmas and a tooth of St Lawrence come far above relics that might have been thought more precious. The likely reason for this is that they were more substantial; they retained the saint's aura, while the other relics were no more than mementoes which preserved only the faintest trace of the power of saints and martyrs.

On first inspection Conrad of Halberstadt brought back a more impressive haul than Abbot Martin. At the top of the list were exactly the same items as there were for Abbot Martin: the blood of Jesus Christ followed by fragments of the True Cross. Then came a series of the relics of the Passion: the stone of the sepulchre; the Crown of Thorns; the shroud and *sudarium*; the scarlet robe; the Sponge and the Reed; and Christ's sandals.[36] These were the most precious relics there were. As we shall see, they passed from the Byzantine emperors into the possession of the Emperor Baldwin I and eventually to King Louis IX of France. It was not possible for Bishop Conrad to have obtained these relics. It is conceivable that on his departure from Constantinople he received from the new Latin emperor some tokens of the relics of the

Passion, but being so highly prized the chronicler placed them at the top of his list. They were followed by portions of St John the Baptist and various apostles. As one might expect, the bishop managed to acquire relics of St Stephen, patron of his church. There are some anomalies: the skull of Mary Magdalene comes near the bottom of the list, but above the hand and arm of St Euphemia and relics of other female saints. That may in itself be an explanation: women came last.

The list of the relics that Bishop Nivelon sent back to Soissons is more limited but shows greater discrimination. They came in two batches. The cathedral of the Blessed Virgin Mary received the head of St Stephen, a finger of St Thomas and the top of the head of St Mark. There was one thorn from the Crown of Thorns, a portion of the towel that Christ used at the Last Supper, and part of the Virgin's robe. Appropriately enough the bishop gave the nunnery of Notre-Dame-de-Soissons the Virgin's girdle and the abbey of St John the forearm of St John the Baptist. The second batch of relics was less impressive, even if it did contain the head of St Thomas. Out of the eleven items recorded no less than four were crucifixes 'made from the wood of the Lord'. Holy roods were missing from the first batch of relics sent back by Bishop Nivelon.[37] Their presence reflected the mission which had brought the bishop back to his see: to rally support for the Latin Empire in the wake of the defeat at the battle of Adrianople. To judge by the few relics that have survived in the West from the conquest of Constantinople, reliquaries and phylacteries containing fragments of the True Cross were among the most popular items brought back. Though self-selecting these remnants bear out the contemporary lists of relics that we have examined. There was a demand for relics associated first and foremost with Christ and His Passion, then for those of the Blessed Virgin Mary and finally for those of the apostles and the major saints. These had always been the most precious relics and had not always been easy to obtain in the West. There was little call for the Old Testament relics, though Bishop Nivelon did gift the staff of Moses to Soissons. There was more or less no interest in Orthodox cults and saints, with one puzzling exception, which we shall come to. Despite the worries of the Fourth Lateran Council there was no explosion of new cults. In most cases, the relics went to reinforce existing ones. The cathedral of Langres had long been a centre of the cult of St Mamas. The acquistion of the saint's head in 1209 did much to enhance an already existing collection of the saint's relics.

The arrival of relics from the sack of Constantinople was regarded as the acquisition of new spiritual power, which worked to the well-being of the community at large. But what concrete expression was it given? It came most obviously in the form of new building works. At Chartres the gift of the head of St Anne by Stephen, count of Blois, allowed the resumption of work on the cathedral, which had been halted by the fire of June 1194. The cathedral was dedicated to the Blessed Virgin Mary. A relic of the Virgin's mother was a more than appropriate gift and extended the range of the cult of the Virgin Mary at Chartres, which helped to increase the donations of the pious. As well as helping his own church of Soissons, Bishop Nivelon donated relics to other churches. He gave the forearm of St Stephen to the cathedral of Châlons-sur-Marne with strict instructions to the chapter that half the revenue generated should be spent on the fabric of the church and the other half on a bridge across the Marne.[38]

An important collection of relics was sent back from Constantinople to Troyes by its bishop Garnier de Trainel. The most important relics were those of the True Cross together with relics of the apostles St Philip and St James the Greater. Also included was the chalice of the Last Supper which was soon identified with the Holy Grail. Besides these the relics of St Helena of Athyra seem a little disappointing. They were not those of Constantine's mother, but of an obscure Byzantine saint. Even so the new Troy needed its Helen! To find out more about this Byzantine saint the chapter commissioned a Latin cleric in Constantinople to translate into Latin a Greek life of the saint. This cache of relics was used in the usual way to generate income for the rebuilding of the cathedral. There matters may well have rested, had not the cathedral still in the process of construction been destroyed in 1228 by a storm. This was remarkable enough for Alberic of Trois-Fontaines to devote a few lines to the incident. The main feature was the miraculous escape of the reliquary containing the head of St Philip; the chronicler says nothing about the casket containing the body of St Helena, though we know that it suffered severe damage.[39] Despite this the chapter decided to promote the cult of St Helena to raise funds for a new building campaign. As late as 1260 it instituted a procession in her honour, which brought in sufficient donations from the faithful to allow the final completion of the cathedral.

The use to which these relics were put is entirely predictable. What is unexpected, as P. J. Geary has shown in an exemplary study,[40] is the successful promotion of the cult of a minor Byzantine saint in a place such as Troyes. Why should Garnier de Trainel have bothered to include her relic among those that he sent back to his church? After all, he was the *procurator sanctorum reliquarum* with responsibility for the safe keeping and distribution of relics. He could within reason take his pick. Maximilien Durand has recently made the intriguing suggestion that what was so attractive about St Helena was her excellent state of preservation, which would have excited comparisons with Helen of Troy. The casket and the silks in which the body was wrapped were also of the highest quality.[41] One should not minimise the aesthetic power exercised by a relic nor an authenticity founded on a *Life* which, it was claimed, originally came from the pen of St John Chrysostom. The success of the cult of St Helena of Athyra is an anomaly. It did not conform to the latest fashions in piety, which stressed the humanity of Christ and His Mother. St Helena was an old-fashioned wonder-worker. Her miracles revolve around her ring and her handkerchief; the former tempered sexual passion while the latter cured toothache. In the age of St Francis and St Dominic, let alone of St Thomas Aquinas, this has a banal ring to it but, in the everyday world confronted by the church, toothache before modern dentistry was almost as much of a problem as sex. St Helena's powers were surely appreciated.

IV

Patrick Geary has raised important questions about the transfer of relics to the West after 1204. He argues that the inflow of relics from Constantinople had the effect of devaluing all but the most precious relics. He concludes that piety in the West sought other forms of expression.[42] His view is that relics belonged to an outdated piety that was being replaced by a devotion to the Eucharist and a concentration on the sufferings of Christ. The danger with this approach lies in too strong a contrast being drawn between the old and the new. They are not necessarily mutually exclusive. Another approach would be to suggest that the influx of relics enriched western religious life in many different ways. In the majority of cases the relics brought from Constantinople gave new allure to existing cults. Exceptionally, as with St Helena of Athyra, they spawned new ones. But they might also act as a stimulus to the new currents of piety. The relics of the Passion provide the best example.

They were the most important relics held in Constantinople. They included the Crown of Thorns, the Holy Lance and a nail from the Cross, the shroud and *sudarium*, the scarlet robe, the sponge and the reed, the sandals, and a stone from the sepulchre. There were other precious relics, such as the *mandylion* – a cloth with Christ's features miraculously imprinted. The Byzantine emperors collected them systematically over many centuries. At the end of the twelfth century they were housed in the Great Palace in the church of the Theotokos Pharos. Their existence was well known in the West. They were seen and described around 1190 by a visitor from northern France.[43] During the sack of Constantinople they remained in the Great Palace – known to the crusaders as the Bucoleon – which was occupied by Boniface of Montferrat who ensured their safety. The palace and the relics of the Passion then passed to the new Emperor Baldwin I. There was no question of them being included with other relics which were handed over to the safe keeping of the bishop of Troyes. We have it on very good authority – that of Nektarios of Casole – that in the immediate aftermath of the conquest of Constantinople the bishop of Halberstadt along with the bishop-elect of Bethlehem found in the treasury of the Great Palace the following relics: the True Cross, the Crown of Thorns, the sandals of Christ, a nail from the cross and the winding cloth, all of which Nicholas was to see when he was in Constantinople in 1206. In addition there was a golden container in which there was preserved the leavened bread of the Last Supper.[44] This is corroborated by Robert of Clari, who visited the Great Palace while it was still in the safe keeping of the marquis of Montferrat. He left a detailed description of the Theotokos Pharos, which he says was called the 'Sainte-Chapelle'. Its interior was dazzling: it was 'so rich and noble that nobody could ever describe the great beauty nor the dignity of this chapel'. Nothing had been touched and the relics of the Passion were intact.[45]

Robert of Clari later gave the monastery of Corbie a crystal cross reliquary which, an inscription informs us, came from the 'Sainte Chapelle'. How he obtained it is never made clear.[46] Perhaps it was a gift from Baldwin I, for the Latin emperors of Constantinople had from the outset control over not only the relics of the Passion, but also other relics preserved within the precincts of the Great Palace. Possession of these precious relics proclaimed the Latin emperors as the inheritors of the patrimony of the emperors of Byzantium. They were a source of considerable prestige to be exercised through carefully judged gifts. The Emperor Baldwin I made a very substantial donation of relics to his former overlord, Philip Augustus, king of France. The most precious relic was a piece of the True Cross. The exact size is given: it was about a foot long and an inch broad – something more than a splinter. Also included was a thorn from the Crown of Thorns together with fragments of the white linen winding cloth of Christ and the scarlet robe given Christ in mockery. In other words, the Latin emperor was making a gift of pieces of the relics of the Passion.[47] In 1208 the Emperor Henry of Hainault sent his agent Ponce de Lyon to the West with relics and other precious objects from the Great Palace. His instructions were to use these for the benefit of the Latin Empire. This might be through judicious gifts, but the need for ready cash was such that Ponce de Lyon was allowed to sell or mortgage relics as he saw fit. He returned the next year with much needed money and supplies.[48]

We know that money was always a problem for the Latin emperors, but they clung on to the relics of the Passion. By the reign of John of Brienne (1231–7) they were just about the only financial resource left to the Latin emperor. In the face of the combined Bulgarian-Nicaean assault on Constantinople of 1235 John of Brienne raised money from a consortium headed by the Venetian *podestà* acting with the approval of the doge. He used the Crown of Thorns and other relics of the Passion as security.[49] The sum raised amounted to 13,134 *hyperpyra*.[50] Repayment fell due in September 1238. By that time John of Brienne was dead and the responsibility for the matter fell on the regency council, which borrowed the sum due from Nicholas Quirino, a Venetian financier. As security the Crown of Thorns was deposited in the church of the Pantokrator in the safe keeping of the Venetian treasurer.[51]

The complicated terms set out for the repayment of the new loan reveal the uncertainties that existed. The regency council was playing for time as its members waited for news of the young Emperor Baldwin II, who had departed in 1236 for the French court where he did not cut an imposing figure. The Queen Mother Blanche of Castile found him childish and unprepossessing. 'An Empire', she is supposed to have said, 'requires a more capable and vigorous ruler.'[52] Baldwin had gone to the French court in search of money, very possibly to repay the original loan taken out on the strength of the Crown of Thorns. He had at his disposal his territories in the Low Countries. The most important of these was the county of Namur, which he immediately pledged to Louis IX for the large sum of 50,000 livres, which worked out as somewhat less than a third of the sum for which the relics had been pledged. The young emperor then let it be known that he wished the Crown of Thorns to go to the French king. The regency council in Constantinople may well have had prior knowledge that the young emperor would make an offer of this kind. What its members could not know was how Louis IX would react, hence their uncertainties about the repayment of the loan. The French king agreed to the proposal and sent two Dominicans to Constantinople to make a formal application for the relic. They arrived late in 1238 to discover that the Crown of Thorns had already been pledged to Venice. According to the terms of the agreement the relic had now to be taken to Venice. The two Dominicans were entrusted with this task; they deposited it in the treasury of St Mark's, while they raised the necessary sums of money. They eventually redeemed it for 10,000 *hyperpyra*, which worked out at 135,000 livres.

The translation of this relic was one of the major events of Louis IX's reign. The reception of the Crown of Thorns was carefully stage-managed. The king, together with his mother and his brothers, went out on 11 August 1239 to receive the relic at Villeneuve-l'Archevêque near Sens. Stripped to the waist and barefooted the king and Robert of Artois, the eldest of his brothers, carried the relic into Sens, a scene that would be depicted in the windows of the Sainte-Chapelle. This episode was modelled on an incident recounted in the *Golden Legend*, when Heraclius brought the relic of the True Cross back to Jerusalem after its recovery from the Persians. Louis IX was presenting himself as a Christian ruler in the line of Constantine, whose mother Helena had discovered the True Cross, and in the line of Heraclius who had recovered it. From Sens the Crown of Thorns was conveyed by river to Paris. Finally on 19 August the king and his brother did their duty once more and carried the relic into the city. They went first to the cathedral of Notre-Dame and then deposited the Crown of Thorns in the chapel in the royal palace. As the relic was paraded through the streets on the shoulders of the king, there were shouts of 'Blessed is he who comes in the honour of the Lord, through Whose agency the kingdom of France is exalted by the presence of so great a gift.'[53] We owe this detail to a leading participant in the event, Cornaut, archbishop of Sens, who left a contemporary account of the arrival of the Crown of Thorns in Paris. His purpose was to establish the deeper significance of the event, which he spelt out in the following words: 'Just as the Lord Jesus Christ chose the Holy Land to reveal the mysteries of his redemption, so he seems and is believed to have specially chosen our France for the most devoted veneration of his Passion.'[54] Around the Crown of Thorns a concept of France as a promised land was quickly taking shape. It was built around new currents of piety which centred on the sufferings of Christ. But the feelings aroused were still triggered and legitimised by relics, even if they were the most precious there were – the relics of the Passion.[55]

Once the Crown of Thorns had come into his possession it was more or less inevitable that the French king would set about acquiring other relics of the Passion belonging to the Latin emperor. Before Baldwin II finally left France in June 1239 he gifted the French king a substantial fragment of the True Cross which had been pawned to the Templars of Syria. Two Dominicans were put in charge of recovering the relic from the Temple house at Acre. They stopped off at Constantinople to pick up letters from the Latin emperor authorising the redemption of the relic, which they passed on to a French knight, whom they entrusted with the redemption of the relic of the True Cross from the Templars at Acre. At the same time the knight was also able to acquire other precious relics which the Latin emperor had also pawned to the Temple. He brought these and the Cross back to Paris, where on 30 September 1241 they were solemnly received at the gates of the city by the king.

Meanwhile the two Dominicans had stayed at Constantinople, where they negotiated with the Emperor Baldwin II about the acquistion of a whole series of other relics of the Passion, which the emperor had pledged for the defence of the Latin Empire. They included the Holy Lance, the Holy Reed, the Holy Sponge, the *sudarium* and the scarlet robe. These were brought back to Paris in August 1242. The king declared the day of their arrival, 29 August, a public holiday. Paris was now 'almost a second Jerusalem'. Consciously or not, it was as though Paris was replacing Constantinople as the New Jerusalem.[56]

Having acquired these precious relics at colossal cost,[57] Louis IX now had to house them fittingly. Work was well under way by 1244 when indulgences were first offered to those preparing to visit the relics in the chapel that was under construction. It was consecrated on 26 April 1248 in the presence of the papal legate. The new chapel was always known as the Sainte-Chapelle. It has been urged that the name was chosen in conscious imitation of the imperial palace chapel at Constantinople. Robert of Clari certainly designates this chapel as the Sainte-Chapelle in his *History*.[58] It is unlikely that this text was known to many outside Picardy, but there is a very good chance that Clari used the term because it was current among westerners. At the French court there would still have been some memory of the splendour of the Great Palace, if only because of the legendary visit of Charlemagne to Constantinople. Louis IX would have set out to emulate the dazzling beauty of the chapel of the Theotokos Pharos, where the relics of the Passion had been housed. But he would also have been conscious of the need to emphasise that his acquistion of the relics inaugurated a new dispensation. The architecture of the Sainte-Chapelle was triumphantly modern. Its resplendence emphasised the bankruptcy both of the Byzantine Empire and of the Latin Empire. Their rulers did not deserve to act as guardians of such sacred relics. Very properly, Baldwin II had admitted his incapacity and had handed them over to the safe keeping of the French king. Like the Byzantine emperors before him, he had proved unworthy of a task that had been handed on by Constantine and Heraclius. The guardianship of the relics of the Passion now fell to the Capetian kings of France. This was one of the themes explored in the stained glass of the Sainte-Chapelle. This followed the history of the relics of the passion, beginning with the discovery of the Holy Cross by St Helena, mother of the Emperor Constantine. Its seizure by the Persian King of Kings Chosroes and its recovery by the Emperor Heraclius. These scenes anticipated the arrival of the relics of the Passion in Paris, where they passed into the safe keeping of the French king. The meaning of the programme of the Sainte-Chapelle stained glass is crystal clear. Sacral kingship was rooted in Israel, but given a new dimension by the Incarnation, which was realised through the Emperor Constantine's conversion to Christianity. Its significance was made plain through his mother's discovery of the True Cross. The mantle of the New Israel had now passed from Constantinople to France as the acquisition of the relics of the Passion demonstrated.[59]

As far as the French monarchy was concerned the true meaning of the fall of Constantinople to the crusaders in 1204 lay in the chain of events it unleashed which allowed Louis IX to obtain the relics of the Passion, thus turning Paris into the New Jerusalem. The implication was that it was a divine judgement on the Byzantine emperors who had failed to fulfil their duties towards God. It was equally a judgement on the Latin Empire which had not proved itself worthy of the responsibilities it had inherited from Byzantium. The transfer of the relics of the Passion into the safe keeping of the kings of France legitimised an unfortunate accident and highlighted France's destiny. It may not just be a coincidence that once the relics of the Passion were safely housed in Paris military help for the Latin Empire almost immediately dried up. The last major expedition that set off from France to go to its aid was in June 1239, as the Crown of Thorns was making its way from Venice to Paris. Nothing could be more contemptuous than a contemporary's dismissal of the Latin Empire as 'the land where people go to play at war'.[60]

V

Religious life in the West was immeasurably enriched by the relics that were brought from Constantinople. They gave new life to old cults and traditional expressions of piety. They equally fed into the new fashions of worship. The West took from Byzantium what it required. It was not a question of religious developments in the West being influenced by Byzantine forms of piety, despite their richer and more varied range of expression. Relics did not enjoy the same primacy as a focus of spiritual devotion in Byzantium that they had in the West. Though of the greatest significance they were complemented by icons which added a visual dimension to spiritual devotions. Before 1204 there is little sign, except perhaps in Rome, that icons had any significant role in Latin worship.[61] Constantinople opened the eyes of at least some of the soldiers of the Fourth Crusade to the importance of icons. The incident that caught the imagination of the chroniclers of the Fourth Crusade was the capture in a skirmish on 2 February 1204 of the icon of the Mother of God used by the Byzantine emperor as a battle standard. It was the cause of great rejoicing. They placed it high on the mast of a galley and paraded it up

and down in front of the walls of Constantinople. Such was its importance that it was alloted to the abbey of Cîteaux.[62] Robert of Clari
provides the most detailed narrative of the event. Images fascinated him.
Unlike any other chronicler of the Fourth Crusade he singled out, as of
special importance, the incident of the icon of the Hodegetria, which
caused such a furore at the time of Henry of Hainault's coronation in
August 1206. He was interested enough in it to report that the Greeks
believed that it was the first image of the Mother of God ever made. He
knew that the Greeks took it on procession – he has every Sunday, when
it should be every Tuesday. He also noted that the Greeks venerated it
and gave it rich presents.[63] He was, in other words, trying to understand
the Greek attitude towards icons, even if the subtleties of Orthodox
teaching on icons are likely to have escaped him.

We have already made use of Robert of Clari's description of the relics
of the Passion in the Theotokos Pharos. But these were not his major
focus of interest. He devotes much more space to three images which
were kept in the church: the Holy Tile, the Holy Towel or *mandylion*
and an icon of St Demetrius, which gave off copious quantities of
myrrh. They were all miracle-working images: the *mandylion* and the
Holy Tile had Christ's features miraculously imprinted on them. Robert
of Clari refers to all these images, including the icon of St Demetrius, as
relics.[64] This provides an insight into his fascination with images. They
were a different kind of relic, one that took visual form. Because they
were relics they were worthy of veneration. This was a point of view that
Innocent III was soon to embrace.

The intense interest shown by Robert of Clari in images cannot therefore have been exceptional. It was almost a natural reaction to being
exposed to unusual forms of piety. Not everybody will have approved
and it did not automatically mean that icons would become popular in
the West, though icons were to be found among the items sent back to
the West after the conquest of Constantinople.[65] But the fact remains
that in the course of the thirteenth century panel painting became popular
in the West as a focus of devotions in a way that had not happened
before. Was this not in some way conditioned by western exposure to
Byzantine icons and the practices associated with them? This line of
thought lies behind Hans Belting's contention that in the aftermath of
1204 western religious art was able to appropriate the Byzantine icon.[66]

Belting has developed his thesis with great subtlety and skill, but
before examining it in greater detail, as a way of measuring the possible
impact that the conquest of Constantinople may have made on the
West, there is a major objection that has recently been given prominence.[67]
The objection is twofold: there is very little evidence either that 1204 was

followed by a mass transfer of Byzantine art to the West – reliquaries excepted – or that there was any real appreciation of Byzantine art in the West in the thirteenth century. The two things are obviously connected. Robert Nelson points out that of surviving illustrated Byzantine manuscripts only two are known to have been in the West in the thirteenth century. One of these – an eleventh-century 'Gospel Book' (Vatican. graecus 756) – reached Sicily via the crusader states. The other is more famous – the 'Cotton Genesis', which, it is generally agreed, served as a pattern book for the atrium mosaics of St Mark's Venice, carried out after 1204.[68] The 'Cotton Genesis' dates from the fifth or sixth century. It may well have been that its recommendation was indeed its antiquity. Its style separated it quite clearly from contemporary Byzantine products. Nor is there any guarantee that it came from Constantinople. It could just as easily have come from an Egyptian or Palestinian church or monastery. The apparent absence of illustrated Byzantine manuscripts in the West hardly suggests that in the thirteenth century western artists had much time for contemporary Byzantine models.

There are almost no imported Byzantine icons documented from this period.[69] In his collection of miracle tales compiled in 1223, Caesarius of Heisterbach has one edifying story about a Byzantine icon. It is a mosaic icon of St Nicholas, which still survives. It belonged to the Cistercian abbey of Burtscheid near Aachen and was known to have miraculous properties. It was particularly helpful in cases of difficult childbirth. It was allegedly brought to the monastery by the founder of the abbey, who was supposed to have been a son of the king of Greece, but this was a pious legend designed to give the icon greater authenticity.[70] In fact, it probably dates from the eleventh century. There is nothing to connect it with the conquest of Constantinople in 1204. Caesarius also has a story about a knight who entered the Cistercian Order and kept for his private devotions an ivory image of the Mother of God – an appellation which suggests that it was of Byzantine origin.[71] These two stories are all that Caesarius's bulky collection has on Byzantine icons. Far more prominent are the statues of the Virgin, which were a more obvious manifestation of western taste and devotions.

But how can we reconcile this apparent indifference to Byzantine art in the early thirteenth-century West with the frontispiece of Matthew Paris's *World History*? This has three images, two of Christ and one of Mary and Child, which reproduce the latest types of Byzantine icons.[72] There is an argument that knowledge of Byzantine art reached the West through pattern and sketch books: the Wolfenbüttel sketchbook is a rare survival from the 1230s, which contains Byzantine material. Another possibility is that the Norman kingdom of Sicily continued to act as a centre of transmission of knowledge of Byzantine art to the West, a role it had played throughout the twelfth century. The famous Byzantine icon at Spoleto of the Theotokos Antiphonetissa reached Umbria in the fourteenth century via Sicily. There is the possibility raised by Anne Derbes that familiarity with Byzantine art may owe something to the presence of the Franciscans in Constantinople from the 1220s.[73] The cycle of St Francis in his order's headquarters at Constantinople – now the Kalenderhane Cami – points to the presence of Italian artists in Constantinople, where at the same time Byzantine artists were working for Latin patrons.[74] The role of the Dominicans who also had a house at Constantinople should not be forgotten. As part of their work among the Orthodox, they took a deep interest in Byzantine art. A Dominican used his knowledge of Byzantine iconographies to find common ground between the two churches over the question of purgatory.[75]

However one looks at the problem, the inescapable conclusion is that – once again, reliquaries excepted – the conquest of Constantinople did not play any very large part in the physical transmission of Byzantine art to the West. But it may well have led to a greater awareness of the spiritual powers accorded by the Orthodox Church to icons. It was a problem that Innocent III was forced to confront in the immediate aftermath of 1204 when the dispute between the Latin patriarch Thomas Morosini and the Venetian *podestà* over the image of the Hodegetria was referred to him. He supported the patriarch's actions, which did not have the full support of the Latin community at Constantinople. The pope thought that some people were paying too much attention to Byzantine ideas about icons. The pope dismissed as superstition 'that opinion by which the Greeks suppose that the spirit of the Blessed Virgin Mary resides in the aforesaid image on account of which they perhaps venerate it more than its due'.[76] This does not mean that Innocent III was hostile to all images. As his promotion of the Veronica demonstrates, he favoured images that could be treated as relics. The image of the Veronica only came into prominence in the late twelfth century. It was kept at St Peter's. At the time, it was supposed to be the towel (*sudarium*) with which on the night before his Passion Christ had wiped away 'His sweat [that] was as it were great drops of blood falling down to the ground' (Luke 22: 44). At first, there was no question of the features of Christ showing up on the towel. Only bloodstains were visible. But well before the end of Innocent III's pontificate there was general agreement that the features of Christ were imprinted on the Veronica. Gerald of Wales was deeply impressed by it and is adamant that Christ had left his image on the Veronica 'as an imprint'. He admitted that it was difficult to see because of the 'veils that were hung in front of it'. Innocent III fostered popular devotion to this relic by displaying it publicly during the procession on the second Sunday after Epiphany to the hospital of the Holy Spirit, which he had founded. In 1216 there was a sensation when it proved impossible to return the Veronica to its reliquary with the features of Christ the right way up. Disconcerted Innocent III composed a special prayer to the Veronica and granted ten days' indulgence to all who recited it. His prayer went as follows: 'Lord, you have left behind for us, who are marked by the light of your face, the image imprinted on the cloth as your memorial.' This provided clear papal approval of the image of Christ imprinted on the Veronica.

The Veronica is central to Hans Belting's argument. In the short space of Innocent III's reign (1198–1216) the Veronica had turned into a miraculous image and, what is more, one which had the papal blessing. But it is a development that seems to lie entirely within a Latin frame of reference. There is no obvious connection to the fall of Constantinople. Belting is far too subtle to argue for any direct Byzantine influence. Instead he isolates the role played by Byzantine reliquaries which were sent back in large quantities after 1204 and were highly prized in the West. These reliquaries provided visual proof of the authenticity of the relics that they contained. Transferred to a western context they forced a reappraisal of the relationship of image and relic. The image served as testimony. It meant that it was now possible to give credence to the conviction of the credulous that the features of Christ could be made out on the Veronica. This was given practical effect at some point before 1216 when the features of Christ must have been dyed into the cloth. To emphasise its status as a relic the Veronica was normally kept in a reliquary of rock crystal.[77]

Hans Belting suggests that Innocent III's recognition of the miraculous powers of the Veronica opened the way to a greater western appreciation of images as devotional tools. But its effect was rather to constrict the role of other wonder-working images, which were treated as potential rivals. Take for example the *mandylion*, which made such an impression on Robert of Clari. It passed after 1204 into the hands of the Latin emperors. It remained in Constantinople until it was gifted in 1247 by the Latin Emperor Baldwin II to Louis IX. It formed part of the treasure of the Sainte-Chapelle and is recorded in its inventories.[78] Beside the relics of the Passion housed in the Sainte-Chapelle it made almost no impact. There is another tradition that the *mandylion* went to Rome, where it came into the possession of the nuns of S. Silvestro in Capite. This exemplar, just like its Paris counterpart, languished in obscurity, completely eclipsed by the power and fame of the Veronica.[79] The difference was that the latter had papal approval. Innocent III's promotion of miraculous images of Christ was not a sign of direct Byzantine influence. The conquest of Constantinople continued to be seen as a triumph of the Roman Church. It undoubtedly produced a greater awareness of the devotional differences that separated the two churches. Building on relics and images that were already present in Rome, Innocent III determined to set the papal stamp on popular devotions associated with relics and icons. This became all the more necessary in the face of the relics, reliquaries and other objets d'art, including a few icons, that arrived in the West in the aftermath of the Fourth Crusade. Innocent III wanted these to be understood in ways that conformed to western tradition; he did not want Byzantine ideas about religious art seeping in.

Innocent III promoted images that were closely connected with relics of one sort or another. He was insistent upon the importance of reliquaries, which provided visual authentification of the relics they contained. He also approved of *acheropita*, such as the Lateran Christ, which he had covered in silver and gilt, so that only the features of Christ were visible. This icon had been in Rome since at least the seventh century and it was supposed to have been the work of St Luke with advice from the Virgin Mary and with the help of an angel. Innocent III's attitude to images was restrictive. It scarcely prepared the way for the growing popularity in Italy of panel paintings, which was a feature of the thirteenth century.

Hans Belting is on much stronger ground when he connects this with the mendicant orders. They were the promoters of a spirituality that centred on the Blessed Virgin Mary and on the Passion. Unlike earlier devotional movements in the West there was much greater use made of panel paintings as an expression of spirituality. The West was experiencing a development which had long been central to Byzantine piety. Byzantine art disposed of an iconographic repertoire that exactly met the requirements of the new devotional practices associated with the mendicants. Is there therefore, as Hans Belting suggests, a Byzantine background to mendicant spirituality? In very general terms, the answer must be yes: Byzantine iconographies of the Passion and of the Blessed Virgin Mary were taken over and adapted by Italian artists, who also generalised the Byzantine practice of depicting the crucified Jesus Christ with His eyes closed as though He were dead. This was done to emphasise the utter humanity of Christ. But Byzantine influences were quickly absorbed. The possibility of the West adopting the Byzantine system of images never arose. Byzantium offered the materials necessary for a quite independent line of development. Hans Belting suggests that the western altar piece – one of the most characteristic forms of late medieval art in the West – had its origins in the Byzantine icon and developed into an 'icon frieze' inspired by the Byzantine iconostasis. He concludes, however, that rather than 'testifying to the existence of an actual image cult', the altar piece 'proves to be its heir and successor'.[80] This is an important qualification, since altar piece and iconostasis serve different purposes and obey entirely different rationales, which emphasise the gulf existing between Latin and Orthodox worship. The iconostasis conceals the altar from the congregation; the altarpiece emphasises its centrality.

Anne Derbes has recently looked at the question from a slightly different perspective. She explains the popularity of the Passion cycle largely in terms of the triumph of Franciscan spirituality. She leaves the Dominicans to one side, but notes the differences between the two orders. Dominicans are known to have kept in their cells devotional images, such as the Virgin and Child or the suffering Christ,[81] while the Franciscans preferred narrative images of the Passion. Both orders promoted the use of panel paintings for devotional purposes, whether private or public. Derbes is doubtful that the conquest of Constantinople has any relevance. She notes that Italian artists displayed little interest in Byzantine iconographies until the 1230s. Even then it was rarely a question of direct borrowing. It was much more that Latin spirituality was evolving under the impact of the mendicant orders in a manner reminiscent of Byzantium. It was understandable that Italian artists would look to the repertoire of Byzantine art to help with the elaboration of new iconographies. However, as Derbes underlines, it was no mechanical transcription. The Italian artists of the thirteenth century were creating their own iconographies and their own styles. Byzantine influences were quickly assimilated.[82]

It was no longer a question of the imitation of Byzantine models, as it had normally been earlier in the Middle Ages. Far from enhancing Byzantium's cultural and artistic influence in the West, the conquest of Constantinople had done much to discredit the primacy it had once enjoyed. Because the elements of Byzantine culture, literary and artistic, had before 1204 been so carefully integrated into a system of thought and ideology, it was difficult for outsiders to make significant borrowings of individual elements. Byzantine claims to cultural hegemony had always provoked an ambivalent response in the West. The conquest of Constantinople exposed their hollowness once and for all, but this had a liberating effect. It meant that it was possible to borrow from the detritus of Byzantine culture without regard for the system as a whole. Paradoxically, the fall of Constantinople enriched the culture of the Latin West in a way that had been impossible previously. Elements of Byzantine culture could be used more freely than in the past to advance independent development. The conquest of Constantinople liberated elements of Byzantine culture by destroying the context from which they derived meaning.

VI

Nowhere in the Latin West had been so continuously exposed to Byzantium as Venice. From the seventh century onwards Byzantium and Venice evolved a complicated relationship of mutual benefits and antagonism. The links between them were constantly reforged, most memorably with the chrysobull of 1082, which tied Venice even more closely to Byzantium. It gave Venice a privileged position within the Byzantine Empire as a means of guaranteeing naval support. Venetian traders reaped the rewards. The commercial privileges granted in 1082 underpinned the rapid growth of Venice in the early twelfth century. This was to produce problems that could scarcely have been foreseen at the end of the eleventh century. Venice needed to preserve its privileged position within the Byzantine Empire in the interests of trade, but it also wanted greater independence from Byzantium in order to exploit that privileged position to the full. The result was continuing friction as the two parties tried to come to terms with a changing relationship, in which the Venetians believed they now held the upper hand. By 1171 Venice had overreached itself. Expulsion from the Byzantine Empire came as a real shock and disrupted Venetian trade for decades. Somewhat chastened the Venetians recovered their privileges in the Byzantine Empire in 1187. They were renewed in 1198, when the Venetians obtained more or less everything they could reasonably expect, including recognition of their separate legal status within the Byzantine Empire.

The conquest of Constantinople formed no part of Venetian plans. As we have seen, it presented the Venetians with enormous problems. They were plunged into a protracted struggle to secure control over the waters of the old Byzantine Empire against its major rivals. This included a long battle to establish Venetian domination over the island of Crete in the face of Genoese ambitions. It would be many years before the Venetians could be sure that their involvement with the Fourth Crusade had worked to their advantage. In the meantime they were blamed by the papacy for the way a crusade had been turned against a Christian power despite the pope's express instructions. Blaming Venice was a way of absolving the crusaders of the conquest of Constantinople, but for a devoted daughter of the papacy it was a hard charge to bear.

The conquest of Constantinople produced a series of challenges which the Venetians succeeded in surmounting, but it equally created uncertainties as the Venetians struggled to come to terms with the consequences of 1204. It is these rather than any need to cover up disreputable actions that lie behind the Venetian failure to produce any sustained contemporary narrative of the conquest of Constantinople. The earliest sustained Venetian account comes from the pen of Martin da Canal, writing in the 1260s. He justified Venice's role in the fall of Constantinople as prompted by its responsibilities to the church. His interpretation conformed to the 'Myth of Venice' which had been taking shape since the late twelfth century. The key was emancipation from imperial control, whether German or Byzantine. Central was the cult of St Mark around which a Venetian identity had come into being. It was given greater resonance by historical events, beginning with the Peace of Venice of 1177, which enjoyed pride of place in the elaboration of the 'Myth of Venice'. It will be remembered that this was the occasion when Venice had paid host to a peace conference which brought together Pope Alexander III and the Emperor Frederick I Barbarossa. The Venetians used this event to underline their independence, which had allowed them to act as honest brokers who had reconciled pope and emperor and had brought peace to Italy. In gratitude Pope Alexander III was supposed to have made a gift of the *Trionfi*. These consisted of a ring, a sword, a lead seal, an umbrella, eight banners and silver trumpets together with the right to carry a white candle in the processsions that marked major feast days. These were the symbols of Venetian autonomy. Needless to say, the list was elastic and took its definite form only in the sixteenth century. There is no contemporary confirmation of Alexander III's grant.[83]

However, by the time Martin da Canal was writing the elements of the story were virtually all in place. The Venetians used the legend of the Peace of Venice to proclaim themselves dutiful servants of the Roman Church. It was a way of counteracting papal criticism of their role in the events leading to the conquest of Constantinople. It was in the light of this legend that the official Venetian version of these events finally evolved. The actions of Enrico Dandolo and the Venetians were prompted all along by their regard for the interests of Christianity and the papacy. Once again Martin da Canal is the first Venetian historian to provide the official interpretation. He makes much of Venice being *au servise de Sainte Yglise*. He has the young Alexius going to the papal curia. Innocent III's response was entirely positive: 'The child is welcome; he comes from the French royal house . . . I shall send [the French and Venetians] my message that they abandon their journey to Jerusalem and take the road to Constantinople and put this child in possession of his City.'[84] However, the people of Constantinople refused to obey the pope's order to receive the young Alexius. The French and Venetians therefore had to resort to force. Finally, when the young Alexius was overthrown, the French crusaders decided to attack the city on their own behalf, but failed. It was left to the Venetians to carry out the conquest. This version is a travesty, but it allowed the Venetians to incorporate the events of 1204 into their developing myth.[85]

It was not possible for the Venetians to disown their part in the fall of Constantinople. The doges assumed the title of *moderator et dominator quarte partis et dimidie imperii romanie*. This was proof of their final emancipation from any Byzantine tutelage. But very little was done directly to celebrate the conquest of Constantinople. Enrico Dandolo was remembered in a new chapel built by his successor Pietro Ziani (1205–29). It stood within the precincts of the ducal palace and was dedicated to St Nicholas. It was supposed to have been decorated with scenes of the conquest of Constantinople.[86] If so, St Nicholas was carefully chosen as the dedicatee of the chapel. While St Mark was the patron saint of Venice, St Nicholas presided over Venice's overseas activities. But the latter's cult was always of secondary importance, which will explain the comparative lack of prominence given in the ritual of the *Serenissima* to the conquest of Constantinople. There was no special ceremonial instituted to celebrate it.

This equivocation contrasts with the decisive way in which the Genoese used their participation in the First Crusade to elaborate their political myth.[87] But the status of the First Crusade as a heroic enterprise under-taken for the benefit of Christendom was never in doubt, whereas the papacy had cast doubts on Venice's role in the Fourth Crusade. Until these were resolved it was difficult for the Venetians to deal openly with their part in the conquest of Constantinople, which nevertheless was a potent – if indirect – influence on the profound changes experienced by Venice in the next half-century. These affected so many aspects of Venice's public life. They were reflected in the changing appearance of the heart of the city around the church of St Mark's. It was deliberately reshaped to provide Venice with a public setting in keeping with its new status. This transformation formed a pendant to the elaboration of the 'Myth of Venice' at roughly the same time. Most striking was the creation of the piazza of St Mark's. The process has quite recently been painstak-ingly investigated by J. Schulz.[88] His major conclusion is that the most important phase occurred after 1204 during the long reign of Pietro Ziani (1205–29), the doge who more than anybody had to confront the consequences for Venice that followed from the conquest of Constan-tinople. Venetian tradition insisted that substantial work had already been completed under the doges Vitale Michiel (1156–72) and Sebastiano

Ziani (1172–8), Pietro's father. But their work was more or less limited to the addition to the ducal palace of a palace of the commune. At the turn of the twelfth century the two palaces along with the church of St Mark's continued to form a separate precinct shut off by a crenellated wall. It is therefore difficult to agree with Schulz's contention that Venice was well ahead of other North Italian cities in the creation of a public space as an expression of communal identity, just as it is to accept *tout court* his argument that the inspiration behind the creation of the piazza of St Mark's came directly from Byzantium.

It was more complicated than this. Over the twelfth century Venice developed in a profoundly un-Byzantine spirit. Communal power increased at the expense of ducal authority. Byzantium scarcely offered a model that Venice could emulate, but it was different after 1204. Once again, it is a question of elements of Byzantine culture being liberated from their original context. It made possible the appropriation of Byzantine elements of town planning in order to glorify the communal ideal espoused by the Venetians. The urban fabric of Constantinople was dominated by the great squares inherited from late antiquity, of which the Augousteon which linked the church of St Sophia and the Great Palace of the Emperors was the most magnificent. These squares were dominated by columns, arcades and arches. Unlike the crusaders the Venetians were anxious to acquire precious marbles, plaques and columns as part of the booty brought back from Constantinople. With their aid over the thirteenth century the piazza of St Mark's acquired various features that one associates with the great squares of Constantinople. There are most notably the two colossal pillars in the piazzetta, but Byzantine influence is apparent in more ordinary ways: the style of the arches used for the earliest buildings round the newly opened up piazza was Byzantine. Perhaps the most interesting addition were the four bronze horses brought from Constantinople and eventually installed over the entrance into the church of St Mark's. It will have to remain a mystery why the Venetians went to the trouble of transporting these horses back to Venice rather than melting them down for coin, in the manner of other crusaders. They had then to store them in the Arsenal for at least half a century. The horses were not in position above the entrance to St Mark's until around 1260. It was only then that the façade of the church had been refashioned in a way that allowed their public display. This was done by the creation of a loggia. The effect of the loggia that now fronts the church is, as has often been remarked, that of a triumphal archway presiding over the piazza – an impression much enhanced by the four horses. The lack of documentation makes it impossible to decide whether the installation of the horses was just a happy accident or deliberately planned.[89] Venetians would have been familiar with triumphal archways from the squares of Constantinople, but a triumphal archway that formed the façade of the main church was entirely Venetian.

The horses were a group that almost certainly came from the Hippodrome. The decision to spare them and then put them in storage for more than half a century must have been done with some purpose in mind. This is strengthened by the care with which other spoils from Constantinople were positioned on the piazza around the church of St Mark's. There was the porphyry group of the four tetrarchs, which came from the Philadelphion at Constantinople; the so-called *pillastri acritani*, which came from the ruined church of St Polyeuktos at Constantinople; and the 'Colonna del Bando', which was the porphyry base of a huge column – in all likelihood from Constantinople. The emphasis on porphyry is important. It was the imperial marble par excellence and underlined Venetian claims. Plunder from Constantinople was to create a public space that was quite different from anything that existed in Constantinople but proclaimed the triumph of Venice. Around the piazza of St Mark's were grouped some of the most important buildings of the city, not only the ducal palace and the church of St Mark's, but also on the northern side the offices of the procurators or administrators of St Mark's, who were responsible for much of the Venetian administration as well as the development of the piazza.[90] It was the Augousteon in Venetian guise.

The spirit of emulation is evident in a new insistence that St Mark's was the most beautiful church in the world. Before 1204 the exterior of St Mark's was of brick in the manner of the great eleventh and twelfth century churches at Constantinople. Spoils from Constantinople in the shape of marbles and reliefs were used to clad the exterior, producing the sumptuous effect that has transfixed the visitor down the centuries. Elaborate decoration of the exterior of a church did not conform to Byzantine taste. The church of St Mark's emerged transformed from the building works undertaken in the aftermath of 1204, as we can see for ourselves from the mosaic over the most northerly of St Mark's five porches – Porta Sant'Alipio – which has preserved a record of its appearance in the mid-thirteenth century. The low flat Byzantine domes of the original church have been replaced by the characteristic tall domes that still dominate its silhouette. The long open gallery above the loggia, already the setting for the four horses, has no equivalent in Byzantium. St Mark's no longer 'proclaimed to all the Christian world the special relationship between Venice and Byzantium', to use Donald Nicol's words.[91] It was now a statement of Venetian independence and inventiveness.

This mosaic above the Porta Sant'Alipio shows the relics of St Mark being transferred into the church and is the only one of the thirteenth-century façade mosaics to survive. These mosaics represented the final stage of a building campaign which had begun after 1204. It was not only the exterior of the church which was transformed, but work was resumed on the interior, even though by the late twelfth century the main decoration of the interior was largely complete.[92] There is good documentary evidence that a new campaign was well under way by 1216.[93] The conquest of Constantinople made available large quantities of gold mosaic and perhaps craftsmen as well. The new compositions constitute some kind of a commentary on Venice's self-image in the aftermath of 1204. The most important was the *Apparitio* – the miraculous discovery of the relics of St Mark. This was a recent piece of myth-making. Apparently, when in 1094 the Doge Vitale Falier (1084–96) came to dedicate the new church, the relics of the saint were nowhere to be found. The saint miraculously disclosed their whereabouts when the south-eastern pier supporting the dome opened up to reveal the saint's sarcophagus. The Feast of the *Apparitio* of St Mark was instituted by Doge Ranier Zen (1253–68) near the beginning of his reign and the new composition was intended as an accompaniment. Otto Demus has pointed out that the interior of St Mark's shown in the mosaic conforms to the arrangements of the thirteenth-century church with its two pulpits, both of which came as loot from Constantinople. He therefore suggests that the doge shown in the mosaic is intended to represent Vitale Falier but in the guise of Ranier Zen. It was designed to honour the latter's part in the institution of the new festival. The purpose was to reinforce the legend of St Mark as central to the public life of the republic by incorporating episodes from recent history. It was a way of putting present achievements into perspective and tying them to the central strand of Venetian civic consciousness, which was always the legend of St Mark.[94]

It was not only the exterior of St Mark's that was enriched by the spoils of Constantinople. The treasury of St Mark's has preserved the richest collection of Byzantine plate and liturgical vessels – many brought from Constantinople. More stunning than any of these was the Pala d'Oro, which served as a retable to the high altar. It is a supreme example of enamel work, mostly Byzantine. In its present form it dates from 1345 when it was remodelled in a Gothic frame. The top register consists of scenes of the Passion on either side of the figure of the Archangel Michael. These enamels are distinctly larger than those of the lower pala, which is arranged around a central medallion of Christ and the four evangelists, who are surrounded on either side by apostles, prophets and angels, all framed by scenes of the life of St Mark. The pala also displays a historical curiosity. Immediately below the central panel the Mother of God is flanked on her right by the Doge Ordelafo Falier (1101–18) and on her left by an Empress Eirene. The figure of the doge has been reworked and is, compared to the figure of the empress, very crude. The presence of these figures is in part explained by the accompanying inscription which provides a history of the Pala d'Oro as it was understood in 1345. It records that the Doge Ordelafo Falier commissioned the Pala d'Oro in 1105 from workshops in Constantinople and that it was remounted in 1209 under Doge Pietro Ziani. Many attempts have been made to reconstruct the appearance of the original Pala d'Oro and there have been many surmises about the changes made in 1209.[95]

Particular attention should be paid to the remarks made by members of a Byzantine delegation who visited St Mark's in 1438 on their way to the council of Ferrara-Florence. They at first accepted the information that the enamels had come from St Sophia. Then one of their number began to have his doubts and insisted that some of the panels must have come from the Pantokrator monastery. Like any other interested observer he might have been wrong, but his arguments were cogent and convinced his companions. He gave as his reason for ascribing some of the enamels to the Pantokrator their inscriptions and the costumes of the Comneni.[96] He must have been referring, on the one hand, to the way in which the enamels in the top register are identified in contrast to virtually all others by Greek inscriptions and, on the other, to the imperial robes of the Doge Ordelafo Falier and of the Empress Eirene at the bottom of the panel. The top register is quite distinct from the rest of the Pala d'Oro because the backing is of gilded silver and not of gold.[97] Its central panel shows the Archangel Michael, who has no special connection with Venice, but who is appropriate in the context of the Pantokrator monastery, where the central funerary church was dedicated to St Michael. There is therefore a very good chance that the top register of enamels did indeed come from the Pantokrator monastery in Constantinople, which was in Venetian hands throughout the period of the Latin Empire.[98] When it was added to the Pala d'Oro is another matter, which brings us to the figures of the Doge Ordelafo Falier and the Empress Eirene. There is an immediate difficulty: the doge's head and title were later insertions of local workmanship, not Byzantine. But the vestments were easily identifiable as appropriate to a Comnenian emperor. Only in that sense does it provide a proper pendant to a Byzantine empress, but who can the Empress Eirene have been? There are two candidates: Eirene Doukaina, the consort of Alexius I Comnenus, or the Empress Eirene, the founder of the Pantokrator Monastery – a Hungarian princess, who became the consort of the Emperor John II

Comnenus (1118–43). The opinion expressed by the Byzantine visitors of 1438 about the provenance of the enamels favours the latter. The absence of the surname Doukaina points in the same direction. If the empress was indeed the second Eirene, then her portrait should have been accompanied by that of her husband John II Comnenus, not one of a Venetian doge.

There is therefore a strong possibility that these enamels came from the Pantokrator, but this leaves two unanswered questions. The first concerns the portrait of the empress. What was the point of retaining it? Could it have been as a dramatic illustration of the fact that Venice now had a share of the Byzantine Empire? But when were the two portraits added to the Pala d'Oro? A possible clue lies in the inscription accompanying it which records that the official responsible for the resetting of the enamels in 1209 was the Procurator Angelo Falier, a descendant of the doge who commissioned the original Pala d'Oro. Would he not have been tempted to replace an enamel of a Byzantine emperor with one showing his famous ancestor? But this would not have been done for family reasons only. In the aftermath of 1204 it proclaimed many things: the eclipse of Byzantine imperial power by Venice and the appropriation of the power and treasures of Byzantium by Venice. It also provided authentification of the tradition that the Pala d'Oro had originally been commissioned by Ordelafo Falier. It was essential that so prominent a piece of liturgical decoration was given a proper Venetian pedigree. Its creation had to be placed in a Venetian setting.[99]

Today the Treasury of St Mark's boasts the richest assemblage of Byzantine liturgical vessels and reliquaries that there is. But only a small proportion of these was acquired in 1204. The collection of relics sent back to St Mark's by Enrico Dandolo was quite modest: the so-called Cross of Constantine; a phial of the Sacred Blood; an arm of St George and part of the head of St John the Baptist. Of these only the arm of St George was missing from the inventory of 1283.[100] The Treasury of St Mark's suffered a serious fire in 1231, but somehow the relics brought from Constantinople were discovered miraculously intact amid the ashes and cinders. There were solemn processions to celebrate the miracle, which is commemorated by a mosaic inserted above the entrance to the Treasury which has two angels displaying a reliquary.[101] It was a way of justifying after the event the acquisition of sacred objects from Constantinople. They had stood the test of fire.

The narrative of the fire of 1231 makes no mention of one of the treasures of St Mark's – the icon of the Mother of God *Nikopoios*, which is often identified with the icon captured by the crusaders in a skirmish in February 1204 from the Byzantine usurper Mourtzouphlos. It was reserved for the abbey of Cîteaux, but there is no evidence that it ever reached that destination. The icon is missing from the 1283 inventory of the Treasury of St Mark's and makes its first appearance in the 1325 inventory. Whether or not the icon in the Treasury of St Mark's was the palladium of the emperors of Byzantium, there is no record of its presence there until long after 1204. Even then it appears to have been neglected. Only at the end of the sixteenth century did Venetian antiquarians begin to pay any attention to it.[102]

The patent neglect of this icon is emblematic of the Venetian reaction to the conquest of Constantinople. At one level it was a glorious achievement. The Treasury of St Mark's soon contained three large standards celebrating the victories of Zara and Constantinople.[103] Against this, there was the problem of appropriation. Byzantine treasures had to be given a Venetian setting and a Venetian meaning. There were difficulties in reconciling Byzantium's imperial legacy, into which Venice had entered, with the constitutional path it had been following ever more clearly from the middle of the twelfth century. These developments had left the authority of the doge subject to the power of the commune represented by the Grand Council and the Lesser Council. It was not feasible for a doge to lay claim to any imperial prerogatives without provoking a reaction. The enamel from the Pala d'Oro showing the Doge Ordelafo Falier in Byzantine imperial regalia is a nonsense, but it reflected imperial claims that were more appropriate to the immediate aftermath of 1204 than any other time of Venetian history.[104] In the twelfth century the doge wore a Byzantine ceremonial robe (*skaramangion*) appropriate for an honorary *protosebastos* of the Byzantine court. Enrico Dandolo added other items of Byzantine court dress, such as a collar (*maniakion*) and wristbands (*epimaniakia*) together with a mantle (*himation*). This is the dress of the doge as shown in three thirteenth-century mosaics from St Mark's, which provide an accurate reflection of the vestments worn by the doge in the aftermath of 1204. The one addition is the *corno* – the ceremonial headpiece – which was to be one of the most distinctive items of apparel worn by the doges of Venice.[105] Its origin is uncertain. It has been normal to assume that it derived from the Byzantine *kamelaukion*, which was a closed crown, but if this was the case then the distinctive imperial marks have been removed. Byzantine court dignitaries were not normally accorded special headgear until the twelfth century, when the mysterious *skiadon* made its appearance. Since there is no convincing description, it is difficult to identify the *corno* with the *skiadon*, as some have been tempted to do.[106]

If 1204 made little or no difference to the dress affected by the doge, official ritual became more elaborate. In his *History* Martin da Canal pays great attention to the splendour of the ducal processions on the main festivals of the Venetian year. It seems unlikely that these were staged in conscious imitation of Byzantine imperial ceremonial, but were more an affirmation of Venice's new sense of power and an assertion of its independence. Even if Constantinople returned to Byzantine rule, the conquest of 1204 destroyed the myth of Byzantium. The Venetians had, in any case, found its imperial and ecumenical claims increasingly irksome, as the charade played out in 1148 showed all too clearly. On that occasion the Venetians mocked their ally, the Byzantine emperor Manuel I Comnenus, by dressing up a negro in imperial vestments and by doing him imperial honours.[107] The downfall of Byzantium underlined Venice's final emancipation from a stage of its history. It was marked by the embellishment of its main church and its surroundings with booty taken from Constantinople. The purpose was not so much to glory in Byzantium's overthrow; more to create a suitable setting for Venice's new sense of itself. Venice came to terms with the fall of Constantinople not by appropriating Byzantium's imperial legacy but by renouncing its Byzantine past.

The meaning ascribed to the fall of Constantinople in the western sources was complicated; it was complicated, if for no other reason, because of the unsatisfactory moral status of the event, but one that worked to the advantage of the West. The Latin West undoubtedly felt that it had a moral right to the relics and other booty taken. The downfall of Byzantium confirmed western superiority, but the failure of the Latin Empire of Constantinople to take root pointed to the moral ambiguity of the enterprise. The conundrum facing western apologists was how to preserve the undoubted gains that followed the destruction of the Byzantine Empire in the face of the doubts raised about its moral propriety. For the French monarchy this was relatively easy because it had never been directly involved in the conquest of Constantinople. In strictly moral terms the Capetian kings of France were the major beneficiaries. The Capetian monarchy was the residuary legatee of the Byzantine emperors. The French kings did not have to justify their acquisition of the relics of the Passion.

The wretched state of the Latin Empire of Constantinople only enhanced their moral standing. To an extent it became a French protectorate. The other major beneficiary of the fall of Constantinople was Venice, even if its leaders could never have anticipated the burdens that the signoria would have to shoulder. In a sense, it allowed Venice to escape from the shadow of Byzantium which from the beginning had hung over its history. The process of emancipation began long before 1204, but the conquest of Constantinople allowed Venice to distance itself from its Byzantine past. Its political evolution could continue untrammelled by its Byzantine connections. How little Venice borrowed in the way of public ritual and ceremonial from Byzantium in the wake of 1204 continues to surprise. If the fall of Constantinople made only a superficial contribution to the 'Myth of Venice', it did provide an opportunity and some of the means for self-assertion. A constant reminder of this existed in the shape of the four horses above the loggia of St Mark's. It was less important that the title of 'Lord of a quarter and half a quarter of the Empire of Romania' would in the course of the later Middle Ages be discretely dropped from the doge's titulature.

VII

How exactly things might have turned out if the crusaders had been sent packing from Constantinople in August 1203 or in April 1204 we cannot know. However, there was an insistent rhythm to Byzantine history, which can be traced back to the fifth century: political weakness followed by the reassertion of the centre and a period of renewed power and stability. This pattern ended with the crusader conquest of Constantinople and only returned in a different form with the establishment of the Ottoman Empire after 1453. 1204 inaugurated a new order, characterised by 'great political fragmentation' and Italian domination of commerce, which imposed a degree of unity over the old Byzantine lands.[108] A combination of the weakness of the Latin Empire and a Byzantine backlash ensured rapid political fragmentation, which became more or less impossible to reverse with the creation of a new commercial system which ensured Italian dominance. If not fully in place until the early fourteenth century, its foundations were laid during the period of the Latin Empire. Michael Palaiologos's failure to rid Byzantium of the commercial stranglehold exercised by the Italians is proof enough of the strength of the foundations laid by the Venetians before 1261. They allowed the Venetians and later the Genoese to exploit other opportunities that opened up. Italian commercial domination owed much to the export of western manufactures to the eastern Mediterranean and perhaps even more to the *Pax Mongolica*. Without the advantages obtained through the conquest of Constantinople it is unlikely that the Italians would have been able to derive such benefit from these other developments. An event cannot be considered in isolation. Its impact will be greater or lesser depending on how it combines with other episodes or circumstances.

The fall of Constantinople was in Le Roy Ladurie's terms a 'key event', because it produced the conditions out of which radically different political and economic structures emerged. Venice provides a clear example of the possibilities that opened up after 1204. It was able to create an empire which in some ways replaced Byzantium, but it was quite different. It was based on control of the sea lanes and its motivating force was commercial advantage. It nevertheless took over some of the functions of the Byzantine Empire. Angeliki Laiou has shown how after 1204 Venice replaced Byzantium as the major producer of luxury items – glass and crystal in particular. But it was a different kind of operation. It was on a larger scale and was more aggressively commercial.[109] In much the same way, the city of Venice was refashioned after 1204 with the help of the *disjecta membra* of Byzantium. But this was done as a statement of its new-found power, not as a conscious imitation of the empire that it had helped to destroy. It proclaimed a new political order.

With its market-orientated economy and its government by assemblies and committees, medieval Venice has a deceptively modern look. It lends itself to modern interpretations of the crusader conquest of Constantinople in terms of structural change. This is an approach that has its virtues, as long as it is recognised as just one more stage in the elucidation of an event. But not only that: there is a very close connection between an event and its elucidation by historians. The way that historians over the centuries have made sense of the facts is part of the definition of an event. Thinking in terms of structures or *mentalités* does not make *l'histoire événementielle* redundant; it just gives it a new twist and adds a new layer of interpretation.

On the facts of 1204 there is broad agreement between modern historians and the original chroniclers. They also concur about the outcome, though they express their opinions differently. For the medieval chronicler it was an act of divine providence; for some modern historians an accident. But there are accidents and accidents; and 1204 was not as accidental as all that. There was a logic to the course events took. The crusader conquest was rooted in a bargain struck between partners with very different outlooks and interests. The Venetians thought in terms of the honour of their *patria* and of commercial interest. These dictated the recovery of the Dalmatian city of Zara. This was of little interest to the crusade leadership conscious of its moral responsibilities, which went further than organising an armed pilgrimage to the Holy Land. It was susceptible to the pleas of the young Alexius Angelos for idealistic reasons, but these were reinforced by other considerations, not least the practical need for Byzantine support. Despite reservations the Venetians had an obligation to support the crusaders in their attempt to restore the Byzantine prince. The diversion of the Fourth Crusade first to Zara and then to Constantinople earned the stern disapproval of Pope Innocent III, which was directed mainly at the Venetians. In the hope of mollifying the pope the crusaders justified their actions in terms of the reunification of the churches of Rome and Constantinople which they claimed to have achieved. They thus brought into play the religious differences that existed between the two churches. These had not hitherto meant very much either to the crusaders or to the Venetians. When in the autumn of 1203 relations between the crusaders and the Byzantines began to deteriorate these differences were used to maintain the cohesion of the crusader army. They fed deep-rooted prejudices against the Greeks, which now began to surface: that they were treacherous and ungrateful and cowardly. They were also schismatics; and this was the main justification for the final assault on Constantinople. The Venetian stance was different. The critical moment came in January 1204 when the Byzantines attacked the Venetian fleet with fire ships. The Venetians dealt with the danger, but they realised how close they had come to disaster. The honour of their *patria* – to say nothing of more material interests – was in peril. This was justification enough for all-out war against the Byzantines.

This is not to rule out the accidental. There were other possible outcomes, but the conquest of Constantinople was the most likely, given the attitudes, assumptions, ideals and experience which the participants brought to the decisions they made. The crusaders had no very clear idea of Byzantium before they set out. Hard information was mixed with romantic notions culled from literature. Proximity was troubling. The crusaders were astonished that Constantinople did not open its gate to the young Alexius. They soon became aware of the contempt and hatred that the people of Constantinople had for them. Nothing had prepared them for this. They expected to be received as 'knights in shining armour'! The Byzantines, for their part, were obsessed with the West, to the point of paranoia. Even Nicetas Choniates – otherwise so urbane and level-headed – understood the Fourth Crusade as a plot against Byzantium engineered by Pope Innocent III and Philip of Swabia.[110] At a popular level hatred of westerners was sheer xenophobia intensified by religious differences. The claims made by the papacy over the Church of Constantinople were deeply resented at all levels of society. But the Byzantine establishment realised that it had to balance this affront to its dignity with the need for Latin commercial expertise and military prowess. This required that from time to time westerners be disciplined in order to emphasise the superiority of the Byzantine order. The treatment of Latins in Constantinople was therefore characterised by a combination of popular hatred and *Realpolitik*. This would make a clash between Byzantines and crusaders more or less inevitable. By the beginning of 1204 the Byzantine leadership was convinced that it had the crusaders at its mercy and now had the opportunity to humiliate them. The crusaders were equally convinced of their moral and military superiority. It was the Byzantines who miscalculated.

A conglomeration of facts becomes an event through the work of historians seeking to make sense of the past. In the first instance, this is the business of contemporary chroniclers. An event has two aspects: action and consequences. First then, there is the question of what happened; this is not just a matter of outlining events, but also explaining them. There will always be accidental elements, but almost always there is a logic and consistency to the way events fall out, which is not entirely a figment of the historian's imagination. It is this logic and consistency that helps to define an event. But the meaning of an event depends very largely on the elucidation of its consequences, which may bring in factors hardly connected with the event itself. Contemporary assessments of 1204 have little in common with modern evaluations, which are made in terms that would have meant little or nothing to people whose criteria were largely moral and religious. Modern interpretations add depth to any understanding of the significance of an event and provide a different dimension, but need to be anchored in the realities of the past. Without a firm grasp of how contemporaries viewed matters they fail to carry conviction.

In the case of the fall of Constantinople the initial reaction on the part of Latin commentators was that it revealed the divinely ordained superiority of the West over Byzantium. It was a standpoint defiantly maintained by the first generation of Frankish settlers in the old Byzantine Empire in the face of a series of setbacks that suggested the removal of the divine favour that had originally surrounded the enterprise. Innocent III had at first hailed the conquest of Constantinople as another example of God moving in mysterious ways His wonders to perform, this time to restore unity to the Church. The pope never wavered in this belief, but became increasingly critical of the crusaders themselves, who continued to flout his wishes. He underlined and exaggerated the brutality of their sack of Constantinople as a way of reasserting his moral supremacy over the crusaders. He was disappointed that the establishment of the Latin Empire brought so little effective assistance to the Holy Land. Instead, it threatened to deprive the kingdom of Jerusalem of valuable manpower and resources. He was also disillusioned by the obduracy of the Greeks. By the end of his pontificate he showed only a waning interest in reconciling the Greeks to a union of churches, whereas in the immediate aftermath of 1204 he showed genuine concern for the needs of the Orthodox Church. Papal disappointment set the tone of western opinion, which adopted an equivocal stance. The conquest could not be disavowed, for that would call in question the justice of the transfer of relics and other treasures from Byzantium to the West. It was exactly this transfer that in retrospect became a major justification for the conquest. But the Latin Empire could be repudiated because of its manner of establishment, which owed more to greed than piety. It was a point of view that was largely dependent on special pleading, but its proponents found support in the growing weakness of the Latin Empire which could be taken as proof of its moral shortcomings. Its emperors were not fit custodians of that most precious prize, the relics of the Passion, which they had inherited from their Byzantine predecessors. It was appropriate that they should pass to the Capetian kings of France, who would use them to elaborate their 'religion of monarchy'. This was not done in conscious imitation of Byzantium, despite some similarities. It represented a new beginning, but one that was possible because of the destruction of Byzantium.

The significance of 1204 lies not only in the political fragmentation that followed in its wake; not only in the ensuing Italian commercial domination, but also in the opportunity it provided the Latin West for self-reflection. It was a complicated business. On the one hand, the transfer of relics to the West was a token of its moral superiority; on the other, there were doubts about the legitimacy of the conquest of the Byzantine Empire. These doubts do not seem to have troubled either the Venetians or the Capetian Louis IX, who were the major beneficiaries of the fall of Constantinople. The Venetians were able to assert their independence and the Capetians to evolve an ideology of monarchy that owed nothing directly to Byzantium, but indirectly a very great deal. The papacy gained less than might have been expected. The conquest of Constantinople apparently secured one of its long-term aims: the resolution of differences with the Orthodox Church. But it became clear that it had solved nothing. Indicative was the muted treatment of the Orthodox problem at the Fourth Lateran Council. Instead, the establishment of the Latin Empire produced new dilemmas. How could it be fitted into a crusading framework? The argument that it provided essential support for the crusader states was hollow. But was its defence a legitimate use of the crusade? The First Council of Lyons (1245) placed the defence of the Latin Empire at the head of its agenda and offered crusading privileges to those going to its rescue, but no military help was forthcoming. Though the papacy continued to feel a responsibility for the Latin Empire, there was always a distinct reluctance in the Latin West to participate in expeditions designed to go to its aid. The Fourth Crusade is of great importance for the way that the scope of the crusade was enlarged. It is equally important for the doubts that this development raised.

The mixed feelings surrounding the conquest of Constantinople arose from the nature of the sack of the city, which contradicted the ideal of the crusade. The savagery of the sack was much exaggerated at the time.

The papacy had an interest in doing this; even more so had the Byzantines. It has become part of the event. It is hardly worth protesting that, all things considered, the crusade leadership did a good job in keeping their followers under control. It was the impression that counted. This emphasises a different dimension to a historical event. Its impact will not only depend on what happened, but also on what was believed to have happened. The sack of Constantinople ensured the alienation of the Orthodox world from the West.

Byzantium was the spectre at the feast. For the Byzantines the fall of Constantinople was the ultimate catastrophe, but nothing demonstrates so well the underlying strength of Byzantium than the heroic efforts made after 1204 at its reconstitution. There were remarkable achievements, but the struggle may have been at the expense of earlier creativity. Byzantine culture increasingly concerned itself with retrieving and preserving what was in danger of being lost.[111] The political and economic conditions created in the wake of 1204 always worked against a proper restoration of Byzantium. Paradoxically, the fall of Constantinople offered the Byzantines the opportunity for self-renewal on a different basis – one where cohesion depended on the Orthodox Church rather than on the imperial administration centred on Constantinople. It was perhaps inevitable that, when Michael VIII Palaiologos returned in 1261 to Constantinople, he would attempt to reconstruct imperial authority as it had existed in the twelfth century under Manuel I Comnenus. But this brought him into conflict with the new forces which had developed within Byzantine society during the period of exile and reinforced that underlying political instability which surfaced with a vengeance in the civil wars of the fourteenth century. Michael Palaiologos also found that the western presence was an issue which refused to go away. Byzantine society divided most deeply over the question of church union. Sadly, the recovery of Constantinople did not bring emancipation from the western embrace, but an ever-deeper entanglement, which Michael Palaiologos's successors for all their efforts were never able to escape. This contrasts with the West, which was able to liquidate any sense of inferiority it had felt towards Byzantium by appropriating in its own way elements of the Byzantine heritage.

Notes

1. Loukaki, 'Première didaskalie de Serge le diacre', 167.104–10.
2. Pachymérès ll.31: ed. Failler, I, 219.5–9.
3. Decisive seems to have been the opinion of O. Demus, 'Zwei Konstantinopler Marienikonen des 13. Jahrhunderts', *Jahrbuch österreichischen byzantinischen*

Gesellschaft, 7(1958), 96, who rejected Thomas Whittemore's belief that it was a work of the early Comnenian period: T. Whittemore, *The Mosaics of Haghia Sophia at Istanbul: the Deësis Panel of the South Gallery* (Oxford, 1952), 27–8, 30–1.

4. L. Rodley, *Byzantine art and architecture: an introduction* (Cambridge, 1994), 326–30. Cf. K. Weitzmann, *Studies in Classical and Byzantine Manuscript Illumination* (Chicago/London, 1971), 146–50, 214–17.

5. H. Belting, *The Image and its Public in the Middle Ages. Form and function of early paintings of the Passion* (New Rochelle, 1990), 120.

6. O. Demus, 'The style of the Kariye Djami and its place in the development of Palaeologan art', in *The Kariye Djami*, IV, ed. P. A. Underwood (Princeton, 1975), esp. 152–9.

7. A. Heisenberg, *Quellen und Studien zur spätbyzantinischen Geschichte* (London, 1973), I, 82–116; E. H. Kantorowicz, 'Oriens Augusti – Lever du Roi', *Dumbarton Oaks Papers*, 17(1963), 160–2.

8. M. McCormick, *Eternal Victory* (Cambridge, 1986), 171–4.

9. Pseudo-Kodinos, *Traité des Offices*, ed. J. Verpeaux (Paris, 1966), 189–247; A. Grabar, 'Pseudo-Codinos et les cérémonies de la Cour byzantine au XIVe siècle', in *Art et Société à Byzance sous les Paléologues* (Venice, 1971), 195–221.

10. Pachymérès, IV, 14: ed. Failler, 369–71.

11. Pachymérès, IV, 13: ed. Failler, 369.2–4.

12. G. P. Majeska, 'St Sophia in the 14th and 15th centuries: the Russian travellers on the relics', *Dumbarton Oaks Papers*, 27(1973), 71–87; M. J. Angold, 'The decline of Byzantium seen through the eyes of western travellers', in *Travel in the Byzantine World*, ed. R. Macrides (Aldershot, 2002), 215–16.

13. A.-M. Talbot, 'Old Wine in New Bottles: the rewriting of saints' lives in the Palaeologan period', in *The Twilight of Byzantium*, ed. S. Curcic and D. Mouriki (Princeton, 1990), 15–26.

14. P. Lock, 'The Latin emperors as heirs to Byzantium', in *New Constantines: The Rhythm of Imperial Renewal in Byzantium, 4th–13th Centuries*, ed. P. Magdalino (Aldershot, 1994), 297–304.

15. R. Spence, 'Gregory IX's attempted expeditions to the Latin Empire of Constantinople: the crusade for the union of the Latin and Greek churches', *Journal of Medieval History*, 5(1979), 163–76.

16. M. J. Angold, 'Greeks and Latins after 1204: the perspective of exile', in *Latins and Greeks in the Eastern Mediterranean after 1204*, 76–9.

17. B. Z. Kedar, *Crusade and Mission* (Princeton, 1984), 97–135.

18. C. Mango, 'Classical statuary and the Byzantine beholder', *Dumbarton Oaks Papers*, 17(1963), 59–64.

19. Gunther of Pairis, 91.

20. Ibid., 111.

21. Ibid., 125–7.

22. Andrea, *Contemporary Sources*, 239–64.

23. Ibid., 223–38.

24. AASS Aug III, 444–5; Longnon, *Compagnons*, 219; Malaczek, *Petrus Capuanus*, no. 21, 298–300.

25. P. Riant, *Exuviae Sacrae Constantinopolitanae*, I (Geneva, 1876), 133–40; P. E. D. Riant, *Des dépouilles religieuses enlevées à Constantinople au XIIIe siècle par les Latins* (Paris, 1875), 121–3; Longnon, *Compagnons*, 219–21.
26. Riant, *Exuviae*, I, 36–44; Longnon, *Compagnons*, 205–6.
27. F. Wormald, 'The Rood of Bromholm', *Journal of the Warburg Institute*, 1(1937–8), 31–45.
28. Lateran IV, §62: *Conciliorum Oecumenicorum Decreta*, 263–4; Foreville, *Latran*, 377–8.
29. Gunther of Pairis, 130.
30. Ibid., 127–8.
31. Andrea, *Contemporary Sources*, 260–1.
32. Gunther of Pairis, 123–4.
33. Andrea, *Contemporary Sources*, 236.
34. Ibid., 237–8.
35. Gunther of Pairis, 125.
36. Andrea, *Contemporary Sources*, 262.
37. Ibid., 235–7.
38. H. Belting, 'Die Reaktion der Kunst des 13. Jahrhunderts auf den Import von Reliquien und Ikonen', in *Ornamenta Ecclesiae: Kunst und Künstler der Romanik*, ed. A. Legner, III (Cologne, 1985), 173.
39. *Chronica Albrici monachi Trium Fontium*, 922.
40. P. J. Geary, 'St Helen of Athyra and the cathedral of Troyes in the thirteenth century', *Journal of Medieval and Renaissance Studies*, 7(1977), 149–68.
41. M. Durand, 'Les fragments des reliques byzantines de sainte Hélène d'Athyra retrouvés au trésor de la cathédrale de Troyes', *Cahiers archéologiques*, 46(1998), 169–82.
42. P. J. Geary, *Furta Sacra. Thefts of Relics in the Central Middle Ages* (Princeton, 1978), 29–30.
43. *Le trésor de la Sainte-Chapelle*, ed. J. Durand (Paris, 2001), 35.
44. J. A. Fabricius, *Bibliotheca Graeca*, V (Hamburg, 1712), 151.
45. Clari, §lxxxii, 81–2.
46. Riant, *Exuviae*, II, 175–6.
47. Rigord, *De Gestis Philippi Augusti Francorum Regis*, 59–60.
48. Henri de Valenciennes, §666, 106–7; Longnon, *Compagnons*, 219.
49. Andrea Dandolo, *Chronica*, ed. Pastorello, 295.1–6.
50. The Venetian *podestà* contributed 4,175 *hyperpyra*; the Cistercian nunnery of Percheio 4,300; two Venetian merchants 2,200; and the Genoese 2,459. On the nunnery of Percheio, the richest Institution in Latin Constantinople, see J.-M. Martin *et al.*, 'Un acte de Baudouin II en faveur de l'abbaye cistercienne de sainte-Marie de Percheio (Octobre 1241)', *Revue des études byzantines*, 57(1999), 211–23.
51. Tafel and Thomas II, 346–9. It has been normal to assume that the original loan by the consortium was arranged by the regency council, but it is clear that this was made well before 1238 by which time the original loan had been expended 'a long time since' (*jamdudum*) to support the Latin Empire.
52. *Récits d'un ménestral de Reims*, ed. N. de Wailly (Paris, 1876), 224–6.
53. Riant, *Exuviae*, I, 55.

54. Ibid., 47.
55. *Trésor de la Sainte-Chapelle*, 38–9, 45; D. Weiss, *Art and Crusade in the Age of Saint Louis* (Cambridge, 1998), 11–15.
56. Riant, *Exuviae*, III, 105–12; *Trésor de la Sainte-Chapelle*, 39–41.
57. The only figure we have is the 10,000 *hyperpyra* paid to recover the Crown of Thorns. This is roughly equivalent to 135,000 livres at a time when the annual budget of the French monarchy was about 250,000 livres. One can reckon that recovering the other relics from pawn would have cost at least as much again. As a point of comparison the rough cost of the Sainte-Chapelle was 40,000 livres: Weiss, *Art and Crusade*, 16.
58. Clari, §lxxxii.10.
59. Weiss, *Art and Crusade*, 16–32.
60. '. . . *la terre ou li foul vont folie guerre Constantinoble, Romenie*': Rutebeuf, *Oeuvres complètes*, ed. M. Zink (Paris, 1989), I, 208–9.92–4.
61. H. Belting, *Likeness and Presence. A History of the Image before the Era of Art* (Chicago, 1994), 311–29.
62. Clari, §lxvi, 65–8; Villehardouin II, §228; Andrea, *Contemporary Sources*, 103, 220, 285, 302–3.
63. Clari, §cxiv.
64. Clari, §lxxxiii.1, 6–7, 26, 28. *Saintuaire* is the word used.
65. *Reg.* VII, cxlvii: Migne *PL* 215, 434A.
66. Belting, *Image and its Public*, esp. 1–40.
67. R. S. Nelson, 'The Italian appreciation and appropriation of illuminated Byzantine manuscripts, ca.1200–1450', *Dumbarton Oaks Papers*, 49(1995), 209–35; A. Cutler, 'From loot to scholarship: changing modes in the Italian response to Byzantine artifacts, ca.1200–1750', *Dumbarton Oaks Papers*, 49(1995), 237–67.
68. O. Demus, *The Mosaic Decoration of San Marco Venice* (Chicago and London, 1988), 162–7.
69. Belting, *Likeness and Presence*, 330–3.
70. Caesarius of Heisterbach, *The Dialogue of Miracles*, ed. G. G. Coulton (London, 1929), II, 77.
71. Ibid., I, 515.
72. Belting, *Image and its Public*, 132–3.
73. A. Derbes, *Picturing the Passion in late medieval Italy: narrative painting, Franciscan ideologies, and the Levant* (Cambridge, 1996), 24–7.
74. J. Beckwith, *The Art of Constantinople*, 2nd edn (London, 1968), 130–2.
75. Migne *PG*, 140, 513D.
76. Tafel and Thomas II, 47; Migne *PL*, 215, 1078B.
77. Belting, *Likeness and Presence*, 215–20; Belting, *Image and its Public*, 218–20; Belting, 'Reaktion der Kunst', 175–8; B. Bolton, 'Advertise the message: images in Rome at the turn of the twelfth century', in *Studies in Church History*, 28(1992), 117–30; F. Lewis, 'The Veronica: image, legend and viewer', in *England in the 13th century* (Grantham, 1985), 100–6.
78. *Trésor de la Sainte-Chapelle*, 70–1.
79. Belting, *Likeness and Presence*, 21–8.
80. Belting, *Image and its Public*, 141–2.

81. Ibid., 57.
82. Derbes, *Picturing the Passion*, 12–24.
83. Muir, *Civic Ritual*, 103–34.
84. Martin da Canal, I, xliii, 50.
85. Pertusi, 'Maistre Martino da Canal', 103–35; Fasoli, 'La *Cronique des Veniciens*', 42–74; Carile, *La cronachistica veneziana*, 172–93, 207–9.
86. W. Wolters, *Storia et politica nei dipinti di Palazzo ducale* (Venice, 1987), 179–85; Muir, *Civic Ritual*, 101–2.
87. Face, 'Secular History'.
88. J. Schulz, 'La piazza medievale di San Marco', *Annali di Architettura*, 4/5(1992–3), 134–56.
89. *The Horses of San Marco Venice*, ed. G. Perocco (London, 1979), 56–64, 127–8.
90. Goy, *Venice*, 60–4, 130–2.
91. D. M. Nicol, *Byzantium and Venice: A Study in Diplomatic and Cultural Relationships* (Cambridge, 1988), 52.
92. Demus, *Mosaic Decoration*, 86–90.
93. Ibid., 193–6.
94. Ibid., 108–14.
95. The most recent and authoritative is by R. Polacco in *La Pala d'Oro*, ed. H. R. Hahnloser and R. Polacco (Venice, 1994), 115–47, but he fails to give due weight to the testimony of Syropoulos.
96. ..., 'ἐκ τε τῶν 'ἐπιγραφῶν, 'ἐκ τε στηλογραφίας τῶν Κομνηνῶν: *Mémoires de Sylvestre Syropoulos*, ed. V. Laurent (Paris, 1977), §85, 222–4. A distinction is clearly intended between *epigraphai* and *stelographia*. That being so, the former must apply to those enamels with Greek inscriptions and the latter to the style of dress of the Comnenian figures.
97. R. Gallo, *Il tesoro di S. Marco e la sua storia* (Civiltà veneziana, 16) (Rome, 1967), 161.
98. S. Bettini, 'Le opere d'arte importate a Venezia durante le crociate', in *Venezia dalla prima crociata all conquista di Costantinopoli del 1204* (Florence, 1965), 157–90.
99. R. Polacco, *Pala d'Oro*, 115–26 argues that the transformation of the enamel into a portrait of Doge Ordelafo was the work of the Doge Andrea Dandolo and dates to the remounting of the Pala in 1345. He detects Gothic elements in the portrait of Ordelafo and argues that it was only the final rearrangement of the Pala that would have allowed the portrait of a Byzantine emperor to be converted into that of a doge. This remains a possibility, but why should Dandolo have drawn attention to the role of Angelo Falier in the 1209 remounting of the Pala?
100. Gallo, *Tesoro*, 12, 20.
101. Ibid., 13–15.
102. Ibid., 133–55.
103. Ibid., 275.
104. A. Pertusi, 'Bisanzio e le insegne regali dei dogi di Venezia', *Rivista di studi bizantini neoellenici*, n.s. 2/3(1965–6), 278–80.
105. Gallo, *Tesoro*, 193–8.

106. Muir, *Civic Ritual*, 207.

107. Nicetas Choniates, 86.77–86.

108. See A. E. Laiou, 'The Byzantine economy in the Mediterranean trade system: 13th–15th centuries', *Dumbarton Oaks Papers*, 34–5(1980–1), 177–222; A. E. Laiou, 'Observations on the results of the Fourth Crusade: Greeks and Latins in port and market', *Medievalia et Humanistica*, 12(1984), 47–60.

109. A. E. Laiou, 'Venice as a centre of trade and of artistic production', in *Il medio Oriente e l'Occidente nell'arte del XIII secolo*, ed. H. Belting (Bologna, 1982), 11–26.

110. Nicetas Choniates, 539.6–15.

111. Belting, *Image and its Public*, 120.

FURTHER READING

This is not intended as an exhaustive bibliography, but as a guide to further reading. Most of the items selected are books published relatively recently and in English. There are detailed bibliographies of the older literature in *Cambridge Medieval History*, IV, pt 1, ed. J. M. Hussey (Cambridge, 1966), 880–97, and of the more recent literature in *New Cambridge Medieval History*, V, ed. D. Abulafia (Cambridge, 1999), 911–30. A. J. Andrea has contributed a valuable bibliographic essay with bibliographies to D. E. Queller (with T. F. Madden), *The Fourth Crusade. The Conquest of Constantinople*, 2nd edn (Philadelphia, 1997), 299–343.

General

Cambridge Medieval History, IV, pts 1 and 2, ed. J. M. Hussey (Cambridge, 1966–7)

J. Gill, *Byzantium and the Papacy, 1198–1400* (New Brunswick, 1979)

A. Harvey, *Economic Expansion in the Byzantine Empire 900–1200* (Cambridge, 1989)

J. M. Hussey, *The Orthodox Church in the Byzantine Empire* (Oxford, 1986)

C. Mango, *Byzantine Architecture* (Milan, 1978)

C. Mango, *Byzantium. The Empire of the New Rome* (London, 1980)

New Cambridge Medieval History, 7 vols (Cambridge, 1995–)

J. J. Norwich, *Byzantium*, 3 vols (London, 1988–95)

G. Ostrogorsky, *A History of the Byzantine State* (Oxford, 1968)

Oxford Dictionary of Byzantium, editor in chief A. P. Kazhdan, 3 vols (Oxford, 1991)

L. Rodley, *Byzantine Art and Architecture: An Introduction* (Cambridge, 1994)

S. Runciman, *A History of the Crusades*, 3 vols (Cambridge, 1951–4)

K. M. Setton (ed.), *A History of the Crusades*, 6 vols (Philadelphia/Madison, 1958–89)

W. Treadgold, *A History of the Byzantine State and Society* (Stanford, 1997)

Byzantium in the eleventh and twelfth centuries

M. J. Angold, *Church and Society in Byzantium under the Comneni 1081–1261* (Cambridge, 1995)

M. J. Angold, *The Byzantine Empire 1025–1204. A Political History*, 2nd edn (Longman, 1997)

J.-C. Cheynet, *Pouvoir et Contestations à Byzance (963–1210)* (Paris, 1990)

C. Galatariotou, *The Making of a Saint. The Life, Times and Sanctification of Neophytos the Recluse* (Cambridge, 1991)

M. F. Hendy, *Coinage and Money in the Byzantine Empire 1081–1261* (Washington, DC, 1969)

A. P. Kazhdan (with A. Epstein), *Change in Byzantine Culture in 11th and 12th Centuries* (Berkeley and Los Angeles, 1985)

A. P. Kazhdan (with S. Franklin), *Studies on Byzantine Literature of 11th and 12th Centuries* (Cambridge, 1984)

P. Magdalino, *Tradition and Transformation in Medieval Byzantium* (Aldershot, 1991)

P. Magdalino, *The Empire of Manuel I Komnenos 1143–1180* (Cambridge, 1993)

P. Stephenson, *Byzantium's Balkan Frontier: A Political Study of the Northern Balkans, 900–1204* (Cambridge, 2000)

Byzantium and the West in the eleventh and twelfth centuries

S. Borsari, *Venezia e Bisanzio nel XII secolo* (Venice, 1988)

C. M. Brand, *Byzantium Confronts the West, 1180–1204* (Cambridge, Mass., 1968)

A. Bryer, 'Cultural relations between East and West in the twelfth century', in *Relations between East and West in the Middle Ages*, ed. D. Baker (Edinburgh, 1973)

G. W. Day, *Genoa's Response to Byzantium, 1155–1204* (Urbana/Chicago, 1988)

J. Harris, *Byzantium and the Crusades* (London and New York, 2003)

J. D. Howard-Johnston (ed.), *Byzantium and the West, c.850–c.1200* (Amsterdam, 1988)

S. Kindlimann, *Die Eroberung von Konstantinopel als politische Forderung des Westens im Hochmittelalter* (Zurich, 1969)

P. Lamma, *Comneni e Staufer. Ricerche sui rapporti fra Bisanzio e l'Occidente nel secolo XII*, 2 vols (Rome, 1955–7)

R.-J. Lilie, *Handel und Politik zwischen dem byzantinischen Reich und den italienischen Kommunen Venedig, Pisa und Genua in der Epoche der Komnenen und der Angeloi (1081–1204)* (Amsterdam, 1984)

R.-J. Lilie, *Byzantium and the Crusader States 1096–1204* (Oxford, 1993)

D. M. Nicol, *Byzantium and Venice: A Study in Diplomatic and Cultural Relationships* (Cambridge, 1988)

S. Runciman, *Eastern Schism* (Oxford, 1955)

The Fourth Crusade

M. J. Angold, 'The Road to 1204', *Journal of Medieval History*, 25(1999)

J. M. A. Beer, *Villehardouin. Epic Historian* (Geneva, 1968)

C. M. Brand, 'The Fourth Crusade: some recent interpretations', *Medievalia et Humanistica*, 12(1984)

J. Dufournet, *Les écrivains de la IVe croisade: Villehardouin et Clari* (Paris, 1973), 2 vols

J. Folda, 'The Fourth Crusade, 1201–1204: some reconsiderations', *Byzantinoslavica*, 26(1965)

A. Frolow, *Recherches sur la déviation de la quatrième croisade vers Constantinople* (Paris, 1955)

J. Godfrey, *1204. The Unholy Crusade* (Oxford, 1980)

J. Longnon, *Les compagnons de Villehardouin: recherches sur les croisés de la quatrième croisade* (Geneva, 1978)

W. Maleczek, *Petrus Capuanus: Kardinal, Legat am vierten Kreuzzug, Theologe (+1214)* (Vienna, 1988)

D. E. Queller (ed.), *The Latin Conquest of Constantinople* (New York, 1971)

D. E. Queller (with T. F. Madden), *The Fourth Crusade: The Conquest of Constantinople, 1201–1204*, 2nd edn (Philadelphia, 1997)

D. E. Queller and S. Stratton, 'A Century of Controversy on the Fourth Crusade', *Studies in Medieval and Renaissance History*, 6(1969)

H. Roscher, *Papst Innocenz III. und die Kreuzzüge* (Göttingen, 1969)

The Latin Empire of Constantinople

B. Arbel, B. Hamilton and D. Jacoby (eds), *Latins and Greeks in the Eastern Mediterranean after 1204* (London, 1989)

A. Bon, *La Morée franque*, 2 vols (Paris, 1969)

A. Carile, *Per una storia dell'Imperio latino di Costantinopoli*, rev. edn (Bologna, 1978)

D. Jacoby, *Recherches sur la Méditerranée orientale du XIIe au XVe siècle* (Aldershot, 1979)

P. Lock, *The Franks in the Aegean, 1204–1500* (Longman, 1995)

J. Longnon, *L'Empire latin de Constantinople* (Paris, 1949)

K. Setton, *The Papacy and the Levant (1204–1571)*, vol. I (Philadelphia, 1976)

R. Wolff, *Studies in the Latin Empire of Constantinople* (London, 1976)

The Greeks in exile

H. Ahrweiler, 'L'expérience nicéenne', *Dumbarton Oaks Papers*, 29(1975)

M. J. Angold, *A Byzantine Government in Exile: Government and Society under the Laskarids of Nicaea 1204–1261* (Oxford, 1975)

A. D. Karpozilos, *The ecclesiastical controversy between the kingdom of Nicaea and the principality of Epiros (1217–1233)* (Thessalonica, 1973)

J. S. Langdon, *Byzantium's Last Imperial Offensive in Asia Minor* (New York, 1992)

D. M. Nicol, *The Despotate of Epiros* (Oxford, 1957)

G. Prinzing, *Die Bedeutung Bulgariens und Serbiens in den Jahren 1204–1219 im Zusammenhang mit der Entstehung und Entwicklung der byzantinischen Teilstaaten nach der Einnahme Konstantinopels infolge des 4. Kreuzzugs* (Munich 1972)

Venice

S. Borsari, *Il dominio veneziano a Creta nel XIII secolo* (Naples, 1963)

S. Borsari, *Studi sulle colonie veneziane in Romania nel XIII secolo* (Naples, 1966)

P. F. Brown, *Venice & Antiquity: the Venetian Sense of the Past* (New Haven and London, 1996)

O. Demus, *The Church of San Marco in Venice: History, Architecture, Sculpture* (Washington, DC, 1960)

O. Demus, *The Mosaic Decoration of San Marco Venice* (Chicago and London, 1988)

R. Goy, *Venice: The City and its Architecture* (London, 1997)

D. Howard, *Venice and the East* (New Haven and London, 2000)

D. Howard, *The Architectural History of Venice*, rev. edn (New Haven and London, 2002)

F. C. Lane, *Venice: A Maritime Republic* (Baltimore, 1973)

S. McKee, *Uncommon Dominion. Venetian Crete and the Myth of Ethnic Purity* (Philadelphia, 2000)

J. J. Norwich, *A History of Venice* (London, 1982)

F. Thiriet, *Histoire de Venise* (Paris, 1952)

F. Thiriet, *La Romanie vénitienne au moyen âge* (Paris, 1959)

Booty, relics and icons

H. Belting, *The Image and its Public in the Middle Ages. Form and Function of Early Paintings of the Passion* (New Rochelle, 1990)

H. Belting, *Likeness and Presence. A History of the Image before the Era of Art* (Chicago, 1994)

A. Derbes, *Picturing the Passion in late Medieval Italy: Narrative Painting, Franciscan Ideologies, and the Levant* (Cambridge, 1996)

J. Durand (ed.), *Le trésor de la Sainte-Chapelle* (Paris, 2001)

P. J. Geary, *Furta Sacra. Thefts of Relics in the Central Middle Ages* (Princeton, 1978)

D. Weiss, *Art and Crusade in the Age of Saint Louis* (Cambridge, 1998)

Sources in translation

A. J. Andrea (ed. and transl.), *The Capture of Constantinople: The 'Hystoria Constantinopolitana' of Gunther of Pairis* (Philadelphia, 1997)

A. J. Andrea, *Contemporary Sources for the Fourth Crusade* (Leiden, 2000)

Eustathios of Thessaloniki, *The Capture of Thessaloniki*, transl. J. R. Melville Jones (Canberra, 1988)

Geoffrey of Villehardouin, *The Conquest of Constantinople*, in *Chronicles of the Crusades*, transl. M. R. B. Shaw (Harmondsworth, 1963)

H. E. Lurier, *Crusaders as Conquerors: The Chronicle of the Morea* (New York, 1964)

H. J. Magoulias, *O City of Byzantium: Annals of Niketas Choniates* (Detroit, 1984)

R. Michell and N. Forbes (transl.), *Chronicle of Novgorod (1016–1471)* (Camden Society, ser. iii. 25) (London, 1914)

Robert of Clari, *The Conquest of Constantinople*, transl. E. H. McNeal (New York, 1936)

P. W. Topping, *Feudal Institutions as Revealed in the Assizes of Romania* (Philadelphia, 1949)

INDEX